KU-483-022

Critical Social Psychology

edited by
Tomás Ibáñez and Lupicinio Íñiguez

NEWMAN COLLEGE
BARTLEY GREEN
BIRMINGHAM B32 3NT

CLASS 302

BARCODE 0107015o

AUTHOR IBA

SAGE Publications
London • Thousand Oaks • New Delhi

Editorial Selection and Preface © Tomás Ibáñez and
Lupicinio Íñiguez 1997
Chapter 1 © Russell Spears 1997
Chapter 2 © Tomás Ibáñez 1997
Chapters 3 and 5 © Rex Stainton Rogers and Wendy
Stainton Rogers 1997
Chapter 4 © Jonathan Potter 1997
Chapter 6 © Stephen Reicher 1997
Chapter 7 © Martin Roiser 1997
Chapter 8 © Susan Condor 1997
Chapter 9 © Lupicinio Íñiguez 1997
Chapter 10 © Ian Parker 1997
Chapter 11 © Valerie Walkerdine 1997
Chapter 12 © Sue Wilkinson 1997
Chapter 13 © Ian Lubek 1997
Chapter 14 © Erica Burman 1997
Chapter 15 © Mike Michael 1997
Chapter 16 © Karin Knorr Cetina 1997
Chapter 17 © Ivan Leudar and Charles Antaki 1997

First published 1997

All rights reserved. No part of this publication may be reproduced,
stored in a retrieval system, transmitted or utilized in any form or by
any means, electronic, mechanical, photocopying, recording or
otherwise, without permission in writing from the Publishers.

SAGE Publications Ltd
6 Bonhill Street
London EC2A 4PU

SAGE Publications Inc.
2455 Teller Road
Thousand Oaks, California 91320

SAGE Publications India Pvt Ltd
32, M-Block Market
Greater Kailash – I
New Delhi 110 048

British Library Cataloguing in Publication data

A catalogue record for this book is available
from the British Library

ISBN 0 7619 5288 8
ISBN 0 7619 5289 6 (pbk)

Library of Congress catalog record available

Typeset by Mayhew Typesetting, Rhayader, Powys
Printed in Great Britain by Biddles Ltd, Guildford, Surrey

Contents

Notes on Contributors

Charles Antaki is Reader in the Language and Social Psychology Department of Social Sciences at Loughborough University. His research interests are in conversation analysis and social psychology, and among his recent publications is *Explaining and Arguing: The Social Organization of Accounts* (Sage, 1994). He is currently editing, with Sue Widdicombe, a book collecting together conversation analytic approaches to identity.

Erica Burman is Senior Lecturer in Developmental Psychology and Women's Studies at the Manchester Metropolitan University. She is author of *Deconstructing Developmental Psychology* (Routledge, 1994), editor of *Feminists and Psychological Practice* (Sage, 1990) and *Deconstructing Feminist Psychology* (Sage, forthcoming), co-editor of *Discourse Analytic Research* (Routledge, 1993) and co-author of *Qualitative Methods in Psychology* (Open University Press, 1994), *Challenging Women: Psychology's Exclusions, Feminist Possibilities* (Open University Press, 1996) and *Psychology Discourse Practice: From Regulation to Resistance* (Taylor & Francis, 1996). Her current interests include: the relations between women's rights and children's rights, (countering) the globalization of childhood; and feminist and psychoanalytic readings of subjectivity.

Susan Condor lectures in social psychology, women's studies and culture and communication at Lancaster University, and runs (with Mike Michael) the MA in Critical Social Psychology. Her research interests include common-sense understandings of time and history, and the relation of cultural constructions of 'heritage' to national and personal identity.

Tomás Ibáñez is Professor of Social Psychology at the Universitat Autònoma de Barcelona (Spain). He has published widely on epistemology, history and critical assessments of social psychology. His books include *Poder y Libertad* (Hora, 1982), *Aproximaciones a la Psicología Social* (Sendai, 1990), *Psicología Social Construccionista* (Universidad de Guadalajara, México, 1994) and *Fluctuaciones conceptuales en torno a la postmodernidad y la Psicología* (Universidad Central de Venezuela, 1996). He is editor of *Ideologías de la vida cotidiana. Psicología de las Representaciones Sociales* (Sendai, 1988) and *El conocimiento de la realidad social* (Sendai, 1990).

Lupicinio Íñiguez is Lecturer in Social Psychology at the Universitat Autònoma de Barcelona (Spain). His work has covered a number of areas such as qualitative methodology, discourse analysis, urban and political psychology. He has edited a special issue on Qualitative Methods in *Revista de Psicología Social Aplicada* (1996).

Karin Knorr Cetina is Professor of Sociology at the University of Bielefeld, former member of the Institute for Advanced Study, Princeton, and current president of the 4S Society. Her books include one of the first laboratory studies of science, *The Manufacture of Knowledge* (1981), *Advances in Social Theory and Methodology* (ed. with Aaron Cicourel, 1982), *Science Observed* (ed. with Michael Mulkay, 1983); and a comparative study of the epistemic machineries of two scientific fields, high energy physics and molecular biology (*Epistemic Cultures*, Harvard University Press, in press).

Ivan Leudar is a Senior Lecturer in Psychology at Manchester University. His main research interests concern pragmatics of activities, collectivities and selves, especially in exceptional circumstances. He has recently co-edited a special issue of *Ecological Psychology* on 'Situated Action'. He is currently working on a book on the phenomenon of 'hearing voices' (to be published by Routledge in the spring of 1997).

Ian Lubek, Professor of Psychology at the University of Guelph (Canada), visiting researcher at GEDISST/IRESCO/CNRS (Paris), co-chaired (1993–95) the International Society for Theroretical Psychology. Interested in theory, metatheory and epistemology, he co-edited *Problems in Theoretical Psychology* (Captus Press, 1996) and *Trends and Issues in Theoretical Psychology* (Springer, 1995), while his work on violence is represented in an article in *Theory & Psychology* (1995, *5(1)*, 99–129) on 'Individualism and aggression'. In addition, he has co-edited special issues of *Canadian Psychology* (1992, *33(3)*) and *Sociétés Contemporaines* (1993, *13*) on the histor(y/ies) of social psycholog(y/ies). Ongoing work focuses on gender and mentoring issues in the social psychology of science: a chapter co-authored with Ross et al. (1996, in *Problems in Theoretical Psychology*, pp. 228–241) traces scientific career differences among a sample of women and men social psychologists. When not advancing human understanding nor proofreading manuscripts, he contemplates antique coloured siphon bottles, real and/or constructed.

Mike Michael is Deputy Director of the Centre for Science Studies and Science Policy at Lancaster University. His research interests include the construction of identities in relation to non-humans, postmodern social psychology and the constitution of the 'public' by expert institutions. He has recently published on the animal experimentation controversy, the public understanding of science and critical social psychological theory. He is the author of *Constructing Identities* (Sage, 1996).

Ian Parker is Professor of Psychology in the Discourse Unit at Bolton Institute. He is author of *The Crisis in Modern Social Psychology – and How to End It* (Routledge, 1989), *Discourse Dynamics* (Routledge, 1992) and *Psychoanalytic Discourse* (Sage, in press). He is a member of Psychology Politics Resistance.

Jonathan Potter is Professor of Discourse Analysis in the Department of Social Sciences at Loughborough University. He has published widely on discourse, conversation and social psychology theory and methods. He is the author, with Derek Edwards, of *Discursive Psychology* (Sage, 1992) and, with Margaret Wetherell, of *Mapping the Language of Racism* (Harvester, 1992); his most recent book is *Representing Reality* (Sage, 1996).

Steve Reicher is a Reader in the School of Psychology at St Andrews University. His work has covered a number of areas such as crowd behaviour, delinquency and mass social influence. However, all of this work relates to two interlinked theoretical issues: developing a social psychology of social change and addressing the politics of psychological practice.

Martin Roiser is a Senior Lecturer in Psychology in the School of Creative, Cultural and Social Studies at Thames Valley University, London. He has recently written (with Carla Willig) about 'The Hidden History of Authoritarianism', which appeared in the journal *History of the Human Sciences*. He also researches the relationship between psychology and Marxism, and the public understanding of science.

Russell Spears is Professor of Psychology in the Department of Social Psychology at the University of Amsterdam. He combines research on social stereotyping, intergroup relations and social influence processes with interests in ideology and power (especially as applied to new communications technology), and has also contributed to debates in critical social psychology. Since 1994 he has been chief editor of the *British Journal of Social Psychology*.

Rex Stainton Rogers deconstructs psychology at the University of Reading and conducts Q methodological discourse analysis. His recent publications include *Stories of Childhood: Shifting Agendas of Child Concern* (with W. Stainton Rogers, 1992) and *Social Psychology: A Critical Agenda* (with Stenner, Gleeson and W. Stainton Rogers, 1995). He is also an aspect of 'Beryl Curt' and a co-author (with others) of *Textuality and Tectonics: Troubling Social and Psychological Science* (1994). Rex and Wendy Stainton Rogers are the editors of a new 'alternative' journal: *The International Journal of Transdisciplinary Studies*.

Wendy Stainton Rogers is a Senior Lecturer in the School of Health and Social Welfare at the Open University, UK. Her 'day job' mainly involves preparing distance learning materials in the field of child care and work with young people, including training in law. Her recent publications include *Children's Welfare, Children's Rights: A Practical Guide to the Law* (with Roche, 1994), 'Critical Approaches to Health Psychology' in the *Journal of Health Psychology* (Vol. 1(1)), and, as a member of the 'Beryl Curt Collective', *Textuality and Tectonics: Troubling Social and Psychological Science* (1994).

Valerie Walkerdine is Professor of the Psychology of Communication in the Department of Media and Communications, Goldsmiths' College, University of London. Her research interests include post-structuralism and the study of subjectivity. Two current research projects on transition to womanhood and children and computer games express this interest. Her latest book, *Daddy's Girl: Young Girls and Popular Culture* (1996) is published by Macmillan (UK) and Harvard University Press (USA). She is currently writing *Psychology, Postmodernity and the Media* with Lisa Blackmar, for Macmillan.

Sue Wilkinson is Senior Lecturer in Social Psychology in the Department of Social Sciences, Loughborough University. She founded and edits the international journal *Feminism & Psychology* and the book series *Gender and Psychology: Feminist and Critical Perspectives*. Her books include *Feminist Social Psychologies* (Open University Press, 1996) and, with Celia Kitzinger, *Heterosexuality* (1993), *Feminism and Discourse* (1995) and *Representing the Other* (1996), all Sage Publications.

Preface

In 1993 we organized a Small Group Meeting in Barcelona on 'Critical Social Psychology' with the financial support of the Universitat Autònoma de Barcelona and the European Association of Experimental Social Psychology (EAESP). The aims of the meeting were to bring together social psychologists and colleagues of other disciplines working in what could very broadly be called a critical perspective, and to create a forum where different positions could be expressed in a friendly, informal, free atmosphere.

We asked each participant to send us a very brief 'position paper' which was handed on to the others so as to set up the context of the debates. Various circumstances, including the charm of the city, came together to create the atmosphere we had hoped to generate. The debates were so intense, in a highly polemical but warm atmosphere, that we asked the participants to draw up their position paper once again some time later in the light of the arguments which had been exchanged during the meeting.

The skilful patience of Ziyad Marar of Sage Publications gave us the opportunity to publish the 'outcomes' of this meeting as a further contribution to the great ongoing debate on new directions in the social sciences.

Tomás Ibáñez
Lupicinio Íñiguez

Acknowledgements

Many people contributed to making this meeting possible. We would like to express our gratitude to our colleagues in the Universitat Autònoma de Barcelona, especially to Mercè Botella, Miquel Domènech, Ana Garay, Luz Maria Martínez, Juan Muñoz, Joan Pujol and Félix Vázquez, who offered their help from the very outset.

1

Introduction

Russell Spears

It is not easy to define critical social psychology, and reading the contributions to this volume further demonstrates the difficulty (futility) of this exercise. Perhaps the most interesting feature of the contributions then is not so much what they share in common, but the differences – in the sense of both variability and debate – between them. This heterogeneity in itself is a refreshing sign of life to be contrasted with much of the mainstream, where meta-theoretical debates about method, theory, epistemology and ontology have long since been forgotten or repressed ('agreed' but rarely discussed assumptions of consensus), allowing its practitioners to get on with the daily process of scientific discovery. The lack of an easily definable defining feature (beyond 'criticality'), let alone consensus, may ironically be one reason for the marginal and marginalized status of critical social psychology. Look at how much importance is attached to unity in party politics! However, debates around these issues provide evidence of vitality and purpose. Despite these differences we can point to a number of features associated with the 'crisis' and its aftermath that unite the projects of critical social psychology. At the very least critical social psychology can be partly seen as defining itself in opposition to the positivistic traditions in social psychology, often identified by quantitative research methodologies and the experimental approach in particular (but even here there are some dissenters). Whilst social psychologists in the more positivist tradition would no doubt dispute the implication that they are not critical (in the sense of having a sceptical attitude to their object of study), criticality is directed at our meta-theory, and our own 'interventionist' role in producing knowledge. Critical social psychologists are thus 'self-critical'. More positively perhaps, commitments to constructionism, analyses of talk and text, critiques of individualism and universalist assumptions of human nature are just some of the recurring themes.

But as Condor points out, it is possible to overplay this consensus. It is not long before it breaks down under closer scrutiny, and some old issues come washing back at us (in new bottles, or with new bottle). For example, although most of the chapters here would seem to underwrite a commitment to some form of (social) constructionism, the totalizing nature of this subscription and whether there is life beyond the text is in hot dispute, with issues of realism and relativism never far from the surface (are constructionism and realism incompatible?). Likewise critical social psychology's commitment to some form of progressive politics or democratization, siding with the exploited and oppressed, is on less than stable or common ground.

Despite a general commitment to constructionism and the more hermeneutic and qualitative methods, there would seem to be little consensus on method either. Many contributors use and advocate qualitative methodologies for sure. Others argue, however, that traditional quantitative research methods can be used in service of the pragmatic progressive agendas (e.g. Lubek; Wilkinson) or even to serve as a sort of panoptic parody of themselves to look at power relations (Reicher). Sometimes talk and text may actually be inappropriate to probe beneath the surface or beyond consciousness (Condor; Spears, 1994). If method is also always theory (Potter), disagreement here would once again seem to signal a more fundamental cleavage in critical social psychology, putting people in different camps. While most approaches reject the individualism and humanism of the Cartesian subject, and point to the self distributed in social relations and discourses, this raises issues of agency and structure, and again different approaches emphasize different sides of this dualism. Postmodernism has not only eliminated some of the old political certainties of the past (the so-called 'grand narratives'), it has also in its various versions done much to eliminate the self itself (i.e. a theory of the subject, independent of social structures and texts). If the author is dead and 'psychology is history', perhaps the individual subject is history also! To what extent, then, has political urgency disappeared along with psychological agency? Or rather, has a lack of political urgency dispensed with the need for agency? Perhaps it is fitting that a climate of few political certainties would have little need of certain agents to act on them.

This breakdown of grand narratives and their associated allegiances has left a space that some have been happy to occupy and celebrate. Thus postmodernism goes hand in hand with post-feminism and post-Marxism (Laclau & Mouffe, 1987). Others seem less sure of the gains of the new 'post-it' culture (why should we jettison feminism and Marxism while patriarchy and capitalism flourish? see Roiser). Perhaps, after all, the one uniting theme is the self-reflexivity of criticality. But this is itself to some extent critical on all the other preceding questions and the nature of the self (if indeed it exists) being 'reflexed'. Reflexivity can be disputed as a research practice, both in whether and how it is practised, and where it means the researcher relinquishing some claims to expertise (Condor; Reicher).

Of course, as I suggested, this quest to find commonality or even essence is doubtless forlorn and misguided. If the object of critical social psychology is to generate a 'climate of perturbation' (Rex Stainton Rogers), it can be argued to be in a healthy state (to be contrasted with the rest of psychology's unfortunate condition of consensus and apparent harmony). In this Introduction I shall try to provide a flavour of some of the issues and debates that have led to a collection of positions and approaches that might rather uneasily be grouped under the umbrella of critical social psychology. A brief look back at the history of the crisis and the critical strands is first necessary to show how we got here, where we are coming from and where we may be going (with the possibility that these are multiple departures and destinations). Then I shall try to explore some of the main themes and motifs that arise throughout the chapters, particularly those where tensions between positions arise.

Critical Roots: A Short History of the Crisis

Many readers of this volume will already be well familiar with the historical developments in psychology surrounding the so-called 'crisis'. Without getting into the issue of to what extent this was itself a condition or a construction, the crisis and its aftermath have influenced the course of critical social psychology. The critical strands in this volume have flowed out of many of these earlier debates and are acknowledged in these contributions (see, e.g., Lubek for an excellent historical overview). Many mention the 1972 volume by Israel and Tajfel, as a landmark of resistance to the American individualistic and experimental approaches (Ibáñez; Lubek; Michael), and the need to look at more social and social contextual understandings of being and behaviour. In a famous article Kenneth Gergen (1973) in the US also challenged the positivist paradigm by arguing that history formed a better model for social sciences such as psychology than the universalizing assumptions of natural sciences (cf. Gadamer, 1975). The mainstream was criticized for the mechanistic models which denied the free will of intentional agents (e.g. Shotter, 1975) and the alienating research methods that did not allow them to express it (Harré, 1974). Thus the clarion call of Harré's (1974) ethogenic attack on meaningless experiments became 'why not ask them?' and formed an important step in helping us to trust the objects of our study to provide a gloss on their own experience.

By the mid-seventies, the crisis was heralded on both sides of the Atlantic (Armistead, 1974; Elms, 1975). As well as methodological and meta-theoretical misgivings, the crisis was also characterized by a clear left/liberal political agenda which was also riding high in the late sixties/early seventies with a post-war generation that had begun to question the old world order and its imperialisms. Psychology and its institutions came for many to be identified with the state itself – what Rose (1985) later termed the 'psy-complex'. Positivist science was not just misguided or alienating, but a state apparatus for social regulation and control (see Roiser). Important political forebears drawn into this analysis were the Frankfurt School and particularly Western Marxists such as Lukács (1923/1971) who had pointed to the evils of rationalist science as an arm of the state fifty years earlier. Writings by Marxists such as Althusser and Gramsci also formed highly influential resources for structuralists and cultural theorists respectively (e.g.

Althusser, 1984; Gramsci, 1985). This climate opened the doors to a number of enriching influences from outside psychology, including sociology, social theory, ideology critique, linguistic philosophy – rather different fodder than the physical sciences that previously formed the extra-disciplinary sources of psychology's models and metaphors (Potter). These influences were being combined with some of psychology's own repressed traditions, such as psychoanalysis, in order to effect a paradigm shift in the analysis of subjectivity (e.g. Adlam et al., 1977; Henriques, Hollway, Urwin, Venn & Walkerdine, 1984).

However, just as these doors were opening, so was the mainstream closing down its shutters on these wayward and destabilizing influences. What should have been a dialogue had turned into a hegemonic struggle, in which ignore-ance was an effective strategy. Although the critics remained active, by the late seventies the momentum seemed to have waned. The political climate and the idealism of the sixties had changed. The hippies had become yuppies, and student activism had faded into apathy and personal advancement. Just as the state had won the political battles of '68 and its aftermath, so it seemed was critical psychology on the defensive and increasingly sectioned off. In retrospect, some of the alternative psychology on offer was more liberal than left: the alternative 'humanistic' psychologies can be seen as more based on the mythical adventure of self-discovery (whatever that was) than about social change.

Perhaps more fundamentally the new paradigm simply failed to challenge the old as a paradigm of production, either in scale or in technique. Isolated critique, no matter how profound, cannot challenge an endless production of knowledge from the paper mills of positivism if this is not tied to new and impactful productive practices. Academics could justify their activity by being caught up in this productive activity (activity also productive of them). The experimental and quantitative methods are paradigms of production par excellence. Even ethogenics, which promised a blueprint for a new method, seemed to encourage few active practitioners, not even its progenitor.

In the meantime influences were percolating through to psychology from post-structuralism and continental social theory (e.g. Foucault, Derrida, Barthes), providing a new impetus for both conceptual and empirical critique. These discursive, textual and semiotic analyses could be combined with the more empirical methods derived from Anglo-Saxon influences (speech act theory, ethnomethodology, conversation analysis) to produce concrete analyses of ordinary discourse (cf. Potter & Wetherell, 1987). At the same time, the postmodern turn, and the academic abandonment of the grand narratives of ultimate truth implied by the analyses of the modernist era (e.g. Marxism, feminism), warranted a rejection of attempts to probe for 'reality' or 'truth' in any ultimate sense. Following Lyotard (1979/1984), the old grand 'meta-narratives' had been replaced by 'paralogy', a focus on understanding of local and historically specific micro-conditions, which only permitted locally contingent understanding. This meta-theoretical climate further encouraged a focus on ordinary language, in its local context and in its own terms. The provision of the methods and the conceptual tools from continental and Anglo-Saxon traditions provided ideal conditions for this linguistic turn to take roots in a productive research paradigm and not just a form of critique. Thus we see in this volume the fruits of this conjuncture, and the many different examples of approaches that study everyday conversation and discourse (e.g. Íñiguez; Leudar and Antaki; Potter). Moreover, what gives the new wave of critical social psychology in the last ten years or so cause for optimism is that critical psychologists have developed methods and knowledge-producing paradigms of their own that can challenge the mainstream on its own terms both empirically and productively. These developments in critical social psychology are cause enough for celebration as it becomes clear that, at least in certain local micro-climates (e.g. the UK, Spain), these new traditions have started to challenge the older traditions such that the critical movement becomes critical mass (and perhaps even the new mainstream?).

But already I am beginning to speak as if critical social psychology can be identified with a particular school or even position, when this is very far from the case. Not only are there critical detractors from those involved in discourse analysis but criticism and debate within this area about what discourse analysis is have quickly opened up. It is time, therefore, to map out some of the terrain of critical social psychology covered in this volume and to sketch some debates that arise out of these different positions. Rather than going through the various chapters presented here in turn, it seems more appropriate to try to organize the ground covered by different themes and issues whilst providing some commentary on these.

The Linguistic Turn: Language, Discourse and Constructionism

As indicated above, most chapters in this volume endorse a commitment to some form of social constructionism, the notion that there is no objective window on reality whereby entities in the social world are directly perceived, or whereby words 'mirror' reality. Rather, our concepts are fundamentally socially produced through language and in communication with others. Moreover, these discourses do not simply spring from our heads, but come from the surrounding social institutions and relations in which we are embedded. One radical version of social constructionism represented would seem to dispute the existence of any independent reality beyond the stories we tell, or at least one we can get at in any meaningful sense, and this position is well captured by the contributions of the Stainton Rogers. This position has strong implications for the nature of critical psychology and the strategies it might adopt, which are further discussed in the following sections. However, language and discourse can also be seen to have a more material dimension in productively constructing individuals in relationships of power (Foucault, 1981; Parker, 1992).

Thus, Íñiguez favours a Foucauldian conceptualization of discourse in which institutional power relations reinforce and elicit discourses which in turn sustain them (see also Walkerdine). He is aware of the problems of suppressing agency implicit in a Foucauldian approach and cites Giddens's work on the duality of agency and structure; as agents not only are we responsible for reproducing social structures/discourse, but we also bear the possibility for resistance and change (I return to this theme at different points below).

A slightly different picture is painted by Potter, where the person is presented more in terms of an active user of discourse; discourse invests the individual with the power to argue back. Challenging Reicher's claim of the ability of power to close off argument, he cites the case of a rape victim resisting the insinuations of the defence counsel. Discourses can thus be seen as providing a repertoire of resources that the individual uses to achieve different functions as well as to interpret the social world. The great variability of discourses used, both between but also within individuals, provides the basis of a radical critique of the stability and structure of many of the psychological concepts of mainstream theory, such as 'attitudes' and other mental structures and states (e.g. Potter & Wetherell, 1987). This line of inquiry, then, has been used to critique mainstream psychology for its own reifications, rather than seeing the discourse as reifying us, fixing us in relation to the discourse.

Here we have (at least) two faces of discourse, both as restraint and as resource. Of course these are not necessarily contradictory, but these approaches have tended to lay different emphasis on these aspects, and, this has been the source of debate between different camps (see, e.g., Parker, 1990, 1992; Potter, Wetherell, Gill & Edwards, 1990). Despite differences within these approaches, neither specifies in any great detail the nature of the subject and its relation to discourse. The tendency to see the person as subjected to discourse or as an external user of it raises the questions of determinism and voluntarism. Although the model of the person as a functional user of discourse would seem to give greater accord to individual agency, this, however, is rarely theorized. There are perhaps a number of related reasons for this reluctance to further specification. The concerns with the subject have to some extent been dissipated by post-structuralist critiques that question the very bases and boundaries of the individual self. If the self comprises a series of socially produced texts that is to some extent independent of our physical embodiment as individuals, then focusing on the discourse of the individual would seem to form an appropriate substitute for any deeper analysis in terms of drives, attitudes, mental states and the like (although integration with constructs from mainstream psychology has not always been ruled out: see Potter & Wetherell, 1987; van Dijk, 1987). Moreover, as the textual inputs proliferate within the information society of late modernity, and communications media such as the Internet transcend the restraints of embodiment and even identity (Walkerdine), the self can come to be seen as increasingly saturated and dispersed (e.g. Gergen, 1991; Wetherell & Maybin, 1996). There would seem to be little reason to restrict ourselves to the psychology of the individual if these are themselves fragmented and distributed discursive products.

Leudar and Antaki provide perhaps a more concrete insight into the diverse and distributed nature of the self within a conversation analytic context by going beyond the utterance and taking into account the multiple roles or 'participant statuses' the individual can assume in discourse. This allows them simultaneously to question the individualistic notion of the subject and show that other identities may be implicated in the expression of speech acts than simply the speaker. This notion of multiple statuses is used as basis of a critique of the experimental context in which the participant status of experimenter and 'subject' are open to multiple interpretation. The question of whom we are speaking as or for puts into question the issue of self-definition. However, the conversation analytic framework provides no way of probing into this psychology beyond the surface text, and several interpretative analyses, including psychoanalysis, are criticized for going beyond the information given, searching for some hidden code.

I shall return to the issue of the subject further below but suffice to say a further theorizing in this area would help to explain how and when subjects use or are 'used by' discourse. Meanwhile, the denial of underlying essence provides a serious obstruction to this project, and one that is closely bound up with broader issues of relativism versus realism. If we adopt an anti-realist stance there is indeed perhaps no need to search for deeper essences either inside or outside the self. It is to such questions that have dominated the stage of critical social psychology that we now turn.

Realism versus Relativism: Is Social Construction Enough?

Many of the chapters touch on the realism versus relativism controversy and some are centrally concerned with it (e.g. W. Stainton Rogers and R. Stainton Rogers). Because many other questions follow from it, it cannot be resisted any longer. Questions around this issue have always been lurking in the background of social science (and its claims to be science), and the celebration of relativism by postmodern theorists, in challenging both the positivists' paradigms and the grand narratives of its critics, has forced the controversy into the forefront (Roiser). Indeed one could argue that this has perhaps become one of the central concerns of critical social psychology, inspiring at least one current contributor to plead that we move on from the 'sterile debates' around this topic (Walkerdine). Is it not time to bypass this issue, as Walkerdine suggests, and get on with a political pragmatics of social change (cf. Squire, 1995a)? Maybe. However, it is precisely because realism and relativism have been linked to an analysis of political positions and effects that this debate cannot easily be ignored. It is not just that these different positions promise to provide the key to our understanding of society, and therefore have implications about how to critique and change it. They also have reflexive effects in prefiguring or curtailing practical political activity. The rhetoric surrounding realism and relativism can paralyse as well as promote the social change sought by critical theorists often precisely because of strong claims to the critical high ground. The scientistic dialectical materialism (diamat) of Second International Marxism is a good example of a mechanically materialist realism, where any critical agency was branded as ultra-left or counter-revolutionary, lest this disturb the material contradictions as they unfold by themselves. The political consequences of this kind of determinist fatalism are clear for all to see. From the other side of the fence, relativism is no less immune from the dangers of promoting political paralysis. In discussing the effect of this resurgent relativism on feminism, Gill (1995) refers to a sceptical 'epistemological correctness' undermining the ability of feminists to challenge 'real' oppression and exploitation (see also Wilkinson). The terms of the debate, then, clearly feed into the political process.

Historically realism has been linked to the certainties of the old world order and positivism has been seen as the standard-bearer of objectivity and truth (although strictly speaking it is wrong to view positivism as a realist philosophy of science – see Bhaskar, 1989; Greenwood, 1989, 1991). In the postmodern era, and within social psychology, the ascendancy of social constructionism, and discourse analysis in particular, has brought these epistemological certainties into question and signalled a renewed respectability for a relativism which casts severe doubt on the possibility of any position or perspective from which to view truth. This 'anti-foundationalism' thus eschews not only the fact-finding of a 'value-free' positivist science, but also the grand narratives of Marxism and feminism, which offered a 'value-relevant' critique of both science and society. What was once called critical theory, or critical psychology, is now seen as too doctrinaire, broad-brush and lacking in critical insight. The paralogy of local and multi-layered interpretation has replaced the 'rent-a-narrative'. It is not just that the quest for 'truth' may prove impossible, but the idea that 'truth' provides the panacea to other moral and political problems of concern to critical theorists may be misguided in the first place.

In their recent article Edwards, Ashmore and Potter (1995) offer a defence of relativism against so-called bottom line 'death and the furniture' arguments invoked by realists. These objections to relativism can be summed up by the moral as well as epistemological problems of denying events like the Holocaust (raised here in a number of chapters – see, e.g., Lubek, Wilkinson) as well as Dr Johnson's habit of kicking things into existence. (An example of Michael's 'dialogue with nature' perhaps? See below.) In arguing that these claims are themselves social constructions, Edwards et al. deny the status of realism and argue that their critical (de)constructionist stance is more consistent with the 'ethic of science'. This position forms an important basis of the chapter by W. Stainton Rogers and R. Stainton Rogers as well as informing Potter's position. The Stainton Rogers defend a critical relativism against the critical realism imported into discourse analysis by Parker (1992; Bhaskar, 1989). At a political level there has been a hard-fought struggle between both sides of this argument, not least for the moral high ground (Billig, 1991; Burman, 1991; Gill, 1995; Parker, 1992; Parker & Burman, 1993; Wetherell & Potter, 1992), and these sides are well represented in this volume. Just as realism can be seen to buttress positivist science and all the sins of certainty and reification, so can relativism be seen to signal an absence of any political commitment or critique, or at least a solid platform (a foundation) on which to ground action.

Both W. Stainton Rogers and R. Stainton Rogers and Potter are surely right to argue that the products of our experience are constructed or 'knowledged', and in this sense are right to render problematic the fact–fiction distinction. The real, as it is experienced, and realism, as it is talked about (and used to do things), is thus (among other things) undoubtedly a discursive practice. However, the more sophisticated realists do not deny the importance of social construction (the trick being to reconcile this with an independent 'reality'). And even if we could only ever show that reality is always constructed by its users, this does not necessarily mean that reality (as it is conceived by realists) is *only* constructed. The question is whether construction, subjective or inter-subjective, is in itself enough to capture what is going on, and whether there is anything else going on outside or independent of it. W. Stainton Rogers and R. Stainton Rogers and Potter would seem to suggest construction is all that can or should be claimed with certainty. However, this in turn is not necessarily to deny that there is anything going on outside or underneath the text, but only whether we can ever get at this, in the sense of getting at 'truth'. The issue is therefore one of correspondence between our constructions and reality (between words and things). Although realists would argue that depth explanation allows us to probe beneath 'empirical' surface relations, the radical relativist would counter that this just gets us into an infinite regress and does little to solve the problem of arbitrating between alternatives.

When relativism is run together with the turn to language and discourse analysis this also starts to sets limits on our object of study as well as our method. Potter argues that in looking at concrete discourse and practice we should only study things when they are topicalized in discourse. This is one guaranteed way of avoiding the dangers of reification. However, are we not missing potentially important things that are deliberately left unsaid, or perhaps even not available to consciousness? What is left out of discourse is sometimes most interesting and ideological (in the sense of being 'repressed' – Parker, in press) and it may take the privileged perspective of the researcher to spot this (Condor; Michael; Reicher; Spears, 1994). The concept of ideology, traditionally an important conceptual tool in the armoury of the critical theorists, becomes problematic in these terms. If there is no underlying reality beyond the construction, no difference between essence and appearance as it were, there can be no ideological tension, no space for ideology critique as such. It is odd therefore that Potter should refer to this concept at all, although the Stainton Rogers seem more wary of it (see also Squire, 1995b). Although the logic of their position prevents them from taking sides with the conviction of certainty, lest they privilege one 'reality' over another, the Stainton Rogers reject an 'anything goes relativism', and when the chips are down acknowledge having to act as if the foundations are actually there (!?). As soon as the issues become a matter of practical political activity, then, there seems to be little difference between this 'critical relativism' and the realist position.

Reluctance to take sides is a possible (but not a necessary) consequence of the preservation of criticality at all costs. Criticality is of course precious but can lead to the charge of preciousness when raised to an almost universal principle (see also Lubek), and above some of the political causes for which it might be put to good use. As Gill (1995) points out, when sceptical criticality is an end in itself, it becomes contentless, ironically akin to the dispassionate scientific scepticism of the enlightenment tradition (Condor also notes that relativism derives from the enlightenment values of tolerance). Thus Gill laments that relativism offers no positive alternative to realism with which to challenge the exploitation and inequalities of the status quo. The consequence of this sort of position is not just to disarm those wishing to criticize the effects of patriarchy (for example), it can actually lead its adherents to attack feminists for the use of such grand narratives (see, e.g., Squire's, 1995b, critique of R. Stainton Rogers & W. Stainton Rogers, 1992). The certainty of a position based on uncertainty is the final reflexive paradox that while sometimes acknowledged seems little more than that. Once again it is not the case that advocates of the relativist position are unable to take a political stand, but for them there would seem to be no clear grounds by which to settle the argument. Moreover, to resolve the argument in line with these political convictions would ulti- mately seem to be premised on realizing the falsity of their more general philosophical position.

Do we have to make a choice between the worst excesses of realism and relativism (at least as presented by opposing camps)? As I have suggested above, at the very least we should not have to choose between social constructionism and a realist stance, and a number of other writers have had fewer problems in reconciling these. Reicher and Michael make perhaps the most explicit case for this in the present volume (see also Condor; Wilkinson; Parker; Roiser; Greenwood, 1989, 1991). Whilst not denying construction, Reicher underscores the importance of nature and biological foundations (cf. Timpanaro, 1976) and an independent social reality beyond. Michael emphasizes the 'natural' as an autonomous actor external to social construction, but impinging on it. He argues that the social has been privileged to the point of almost ignoring any biological materialism, although these material constraints are not restricted to the biological: the materiality of our environment, including technology, offers gradients of resistance which form part of the tendency and constraint on human behaviour. He draws on Marx, Gibson and Latour to argue for a more mutualist interaction between environment and organism and sees nature as a neglected semiotic player in this dialogue. In sum, the natural limits of and on the body require a corporeal semiotics beyond the purely linguistic discursive realm. Viewing nature as part of the conversation presents a refreshing realist edge to counter the tyranny of the text. However, we should also be wary of dissolving the analytic distinction between the natural and the social (Cohen, 1978). The tension between them (as in the contradictions between forces and relations) provides a cleavage for critique, as well as preserving the 'human' nature of intention and agency for the social dimension (Callinicos, 1987). This is surely one analytic dualism worth preserving.

The realism–relativism debate is also a struggle to (re)construct classical recruits. For example, although Wittgenstein is seen by many in the discursive tradition as a social constructionist, in the radical relativist sense (cf. Gergen, 1988; Shotter, 1991), others have disputed this claiming he was (like Marx) a social materialist, because his language games were firmly located in particular forms of social life (Jost & Hardin, 1996; Rubinstein, 1981). In relativist writings, these social relations are sometimes over-shadowed by the act and content of construction itself. Thus although it is not excluded by the Stainton Rogers, there is little mention of the shared collective activity that locates 'knowledging' in the social and not just the subjective psychological domain. To the extent that this reality is *socially* constructed and negotiated, this social validation from others allows for social reality testing that arguably sets constraints on one's constructions. Moreover, although the struggle over different stories or constructions is undeniable, the fact that these do not take place in an ideal speech com-munity where everyone has equal voice or ability to speak demonstrates not only the power of construction, but also the importance of power (Reicher; Spears & Parker, 1996), and the relation of power to material interests. One reason why not 'everything goes' is therefore arguably because of the tendency and constraint imposed by social realities, which support some constructions more than others. Moreover, we do not need a transcendental position outside of social relations to understand these relations and how they might change – this understanding can be immanent, collective and concrete. Transcendental arguments are, however, useful and perhaps necessary, in the sense that we often have to assume certain realities for things to make sense or to be possible at all (Bhaskar, 1994; Callinicos, 1987).

Nevertheless, the fact that different groups have different understandings of reality suggests that reality can itself be a function of social position and interests. In this sense reality itself is relative, because the reality of group interests actually varies with social position in asymmetrical social relations (Spears, 1995; Spears, Oakes, Ellemers & Haslam, 1997). The material interests, as well as the experiences, of different groups (males and females, whites and blacks, middle-class and working-class people) are likely to be different and reflect different social realities. If this argument resolves the apparent contradiction between realism and social relativism in one sense, this would still seem to leave the problem of choosing between the reality-based constructions of different sides. Although critical theorists may be politically inclined to side with the exploited and oppressed (cf. Gill's, 1995, 'politically informed relativism'), is there a warrant for this beyond pragmatic preference? Certainly if truth is beyond reach (as some postmodernist sceptics have concluded), perhaps a politically informed relativism may be the best we can hope for. The alternative is to return to the grand narratives of feminism and Marxism for our foundations. However, perhaps the postmodernist radicals are being unrealistic if they think that focusing on politics and justice allows us to side-step judgements of truth; in deciding rights, the question of 'rightness' is (in the last instance) probably unavoidable (cf. Geras, 1983).

Whatever the answers to this realism–relativism controversy, if not aware of these issues already the reader will quickly realize that this complex debate both plagues and enriches critical social psychology. Unlike the mainstream, there is at least an acceptable space for this debate to take place.

Method, Research Practice and Reflexivity

As we have seen, the terms of this debate are far-reaching and sometimes threaten to strangle rather than promote a critical psychology. This debate spills over into many other questions, including questions of method (as well as sometimes itself stemming from such questions). Some realists are wont to claim the experimental method as the only true means of isolating the causal mechanisms operating in open systems such as society (see, e.g., Bhaskar, 1989; Greenwood, 1989, 1991; and also Knorr Cetina, this volume). However those in the more hermeneutic tradition clearly view this quest as misguided from the start, questioning not just the applicability but also the very realist assumptions associated with importing natural science models and metaphors into the social domain (theorists such as Dilthy, Simmel, Winch and Gadamer predate the current school of social constructionism and discourse analysis in taking this tack). Thus many of the current flux of constructionist and discourse analysts, including Potter here, see the study of natural discourse as the natural and perhaps only means of proceeding. Clearly the turn to language and the crisis critique of the artifice and artificiality of experimentation, and the violence of abstraction it brings with it, have meant a move away from 'mainstream' quantitative methods, towards more qualitative and ethnographic techniques. These qualitative methods have thus become the mainstream of the critical repertoire, and method has almost become the ultimate loyalty test of criticality.

When method, like criticality, becomes raised to the status of end in itself rather than serving the research questions dictated by a critical analysis, this can be problematic. On the other hand, as Potter is right to observe, method is often theory disguised as method so we should always be wary of methodology wolves in sheep's clothing, bearing gifts of value-free facts. Once again reification is clearly a legitimate concern here reinforced by a number of authors (see also Reicher). Where critical political objectives are at stake, however, pragmatism is probably better than purism. Despite his critique of empiricism and his suspicion of surface 'facts', Marx was not above the use of quantitative methods and used official statistics to add concrete empirical body to his analyses (Triesman, 1974). It is therefore refreshing to see not only the range of methods used to advance critical arguments and critique in the present volume, but also that some contributors have not been afraid to cock a snook at 'methodological correctness' and recuperate some 'enemy' tools. Lubek demonstrates perhaps most clearly the use to which quantitative methods can be put in order to expose and undermine the hegemonic forces operating on and in the academy. He uses his social psychology of science model to examine the asymmetrical power relations in academia and the gate-keeping practices that can reinforce this. These methods complement the equally compelling case studies, such as that of John Garcia. This account of the helplessness of a high-status individual, aligned against the power of prevailing institutional forces, puts our worst nightmares of the review process into perspective, and demonstrates the difficulties of getting critical work into the public domain. The solution of setting up 'critical' journals does not always offer the best option if these are marginalized or even used as an excuse by more established and accessible outlets to siphon off 'critical' pieces (why not try journal *x*?).

Lubek underlines the importance of the political ends and practical use to which research can be put, rather than getting bogged down in issues of methodological purity (see also Ibáñez). However, he does remain critical of the experimental paradigms that have formed straitjackets for research, and the fetish of standard procedures encouraging trivialization and displacement of issues of genuine interest. In the present context and company it would be something of a brave person who would have as the main motif the defence of experimentation (the critical equivalent of swearing in church?). However, this is the distinctive message of Reicher's contribution and his defence is partly the realist defence of experimentation alluded to above. The privileged position and perspective of the researcher allows an access sometimes denied to the participants of research themselves; not all evidence is open to or produced through discourse and personal testimony, so the researcher and the experimenter in particular has access to both social (supra-individual – Condor) and subconscious products that may be inaccessible to the participant (Condor; see also Spears, 1994). These points link up with some of the warrants for realism discussed in the preceding section. It may therefore sometimes be disingenuous to suggest that researcher and researched are on an equal footing when the former is (legitimately) claiming special insights deriving from expertise or perspective.

However, Reicher's argument is more than this because he considers reflexivity as part of the object (subject!) of research within the experimental context. He has the same concerns with reflexivity, power relations and politics that concern Lubek and many other contributors, but argues that, as classical and explicit paradigms of power, experiments allow us both to use and to examine the nature of the power relationship (between experimenter and 'subject'), and to acknowledge our own role and reflexivity in the research process. The laboratory as a place which typically denies the participant a voice (Billig, 1994; Bowers, 1991) therefore offers a context within which to use and dissect this panoptic power (see also Condor; Spears, 1994). Moreover Reicher argues that this power relation and the typical lack of reflexivity of the researcher is not unique to experimentation, but is characteristic of most methods. The unacknowledged role of the researcher in (co)producing the outcome of research is also evident in questionnaires but also in more qualitative methods such as discourse analysis. Simply acknowledging the role of the interviewer and the reflexivity of the research relation is often more a gesture than a solution (see also Condor; Gill, 1995). Certainly, the participants of research rarely if ever have any say over the final text (Billig, 1994; Condor; Spears, 1994). Reicher therefore proposes the experiment as a way of making this asymmetry explicit and to use it as a model of the asymmetrical power relations in society, with the proviso that the experimenter's role becomes acknowledged as a crucial part of the process.

Perhaps not surprisingly, this may seem hard to swallow for those wary of the track record of experimental psychology, who see it as part of the problem; as noted earlier, Potter explicitly challenges this move. As we have seen, the relativist is hardly likely to be persuaded by realist justifications for experimentation, and finds the study of people in artificial contexts in which they have little stake a poor substitute for studying people in their 'real' lives. A concern with context is a prime concern of critical theorists and Condor recommends that we keep on our 'context lenses' as an antidote to universalizing tendencies in both mainstream and critical psychology (although it is unclear whether the lack of interests and 'mundane realism' is a generic feature of experimentation or just a feature of poorly designed research). However, at a time when the distinction between the artificial and the real has been questioned and deconstructed by such godfathers of postmodernism as Baudrillard, so that the veridical and virtual are increasingly mixed up (Roiser; Walkerdine), one may indeed begin to wonder whether reality has not in certain respects come to mirror some aspects of the experimental situation, if not always the reverse. Is the research paradigm itself not a regulatory and normative 'story' that is itself worthy of reflexive self-examination?

This has indeed been the subject of some of Potter's own discourse analytic work, and in this volume Knorr Cetina also devotes her attention to the sorts of things that researchers get up to. Like this earlier work on 'scientific' construction (e.g. Potter, 1992), we find the 'opticist' image of the scientist as the dispassionate and passive observer uncovering neutral facts of the hypothetico-deductive ideal often diverges from the reality. However, the notion of scientists as interested, actively intervening and aware of that to which they are working towards is less problematic for the 'retroductive' philosophy of science characterized by some realists (cf. Bhaskar, 1989; Sayer, 1983). What is clear is that science is a messier business than it is presented to be, where knowledge production and the building and maintenance of socio-technical networks (Latour, 1992) play just as important a role as the building of other pieces of apparatus. A reflexive socio-political analysis of what scientists, both natural and social, do is therefore necessary if we are to monitor and resist their productive support for the psy-complex.

As suggested earlier, reflexivity has become the new buzz-word of critical psychologists, and would seem to be something that all can agree on. Going critical means getting self-critical: the model of the disinterested scientist has been replaced by the researcher reviewing his or her role as part of the process if not part of the problem. The power of the researcher, both in the research context, and in control of the texts that arise from it, is just another of the asymmetrical relations of interest to the critical psychologist. Such reflexivity is often difficult to reconcile with the role of researcher and the claims to expertise that this entails. A number of contributors touch on reflexivity, but Condor provides perhaps the most thorough analyses of the issues and problems of reflexivity in her critique of Sampson's work (Sampson, 1991, 1993). She argues that claims to democracy and dialogism made by Sampson can be analysed for the rhetorical devices they use to buttress his authority, by claiming expert knowledge and the right to speak for others ('translation'). The rhetoric of dialogism and democracy can be used to obscure the fact that the author is himself claiming 'an a-contextual, universal' voice (Nagel's, 1986, 'view from nowhere') characteristic of the 'sanctioned sciences' (cf. Latour, 1992). In advancing his own dialogical blueprint over the Western project of cognitive psychology, Condor thus shows that critical psychologists are often ultimately as prone to the same unreflexive and universalizing tendencies criticized by critical theorists. All this serves to show that claims to self-reflexivity should themselves be critically interrogated.

Not Forgetting the Subject . . .

There is perhaps an even more fundamental issue arising from the question of self-reflexivity and this is (once again) the notion of the self or 'subject' itself. This is yet another area where critical theorists seem as divided and dispersed as some of their notions of the self. On the one hand, many or most of the contributors are critical of the preformed unitary Cartesian subject (see, e.g., Condor; Burman; Reicher; Walkerdine) familiar to main-stream psychology, and Western thought and culture in general. A critique of this assumption seems to be a starting point and to provide much common ground for critical psychologists keen to avoid the essentialism and voluntarism implied by this position as well as the liberal and right wing politics that it is all too often woven into (see Roiser). Questioning the individualistic myth that we are masters of our own destinies and can pull ourselves up by our bootstraps is paralleled by an even more fundamental questioning of whether the individual self, *sui generis*, actually exists (or is just a figment of our cultural imagination). If there are no certainties associated with the grand narratives, why should the subjective certainties of individual authenticity and experience be anything more than an illusion? As we have seen, one radical course therefore seems to have been to deny the existence of the self or the individual, beyond the textual construction, or at least to omit it or leave it untheorized. Post-structuralism has been so busy talking up the power of social structure, language and discourse that there seems at times to be little room for the individual agent. Agents come to be seen all too easily as passive bearers of social structures, a legacy of the structural Marxism of Althusser, the discursive tradition of Foucault, and 'psychology as history' of Gergen (1973). For activists keen to engage in change, these influences continue to cast a rather pessimistic pall over critical psychology.

Within this context, generating a theory of the subject has, as I have argued earlier, not always been the first priority of theorists coming out of the bend of the linguistic turn. Discourse analysts, and even more so conversation analysts, have been reluctant to stray too far from the surface of the spoken word, rightly wary of the dangers of psychologizing and reification (see Leudar and Antaki, discussed earlier). Fresh from a critique of psychology, these writers are hardly likely to turn back to it for the meanings and motives behind the talk. This wariness goes hand in hand with the debates around realism and relativism, discussed above. To admit of essence driving behaviour would be to reinvent realism in the psyche. Rather than using conversation or discourse to reveal some-thing underneath, then, we should see it for what it is, and see ourselves in this talk. Discourse analysts are prepared to refer to the local functions realized by agents in talk but again there is still little theory of how these local functions might relate to a more general theory of functional being. However, as Condor remarks, the whole discursive exercise is based on the problematic assumption that subjects are perfectly conscious intentional agents. The willingness to see individuals as generators of talk, but not to probe too far beyond this, reflects and often results in what Parker (in press) has recently called 'blank' or 'simple subjectivity'.

But to repeat our earlier question, why do we need a theory of the self anyway? If we don't need to dig beyond the surface to deeper essence or motives, then it is unnecessary. The abandonment of attempts to find consistency and coherence in discourse combined with the distributed and fragmented self (Burman; Leudar and Antaki; Walkerdine) suggests the subject may just get in the way, while we should look elsewhere for our unit of analysis. The discourse becomes both explanandum and explanans in a world where there is nothing but or beyond text.

The concern with micro-functions and local projects of situated action means that some of the grander metaphors that gave self-projects a greater purpose have similarly been eroded along with the grand narratives. But is it enough to look at what people say and do, without relating these to grander schemes inside or outside the self? This position seems unsatisfactory for several reasons. First, as Condor observes, much language work treats people as if they are intentional agents, and to fail to analyse the cause of their functional and strategic behaviour may therefore dissolve into some form of voluntarism, which moves us no further than more structuralist accounts in resolving the relation between agency and structure. Second, evidence of variability in discourse does not rule out consistencies at other levels. To be sure, consistency should be sought less in psychometric than in discursive and ideological forms. If we are to avoid the twin dangers of voluntarism and structuralism, we need to understand the ways that agency both is constructed by and can resist these discourses. More fundamentally perhaps, Reicher suggests we need a theory of the self to know which side we are on, both epistemologically and politically. Epistemologically we need to know who we are in order to act; we need first to make sense of ourselves in order to make sense of the rest. Selfhood therefore provides perspective and sense of identity, which are necessary for conscious agency. In political terms this means a division into us and them, and the ability to take sides. A theory of the subject in these terms, then, would seem to be an important ingredient for a critical psychology if it is to have bite, and allow us to descend from the fence.

Traditional psychology has not been short of attempts to define 'human nature' and critical psychology has been understandably wary if not hostile to these candidates. Ironically what we now regard as mainstream has often itself been seen as critical opposition at earlier junctures. Some critical voices held out early hope that cognitive psychology might prove to be a radical alternative to behaviourism (Sedgwick, 1974; Shallice, 1984), precisely because it appeared to reinvest the subject with some agency (just as behaviourism was held up by many seeking to counter the hereditarian notions of personality and intelligence). This seems rather optimistic in retrospect. Now the pendulum has swung and alternative critical traditions must take the role of opposition to cognitivism, whose mechanistic and computational metaphors expunge the agent from the inside as effectively as behaviourism had expunged the self from the external world. A classical recourse for many critical theorists seeking a theory of the subject beyond the mechanistic metaphors of positivism is psychoanalysis. A number of the current contributors have developed this possibility here and elsewhere (Parker, Walkerdine). Parker sees psychoanalysis as a counter to attempts to suppress the sensual organic nature of our being and this biological underpinning is echoed by Michael and Reicher.

Do psychoanalytic categories do the trick or do they, as Tajfel (1978) once suggested, provide a drama that has been played out before the actors have come on stage? To be sure, they capture the motivations that allow us to move beyond simple and blank forms of subjectivity to more 'complex' forms, and such ideas and analyses can be usefully integrated with discourses and their hold on us (Parker, in press). These motives do not have their sources just in biology, but also in the recursive filtering back of metaphor in society (Moscovici, 1976). What is sometimes unclear in these culturally reconstructed psychoanalytic approaches is whether their advocates believe in the power of the primary biological model as well as the secondary cultural metaphor (or are these inseparable?). At a political level it is perhaps clearer, as Parker points out, that psychoanalysis has itself a dubious, often misogynistic political history, requiring a certain critical distance.

Psychoanalysis is not the only available resource for critical theorists looking for a theory of the self. Reicher and his colleagues (Reicher, Hopkins & Condor, 1996) have advocated integrating a discursive approach with a theory of the social subject arising out of social identity and self-categorization work (e.g. Turner, Hogg, Oakes, Reicher & Wetherell, 1987). Again, the more dynamic constructionist and dialogical aspects of the discursive tradition provide a useful counter to some of the perceptualist/cognitivist tendencies within this tradition, while the analysis of social identities, or self-categories, provides a theory of the subject to motivate the struggle, not least over the meaning of self and identity itself. Attempts to theorize the social subject also reflect an effort to move away from the individualistic conceptions of selfhood and subjectivity, linking in to collective behaviour.

Psychoanalysis and self-categorization are not the only options of course but the fact that critical social psychology is not overwhelmed with options here reveals the continued emphasis on structural constraint and under-recognized or undertheorized agency. For the more structurally inclined constructionists and Foucauldians this wariness doubtless relates to a fear of letting the individualistic Cartesian subject back in. This has resulted in attempts to develop not only more social forms of subjectivity, but also more mutualist understandings of agency, taking into account the inter-action of the person and the material and social context (see Costall & Still, 1987; Leudar, 1991; Michael; Reed, 1996). Reclaiming the subject and the self from mainstream psychology will no doubt be a continuing and growing concern to critical psychologists.

. . . and Finally Politics (Again)

Formulating a theory of the subject provides agents and agency that can be the vehicles of resistance and change, and this returns us to the issue of a progressive politics. However, once again we should be wary of the dangers of idealism and voluntarism. If (to paraphrase Marx) people make history, but not under conditions of their own choosing, then we should not forget the external structural constraints on agency, nor the ability of social structure to infuse our very being through the social practices and discourses it fosters. One of the major contributions of the postmodernist turn, as well as one of its dangers, is to blur this boundary between structure and agency. Foucault makes this point when underlining the productive and not just the repressive aspects of the ideological discourse enveloping the individual. Other structuralists like Althusser also capture the essence of ideology as embedded in lived, material practices rather than reflecting 'ideas' imposed by powerful interests through 'false consciousness'. The agency that can produce change is thus the same agency that maintains the status quo, and both are willing intentional processes that follow from the contents of our identities. In this way political change is bound up with the possibilities contained in identity.

This agency/structure dualism is further blurred because external aspects incorporated within the self become a party to our agency as subjects. Not only are agents comprised and influenced by social structures and discourses; these social structures, once incorporated in the self, can themselves have the properties of social agents in the sense of being able to resist or enable (Ibáñez; Michael; see also Callinicos, 1987; Giddens, 1984). New and more collectivist definitions of the 'social' self (social identities) mean that social structures (groups, collectivities) may also form part of the resources of the self, including a transformed sense of agency. People are often able to resist or challenge politically precisely because of the knowledge of collective support, both physical and psychological, through shared identity with others trapped in similarly exploitative or oppressive relationships. Collective identity thus evokes a potentially powerful social reality beyond the individual and prevents agency dissolving into individualistic idealism. In these terms political resistance and change transcend the agency/structure dualism, by demonstrating the social dimensions of self, and the agency of social structure.

Thus when we reconsider Potter's example of the rape victim 'arguing back', and resisting the constructions of the defence counsel, we should be wary of identifying this as a simple individual voice, thereby of overestimating the powers of untheorized 'individual' resistance. The fact that this example 'proves' the rule of the majority of such cases that never make it to the legal stage reflects the institutional and hegemonic powers of a society and legal establishment that consciously and unconsciously check such challenges. Moreover, when the victim *is* prepared to confront legal power/knowledge in courts, we should not neglect the role of the collective agents supporting the individual from outside and from within that make much of this individual resistance possible. It is therefore arguably in spite of the institutional forces of patriarchy ranged against her and at least partly because of this collective strength of others that resistance is possible.

While it is politically important to preserve a conceptual distinction of agency (the intentional subject), then, it is important to acknowledge the elements from outside that both help to constitute this agency as well as keep it in check.

Political possibilities are therefore closely bound up with the models we present of psychology and the self, and there is a close interplay between these models and societal forces ('ideological discourses'). Using the themes of psychoanalysis, Parker takes this reflexivity a step further and analyses the recuperation of psychoanalysis by the psy-complex. There are instructive parallels between repression of the sensual dimension in ourselves and how the psychological community has disarmed and stripped psychoanalysis of its sexual *jouissance* and radical edge, tailoring it to conservative Western values (as in 'ego-psychology'). The idea that our psychology can serve as a metaphor for the social forces of which it is a part is a theme also picked up by Burman. She relates the discourse surrounding developmental stage models to discourses of colonialism in the Third World, arguing that these cultures can be drawn into adopting these discourses themselves, reproducing the oppressive power relations (and thus adding a Foucauldian twist). Similarly hierarchical models of cognitive science have been incorporated into militaristic programmes such as 'Star Wars' (Bowers, 1990) and the tailoring of psychology to capitalist society includes links between cognitivism and 'Taylorism' (Shotter, 1987). The complicity of psychology as a part of societal and institutional defence and control mechanisms makes clear why critical social psychologists have been so concerned to look 'inwards' at what psychology is up to. Although critical psychology can, as Parker and Burman show, provide a critical gloss on more macro-social processes, we should be wary of overplaying the anthropomorphism; these metaphors are useful up to the point where they deflect us from other heuristic levels of analysis. However, what this and the earlier analysis of agency show is that both resistance and critique are not something we derive from external insights or vantage points – they are internal to ourselves as political agents and as critical theorists, 'fashioned from available cultural resources' (Condor). The idea of a culture-free perspective is a myth of positivism, while the 'emigration fantasies' of finding such a view from other disciplines only perpetuate this myth. A commitment to immanent critique thus provides some common ground for postmodernist and Marxist strands of critical thought.

Closely related to the power of theory, both as part of the problem and as an analytic tool with which to examine it, is our own contradictory 'critical' role as academics and practitioners. A number of contributors are sensitive to our potential complicity by virtue of our position in 'state apparatuses' and institutions – as a part of the psy-complex which feeds into and is shaped by the institutions and the knowledge they produce (Ibáñez; Lubek; Reicher). Just by 'being there' is there not a danger that we do more to sustain rather than subvert? The tolerance of criticality in the academy is arguably a small price for the state to pay compared to the possibility of wider unrest in more economically productive quarters. Critical psychologists have to fight with the uncomfortable realization that their own resistance sometimes only serves to strengthen the semblance of critical freedom whilst leaving the major power relations intact (Reicher, 1996). Our role is an inherently ambiguous one, in which we habitually occupy something akin to 'contradictory class locations' (Wright, 1985). This calls for a range of different tactics and struggles on different fronts; the possibility of direct political action in certain contexts may not be consistent with preserving our position of power within the academy (which may have its critical uses) in other contexts. Managing these contradictions is sometimes a difficult balancing act, and it is all too easy to become seduced by the realities and interests of this relatively privileged position.

This acceptance of things as they are (and being a part of this) is made all the easier by the wider context of the defeat of communism in the East and socialism in the West. Against this backdrop, postmodernism can be seen as an understandable reaction to both the excesses and failures of state communism and other forms of 'Big P' politics. One of the reasons the grand narratives have fallen from grace among large sections of the critical community is because they were seen as crude and heavy-handed, with some revolutionary groups' predictions about the imminent collapse of capitalism too embarrassingly reminiscent of those of Armageddon cults to inspire much confidence in the analysis. Moreover, the terrors of Stalinism provided not only doubts about the ultimate destination and its foundations, but legitimate fears that the journey there might be even worse ('the end justifies the means'). However, we are perhaps now far enough to be able to cast a critical eye back at postmodernism, the critical heir apparent. Perhaps now we can see its own concerns as a sign of its own historical times (see, e.g., Condor) rather than as the ultimate critical vantage point from which to judge others. To be sure, many crimes were committed under the name of communism, but the banner of postmodernism offers no guarantee against the abuse of power either (a minor recent example is that of the cult Church of England cleric Chris Brain, who combined postmodernist and New Age rhetoric with religion to provide a cloak for the abuse of women in his 'Nine O'clock Service'). The lesson here perhaps is that almost any discourses can be put to almost any ends (the arbitrariness of the sign?) if the power and will are there. This would seem at least to warrant an analysis acutely attuned to power relations. Both the deficit, and thus danger, of much postmodern criticality, then, is that it does not appear to have an explicit politics or political agenda. That this is a problem is perhaps made most explicit by Wilkinson, who emphasizes the contrasts if not conflicts with the feminist agenda(s), and is not the only one to be exasperated by some of the positions this can lead to (Roiser; see also Gill, 1995, discussed above). Thus, for the more politically oriented, the political insouciance of postmodernist strands of critical social psychology can be seen sometimes as as much part of the problem as of the solution ('modernism without the politics' as Roiser puts it). As we have seen, by rejecting these grand narratives, postmodernists can all too easily find themselves arguing against what many others of more pragmatic or political persuasion consider self-evident progressive causes, or simply providing a recipe for 'nihilism and quietude' (Wilkinson).

Some of the contributions to this volume advocate a less purist and more pragmatic stance prioritizing the political objectives of liberation above the theoretical issues (see also Squire, 1995a). As we have seen, this pragmatism also carries over into method with a few arguing that anything goes that attacks the hegemony of the psy-complex, even where this means using the standard methods (Ibáñez; Lubek; Reicher; Roiser; Wilkinson). Unholy alliances are a way of breaking from strictures of critical thought as much as from the mainstream. The end justifies the means may be an ominous slogan, but there is perhaps a greater danger of purism, that means and method become ends in themselves, taking our eyes off the prize. If taking sides has come to mean making a choice between political versus epistemological correctness, there is a danger that these internal debates will obscure and overshadow the use value of critical social psychology.

Once again reflexivity and pragmatism are essential antidotes to such paralysing stand-offs, helping us consider how our work as critical psychologists can facilitate, inspire or prefigure political changes. The critical issue is to what extent our psychology is useful to those who need it to resist, raising the question of accessibility and user-friendliness to ordinary people and not just expert practitioners. Lubek points out that critical writing all too often seems to require subtitles or originate from another planet: if much of psychology uses its own alien and alienating jargon, this seems alas no less true of critical social psychology. I will let the readers judge for themselves whether some contributors might have overstepped the mark (and I do not claim to be exempt). If translation into practice is the criterion, our critical approaches must be accessible and come *prêt à porter* (it's all very well bringing out the Lyotard, but will the people wear it?). Abstraction is often the enemy of simple action, and critical theorists have an important role as the organic intellectuals tuned in to real struggles, translating theory and research into resistance, or at least attempting to inoculate psychology's consumers against complicity. Theoreticians and politicians, radical and right, from Gramsci to Berlusconi, have understood only too well the need to touch on the experience of ordinary people in order to interpellate them and turn them to their causes. The hold of Mao and Stalin beyond their obvious power base lay not so much in their knowledge of the finer points of Marxist theory, as in an affinity with their own culture, the folklore and icons which enabled them to tailor a rhetoric and analysis to the local context and their own ends. The 'practical adequacy' of the message, and its resonance with real and potential struggles, is an important criterion for the radical as well as the reactionary. This struggle of meaning is clearly an ideological struggle precisely because many of the discourses that come ready to wear, 'off the peg', are inevitably not made to fit the interests of the exploited and oppressed.

If aspects of popular culture and the like can be used conservatively to reinforce prejudices and established social relations, these resources can equally be mobilized to social and political change, by providing a language that is both understood and appealing. Humour can be more than a sugar coating for a bitter political pill; it can be a useful form of mobilizing resistance in itself (and a resource sometimes under-used by critical psychologists). This is not to say that the use of humour and the popular in the mobilizing discourses should be ends in themselves or devoid of theoretical analysis (and there is indeed a danger that strategies solely premised on playfulness will lead to its proponents being dismissed as juvenile). Theory, and theoretical debate, are necessary of course, lest pragmatism dissolve into pure populism. However, one of the lessons of theory is that it must also stay closely tied to the political practice and experience of those using it. The notion that thought (theory) is a moment in practice protects against the dangers of this dualism, and helps to explain why theories, just like words, do things and have political consequences. If we act as if they are real they may already have come true. Thus, following Gramsci, while 'pessimism of the intellect' is the realist's antidote to idealism, 'optimism of the will' shows that the idea of change must be born through practice. Critical psychologists have to square the circle of both ideas and action if they are to change and not just interpret the world. One of the many encouraging features of the collection in this volume, then, is that it presents a wealth of theoretical ideas, all of which give pause for thought, and many of which provide cause for action.

This introductory chapter provides only a mere hint of some of the goods in store. I have tried to provide a flavour of many of the themes addressed as well as put my own gloss on some of them. If this attempt comes across itself as rather discursive, my excuse is that this appropriately reveals both the range and variability of the issues addressed and the fact that the issues and debates interleave at multiple points and in many ways. Although critical social psychology is united in trying to get 'clear water' between itself and 'mainstream' psychology and its practices, it should be clear by now that the reader who looks in these pages for consensus and common ground is likely to be disappointed. I have probably overemphasized the opposition between the postmodernist and more political wings, but critical social psychology is a rich source of many other instructive antagonisms and alliances. It should be clear that this argumentative atmosphere is a strength and not a weakness, because as well as being a topic of study, argument is the basis of inquiry and of political change. These contributions are therefore about the power of argument and also the argument of power (and as we have seen this difference is an argument in itself). Whether used as a course book, a source book or just a good read, I trust that the issues and debates in this volume will enrich understanding of the diverse questions raised by a critical social psychology. However, hopefully it should also do more than just raise consciousness. In their nature many of these contributions furnish the motivation and means to change the discipline of psychology and society by entering into the argument.

References

Adlam, D., Henriques, J., Rose, N., Salfield, A., Venn, C., & Walkerdine, V. (1977). Psychology, ideology and the human subject. *Ideology and Consciousness, 1*, 5–56.

Althusser, L. (1984). *Essays on ideology.* London: Verso.

Armistead, N. (Ed.). (1974). *Reconstructing social psychology.* Harmondsworth: Pelican.

Bhaskar, R. (1989). *Reclaiming reality: A critical introduction to contemporary philosophy.* London: Verso.

Bhaskar, R. (1994). *Plato etc.: The problems of philosophy and their solution.* London: Verso.

Billig, M. (1991). *Ideology and opinions: Studies in rhetorical psychology.* London: Sage.

Billig, M. (1994). Repopulating the depopulated pages of social psychology. *Theory & Psychology, 4*, 307–335.

Bowers, J.M. (1990). All hail the great abstraction: Star Wars and the politics of cognitive psychology. In I. Parker & J. Shotter (Eds.), *Deconstructing social psychology* (pp. 127–140). London: Routledge.

Bowers, J. (1991). Time, representation and power/knowledge: Towards a critique of cognitive science as a knowledge producing practice. *Theory & Psychology, 1*, 543–569.

Burman, E. (1991). What discourse is not. *Philosophical Psychology, 4*, 325–343.

Callinicos, A. (1987). *Making history.* Oxford: Polity/Blackwell.

Cohen, G.A. (1978). *Karl Marx's theory of history: A defence.* Oxford: Clarendon Press.

Costall, A., & Still, A. (Eds.). (1987). *Cognitive psychology in question.* Brighton: Harvester.

Edwards, D., Ashmore, M., & Potter, J. (1995). Death and furniture: The rhetoric, politics and theology of bottom line arguments against relativism. *History of the Human Sciences, 8*, 25–49.

Elms, A. (1975). The crisis of confidence in social psychology. *American psychologist, 30*, 967–975.

Foucault, M. (1981). *The history of sexuality. Vol. 1: An introduction.* Harmondsworth: Penguin.

Gadamer, H.-G. (1975). *Truth and method.* London.

Geras, N. (1983). *Marx and human nature: Refutation of a legend.* London: Verso.

Gergen, K.J. (1973). Psychology as history. *Journal of Personality and Social Psychology, 26*, 309–320.

Gergen, K.J. (1988). If persons are texts. In S.B. Messer, L.A. Sass & R.L. Woolfolk (Eds.), *Hermeneutics and psychological theory: Interpretive perspectives on personality, psychotherapy and psychopathology* (pp. 28–51). New Brunswick, NJ: Rutgers University Press.

Gergen, K.J. (1991). *The saturated self.* New York: Basic Books.

Giddens, A. (1984). *The constitution of society: Outline of the theory of structuration.* Cambridge: Polity.

Gill, R. (1995). Relativism, reflexivity and politics: Interrogating discourse analysis from a feminist perspective. In S. Wilkinson & C. Kitzinger (Eds.), *Feminism and discourse: Psychological perspectives* (pp. 165–186). London: Sage.

Gramsci, A. (1985). *Selections from cultural writings.* London: Lawrence & Wishart.

Greenwood, J.D. (1989). *Explanation and experiment in social psychological science: Realism and the social constitution of action,* New York: Springer-Verlag.

Greenwood, J.D. (1991). *Relations and representations: An introduction to the philosophy of social psychological science.* London: Routledge.

Harré, R. (1974). Blueprint for a new science. In N. Armistead (Ed.), *Reconstructing social psychology* (pp. 240–259). Harmondsworth: Pelican.

Henriques, J., Hollway, W., Urwin, C., Venn, C., & Walkerdine, V. (1984). *Changing the subject: Psychology, social regulation and subjectivity.* London: Methuen.

Israel, J., & Tajfel, H. (Eds.). (1972). *The context of social psychology: A critical assessment*. London: Academic Press.

Jost, J.T., & Hardin, C.D. (1996). The practical turn in psychology: Marx and Wittgenstein as social materialists. A commentary on Ian Parker's 'Against Wittgenstein: Materialist reflections on language in psychology'. *Theory & Psychology*, 6, 385–393.

Laclau, E., & Mouffe, C. (1987). Post-Marxism without apologies. *New Left Review*, 166, 79–106.

Latour, B. (1992). Where are the missing masses? A sociology of a few mundane artifacts. In W.E. Bijker & J. Law (Eds.), *Shaping technology/Building society* (pp. 225–258). Cambridge, MA: MIT Press.

Leudar, I. (1991). Sociogenesis, co-ordination and mutualism. *Journal for the Theory of Social Behaviour*, 21, 197–220.

Lukács, G. (1971). *History and class consciousness*. London: Merlin. (Original work published 1923)

Lyotard, J.-F. (1984) *The postmodern condition: A report on knowledge*. Manchester: Manchester University Press. (Original work published 1979)

Moscovici, S. (1976). *La psychoanalyse: Son image et son public* (2nd ed.). Paris: Presses Universitaires de France.

Nagel, T. (1986). *The view from nowhere*. New York: Oxford University Press.

Parker, I. (1990). Discourse: Definitions and contradictions. *Philosophical Psychology*, 3, 189–204.

Parker, I. (1992). *Discourse dynamics: Critical analysis for social and individual psychology*. London: Routledge.

Parker, I. (in press). Discourse analysis and psychoanalysis. *British Journal of Social Psychology*.

Parker, I., & Burman, E. (1993). Against discursive imperialism, empiricism and constructionism: Thirty-two problems with discourse analysis. In E. Burman & I Parker (Eds.), *Discourse analytic research: Repertoires and readings of texts in action* (pp. 155–172). London: Routledge.

Potter, J. (1992). Constructing realism: Seven moves (plus or minus a couple). *Theory & Psychology*, 2, 167–173.

Potter, J., & Wetherell, M. (1987). *Discourse and social psychology: Beyond attitudes and behaviour*. London: Sage.

Potter, J., Wetherell, M., Gill, R., & Edwards, D. (1990). Discourse – noun, verb or social practice? *Philosophical Psychology*, 3, 205–217.

Reed, E. (1996). The challenge of historical materialist epistemology. In I. Parker & R. Spears (Eds.), *Psychology and society: Radical theory and practice* (pp. 21–34). London: Pluto Press.

Reicher, S.D. (1996). The reactionary practice of radical psychology: Revoking the Faustian contract. In I. Parker & R. Spears (Eds.), *Psychology and society: Radical theory and practice* (pp. 230–240). London: Pluto Press.

Reicher, S.D., Hopkins, N., & Condor, S. (1996). Stereotype construction as a strategy of influence. In R. Spears, P.J. Oakes, N. Ellemers, & S.A. Haslam (Eds.), *The social psychology of stereotyping and group life* (pp. 94–118). Oxford: Blackwell.

Rose, N. (1985). *The psychological complex: Psychology, politics and society in England 1869–1939*. London: Routledge & Kegan Paul.

Rubinstein, D. (1981). *Marx and Wittgenstein: Social praxis and social explanation*. London: Routledge.

Sampson, E.E. (1991). The democratization of psychology. *Theory & Psychology*, 1, 275–298.

Sampson, E.E. (1993). *Celebrating the other: A dialogic account of human nature*. Hemel Hempstead: Harvester Wheatsheaf.

Sayer, D. (1983). *Marx's method: Ideology, science and critique in 'Capital'*. Brighton: Harvester.

Sedgwick, P. (1974). Ideology in modern psychology. In N. Armistead (Ed.), *Reconstructing social psychology* (pp. 29–37). Harmondsworth: Pelican.

Shallice, T. (1984). Psychology and social control. *Cognition, 17*, 29–48.

Shotter, J. (1975). *Images of man in psychological research.* London: Methuen.

Shotter, J. (1987). Cognitive psychology, 'Taylorism' and the manufacture of unemployment. In A. Costall & A. Still (Eds.), *Cognitive psychology in question* (pp. 44–52). Brighton: Harvester.

Shotter, J. (1991). Wittgenstein and psychology: On our 'hook up' to reality. In A.P. Griffiths (Ed.), *Wittgenstein centenary essays* (pp. 193–208). Cambridge: Cambridge University Press.

Spears, R. (1994). Why depopulation should not (necessarily) be taken personally. A reply to: 'Repopulating the depopulated pages of social psychology' by Michael Billig. *Theory & Psychology, 4*, 337–344.

Spears, R. (1995). Social categorization. In A.S.R. Manstead & M. Hewstone (Eds.), *The Blackwell encyclopaedia of social psychology* (pp. 530–535). Oxford: Blackwell.

Spears, R., Oakes, P.J., Ellemers, N., & Haslam, A. (1997). The social psychology of stereotyping and group life. In R. Spears, P.J. Oakes, N. Ellemers, & S.A. Haslam (Eds.), *The social psychology of stereotyping and group life* (pp. 1–19). Oxford: Blackwell.

Spears, R., & Parker, I. (1996). Marxist theses and psychological themes. In I. Parker & R. Spears (Eds.), *Psychology and society: Radical theory and practice* (pp. 1–17). London: Pluto Press.

Squire, C. (1995a). Pragmatism, extravagance and feminist discourse analysis. In S. Wilkinson & C. Kitzinger (Eds.), *Feminism and discourse: Psychological perspectives* (pp. 145–164). London: Sage.

Squire, C. (1995b). Review of 'Stories of childhood: Shifting agendas of child concern' by R. Stainton Rogers & W. Stainton Rogers. *British Journal of Psychology, 86*, 550–551.

Stainton Rogers, R., & Stainton Rogers, W. (1992). *Stories of childhood: Shifting agendas of child concern.* Hemel Hempstead: Harvester Wheatsheaf.

Tajfel, H. (1978). Intergroup behaviour. 1: Individualistic perspectives. In H. Tajfel & C. Fraser (Eds.), *Introducing social psychology* (pp. 401–422). Harmondsworth: Penguin.

Timpanaro, S. (1976). *On materialism.* London: Verso.

Triesman, A. (1974). The radical use of official data. In N. Armistead (Ed.), *Reconstructing social psychology* (pp. 295–311). Harmondsworth: Pelican.

Turner, J.C., Hogg, M.A., Oakes, P.J., Reicher, S.D., & Wetherell, M. (1987). *Rediscovering the social group: A self-categorization theory,* Oxford: Blackwell.

van Dijk, T. (1987). *Communicating racism.* London: Sage.

Wetherell, M., & Maybin, J. (1996). The distributed self: A social constructionist perspective. In R. Stevens (Ed.), *Understanding the self* (pp. 219–279). London: Sage/Oxford University Press.

Wetherell, M., & Potter, J. (1992). *Mapping the language of racism: Discourse and the legitimation of exploitation.* Hemel Hempstead: Harvester Wheatsheaf.

Wright, E.O. (1985). *Classes.* London: Verso.

2

Why a Critical Social Psychology?

Tomás Ibáñez

I have a rough idea of what social psychology has come to be at present, and I also have a more or less definite sense of what 'being critical' means, but I am not at all sure what a 'critical social psychology' might look like.

It seems that there are those among us who are concerned with making social psychology 'critical', but does this make any sense? Is it worthwhile? How can it be made possible? What should it criticize? What effects are we looking for? Why get caught up in such a project? Why should a 'critical' social psychology be better than a 'non-critical' one? What does 'better' mean? Taken together these questions involve a host of ontological, epistemological, ethical and political issues through which I shall try to sail and in which I will probably sink.

Social Psychology as It Stands Now

I do not think that this area requires lengthy discussion, so, for the sake of my argument, I will only stress three constraints which have played a strong role in shaping the discipline.

Whatever else it may be, social psychology is first the activity (with its outcomes) of a community of workers who are paid wages by academic/scientific institutions, government departments and/or private corporations to produce supposedly useful and valid knowledge on a certain range of social phenomena. This obviously does not mean that social psychologists are strictly required to supply their employers with 'what is good for them' as in most cases they themselves do not know exactly what is 'good for them' and knowledge-production activities require a somewhat fuzzy context of social control. Obviously, too, any construction of a corpus of knowledge follows a logic which is partly autonomous.

At any rate, the effects of our condition as salaried employees on the shaping of the discipline should not be underestimated. The so-called 'peer' evaluation in academic settings, on the one hand, and the journals' referee networks, on the other, ensure that we cannot be promoted or simply remain in our professional community unless we produce roughly what we are paid for. This has left a deep trace on what social psychology has come to be, and is a serious constraint on its possible appearance, whether or not it be critical.

Second, as we all know, the epistemological standards prevailing in each epoch affect what is considered to be valid knowledge. Since the end of last century the so-called 'short history' of social psychology has been largely contemporary and dominated by positivist and empiricist assumptions (including neopositivism, logical empiricism and the like). Therefore it is not surprising that the discipline broadly shares these assumptions and that social psychological knowledge is coined by them; the contrary would be amazing.

Third, on a more general level, social psychology belongs to a wider epoch (i.e. modernity) whose ideology with regard to knowledge has stressed the self-contained value of the 'disinterested quest for knowledge', on the one hand, and the intrinsic value of knowledge for promoting social welfare and progress, on the other (the supposed emancipatory and liberating effects of knowledge per se).

For the moment, we social psychologists are still salaried employees with all the consequences that this entails; positivist assumptions are far less dominant than some years ago, but modern ideology remains strongly pervasive. I will return to this at a later stage.

The Impressive Surge of Criticisms against Social Psychology as It Stood Some Years Ago

I am not going to make another flashback to the 'crisis' of social psychology and to the internal and external factors which have triggered off the wave of criticisms, but I think it is important to stress that a good deal of these criticisms have been directed at social psychology from within the very values sustained by mainstream social psychology. The main worries were about the fact that social psychology had not fulfilled its promises, and that it had to be reconstructed so as to fulfil them.

The knowledge built by social psychologists was intended to progressively increase the understanding of social psychological phenomena. Despite many decades of continuous work this aim was clearly unattained by the late sixties. As a result, on the one hand, the criticisms focused upon the reasons for this failure (positivist assumptions on the level of methodology and theory were mainly accused), and on the other hand, the critics tried to establish the basis of 'alternative ways of doing and thinking' for the discipline. These 'new ways' were supposed to enable social psychology to attain what it had failed to fulfil because of its inadequate epistemological and methodological assumptions. However, the aims were still roughly the same.

Of course, social psychology was not only concerned with the production of knowledge; it was also deeply concerned with making social life less wicked. Many social psychologists were clearly 'progressivists' in the plain modern sense, and they were quite confident of the 'social relevance' of their discipline. Social psychology was seen as a tool which would contribute to solving social problems, discrimination, prejudices, intergroup hostility, and so on. However, once again, towards the end of the sixties it became clear that this promise stood a long way from being fulfilled. Consequently criticisms stressed the discipline's lack of relevance and the more radical criticisms raised the suspicion that social psychology was actually doing the contrary of what it claimed, that is, it was helping to maintain the status quo. It became clear that new ways of 'doing and thinking' were badly needed if social psychology was to promote social welfare and social equity.

By way of a summary, social psychology had not succeeded in becoming an emancipatory tool, which was its original end, and therefore had to be changed in order to do so. Obviously, the end remained the same.

Striving to do Something Else

Since the late seventies a number of social psychologists who had either been active in the contest against the established social psychology (the 'crisis' period) or who began to be highly productive in the time after the crisis put aside their attacks against the mainstream orientation and took a more positive stance by trying to develop new research practices. In short they began to construct a truly 'different' social psychology. Post-positivist assumptions were largely taken for granted, new methodologies were put to use and new topics were adopted: discursive productions, conversation analysis, social construction of a vast array of formerly 'naturalized' psychological entities (emotions, mind, cognition . . .), narratives, and so on.

On a very general level, this 'different' social psychology assumed a 'constructionist turn' (in the realm of ontology), a 'language/interpretative turn' (on the level of methodology) and a 'non-foundationalist turn' (on an epistemological plane, even though the most radical of the critics challenged the very concept of 'epistemology').

All these 'turns' doubtless lent more excitement, interest and life to social psychology (the tedious atmosphere of mainstream social psychology had become somewhat asphyxiating for many of us . . .). Many positive outcomes emerged from the activity of the 'unorthodox' social psychologists: alternative journals became available for interesting papers which would never have been accepted by mainstream journals; publishers published collections of this new social psychology. We were able to organize alternative conferences, like the one that gave rise to the present volume, or even symposia within mainstream meetings, without being a priori disqualified by our more orthodox colleagues.

To sum up, the activity of marginalizing devices against unorthodox views is now far weaker than a few years ago, and one can be 'different' without being rejected as a meaningless outsider.

This is all very comforting, but if everything continues along these lines, I fear that in a few years we will have a new 'mainstream' social psychology which will be quite different from the previous one in terms of content and methods but with the same structural characteristics and the same effects! The defining criteria of what constitutes legitimized psycho-social knowledge will have changed but the only rules of the scientific game which will have changed will be the rules of disciplinary working.

Some Points of No Return Moulding the Emerging 'New Mainstream Social Psychology'

Whatever the infinite play of discrepancies between critical social psychologists may be, it seems that they all take for granted a new set of evidence including at least the following.

The Symbolic Nature of Social Reality

The distinctive mark of what is social cannot be established through a typology of objects because it is not the nature of the object but the type of relation in which the object is caught which gives it a social dimension, and this relation is of symbolic nature. In effect, a social dimension does not appear until a world of shared meanings is established among people. It is this common background of meanings which allows individuals to invest the objects with social properties that they do not possess in themselves but which are constructed jointly through communication and are thus located in the sphere of symbols.

From the connection with the dimension of symbols and with the construction and use of meaning it is clear that anything defined as social must, by necessity, be intimately related to language and culture. Nothing is social if it is not instituted within the sphere of shared meanings which belongs to a collective of human beings. This suggests that what is social is neither to be found *in* people, nor *outside* them, but is rather situated *among* people, that is, within the shared meanings people construct together, just as Vygotsky clearly saw.

From the moment the symbolic dimension becomes part of the agenda of social psychology, it is obvious that the discipline finds itself under threat of giving preferential attention to the role of language and communication in the production and working of social reality. Of course, symbolic productions are as real as any other object which we refer to as 'real'. This is why one of the political problems of our time is precisely acceding to the means of the symbolic production of reality. It is also for this reason that the knowledge developed by the social sciences can change the actual characteristics of reality. If social reality did not have a symbolic dimension, and if what is symbolic did not have the capacity to generate realities, there would be no sense in talking about enlightenment in Gergen's sense.

The Historical Nature of Social Reality

Since Giambattista Vico, the idea that, far from being independent of human practices, what we call 'social reality' is precisely the result of these practices has become progressively more consolidated.

As Vico pointed out, the realization that social reality has no other origin than the actions of human beings has consequences in regard to the kind of knowledge we can create about it. But, above all, this realization leaves us no option but to recognize the unavoidable historical dimension of social phenomena with all its implications. Insofar as the human practices which constitute social objects have the peculiarity of being processes which create, through their very development, the conditions for their own transformation, social objects must necessarily change with time. However, social phenomena are not only historical because they change with time and because they are relative to the historical period in which they manifest themselves. They are also intrinsically historical in the sense that they have memory. The current characteristics of a phenomenon are not independent of its genealogy, or, rather, the present form of social phenomena results from the social practices and the social relations through which they have been constituted. In this sense, all social phenomena can be considered to incorporate the memory of the social relations which instituted them and which are deposited within them. As the post-structuralists, among others, have so well elucidated, a phenomenon cannot be adequately accounted for without its process of formation being elucidated. Nevertheless, while this elucidation is necessary, it can by no means be fully grasped.

In effect, certain social phenomena constitute non-events in the sense that they are literally invisible at a given historical time and only become 'events' in the light of later developments. At any moment, various futures exist of which only one will come to pass. In this way it can be said that, like the future, the past is not yet written, given that some of its characteristics come into existence as a result of specific further developments which do not exist when we talk of the past. It is not true either that the future depends in part on the past, but that the past acquires some of the characteristics of the actual future coming to pass. Of all the non-events which are present in any given historical situation, only those which can be seen from the effectively realized future turn into real events. The others remain obscured for ever because none of the possible futures which would have revealed them has been realized. In this way the genealogy of the social phenomenon changes via the events which are produced later and, at the same time, a total knowledge of this genealogy cannot be gained. In simple terms, this means that psychosocial knowledge is necessarily incomplete.

The Importance of Reflexiveness

Of all the qualifying adjectives which have been used with the word 'animal' to designate the property which distinguishes human beings (rational, political, social, hermeneutical, etc.), one of the most adequate is the one which qualifies humans as *reflexive animals*. In effect, human beings could not become social beings if they did not have the ability to break the object/subject distinction and join both terms in a circular relationship. It is because subjects are capable of taking themselves as objects of thought that they can build a world of shared meanings and an inter-subjective space without which the social dimension could not emerge as such. To see oneself *through* the eyes of others, to see oneself *in* the eyes of others, to anticipate the 'sense effects' (*effets de sens*) we produce in others, to understand what others do or claim, and, in short, to make ourselves intelligible to others and vice versa would all be impossible without the self-consciousness which arises from reflexiveness. In the final analysis, the recursive loop which closes the 'knowing I' over the 'known I' makes up the very possibility of the social dimension.

Of course, reflexiveness must be extended to the social sciences themselves. Social psychology, as a discipline formed at one particular social and historical moment, constitutes part of the same social dimension that social psychology proposes to elucidate. For this reason, social psychology must take itself as an object of analysis, and it is perhaps the fact that it began to do so which brought about the famous 'crisis' that shook it so profoundly.

The question of reflexiveness, like any other question which implies a self-referential loop, is certainly not an easy one. Nevertheless, it constitutes another of the points of no return which mould the new social psychology.

Human Agency

With Brentano the idea that human behaviour is essentially purposive was already present at the beginning of modern psychology, before it fell out of fashion with the hegemony of behaviourism. But once it was reactivated by the followers of the second Wittgenstein, the discussion about the intentional character of human behaviour had to handle the question of the type of causality which mediated between behaviour and intentions. In this way it was driven to emphasize the relative self-determination of behaviour by its agent. The recognition of the intentional character of behaviour gave an image of human beings as agents capable of constituting themselves as the ultimate source of determination of their own behaviour.

The fact that humans can act for reasons destroys all possibilities of formulating an explanation of behaviour based on universal causal determinism, which was assumed by positivism as one of the conditions of a correct scientific explanation. In fact, the relative autonomy of humans obliges us to accept that there can be cases in which no condition is ontologically sufficient to produce an effect; that is, that there are cases where, all causes being present, the effect may or may not work out. This is why the perseverant dream of so many psychologists to be able to predict human behaviour through elucidating stimulus–response links or cognitive structures has no place in critical social psychology.

The Dialectical Character of Social Reality

For whatever reason, it is clear that it is much easier to see and to think in terms of objects than in terms of relations. This may account for the tendency to constitute entities which can only exist by virtue of their reciprocal relationships as independent ontological categories and to represent ourselves in the form of objects when, in reality, we are a framework of relations. This lead us to conceptualize individuals as independent ontological realities, on the one hand, and as society on the other, giving rise to the sterile debate between methodological individualism and sociological holism.

The dialectical concept of social reality emphasizes two aspects: the *relational* nature of social phenomena and the *processual* character of these phenomena. In this sense we must reject the ontological dichotomy between the individual and society, given that neither of the two terms is definable independently of the other; society only acquires the status of existence by means of the practices developed by individuals, which in turn do not exist as social beings unless through their production by society. This suggests a process of mutual construction in which causes and effects exchange status continually. For this reason the dichotomy between an exterior space, society, and an interior space, the individual with internalized characteristics of society, does not fit. In the same way, if it is true that acts only acquire meaning in the context in which they are expressed, it would be wrong to attribute to the context a status independent of the acts. The context is made up of the acts constituted by it. We again find a recursive loop which reminds us of the problem of the hermeneutic circle and Gadamer's description of it.

On the other hand, the emphasis which dialectics puts on the processual character of phenomena leads us to consider that, far from being constituted once and for all, social objects are in a continual process of becoming, of constant creation and re-creation, of reproduction and transformation. Hence we encounter the historical dimension of social reality just as we have noted before.

Giddens's concept of structural duality, which accounts for the simultaneously structured and structuring character of society and of social practices, is linked in the agenda of the new social psychology with the concept that social phenomena are constituted in the process of their development in such a way that they are not entirely predefined by any of the preceding conditions. As Shotter says, what is already made opens, but does not determine, the possible lines of development of what will happen.

The Constructionist Perspective

Nobody doubts that society constitutes human production. Nevertheless, it continues to be difficult to resist the temptation to naturalize what are no more than cultural constructions. Although no-one will accept naïve realism, one continues to fall into the traps of language and continues to attribute the status of natural categories to certain entities merely because they form part of our vocabulary. The acceptance of the constructionist point of view requires an attitude of methodical doubt of any attribution of reality to phenomena or objects whose existence seems to have a solid base in our language. In keeping with this systematic suspicion, it appears that one of the fundamental aims of social psychology is to clearly show the role played by cultural constructions and linguistic conventions in the generation of a series of evidence which demands our respect as much as natural things used to. Michel Foucault on a more general plane and Kenneth Gergen within the framework of the social sciences have contributed decisively to dispel the supposed natural character of certain phenomena, and have placed them in their particular historical, discursive, social and cultural dimensions.

This preoccupation with denaturalizing social phenomena is all the more important given the fact that all social phenomena are intrinsically historical and that historicity implies that every phenomenon of this type arises, at least partially, from linguistic conventions, from language games and from the cultural traditions which make up a way of life, in Wittgenstein's sense. To account for these phenomena, at least three questions must be dealt with:

- The first is none other than the determination of the role that linguistic conventions play in the production of the different social phenomena.
- The second consists of elucidating the nature of the process by which discursive processes have the ability to engender, if only partially, social objects.
- The third goes on to specify the mechanism by which we confuse the properties of our way of speaking about things with the properties of things we speak about.

The Social Nature of Scientific Knowledge

The forceful arguments in favour of a non-representational conception of scientific knowledge seem more and more difficult to refute. Not only is it clear that the theses about truth-as-correspondence are unable to resolve the question of a supposed independent access to reality, but they also have serious problems in making a complete assumption of the consequences of two firmly established points: the constructed dimension of scientific facts, on the one hand, and the partial osmosis between observational language and theoretical language, on the other. As if that was not enough, the contribution of the second Wittgenstein and of Gadamer mutually reinforce each other to establish that it is impossible that scientific knowledge could transcend either the constrictions imposed on it by natural language or the preconceptions inherent in a particular cultural tradition. This means that at least some of the conditions of possibility and intelligibility of scientific knowledge are definitively of a social nature and thus historical. Moreover, the operation to deconstruct epistemology achieved by Rorty is thus justified by the need to substitute the philosophy of scientific knowledge for a sociology of that knowledge.

One of the consequences of the reinsertion of science in the body of social phenomena is that of rendering unsustainable any attempt to establish the supposed neutrality of scientific knowledge. The distinction between factual and value questions ceases to have the clarity it had before. But if scientific knowledge in general loses its attributes of neutrality, it obvious that, a fortiori, social scientific knowledge is to be considered in its normative dimensions.

The Self-organizational Nature of Social Reality

Self-organizational systems are basically characterized by their property of eluding the second law of thermodynamics by virtue of a series of internal mechanisms which, alone, generate neguentropic processes. These processes lead to internally self-generated increments of complexity. This means that we are dealing both with systems endowed with sufficient redundancy or internal variability, among other things, to transform the input provided by the environment into structuring processes and also with systems which maintain their structure and make it ever more complex through the very forces and energies which act against the maintenance of the system. Although this may appear paradoxical, self-organization is not possible if it is not carried out by means of the simultaneous presence of antagonistic forces and mutually incompatible elements. In other words, a system which does not produce errors in its function, which does not experience noise, and which cannot enrich itself precisely because of these errors and of the noise, is incapable of accomplishing internal neguentropic changes by itself. A system which does not produce errors, or cannot enrich itself by means of these errors, can only change towards greater complexity or a readaptation to the changeable characteristics of the environment through an agent exterior to the system, or by means of a programme of change incorporated therein from the very moment of its constitution.

One of the most interesting characteristics of self-organizational systems is rooted in the unpredictability of the effective changes which the system undergoes. This unpredictability does not arise from insufficient knowledge of the processes experienced by these systems, from an insufficient mastering of their laws of functioning, nor from imprecision in relation to the definition of their initial states, but it is the result of their sensitivity to random influences and to evolution, which responds to non-linear equations with several solutions that are equally possible.

Bearing in mind the characteristics of self-organizational systems, it seems sufficiently clear that societies exhibit a series of properties which brand them as such systems. I will cite a few:

- Society is neither designed nor regulated by the art or magic of any exterior agent or will (clearly the figure of colonialism does not constitute a counter example).

Society is not implemented from its beginnings by a programme which incorporates the instructions for its functional evolution:

- Society maintains itself, by definition, in a state of non-equilibrium, that is, a state remote from maximum entropy.
- There is no society without social differentiation and social structures. Moreover, modern societies are characterized by a strong internal differentiation with a high degree of redundancy or structural and functional variability;
- Society evolves historically towards greater complexity, and this social evolution constitutes an irreversible process (except, obviously, if society is destroyed).
- As Popper argued, there are reasons of principle which make precise knowledge of the evolution of a society impossible.

Until now, it has not been very fruitful to import concepts originating in the natural sciences into the field of social science. It is understandable, then, that a certain reluctance is exhibited even among critical social psychologists about the idea of looking to the dynamics of meta-stable systems to develop a new social psychology. Nevertheless, I am convinced that this reluctance is not justified, because the failing hitherto has been not the choice of the natural sciences as a model for the social sciences, but the use of analogies based on positivist–naturalist knowledge.

Internal Tensions in New Social Psychology: The Case of Realism

As we have seen, critical social psychologists share many assumptions but there are also serious tensions between them. One of the most striking of these tensions relates to the issue of realism versus relativism. Apart from the fact that modernity has devoted so much effort to demonizing relativism that intense and deep resistances must be overcome for it to be adopted, it must be acknowledged that some realist arguments are quite attractive. For instance, realism has the advantage of being compatible with a belief based firmly on common sense and whose practical truth commands respect from a child when he burns himself for the first time:

- 'Things are as they are, independent of what we imagine them to be.'

The simple fact that survival is impossible if one does not act according to this proposition is a good argument for accepting it as true. But it is also true that things are partly the result of how we see them, not only because their effects on us partly depend on the representation we have of them, but much more radically because what we think and say about them forms part of what they really are.

Another realist proposition which seems to deserve some confidence is as follows:

- 'The acceptability criterion for valid knowledge consists of accounting for reality such as it is under one of its possible descriptions.'

Even if realists admit that it impossible to gain independent access to reality to see if it looks like its description, and even if they accept that the same reality can be grasped in different ways, they maintain that the above proposition must be accepted as the only means of making intelligible the fact that one can use valid knowledge to act purposively and efficiently upon reality.

One of the inconveniences of this formulation is that it renders true theories indistinguishable from theories which are false but which enable true predictions to be made and have efficient practical consequences. Moreover, this formulation suggests, as does the false theory, that reality is necessary. The realist conception of truth as reality raises even more problems than the empiricist conception of truth as phenomena.

One final proposition which is more difficult to deny is the following:

- 'A realist conception of causality (generative power) must be held if sense is to be given to the affirmation that some causal factors are present in a situation even if they do not produce manifest effects.'

It effectively seems that a realist conception avoids the masking effect which other conceptions produce in the analysis of some situations. It must be admitted that causes have a real existence if we are to argue that they are effectively present in a situation when no sense effect is perceptible. We all know that the suppression of an effect does not mean that its cause has been eliminated. When protest movements are wiped out by repression, the causes of public unrest are still there. However, this 'invisibility argument' may not disturb relativists. In effect, relativism finds no problem in constructing explanations in terms of underlying and invisible causal factors without deifying them. To say that the most convincing explanation of a situation passes through reference to sleeping causal factors, does not imply that these factors have a 'status of existence' which goes further than the one usually established by our discursive practices.

Even the most sophisticated and liberalized realism eventually refers to some principle which is independent of us as human beings and which forces our submission. In this sense, it bears some resemblance to all the foundationalist positions which try to situate the criterion of truth outside the rationale of contingent human decision. Relativism raises the assumption that any attempt to base 'truth' on anything which transcends human decisions constitutes a power operation aimed at restricting the decisional capacity of social communities.

In effect the formulation of an ultimate foundation for truth implies that the criteria for the acceptability of knowledge are situated above the decisions rationally and consensually developed by social communities. The only route open is submission and adhesion to a principle which transcends human communities.

Why Are We Doing Something Else and What Are We Actually Doing?

Instead of testing hypotheses drawn from narrow theories, instead of conducting nice, well-controlled experiments, instead of submitting to the rituals of statistics and, finally, instead of writing standardized research reports moulded in the rhetoric of objectivity, we now tell stories, we analyse discourses, we make people talk, we play with qualitative methods, we observe what is going on in everyday life or in specialized settings, we discuss broad cultural issues, and so on. This is certainly far more enjoyable and now we can do this without losing our professional credibility and the esteem of our peers.

To enjoy what one does seems a good enough reason for doing it, but I doubt that this would be the main argument offered to somebody who asked 'Why are you doing this kind of social psychology?' I wonder if our legitimizing claims would not stress the fact that we are constructing more elucidating knowledge than the mainstream does, better and more reliable knowledge, and that this knowledge is more socially relevant or even more politically correct than the other. If this was the case then the difference between our new social psychology and the established one would be more apparent than real. No more than a 'cosmetic' difference . . .

Putting aside the legitimizing claims, there is no doubt that we are actually widening, opening and renovating a social psychology which had become quite sterile, narrowly limited and highly reiterative. We are introducing fresh air into the discipline and opening it to new realms of social life. This is, I think, highly positive for our employers. We are also participating in updating the epistemological assumptions of the discipline, and this is not bad for our employers. I am not completely sure how to interpret this coincidence of interests but I cannot avoid the suspicion that what is good for employers in general is probably bad for all other people, including myself. Through this consideration we can point to the subversive trends which are generally present in the kind of knowledge constructed by non-orthodox social psychologists; but is this a guarantee? I do not think so. I am more inclined to think that our employers can afford the risks associated with these subversive trends insofar as the effectiveness of knowledge for changing social life is so very limited. People's acceptance of a social order is not so much a question of beliefs and knowledge as a question of 'habits' founded on the continuous experience of its solidity and its enabling conditions for developing unproblematic daily actions. Existing social conditions have tremendous inertia due to their ability to ensure the routine nature of ways of living, and cognitive and moral legitimization plays a secondary role in the acceptance of the established social order. This is why discourses are largely unable to change social practices and situations, even if they argue convincingly about their unfairness.[1]

As usually happens with people who are engaged in doing new things, changing established situations, opening new frontiers, and the like, non-orthodox social psychologists are quite enthusiastic about what they are doing, highly motivated and somewhat activist. From what I have said, all this excitement does not seem to be very justified, but I think it is, and I will try to explain why.

The Political/Normative Grounding of Critical Social Psychology

If we abandon faith in the self-contained value of the 'quest for knowledge', and if we depart from the emancipatory power of knowledge then we must also reject the proclaimed aims of mainstream social psychology. It does not make much sense to strive for a more elucidating knowledge and to believe that this knowledge can be a potential emancipatory tool. These aims were suitable to the modern ethos of established social psychology but they can no longer support the 'why' of an alternative social psychology. Other justifications must be found unless we feel totally satisfied with the hedonistic arguments of enjoyability.

Once the modern illusions have been swept away what remains is no more (and no less) than a (Foucauldian) concern with an 'art of existence' and an ethos of living founded on the ethical concern with constructing one's own life as a nice object of value; it is precisely from this perspective that critical social psychology makes sense. Several steps are needed here to outline my argument. The first is related to structures of domination, the second is linked with the scientific institution, and the third is tied to practices.

Structures of domination in all realms of existence, from economic to affective domains, prevent the very chance of constructing valuable ways of living for all people, including myself, who are caught in these structures. I may or may not engage in active opposition to what hinders the 'art of existence', but if I decide to do so, I cannot make a schizophrenic split between 'me' as a social psychologist and 'me' as anything else; this engagement also stands in my professional life. In this sense a critical social psychology (or any other label I choose to refer to what I want to do in my professional domain) is founded on the political/normative struggle against the structures of domination which prevent any 'art of existence' at all. Of course, this struggle is not to be seen as a 'duty' and neither as a 'moral obligation', it is just the way to be what one feels is of value.

There is no doubt that Science, Reason, expert knowledge, constitute together one of the most powerful structures of domination existing today. This domination device widens the gap between North and South (and between the many Norths/Souths within both the North and the South) and makes the gap almost insurmountable, while it also fosters new ways of domination (through computers and biotechnologies, for instance). To the extent that we work within the broadly defined scientific enterprise, it seems that opposition to *this* structure of domination should be a clear priority.

But this opposition cannot achieve its aims through the production of more knowledge (papers, books, and so on); knowledge is not efficient as such, it is efficient through its uses, through the practices it allows.

In this sense, critical social psychology is more a question of practices than a question of general claims and of knowledge production; it is based upon a set of practices tending to weaken the power effects of science, and upon practices which try not to reproduce structures of domination. This means that critical social psychology is not so much a tool for criticizing contemporary society (critical discourse is not efficient by itself), neither is it a tool to produce emancipatory knowledge (knowledge has no emancipatory effects by itself), but is better conceived as a tool to counter the domination effects of science and naturally includes social psychology as a part. Consequently, critical social psychology has to develop a permanent critique of social psychology itself, but a critique in practice insofar as a solely discursive critique lends no credibility to its practitioners and can become tedious. This means that it has to constitute itself as a weakening device against the discipline as such.

What form can all this take? There is, of course, no cookbook formula for a critical social psychology, but deconstruction, critical thinking and transdisciplinarity certainly stand in its agenda.

Focusing, reflexively, upon the productions of social psychology (both the old and the new) so as to make their implicit assumptions, short-comings, biases, and so on, salient is certainly a healthy exercise. Insofar as all knowledge is necessarily limited and, in some sense, 'false', a rethinking of knowledge is very likely to bring to light its shortcomings.

Paradoxically, this may have the perverse effect of constantly improving the knowledge of the discipline, but at the same time challenging the authority of its discourses by pointing to their instability. As we are concerned not so much with the issue of knowledge but rather with 'weakening practices', this seems acceptable.

On the other hand, setting up as many links as possible with other disciplines so as to weaken the disciplinary boundaries, weaken the power structures inside each discipline and partly dissolve the identity of the discipline also seems to be a healthy practice. Of course, this trans-disciplinarity can also be justified from purely epistemological viewpoints, but in this case political and epistemological concerns seem to go in the same direction.

Finally, topics such as racism, sexism, exploitative behaviour, discrimination, and the like, seem to be especially relevant for critical social psychology, but in fact 'anything goes'; a very large array of topics, theories and methods can inspire specific research insofar as what is at stake is not so much the kind of knowledge produced, as the uses to which this knowledge is put, and the practices it can feed. 'Anything goes' if it allows the power effects of our own scientific activities, as well as those of the others, to be weakened. This standpoint goes hand in hand with matters such as non-authoritarian sensitivity, irony towards the status of our own productions, the questioning of any rhetoric of truth, the dismissal of the superiority of specialized knowledge over folk knowledge, and so on.

Obviously not all social psychologists engaged in post-crisis trends are also engaged in a critical social psychology as I see it. They may develop their research with the conviction that a change of content and methods is necessary in order to fulfil the unfulfilled promises of the discipline, that is, the production of both elucidating and relevant, or even emancipatory, knowledge. But for those who have abandoned these aims the question of how to justify our activity is, I think, largely open. My trip around the 'why' of doing the kind of social psychology we do has had no other aim than to explore a possible path.

Note

1. Two qualifications must be made here. First, I cannot deny that the production of knowledge, and especially scientific knowledge, is a powerful device for social change. But change emerges from use and the outcomes of this knowledge more than from its mere formulation. Second, I do not deny that discourses have strong social effects. Social objects are constituted and maintained through discourses, at least partially. But the belief in the discourses which sustain our practices is far from being a necessary condition for engaging in these practices.

3

Going Critical?

Rex Stainton Rogers and Wendy Stainton Rogers

Critical Potentials?

This book attests to the complex of connotations that attach to the term critical, rendering the equation *critical + social psychology = ?* both troubling and troublesome. As a relative late-comer to the party celebrating the troubled condition of the social disciplines, critical social psychology cannot escape those already sedimented associations. It can, however, employ that stratiformity, seeking to be critically informed by its tectonics, its predications upon the 'climate of problematization' that emerged in the 1960s (cf. Curt, 1994).

Critical social psychology's closest, and elder, relation could be said to be critical sociology – very much a 'child of the sixties'. Andreski (1977) rather cruelly dubbed it

> . . . a label for denigration (rather than a discerning and original criticism) of the status quo in the West, usually inspired by uncritical Marxism. (p. 146)

It is worth, however, emphasizing that Andreski began this digest by noting that critical sociology was

> An expression which in principle is a pleonasm, since all good sociology must be critical in the sense of insisting on probing and being ready to challenge current opinions. It is only because the main current of sociology had become apologetic that the justification for 'critical sociology' has arisen. (p. 146)

Critical social psychology (CPS), on such an analysis, also escapes pleonasm only insofar as the now contemporary 'main current' of social psychology is similarly conservative. This is far from the only sense (and not, it will be suggested, the most productive sense) in which CPS can be understood as critical. Unlike a 'critical period' in the ethological sense, the 'climate of problematization' encompassed possibilities not only of 'attachment' but also of disenchantment (cf. Curt, 1994).

Concern over the condition of the mainstream, whether resulting in a continued critical attachment to it or disenchanted detachment from it, is, nevertheless, probably the modal theme in terms of where CPS, and critical psychology more generally, is seen to be 'coming from'. In several senses, the conservatism of psychology – whether we are talking of its developmental, personological, social or therapeutic branches – is paradigmatic. As Harré (1993) puts it:

> Every science is shaped by its ontology, that is by a set of assumptions about the nature of its subject matter that are shared by the community of practitioners. . . . In the history of the physical sciences the demonstration of the inadequacy or incoherence of an ontology has led to its abandonment, usually within a fairly short time. Psychology is unique, even among the human sciences, for the fact that this does not happen. (p. 13)

Even given that such concerns form a 'condition of plausibility' in the accounting of, or storying of, from whence CSP might be coming, they give no indication as to the manifold of where or how it might be going. These 'conditions of possibility' – the 'going critical?' of the title – are where our attention must now turn.

Criticality and Techno-science

In any ruminations about the notion of criticality, one set of connotations is inescapable. The complex of modernism and its discontents is not just the Zeitgeist of contemporary social science, it is our collective life-world. The title of this chapter, specifically, reminds us that modernism also implies techno-science. It does so by drawing upon one of the great icons of our times, nuclear fission. Unstable isotopes, like U235, bombarded with neutrons, split into fission fragments, giving off further neutrons, which can promote further uranium nuclei to fragment – leading to a chain reaction. Implode together fragments of U235 to make above a critical (or minimal) mass and you have a first-generation atomic bomb; control (moderate) the disintegration and you have a nuclear reactor (so long as you can maintain its temperance!).

Is it this kind of resonance with the nuclear horrors, with the threat of ultimate disorder, which mediates the tendency for criticality (cf. Andreski, 1977) to 'get a bad rap'? More germane to those themselves involved in CSP, might there be a narrative lesson to be learned from nuclear techno-science about the risks of meddling with criticality? These questions become easier to deal with if we look back to the conditions of plausibility for CSP.

The Climate of Perturbation

Techno-science, as we have seen, is a major resource for the provisioning of contemporary forms of narrativity. It is one that may be further scavenged for the purpose of storying the conditions of plausibility for CSP. Within biological science, one of the great narrative schemas is that of climate. Climatic stability tends to be associated with a more broadly stable ecosystem, while climatic change provokes either adaptation or migration (the alternative, of course, is extinction). This metaphoric permits the narrative device of treating CSP as phenomenon reflective of a shifting weather system in the meteorology of ideas – a climate of perturbation. This is a piece of shorthand which is deliberately porous; it absorbs a salmagundi of critical, perturbating and radical thought to which one can attach such labels as: feminism, French theory, neo-Marxism, post-structuralism, post-phenomenology, postmodernism and the sociology of scientific knowledge. That climate of problematization (CoP), considered as three decades of the shaking and stirring of confidence, is, in the broadest sense, what has enabled what now passes as CSP.

Such biological story-telling is, of course, no more than an analytic. What is being ventured is far from a natural history, with all its implications of evolutionary laws, of a nomic development. The weak agenda is, rather, the *unnatural* history of social psychology (and its linked disciplinarities). The stronger agenda concerns its possible futurities – its conditions of possibility. This latter must encompass questions as to whether such a species as social psychology (indeed the very notion of speciation) can survive in a post-CoP ecosystem.

Textuality and Tectonics

We have, then, offered an account of the CoP as the conditions of plausibility for a changing, shifted intellectual ecosystem. We now need to consider what is added by regarding such a concourse as one of criticality – of a condition of paradigmatic warp. Returning to our first metaphoric, we would find ourselves talking about the dialogics operating between active elements capable of mutual destabilization. This would indeed be a kind of 'going critical'. What we have here is one reading of the notion of postmodernism. In the critical dialect of textuality and tectonics (Curt, 1994), the tectons (the 'plates' of cultural tectonics) of the CoP are mutually disturbing. Those tectonics (e.g. the tensions between the 'plates' of critical pluralism and critical realism, or post-Lacanian feminism and post-Marxist feminism) are yielding a fluxional, unstable topography of knowledging.

The heavy use of conditionals (e.g. notions of reading, warning marks) here is deliberate. For one thing, there is no implication of actual subterranean events; the notion of tectonics is being employed as an analytic. Tectonics are not constructs or variables in theory, but devices in and on narrative. They are dependent upon reading, where they express in the domain of our second analytic, that of textuality. Textuality implies more than text, as sexuality implies more than sex. One can think about the analytic of textuality as a way of addressing the expressive lithosphere, the crust or surface of textedness. But again it is not taken as actual, rather it 'has actuality'. This shift in part-of-speech works better in French, where *actualité* carries the sense of 'news'. We could, for example, talk of the textuality of this book as 'the critical news'.

Supercriticality as a Lead Story

While the conditions of plausibility of the CoP belong, if you will, to commentary upon or interpretation of 'the news', to its contextualization – they are not, in and of themselves, 'the news'. The 'news' is (or should be) immanent with the conditions of possibility, the futurities of CSP. Once again, techno-science gives us a metaphoric. Currently to be found in the techno-science news is the notion of supercriticality. While the key to criticality is minimalism (such as the minimum mass for a self-sustaining nuclear reaction; the minimum temperature at which a gas cannot be liquefied by pressure alone), the key to supercriticality is the strange world just above the minimal, a place of fluids neither, strictly, gas or liquid. In the case of, say, supercritical fluid water, the hydrogen-bonded structure, the links between hydrogen in one molecule and a contingent other molecule, break down. The result is a wa-X-ter which is no longer lipophobic (one in which lipids, fatty organics, are insoluble) but lipophilic. What, then, might dissolve in a supercritical social psychology? (Stainton Rogers et al., 1995). Two candidates, at least, spring to mind – authority and disciplinarity.

Dissolving Author-ity?

Being here 'authors in our own write' (cf. Pfohl, 1992) is a decidedly uncritical location. No warrant of author-ity is thereby troubled – quite the reverse! To 'author' is to claim identity (an academic identity, a legal identity, an identity with the text, and so on). Yet to claim such an identity is to gainsay other claims (e.g. that ideas were shared at the germinal Small Group Meeting from which this book stemmed, that this book is more than set of unconnected essays). More generally it is like claiming ownership of the text of a dinner party conversation – it is to deny that textuality is always–ever intertextual.

Yet if the CoP takes us beyond grand narratives, it also takes us beyond grandiloquent gestures. One cannot have 'attitude' (as Potter might say – e.g. Potter & Wetherell, 1987), save as a 'discourse dynamic' (as Parker, e.g. 1992, might say). In other words, authoriality cannot simply be discarded – we live in practical realities that enjoy the dialogics (cf. Sampson, 1993) of both/and. One cannot, that is, avoid being both an author and not an author.

In an attempt to do just that, several of us abrogated authorship of a series of dinner parties and endowed their authorship to a fictive identity – Beryl Curt. This teasing strategy gave us (to borrow Game's, 1991, phrase) much ongoing 'disturbing pleasure' as we acted as Beryl's amanuenses. The 'book that Beryl wrote', *Textuality and Tectonics* (Curt, 1994), was an attempt to find ways-of-writing-about ways-of-working in the wake of the CoP.

To allow, in that practical reality, that matters have gone 'critical' also permits another possible – the 'supercritical' dissolution of author-ity. However, it is important to resist any singular reading of this venture. There are, in the reading and hence (in criticality) rewriting of any text, a manifold of possibilities. Thus, it also enables other, more overtly 'political', agendas – for example, the subversion of the monitoring of academic performance. Beryl, in challenging the author function, will (we hope) gain a place in citation indices and already has a registration in the US Library of Congress. What, quite, she will do to our (and our academic institutions') performance assessments we do not yet know, but the possibilities are certainly disturbingly pleasurable to us!

Dissolving Disciplinarity?

Beryl's book, *Textuality and Tectonics*, aims to ride the flux of being without foundations (the minima of criticality), of no longer importing the corporate warranty of social psychology. It is a speculation in transdisciplinarity. However, it is important to distinguish between our 'supercritical' notion of transdisciplinarity and both the modernist call to interdisciplinarity (liberal-humanistic dialogue between the parties to an ongoing governance) and the early critical reaction against discipline per se (as set out at the start of this chapter). Interdisciplinarity owes nothing to criticality, being no more than free trade in academic goods. Anti-discipline is part of the predication of CSP. Both (and their interrelations) can be usefully approached by means of an allegory of academic modernism.

Imagine 'the human condition' as the current physical geography of the Americas and then let it be 'discovered' by academic adventurers. Picture the land to the north of 'Panama' as having been colonized and divided into dependencies called bio-natural disciplines (such as medicine, biology, physiology). Further imagine that the south of 'Panama' has similarly been colonized into territories called social disciplines (economics, sociology, anthropology). Finally, position psychology on the isthmus, covering Panama.

The 'Panama Canal' now becomes the topological divide – the hiatus between the biological and the social – that both fracts psychology itself, and makes possible all manner of constituted tensions. What then happens is that every manner of mentor comes along claiming to offer ways of transducing the divide. Some have called themselves social psychologists. (There are even those who claim to have methods that can reveal how much of the variance in the human condition is explained north of the divide and how much to the south!) It was over just this mapping of intellectual imperialism that the CoP has offered what seems like a vision of literal and figurative decolonization. Radicality and criticality were, in the late sixties, blurred in just this way. Faced with a seeming choice between an old order 'rapidly fadin'' and the 'Aquarian Age' – back, in other words, in the time of dreams (and not just of *Reconstructing social psychology* – Armistead,

1974 – but everything) – protest and prophecy seemed that easy. Dylan (1974: 216) captured the nostalgia of those simple choices beautifully when he wrote:

Good and bad I define these terms
Quite clear, no doubt, somehow.
Ah but I was so much older then,
I'm younger than that now.

Here, now, in the lean and hungry nineties, the affirmative hymns of the sixties like 'We shall overcome' sound only acute embarrassment. (Some of us, indeed, have taken to singing 'We may undercome' instead!) Social psychology is not so much to be reconstructed as deconstructed (cf. Parker & Shotter, 1990). To story that transit is also to make the jump from dream to myth. If proactive dreams (utopianisms) are troubling in the nineties, myth (from the genre of 'sword and sorcery' to the *Realpolitik* of fascisto-nationalism) is very much alive and well. Where, then, has the CoP delivered us in terms of mythic textuality?

Boldly Going

As in many myths, we find a group of travellers traversing a topography that raises dilemmas of 'reality'. This often actualizes in the form of the threat and the promise of the door to the beyond. Who, then, might we find in our merry band? Clearly not the bio-natural psychologists – they have no interest in 'taking a trip', as there is still so much 'more research' waiting to be done! Nor should we expect to find the practitioners – they are too busy building a profession, insinuating the 'harm warrant' around the traumas, stresses and abuses of contemporary life. But if they are absent, their tellers will be present. They are present on every journey and their interest lies in what can be seen through the rear-view mirror, the past in the making.

Present, too, are the critical realists – they will risk the door – but only with the protection of talismanic transcendentality. To venture through the portal without it, they argue, is like drinking a draught which makes one amnesiac. For some there is the worry that to traverse is to emerge into a mere 'land of textual lotus eating' in which one forgets home; in which power and oppression become mere chimera. For others of this ilk the worry is of emerging into some new, discursive 'dark [*sic*] continent', but without a 'Heart of Darkness'. To the hero cloaked in rationality either of these can be tamed and plundered to revitalize old seats of power – perhaps to yield a 'discursive psychology'.

For us Beryllians, the position of the traveller is different again. What lies on the other side of the portal is profound change – not paradigm shift, but paradigmatic warp into transdisciplinarity. Situated on that other side, it is not so much that the portal then disappears (the archetypal afright of being trapped) but that the start, the journey and the transit are transformed.

Critical Polytextualism

It is important to try to make it possible to read that shift, as it has seemed to us, from off this text where it is being told. A useful raconteurial device to provoke engagement is emotion. What is being described has links to the medieval emotion of acedia (cf. Harré, 1986). What the warp means for the critical polytextual traveller is not amnesia. We still know how to be, say, experimental social psychologists, ethnomethodologists or existential psychoanalysts, but the thought of engaging in those practices brings us no joy. We know that engaging in them would not result in any sustainable affirmation or revelation. We have, in that other place, become critically polytextualized – acclimatized to fluxion, to change, to transformation. Unlike acedia, however, the emotionalizations of being positioned as critically polytextualized are positive. We find ourselves revelling in, rather than suffering through; losing all foundationed faith – becoming agnostic. This reverie itself is an intellectual joy, a disturbing pleasure, a love of the thereby realized possibilities of 'nothing goes', not a mere celebration of that specific possibility whereby in transiting the CoP 'anything goes'.

Critical polytextualism is, to reach back to our very first metaphor, a venture in reflexively moderated criticality. It is instructive to remind ourselves that nuclear chain reactions were laboured into being by what followed upon the downfall of a far more substantial intellectual edifice than human science has ever been – namely classical physics. The vagaries of U235 were harnessed by relativity physicists, people for whom in Eddington's words (1928/1932):

> . . . the world of physics is a world contemplated from within, surveyed by appliances which are part of it and subject to its laws. What the world might be deemed to be like if probed in some supernatural manner by appliances nor furnished by itself we do not profess to know. (p. 225)

Transfer that perspective to the 'social world' and substitute 'local and contingent orders' for 'laws' and you have the social constructionist position of sixty years later. The appliances are both ourselves and the tools we create from the 'subtle substance/energy' of sociality.

One of the arguments we develop in *Textuality and Tectonics* is that classically scientized psychology operates through alienation; that is, via a denial (through false objectification) of the social constitution of its concerns and its methods. But even where that constitution is accepted, it does not follow that the result is a radical constructionism.

It is worth reminding ourselves that Berger, who first popularized the term 'social construction' (Berger & Luckmann, 1966/1967), was to go on to co-write the most decidedly unradical *The War Over the Family* (Berger & Berger 1983/1984). Perhaps we should not have expected anything else. Berger himself makes clear (e.g. 1963/1966, 1981/1982) that he sees the stance of 'things are not what they seem' as the necessary and desirable condition for a social science. But he also stresses that he regards its politicization (its application to 'everyday social life') as only able to lead to a de-legitimation which 'contributes to the disillusion, anomie and normative disintegration of modern society' (1981/1982, p. 159). Indeed, Berger regards 'universal' (as opposed to factionalized) social science as a powerful protector against radicality because it debunks everything (apart, we would argue, its own pretensions, of course).

Radicals of various persuasions (e.g. Kitzinger, 1987; Parker, 1989) have challenged this 'dual citizenship' analysis (debunking social scientist and value-pursuing member of everyday social life). However, they are often themselves troubled by the potential of the CoP transition to seem to be positioning them as just as prone to foundational deconstruction as the liberal science they vilify. It is not necessary to further précis (and hence distort) these debates in order to establish the core point – that radicality and criticality have a troubled and troublesome relationship.

They do so in part, it could be argued, because much of our sense of radicality is predicated upon the modernist notion of a metricated politics, in which radicalities are 'extreme' (i.e. far from the norm). The consequence is a constitution of the radical in which any given radicality is delivered to us in terms of its particular manifesto – in other words, where its 'extremity' lies, where it 'deviates' from the modal bedrock. In turn, this tends to bring into focus both its particular metaphysics (its ontological and epistemological foundations) and its particular utopian vector (such as its instrumental and terminal values – cf. Rokeach, 1968). In the case of social psychology, much radicality is as much a mission (cf. Stainton Rogers, Stenner, Gleeson & Stainton Rogers, 1995) as the mainstream liberal-humanistic project it challenges and, which in turn, resists it.

Their respective positions over whether a clear mission can and should be drawn from problematization is one common area of dispute between criticality and radicality. At the moment of criticality, 'missioneering' becomes a concern. At the moment of radicality, to perturb any and all foundations to commitment is equally troublesome. The response to this tension favoured here is to argue that not just our scrutiny but also our concern can work in tension – in reflexive moderation. Such a 'critical pluralism' (under erasure, of course) works upon polytextual possibilities in terms of a counterpoint of analytics.

The metaphor of moderating a chain reaction is our best working shot at describing what it means for us to take from the CoP and rework the problematic of: 'a world contemplated from within, surveyed by appliances that are part of it' (Eddington 1928/1932, p. 225). Such a universe is infinite in its fluxional possibilities and also doubtfully bounded. Being infinite in its fluxional possibilities means its futurity is generative and hence neither its lineaments nor its iconographic conventions are open to extrapolation. Being doubtfully bounded is being agnostic over the possibility that it can be shown to have either an 'inside' (in the sense of a foundational reality) or an 'outside' from which a supernatural observer could instrument what is truly going on.

With those affirmative doubts comes the doubtful affirmation that flux is what we have and where we have our Being. If you detect in that minimal equipment a certain Heraclitean tendency, you have not made a unique reading. The CoP may have originally encompassed in its forum an 'Aquarian conspiracy', but what has passed through it is more of a 'bonfire of the vanities'. To shift position on the bookshelves again, John Fowles, whose novels from the early *The Magus* (1977) to *Mantissa* (1982) capture so many themes of troubled late modernity, at one point tried his own doubtful affirmation of Heraclitus in *The Aristos*. The motif of movement is also strong in a number of recent critical glosses (or we could say thick descriptions) on the idea of a social discipline. An obvious case in point is Ann Game (1991), who also provides a neat 'shifty proposition' for the introduction of fiction into the argument at this point:

> As an initial move in shifting the codes of sociology I will propose a reversal: that we think of sociological writing as fiction and fiction as social analysis. (p. 18)

The fluxional investment in Game is formidable. In her Preface she asserts:

> Reading a text is a writing practice, and in this lies the possibility of a rewriting of the texts of the culture, in the now. A deconstructive strategy is a positive strategy of transformation: undoing is simultaneously an unmaking and a making, a process without end. (p. x)

Getting Changed

Of course, 'transformation' is a not a singularity. The agenda that flows from Ann Game's 'desire' is but part of a polytextuality. Beryl Curt, you may think, has her very 'desire' undone, along with her body, in her fictivated authorship. This was not just a response to collective writing but a distinct utilization of what that undid. It is hard (outside of Jungian concepts anyway) to think of a collective as having an unconscious, let alone the kind of unconscious (out of French feminism) that is said to be capable of being unleashed as positive (radicalizing) desire. In any case, psychoanalytically informed (specifically post-Lacanian) feminism has its critics within feminism. Frazer (1992: 65) argues that 'the mere addition of an anti-structuralist force doesn't lead beyond structuralism'. For her, that is a moment without progress, without movement. Hence, she argues for a discursive rather than a structural analytic.

This text is itself taking on fluxional qualities. On the one hand, it celebrates polytextuality. On the other hand, it argues one text of trans-formation against another. (So, by the way, does Ann Game.) It is an inconsistency only in a logic of permanence, which requires a singularized viewer and a singularized viewpoint. Fluxionally, this is how the chain reaction – the going critical – is reflexively moderated, so that it neither stops nor produces 'melt-down' but yields a permanent auto-critique.

There are, of course, no guaranteed, money-back prescriptions for auto-critique. If one knew how to achieve it (like Tao), that certitude of knowledge would immediately demand deconstruction! Nor can there be any guarantee that we shall like the view we will see through the rear-view mirror. Indeed, under auto-critique we should not, necessarily, *expect* to like it. At best we can hope we have not helped to launch a textual chlorofluorocarbon – a compound which eats the very flux in which we live!

Going Critical?

The notion of 'going critical', then, of the mass of problematizing texts creating a self-sustaining criticality, can be read in a variety of ways. One, which we would obviously want to avoid, is too literally – that is, as if it were a causal proposition derived from the (non-existent) covering laws of textuality and tectonics. Our possibilizings about textual CFCs or super-criticality are not meant as oracular utterings to be read in some future as 'crises' predicted. The idea that, so long as certain criterion conditions are met, the future will happen is best left to the realm of science fiction, where such myths belong (cf. Asimov, 1951/1960 and the 'psycho-historian' Hari Seldon). A second reading, which also gives us grief, is that of linking 'going critical' to the grand theme of 'endism' – that particular present-valorizing arrogance which says that we live in interesting, millennial times. We are very aware here of the bones of Asimov's Foundation myth:

> The Old Empire is crumbling into barbarism and Hari Seldon and his band of psychologists see before them only the despair of thousands of years of anarchy unless they can create a new force – the Foundation – dedicated to art, science and technology – the foundation of a new empire . . . (Asimov, 1960, dust cover)

A third reading of 'going critical?' which also gives cause for concern is as a political description or, indeed, prescription. It is not a mantra which can release an outbreak of peace and understanding – it cannot be traded for 'a flower with every cheque', nor will it enable levitation or yogic flying which will heal all the world's ills. But it just might leaven something of the world outwith the textualists (who are yeasty enough in any case!) if it can be seeded beyond the boundaries of high culture.

What, then, is the reading that we would want for it? Our view is that 'going critical?' should be a matter of asking questions without expecting finite answers – engaging in a quest which is an end-in-itself not a search for anything. Under critical polytextualism there is no 'Holy Grail' of truth to be sought, no 'problem' to be solved. Indeed we have been criticized (Domenech and others, personal communication) for our adoption of the term 'climate of problematization' because the word 'problem' implies a solution – perhaps we should shift to calling it a 'climate of perturbation', though this would undoubtedly result in criticism for bringing in yet more 'insufferable jargon' from other quarters.

This shift is uncomfortable, given the extent to which we are all so steeped in modernism that the idea of a 'questless quest' can come over as self-indulgent and lacking in serious purpose. And yet, it is the inevitable consequence of 'going critical?' in its most radical form. Once we agree to give up 'God tricks' (Haraway, 1989/1992), there can be no 'solutions', only ever more questions.

Critical + Social Psychology = ?

Where then does 'going critical?', if at all, relate to critical social psychology? The word 'critical', as we have seen, is deeply polysemic, and some of its glosses are obviously troubled when juxtaposed against the metaphoric senses in which we have employed it thus far in this chapter. Most obviously, to transit the CoP perturbates the roles both of the critic and of criticism as arbiters of quality and taste or as mentors of meaning.

Clearly, then, there is nothing of 'going critical?' in a critical social psychology, taken as meaning the provisioning of a kind of Michelin Guide or concordance to the discipline, however analytically well formed or ideologically well informed. Nor can we get much enthused about the idea of a critical social psychology taken as a catalogue of all that is wrong (from some position of assumed politico-moral superiority) with the discipline as constituted.

It is true that, biographically speaking, such dis-ease often seems a necessary condition for 'going somewhere', but those movements can as easily be into, say, established singularizing heterodoxies (such as libertarianism) rather than being 'out of' the CoP. Another sense in which critical social psychology is sometimes taken is as addressing some, variously glossed, 'crisis' in social psychology.

We need to be cautious of the bio-medical warrant often haunting such diagnoses. The idea that the body of social psychology needs some 'critical treatment', perhaps even a 'critical operation', raises several worries. The first is that the purported patient shows every sign of health – for a nonagenarian. Nor should we trust those self-satisfied and self-satisfying narrative subject positions which accord us some unique powers to see the underlying sickness. That sounds too much like 'where we came in', too much like the technology of regulation that is the psychology we criticize. Received social psychology is not so much 'diseased' as arousing critical dis-ease – and not only do we need to trouble criticality, we also need to worry the algebra of its additions to social psychology. The questions need to be raised:

- Do we want social psychology?
- Do we need it?
- Is it more than a biographical contingency, like being brought up in the Church of England?

- Does it (except in terms of hard cash) serve us as more than a predicate, a set of training reins that enabled us to 'kick over the traces'?

These questions are, of course, part of the agenda behind posing the transit of a CoP, for they suggest a loose, disputatious promenade – projected on all fronts from a rejection of the received (effectively no matter what that received was across the humanities and social sciences).

On this reading, social psychology may be substantively where we are but only trivially 'where we are at'. Critique of our provenance may be only a condition of plausibility for the going-of-our-criticality/criticality-of-our-going – our critical scrutiny. What we mean by critical scrutiny is picked up in Chapter 5.

References

Andreski, S. (1977). Critical sociology. In A. Bullock & O. Stallybrass (Eds.), *The Fontana Dictionary of Modern Thought*. London: Fontana.

Armistead, N. (Ed.). (1974). *Reconstructing social psychology*. Harmondsworth: Penguin.

Asimov, I. (1960). *Foundation*. London: Grafton. (Original work published 1951)

Berger, B., & Berger, P.L. (1984). *The war over the family*. Harmondsworth: Penguin. (Original work published 1963)

Berger, P.L. (1966). *Invitation to sociology*. Harmondsworth: Pelican. (Original work published 1963)

Berger, P.L., & Kelner, H. (1982). *Sociology reinterpreted*. Harmondsworth: Pelican. (Original work published 1981)

Berger, P.L., & Luckmann, T. (1967). *The social construction of reality*. Harmondsworth: Penguin. (Original work published 1966)

Curt, B. (Pseud.). (1994). *Textuality and tectonics: Troubling social and psychological science*. Milton Keynes: Open University Press.

Dylan, B. (1974). *Writings and drawings*. St Albans: Panther.

Eddington, A.S. (1932). *The nature of the physical world*. Cambridge: Cambridge University Press. (Original work published 1928)

Fowles, J. (1977). *The magus* (rev. ed.). St Albans: Triad/Panther.

Fowles, J. (1982). *Mantissa*. London: Jonathan Cape.

Frazer, N. (1992). The uses and abuses of French discourse theories for feminist politics. *Theory, Culture & Society*, 9, 51–71.

Game, A. (1991). *Undoing the social*. Milton Keynes: Open University Press.

Haraway, D. (1992). *Primate visions: Gender, race and nature in the world of modern science*. London and New York: Verso. (Original work published 1989)

Harré, R. (Ed.). (1986). *The social construction of emotions*. Oxford: Blackwell.

Harré, R. (1993). *Personal being* (2nd ed.). Oxford: Blackwell.

Kitzinger, C. (1987). *The social construction of lesbianism*. London: Sage.

Parker, I. (1989). *The crisis in modern social psychology – and how to end it*. London: Routledge.

Parker, I. (1992). *Discourse dynamics: Critical analysis for social and individual psychology*. London: Routledge.

Parker, I., & Shotter, J. (Eds.). (1990). *Deconstructing social psychology*. London: Routledge.

Pfohl, S. (1992). *Death at the parasite café*. Basingstoke: Macmillan.

Potter, J., & Wetherell, M. (1987). *Discourse and social psychology: Beyond attitudes and behaviour*. London: Sage.

Rokeach, M. (1968). *Beliefs, attitudes and values*. San Francisco: Jossey-Bass.

Sampson, E.E. (1993). *Celebrating the other: A dialogic account of human nature*. New York: Harvester Wheatsheaf.

Sarbin, T.R. (Ed.). (1986). *Narrative psychology*. New York: Praeger.

Stainton Rogers, R., Stenner, P., Gleeson, K., & Stainton Rogers, W. (1995). *Social psychology: A critical agenda*. Cambridge: Polity.

4

Discourse and Critical Social Psychology

Jonathan Potter

This chapter explores some of the implications for and within critical social psychology of discourse analysis. It is rhetorical. Some of its countertexts are diffuse (realism in psychology); some are specific (arguments in other chapters in this collection).

Anti-foundationalism

The discourse analytic and rhetorical position draws on a number of developments in post-structuralism, linguistic philosophy, ethnomethodology and sociology of science (Billig, 1987; Edwards & Potter, 1992; Potter & Wetherell, 1987). In a sense, it is exploring a space where the problematics of these different fields intersect. None of these developments originated from within the discipline of psychology. However, a characteristic of psychology is that it is continually reconstructed by systems of thought from elsewhere: Chomskyan linguistics, neurophysiology and computer science are just three recent examples.

For theoretical, analytic and reflexive reasons I take discourse analysis to be an anti-foundationalist position on knowledge. At its simplest, this means that there is no touchstone, bedrock or set of logical principles which provides an unproblematic arbiter of knowledge claims. Foundations for knowledge are not simply *there* – they have to be built; and there are different building systems. Houses of knowledge can fall down; sometimes earthquakes reduce whole cities to rubble.

Across the human sciences truth is being dismantled – although what is to replace it is less clear (Bruner, 1990; Lawson & Appignanesi, 1989; Rorty, 1989; Second of January Group, 1986; Shotter, 1993a; Woolgar, 1988). Yet this is not so in much of mainstream empiricist psychology (social or otherwise), where stories of truth frame textbooks and methodological discussions are policed as vigorously as ever; neither is it so in various more critical developments organized around some sort of realism (e.g. Harré, 1993; Parker, 1992; Reicher, this volume).

For discourse analysis, realism is not an abstract philosophical position. Rather, it is a farrago of more of less related discursive practices which can be used by both analysts and participants to do particular things. These practices can be analysed and criticized. Analysis can unpick the workings of realism's central tropes: the Word-and-Object story and the image of the Mirror (Potter, 1992; Rorty, 1980); and it can undermine realism's central modes of attack: the Furniture Argument ('see this table [*bang*], is that a social construct?') and the Death Argument ('what about misery, genocide, power . . .', Edwards, Ashmore & Potter, 1995).

This critique of realism's story about itself does not require discourse researchers to engage in a moral programme for purging realist discourse from their texts. At times realism can be used positively. Take the analogy with liberal discourse: a weave of notions organized around rights, the sanctity of the individual and freedom. This can certainly be used to reactionary and racist ends; but the appropriate response is not necessarily its abandonment. Racism and reaction are not *inherent* within it; rather, they can be *accomplished* by it in certain practices (Wetherell & Potter, 1992). Likewise, realism can be a good story.

Rhetoric

One of the standard criticisms of anti-foundationalist positions is that they lapse, slide, fall, descend into or end up in relativism. For traditional psychology, relativism's problem is that it puts into question the powerful and legitimating story of accumulating facts and orderly scientific progress. Social psychologists often marshal the Furniture Argument against relativism and constructionism. For modern psychological realists the Death Argument is more apt. For them the anti-foundationalist's problem is a moral and political one; it is taken to promote inactivity or moral vacuousness, or to question the reality of social structure or of crucial events such as the deaths of fleeing Iraqis on the Basra Road (e.g. Parker & Burman, 1993).

There are various arguments that counter both of these constructions of relativism. Some of these arguments point out that the relativists can take positions, have commitments, attack inequality and exploitation without having to buy into the story that to do so they require neutral, exterior arbiters (God, experimental findings or whatever) of their knowledge and knowledge systems (Edwards et al., 1995; Smith, 1988; Wetherell & Potter, 1992). *Commitment makes at least as much sense to a relativist as a realist, perhaps more!* There is certainly no sense in a relativist adopting an over-arching principle such as 'equal validity for all knowledge systems'. Other arguments involve an examination of the rhetorical devices used to shore up realism and cover over the necessary uses of non-realist rhetoric when realists clash with one another (Latour, 1987; Woolgar, 1988).

One traditional picture treats the 'problem' of relativism as being its failure to provide any ruler with which to compare separate systems (cultures, paradigms, religions). Without such a ruler, the argument runs, what is left is a collective, or even an individual, solipsism. Discourse researchers can respond to this by emphasizing the centrality of rhetoric: systems (personal, social, scientific) are constantly being broken down through diverse processes of argument. This does not mean that a foundation has been found beyond contingent human processes of construction, that a neutral ruler has been manufactured; but it does show that relativism does not lead to a set of disinterested analysts, sitting in Zen-like calm, each sealed in her own universe. An active relativism can engage in the task of undermining the grounds of alternative systems of knowing.

It is possible to take a rhetorical approach to social science knowledge generally. This can emphasize how much positions and claims – including this claim – are structured by their argumentative context. However much they are presented as about the world, they are also analysable as about competing positions and claims, doing alignment and admonishment, building communities and designating outgroups. In this way, the debates in social psychology are paralleled by, and interdependent with, the debates and dilemmas of everyday discourse (Billig, 1991; Billig et al., 1988). And discourse researchers are here wary of the social representations story which has everyday understanding a product of knowledge drifting down to the masses from the ivory towers of social sciences (Moscovici, 1984). They stress that these parallels may be there because researchers face the same ideological dilemmas when they construct their theories as non-academics do when they argue about their worlds (Wetherell & Potter, 1992).

Criticism and Experimentation

Given the emphasis on rhetoric and anti-foundationalism it would be odd to say that only one research method is appropriate, let alone that only one method is intrinsically *radical*. Social psychologists such as Tajfel and Moscovici have combined both experimental research and trenchant social criticism. Feminist psychologists have frequently demonstrated the radical possibilities of traditional number crunching and survey work (e.g. in the area of sexual violence – Kelly, 1988). Moreover, from a discourse and rhetorical perspective the idea of method as a discrete category (as it is traditionally understood in social psychology) becomes untenable (cf. Billig, 1988). *Method is theory in disguise.* However, that is not to say that the force of well-known critiques of experimental work in social psychology need be ignored (Gergen, 1978; Harré, 1992); nor that questions should not be raised about specific experimental proposals.

Reicher (this volume) makes the argument that experiments are an excellent way of investigating power because of their 'accurate representation' of the power relations in society: in both experiments and society power is exercised to close down argumentation. Whether or not Reicher is able to initiate a radical programme of experimentation into issues of power, this argument begs some of the most interesting and potentially important questions that a radical social psychologist might ask. For example, how do people sustain argument in the face of attempts to close it down? How does closing down argument, if and when it happens, work? One of the common conclusions of studies of talk and social structure is that even in situations of heavily pre-structured asymmetry people can resist and argue back. For example, against the institutional backdrop of the courtroom, a rape victim can, through the design of her testimony, resist attempts by a high-status, highly skilled and highly paid defence attorney to depict her as having a prior relationship to the victim (Drew, 1990; see also, McHoul, 1987). What is striking is how subtle and well organized such resistance is.

Two characteristic features of experiments make them particularly poor tools for such an investigation of the workings of power. The first is that experiments have overwhelmingly been done with people who have exceedingly little stake or interest in the materials that they are dealing with. The sorts of concerns that form a backdrop to everyday life and familiar settings are largely absent. Power may come to seem irresistible if the participants have no stake in resisting it. The second is that, far from being in the position of Foucault's/Bentham's all-seeing panopticon, the experimenter deliberately blinds him- or herself to virtually everything the person ('subject') does. Overwhelmingly, experimental results are structured 'responses' limited by small sets of available categories: dials on shock generators, ticks in boxes, choices between descriptions. Resistance to the experimenter's demands may well go on; but it is likely to be entirely invisible in this monocular universe.

If power is the research topic, why not study families, the army or everyday interaction? Psychologists have spent a hundred years largely avoiding studying people living their lives. With the advent of cheap tape and video technologies, and the breakdown of the positivist story that ruled 'subjective' ethnographic research out of court, there is no excuse for spending the next hundred years repeating this mistake.

Criticism, Discourse and Some Cautions

A common claim in recent critical works in social psychology is that analyses must be related to social context or social structure. As a general suggestion this is unproblematic. There is nothing in an anti-foundationalist position that precludes such concerns. For an anti-foundationalist social structure has no more and no less an objective status than a table. It would be entirely realist to claim that social structure, power or whatever does not exist.

Nevertheless, there is something unsatisfying about some recent conceptualizations of this issue by critical social psychologists (e.g. Parker, 1992). There is an elision between realism as an abstract philosophical position and a particular story about social structures and processes. However, this story of social structure is not topicalized in this work; it is made to stay as a taken-for-granted background to analysis. Political issues are not raised for debate; rather a political stance is presupposed under the cover of a classical metaphysical story about facts and the real. One of the arguments of recent discourse work is that a lot of politics is done through constructing particular stories about social structure and social processes (Billig, 1995; Wetherell & Potter, 1992). This suggests we should attend more to our own constructions of this kind.

At a more specific level, there has been a very productive debate across the human sciences about the relations between talk, institutions, context and structure (Boden & Zimmerman, 1992; Drew & Heritage, 1992; Duranti & Goodwin, 1992; Markova & Foppa, 1991; Watson & Seiler, 1992). This has attempted to map a path between two positions: on the one hand, that discourse is soft stuff that is contained by a hard box made up of social structure or context; on the other, that only talk is real and all around it is made up or imaginary.

As a final caution, I should stress that, although important, I do not view social critique as the *exclusive* goal of studies of discourse and rhetoric. When researching the practices of, say, education, couple counselling or social work it may be positively unhelpful to *start* with the assumption that there is something wrong with those practices that must be corrected, or that those practices are inevitably organized into structures of domination. For example, an analyst might look at the procedures through which both social workers and clients warrant versions of risk without starting with the assumption that current practices are flawed. The point is not to preclude critical studies, merely to avoid making the a priori assumption that all current practices are flawed. There is another way of putting this. Criticism can turn into a kind of arrogance, where the researcher knows already what is wrong (and how it can be put right) and the research is merely a device for passing off what was already known as a product of investigation.

Given these cautions, how can discourse and rhetoric work be critical? I will emphasize three interrelated research strands that could be part of a critical social psychology: (1) ideological critique; (2) fact critique; and (3) disciplinary critique and reflexivity.

Ideological Critique

One of the central themes in discourse and rhetoric work is social and ideological critique. Billig (1992) and Wetherell and Potter (1992) are examples of this. They are studies concerned with discursive resources and their organization in social practices. These resources range from broad interpretative repertoires (e.g. Culture-as-Heritage) to relatively discrete rhetoric commonplaces (such as 'the Royal Family promotes tourism'). Their goal is to provide clear and persuasive accounts of the workings of various discursive forms that work to 'settle' the population into the acceptance of particular social arrangements or to treat inequalities as a necessary part of 'living in the modern world'. Analysis of this kind is exploring the common sense of a culture or group, what Roland Barthes calls the 'doxa' or 'Voice of Nature' (1977). The ideological significance of this work lies in its potential for showing how issues of legitimacy, inequality and exploitation are managed.

A striking thing about analyses of this kind – whether of New Zealand race talk, UK talk about the Royal Family, or everyday explanations of riots – is the complex and fragmented organization of common-sense reasoning. Billig (1992) talks of the 'kaleidoscope of common sense': a swirling pattern where premises and inferences regularly change places, where shifts are fluidly made between arguments from principle and practice, and where liberal, humanistic or egalitarian 'values' are drawn on for potentially racist effect or to legitimate inequality.

This picture does not sit well with traditional accounts which see common sense as essentially a reproduction in individuals of broad coherent ideologies: liberalism, conservatism, and so on. It forces a consideration of practices themselves and the important role of contradictions and tensions within and between discourses. One way of exploring this is with the productive notion of ideological dilemmas (Billig et al., 1988). For example, this can help show how 'liberal' principles and the 'practical considerations' which arise from having to live in 'the modern world' can be combined to legitimate a range of inequities (Wetherell, Stiven & Potter, 1987). The power of this form of accounting is that it can be explicit, public and accountable – for example, it does not need to be disguised and hidden behind a variety of disclaimers, as do more traditional racist or sexist claims (Gill, 1993; Wetherell & Potter, 1992).

It could be argued that this is an exemplary picture of the 'postmodern condition': the grand narratives have been dispersed to leave varied and fragmentary 'language games' with their own patterns of 'pragmatic valences' (Lyotard, 1979: xxiv). There are some interesting questions raised by this comparison, yet from a discourse analytic perspective it is possible to question the widespread lack of attention to concrete analysis as well as the surprisingly unreflexive set of stipulations and claims about social transformation and the role of technology found in much existing critical social psychology. An understanding of common sense as a swirling kaleidoscope need not blunt criticism; indeed it has opened up new critical paths, including radical new stories about subjectivity (Walkerdine, this volume). It is also important to emphasize that discourse researchers are not here assuming a 'free play of meaning' (cf. Wilkinson, this volume) in the manner of some American literary theorists; they are concerned to enter arguments about the meanings that are actually constructed, and what they are actually used to do.

Fact Critique

The second critical theme in discourse and rhetoric studies is on facts and fact construction (see Potter, 1996, for overview). This should not be seen as separate from the analysis of discursive resources. Indeed, one of the central traditions involved in the study of fact construction has been precisely a post-structuralist study of resources. Here realism is treated as the product of historically developed familiarity with sets of resources or interpretative repertoires. The representation ceases to be treated as a representation and becomes merely an index of the real 'because it is so familiar it operates transparently' (Shapiro, 1988: xi). On this analysis, part of the success of discourses of 'practical considerations' and 'the modern world' is that they are so familiar that they have become 'obvious' truths.

This post-structuralist approach to facts and their ideological role is not sufficient as it stands. For one thing, it does not explain why some widely familiar discourses are abandoned, or how they become familiar in the first place. Or, out of two familiar discourses, why should one be used in a particular setting and one not? For another, it treats the discourses as abstract entities separated from social practices altogether (Potter, Wetherell, Gill & Edwards, 1990). This approach can be modulated and supplemented by a more rhetorically based perspective, which treats talk and texts as organized in particular ways to make a version of reality appear solid, factual and stable. To accomplish this reality construction they draw on a range of techniques and devices: effects from categorization and particularization, the use of combinations of detailed and vague formulations, narrative techniques, constructions involving consensus and corroboration, and various basic rhetorical forms such as contrasts and lists (Atkinson, 1989; Edwards and Potter, 1992; Smith, 1990; Wooffitt, 1992). It is here that ethnomethodology and conversation analysis have made a substantial contribution.

It is important to combine analysis of the rhetorical work of fact construction with analysis of the sorts of activities and interaction sequences that factual versions or reports are embedded in. Indeed, it is difficult to do analysis of one without the other. One of the points emphasized in recent studies is that in many situations of conflict, or where potentially sensitive or threatening actions are being performed, there is a *dilemma of stake* (Edwards & Potter, 1993; Potter, Edwards & Wetherell, 1993). This results from the potential for an action or claim to be discounted by referencing the stake or interest of the individual or group doing the action. The point is not that traditional social psychologists have failed to treat people's claims and accounts as interested, but that *people treat each other in this way*; they have failed to recognize the extent to which stake and interest is a pervasive participants' concern. The answer is not for discourse analysis to attempt to establish its own competing theory of interests, but to address interests as a participants' topic.

One principal role of factual versions is the management of this dilemma of stake. Methods of fact construction can be used to make a version seem out-there, disinterested, a mere feature of the world and not something the speaker or representative desired or even expected. This is neatly illustrated in Gill's (1993) study of the varied techniques broadcasters use to account for, and justify, the desultory proportion of women DJs on British radio. Fact construction need not always be analysed for its ideological significance; managing the dilemma of stake through factual versions can be an important task when flatmates sort out who should be doing the dishes. Yet, even such a prosaic topic area as this is implicated with questions of rights, duties and notions of individual responsibility which can be explicated through this approach. One of the general aims of this work is to provide a new take on a variety of broadly ideological questions to do with the legitimation and encouragement of exploitation, war, racism and gender inequality.

In terms of the discipline of psychology this approach undermines the traditional distinction between the cold outer world of facts and the warm inner psychology of attitudes and evaluations. Rather than seeing facts as marking the *edge* to psychological interest, because they are simply reflections of the way the world is, we can see that this idea is, *itself*, part of a move in a social practice which psychologists use to manage their own dilemma of stake (Potter et al., 1993).

More generally, we can turn this sort of analysis round onto psychology and look at the way particular sorts of epistemological privilege are generated in the course of standard 'methodologies'. For example, we have argued that in much memory and attribution research pertinent, and sometimes political, issues of fact construction are obscured through the researcher legislating as to the meanings of 'vignettes' or 'stimulus materials' (Edwards & Potter, 1992). This sustains, and is sustained by, the foundationalist epistemology characteristic of modern psychology.

Disciplinary Critique and Reflexivity

The third critical theme in discourse work relates to its reflexive role in addressing the practices and texts of social psychology. In part, this is a distinctive contribution to a larger tradition of ideological critique of social psychology and social science more generally (Henriques, Hollway, Irwin, Venn & Walkerdine, 1984; Rose, 1989; Shotter, 1993b). One critical move has been to highlight the way social psychologists have treated people's talk and texts as literal and straightforward, failing to address their orientation to action. Such traditional research frequently ends up obscuring a central moral and political dimension of human life. At the same time the researcher often ends up aligned in some conflict without realizing it; he or she is 'captured' by one side in a dispute (Ashmore, 1996).

An example of discourse research on social psychology itself is Stringer's analysis of the construction of Irving Janis's well-known study of the social psychological processes that led to the Bay of Pigs 'fiasco' (Potter, Stringer & Wetherell, 1984: chap. 6). Janis explains such events as a product of 'groupthink' (a constellation of 'small group processes' and 'mental biases'); and his evidence of what went on is taken from narrative and biographical sources, notably the account of one of the major participants. What Janis fails to do is theorize how those sources are constructing local social psychologies and, moreover, how these social psychologies are *themselves* oriented to actions. For example, the central source text foregrounds *group* processes in a way that preserves the reputation of the President. Janis attends to the way attribution of responsibility is done *in* these texts, but not how it is done *by* them. In Janis's version, the social psychology of groupthink becomes another way of sustaining the myth of John F. Kennedy's presidency. The problem is not, of course, that Janis has taken sides; it is that he has done so in an unexplicated and unacknowledged manner hidden behind a veil of empiricist rhetoric.

This sort of disciplinary critique involves considering social psychology from the theoretical and analytic perspective of discourse analysis. In some ways Janis's work is a safe target. He is a representative of a mainstream North American tradition who has applied its familiar theoretical apparatus to an incident of major political implications. What is more contentious, however, is a more fully reflexive turn. Should we turn a discourse perspective onto our own texts, or onto the texts of other social psychologists who have critical aims? In more reflexive writing there is an attempt to work by displaying textual workings rather than describing them, and to consider the implications of the arguments and claims that are being made for the discourse in which those arguments and claims are constructed (see Ashmore, Myers & Potter, 1995, for a review and demonstration). For example, if I criticize the operation of realist discourse, is it appropriate that I use realist discourse in which to construct the critique? Or, if I attempt to show facts are discursive constructions, what about the discourse in which I construct the fact that facts are discursive constructions? There are difficult issues here, for which there are no easy answers.

Such a reflexive concern has been described as 'self-referential futility' (Wilkinson, this volume) and simply 'going round in circles' (Parker, this volume). In contrast to this I would argue that, far from being futile and circular, this sort of reflexivity is *required* if we are to critically address our *own* constructions of the social world, our *own* constructions of what is radical and what is reactionary, and the authority relations produced by our *own* texts. The alternative would be to claim a special privilege: a position beyond the sorts of questioning and criticism that our research participants undergo.

The way this issue is understood is bound up with judgements about politics and theory. For example, if radical politics is taken as equivalent to the mobilization of individuals around a unitary programme of action, then critically exploring one's own rhetoric can be seen as a corrosive distraction. It can be seen as leading to weakness and doubt when strength and resolution are needed. However, if politics is understood more broadly, then a critical interrogation of our own constructions of authority might be a radical place to start. Indeed, Ashmore (1989) demonstrates that, far from avoiding facing up to theoretical, moral and political issues, one's own practice is a place for exploring precisely these things – and one which often turns out to have much wider relevance.

This is paralleled in certain important ways by post-structuralist and discursive approaches. For here ideology and politics are theorized not as a separate realm, but as something inscribed in common sense and subjectivity. This again suggests that we run considerable risks if we insulate our own practices, understanding and texts from scrutiny; not least because we may end up reproducing precisely the assumptions we have set out to criticize.

Undoubtedly there are tensions between this form of work and the more 'straightforward' ideological critique described above. One of the future directions for discourse and rhetoric theorizing will be creatively to explore this tension, and to build on the softening of disciplinary boundaries and methodological constraints that allow new alignments and critical possibilities.

Note

This chapter has benefited from many arguments with Malcolm Ashmore, Michael Billig, Derek Edwards, Dave Middleton and Margaret Wetherell. I would like to thank Margaret Wetherell in particular for detailed comments on a first draft.

References

Ashmore, M. (1989). *The reflexive thesis: Wrighting sociology of scientific knowledge*. Chicago: University of Chicago Press.

Ashmore, M. (1996). Ending up on the wrong side: Must the two forms of radicalism always be at war? *Social Studies of Science*, *26*, 305–322.

Ashmore, M., Myers, G., & Potter, J. (1995). Discourse, rhetoric and reflexivity: Seven days in the library. In S. Jasanoff, G. Markle, T. Pinch & J. Petersen (Eds.), *Handbook of science, technology and society* (pp. 321–342). London: Sage.

Atkinson, P. (1989). *The ethnographic imagination: Textual constructions of reality*. London: Routledge.

Barthes, R. (1977). *Roland Barthes by Roland Barthes*. New York: Hill & Wang.

Billig, M. (1987). *Arguing and thinking: A rhetorical approach to social psychology*. Cambridge: Cambridge University Press.

Billig, M. (1988). Methodology and scholarship in understanding ideological explanation. In C. Antaki (Ed.), *Analysing lay explanation: A casebook* (pp. 199–215). London: Sage.

Billig, M. (1991). *Ideologies and opinions*. London: Sage.

Billig, M. (1992). *Talking about the Royal Family*. London: Routledge.

Billig, M. (1995). *Banal nationalism*. London: Sage.

Billig, M., Condor, S., Edwards, D., Gane, M., Middleton, D.J. & Radley, A.P. (1988). *Ideological dilemmas: A social psychology of everyday thinking*. London: Sage.

Boden, D., & Zimmerman, D. (Eds.). (1992). *Talk and social structure*. Cambridge: Polity.

Bruner, J. (1990). *Acts of meaning*. Cambridge, MA: Harvard University Press.

Drew, P. (1990). Strategies in the contest between lawyers and witnesses. In J.N. Levi & A.G. Walker (Eds.), *Language in the judicial process* (pp. 39–64). New York: Plenum.

Drew, P. & Heritage, J.C. (1992). *Talk at work: Interaction in institutional settings*. Cambridge: Cambridge University Press.

Duranti, A., & Goodwin, G. (Eds.). (1992). *Rethinking context: Language as an interactive phenomenon.* Cambridge: Cambridge University Press.

Edwards, D., Ashmore, M., & Potter, J. (1995). Death and furniture: The rhetoric, politics and theology of bottom line arguments against relativism. *History of the Human Sciences, 8,* 25–49.

Edwards, D., & Potter, J. (1992). *Discursive psychology.* London: Sage.

Edwards, D., & Potter, J. (1993). Language and causation: A discursive action model of description and attribution. *Psychological Review, 100,* 23–41.

Gergen, K.J. (1978). Experimentation in social psychology: A reappraisal. *European Journal of Social Psychology, 8,* 507–527.

Gill, R. (1993). Justifying injustice: Broadcasters' accounts of inequality in radio. In E. Burman and I. Parker (Eds.), *Discourse analytic research: Repertoires and readings of texts in action* (pp. 75–93). London: Routledge.

Harré, R. (1992). *Social being: A theory for social psychology* (2nd ed.). Oxford: Blackwell.

Harré, R. (1993). Reappraising social psychology: Rules, roles and rhetoric. *The Psychologist, 6,* 24–8.

Henriques, J., Hollway, W., Irwin, C., Venn, C., & Walkerdine, V. (1984). *Changing the subject: Psychology, social regulation and subjectivity.* London: Methuen.

Kelly, L. (1988). *Surviving sexual violence.* Cambridge: Polity Press.

Latour, B. (1987). *Science in action.* Milton Keynes: Open University Press.

Lawson, H. & Appignanesi, L. (1989). *Dismantling truth: Reality in the post-modern world.* London: ICA.

Lyotard, J.-F. (1979). *The postmodern condition: A report on knowledge.* Manchester: Manchester University Press.

Markova, I., & Foppa, K. (1991). *Asymmetries in dialogue.* Hemel Hempstead: Harvester Wheatsheaf.

McHoul, A.W. (1987). Why there are no guarantees for interrogators. *Journal of Pragmatics, 11,* 455–471.

Moscovici, S. (1984). The phenomenon of social representations. In R.M. Farr & S. Moscovici (Eds.), *Social representations* (pp. 3–70). Cambridge: Cambridge University Press.

Parker, I. (1992). *Discourse dynamics: Critical analysis for social and individual psychology.* London: Routledge.

Parker, I., & Burman, E. (1993). Against discursive imperialism, empiricism and constructionism: Thirty-two problems with discourse analysis. In E. Burman & I. Parker (Eds.), *Discourse analytic research: Repertoires and readings of texts in action* (pp. 155–172). London: Routledge.

Potter, J. (1992). Constructing realism: Seven moves (plus or minus a couple). *Theory & Psychology, 2,* 167–173.

Potter, J. (1996). *Representing reality: Discourse, rhetoric and social construction.* London: Sage.

Potter, J., Edwards, D., & Wetherell, M. (1993). A model of discourse in action. *American Behavioral Scientist, 36,* 383–401.

Potter, J., Stringer, P., & Wetherell, M. (1984). *Social texts and context: Literature and social psychology.* London: Routledge & Kegan Paul.

Potter, J., & Wetherell, M. (1987). *Discourse and social psychology: Beyond attitudes and behaviour.* London: Sage.

Potter, J., Wetherell, M., Gill, R., & Edwards, D. (1990). Discourse – noun, verb or social practice? *Philosophical Psychology, 3,* 205–217.

Rorty, R. (1980). *Philosophy and the mirror of nature.* Oxford: Blackwell.

Rorty, R. (1989). *Contingency, irony and solidarity.* Cambridge: Cambridge University Press.

Rose, N. (1989). *Governing the soul: The shaping of the private self.* London: Routledge.

Second of January Group (1986). *After truth: The post-modern manifesto.* London: Inventions Press.

Shapiro, M. (1988). *The politics of representation: Writing practices in biography, photography, and policy analysis.* Madison: University of Wisconsin Press.

Shotter, J. (1993a). *Cultural politics of everyday life: Social constructionism, rhetoric and knowing of the third kind*. Buckingham: Open University Press.

Shotter, J. (1993b). *Conversational realities*. London: Sage.

Smith, B.H. (1988). *Contingencies of value: Alternative perspectives for critical theory*. Cambridge, MA: Harvard University Press.

Smith, D.E. (1990). *Texts, facts and femininity: Exploring the relations of ruling*. London: Routledge.

Watson, G., & Seiler, R.M. (Eds.). (1992). *Text in context: Contributions to ethnomethodology*. London: Sage.

Wetherell, M., & Potter, J. (1992). *Mapping the language of racism: Discourse and the legitimation of exploitation*. Hemel Hempstead: Harvester Wheatsheaf.

Wetherell, M., Stiven, H., & Potter, J. (1987). Unequal egalitarianism: A preliminary study of discourses concerning gender and employment opportunities. *British Journal of Social Psychology*, *26*, 59–71.

Wooffitt, R. (1992). *Telling tales of the unexpected: The organization of factual accounts*. Hemel Hempstead: Harvester Wheatsheaf.

Woolgar, S. (1988). *Science: The very idea*. Chichester: Ellis Horwood/London: Tavistock.

5

Does Critical Social Psychology Mean the End of the World?

Wendy Stainton Rogers and Rex Stainton Rogers

One of the most critical concerns of critical social psychology is what to make of the 'real world' – what Mulkay (1985) describes as 'that beyond textuality'. Behind and beyond our dalliances with discourse and our trysts with text, our disdain for 'truth games' and our enjoyment of 'language games', the issue of the 'real world' refuses to go away. Indeed, even were we tempted to ignore it, our detractors never fail to bring it up. In what Jonathan Potter and his colleagues have so nicely termed their 'death and furniture' arguments (Edwards, Ashmore & Potter, 1995), the more we talk of 'the social construction of reality' the more they slap the table (*bang!*) and say 'Go on, argue that away.' The more we discourse on the discursive production of knowledge, the more they get hot under the collar and start shouting, 'So you're trying to claim that the Holocaust never happened, then, are you? Nobody died, did they?' This 'death and furniture' line of argument is, they assert, the 'bottom line', which criticality cannot counter. Claiming 'there is nothing outside the text' simply will not do, they say, because the extra-textual 'world' of physical things and real events cannot be textualized out of existence. All the discourse in the world will not stop you bumping into things, nor will it bring the dead to life. It is bullets, bombs and famine which kill, not words.

In this chapter we will consider a number of (interlinked) aspects of 'the real world' which we think critical social psychology needs to address:

- How can criticality counter 'death and furniture' arguments in relation to social psychology?
- Does 'critical realism' offer a solution – and if not, why not?
- What has critical social psychology to say about the place we, as persons, occupy in 'the real world', in terms of ourselves both as academics and as 'real-world actors' in everyday life?
- How can we progress beyond abstract critique and address the sub-stantive? In other words, what methods of scrutiny can critical social psychology employ, once it has dispensed with empiricism?
- Do we (can we?) 'realistically' have any solutions to offer to 'real-world' problems (such as human suffering, the exploitation and oppression of the weak by the strong, and the harms being done to the planet)?

Down with 'Death and Furniture' – Dissolving the Fact/Fiction Distinction

For us, 'death and furniture' arguments are based on a fundamental mis-understanding of the critical position (or at least of our critical positions). What we read into the assertion that there is 'nothing outside the text' is not a claim that there is no such thing as 'reality' – that there is no existence of things and events outside of discourse. To do so would be to make the 'atheist's error' – to make a foundational claim about non-Being. Rather, it is a call to doubt, a radical agnosticism (not Huxley's material-ism), which directs attention somewhere else – specifically, towards an appreciation that 'reality' comes about for us through the always contested ways we *know about* reality. It is not an argument that 'the real world of facts' does not exist, but that 'the real world of facts' and 'the imagined world of fiction' cannot be treated as *factually* separate and different, the first based on a one-to-one mirroring of things-as-they-exist-in-the-world, and the second 'imaginal'. This is what we take Mulkay (1985) to be saying when he claims that:

> Fact and fiction . . . are . . . forms of discourse . . ., neither of which has a privileged relationship to the world in which we are interested. (p. 12)

In other words (itself a telling phrase), we cannot 'factualize' facts into existence, or 'fictionalize' fiction out of existence. Both are forms in and of 'knowledging' – the active construction of knowledge. A fact is not a-thing-in-itself, but knowledge-of-a-thing, and always predicated on, always inter-textual with, other forms of knowledge. A fiction is equally not a-non-thing-in-itself. Fiction is only 'imaginal' in the sense that the 'imaginal' is itself imaginal. This is not to say that it, or anything else, is 'all in the mind', but rather that it has been knowledged about (not, of course, 'by the mind', unless it is also reflectively allowed that that 'mind' also has the status of the knowledged-about).

This worrying of the fact/fiction distinction is crucial to critical social psychology (as critique of social psychology) since it troubles the idea that we can know about 'the social' in terms of 'the Fact' without reflexively un-addressing knowing about 'the Fact' in terms of 'the social'. In the preface to her book *Undoing the Social* (1991), Ann Game draws an analogy between the social analyst and a sea-captain, bustling around on the bridge, adjusting steering devices and shouting orders 'below', in the belief that all this frenetic activity is directing the ship – when, in fact, there is no crew, no engine room, no machinery at all. The ship's course is merely being buffeted by the sea itself. Attempts to analyse the social, she suggests, are similarly adrift:

> There is no deep real (or engine-room) below the surface; there is no extra-textual ground for social analysis to cling on to. We, like the writers of 'fiction', are at sea. (p. xii)

This is to assert that there is no external (extra-discursive) benchmark that can ever show that a foundational 'Truth' has been revealed. Any act of discovering is also always an act of covering; discovery of knowledge is a 'Truth game', in which Truth is actively and purposively knowledged into being (cf. Curt, 1994).

This is what makes the critical approach a challenge to the mainstream, received, scientized social psychological approach, which regards 'the facts of personal and social life' as waiting-out-there-to-be-discovered 'things' which have an independent existence from the act of discovering them. The crux of argument is not, then, about the being-in-the-world of physical entities (such as furniture) and the happening-in-the-world of events (such as death), but about how we may come to know about them. Mulkay (1985) explains this thus:

> There's no way of separating reality from the symbolic realm of human discourse and no way in which reality as such can be used to check our factual claims. . . . The propositions of factual texts are no more direct representations of the real world than are the contents of fictional texts. Both kinds of text are imaginative reconstructions of the world, in so far as that world is mediated through our own and others' interpretative work. My view is that 'fact' and 'fiction' are not distinguished by some radically different relationship with an independently real world, or even by some radically different use of empirical evidence, but are rather labels which we attach to forms of discourse which formulate and present their propositions through significantly different conventions. (pp. 11–12)

Critical Realism

Parker (1992), one of the most vocal proponents of 'critical realism' (cf. Bhaskar, 1989), cautions us against the kind of realist analysis which can 'turn . . . into a series of rhetorical devices which butress reductionism' (p. 95). He is particularly concerned we should avoid what he sees as harking-back to scientism and its 'representation of the world as organized by the metanarratives of humanized science, progress and individual meaning' (Parker, 1989, p. 54). None the less, Parker views 'critical realism' as a necessary analytic for critical social psychology, and devotes his second chapter of *Discourse Dynamics* (1992) to setting out the critical realist position, and showing how it can be used.

What needs to be recognized here is that the argument *within* critical social psychology is a different one than that between critical social psychologists and the mainstream (what Edwards et al, 1995, call the *ontological* argument). The case Parker is making against what he terms 'relativism' arises from his view that the purpose of criticality is a political one – challenging the complacency of liberal humanism by bringing injustice and oppression into visibility (and thus to our attention). From this perspective 'critical realism' is essential to 'bar the gate to the polis and keep the night, the jungle and the jackals at bay' (Smith, 1988, p. 154). Others who take a similar 'critical realist' line do so from somewhat different political stances – for instance, Kitzinger, Wilkinson and Perkins (1992) write as separatist lesbians. For them, criticality must serve the purpose of exposing the oppressive potential of heteropatriarchy (as they term it), and be used to fight it.

The 'critical realist' rejection of a criticality which admits no foundation is therefore not a call to naïve materialism, but a foreboding over relativism as a 'slippery slope' where

> . . . those fascinated by the power of discourse cut loose from any connection with a real outside. Texts are becoming the vehicles for the 'radical' expression of a purely pragmatic 'new realism' which has lost any desire to take underlying structures of oppression and resistance seriously. (Parker, 1992, pp. 40–41)

The nightmare scenario here is a world in which the very people who should be resisting the 'horrors' of death and destruction get so beguiled by the postmodern carnival that they give up on radical politics altogether. Such irresponsible hedonism is held to be made possible by the detachment that follows from arguments which fail to address the material conditions which render some people oppressed. Put crudely (very crudely), a relativism which admits no bombs, no torture, no oppression – only text upon text – is 'dangerous' and irresponsible:

> As I write this, an area of Tripoli has been laid waste by a number of aircraft currently (I hope) sitting on the ground a few miles down the road from my Ivory Tower. Some 100 people (not very many by modern standards) have been killed. They were not killed by words, neither are they dead because the rest of the world decided to call them dead. Their death was brought about by the employment of a disproportionately immense amount of scientific and technical knowledge. If we can only see this knowledge as just another story, then we too deserve to fall victim to it. (Craib, 1986, p. 48)

Seemingly, the inscription of discourses upon the body (direct in the Kafka-esque sense, or more distally) can claim no special status or concern. The feature of so-called 'relativist' positions which seems to worry 'critical realists' most is the profound doubt implicit in the relativist position. In particular, it is the argument that there is no *extra-discursively palpable* infrastructure of 'really-real reality' upon which the social gets laid, no 'safety rail' of the real (Frow, 1983) to which we can cling in our attempts to explain it.

It is not 'alternative realities' which are at issue, for Parker accepts that '[t]he realist conception of social structure offers a version of materialism which takes account of different senses of reality, and of reality outside of sense' (Parker, 1992, p. 36). In other words, he accepts, as do 'critical pluralists/relativists', the notion of multiple realities. The dispute is (or seems to be) centred upon the need for asserting the extra-textual 'reality' of the material conditions of oppression. It is, for the 'critical realists', both about asserting that criticality must *be* politicked; and valorizing a particular reading of *how* criticality must be politicked.

The Holocaust is possibly the bench-mark 'horror' for realist (including critical realist) argument. Uncapitalized, the word 'holocaust' (literally, a great destruction or loss of life) carries a massive weight of meanings. For example, it has come to stand for all the terrors of an imagined global nuclear war and its aftermath (e.g. nuclear winter) in the genre of 'post-holocaust' science fiction. Capitalized as 'The Holocaust', it stands in for the more than a decade of genocidal horrors that Hitler's National Socialism unleashed upon the Jews of Europe.

To pursue the claim that 'The Holocaust' is a discursive production is certainly discomforting, for it risks being associated with the apologists for Nazism and anti-semitism who seek to argue that 'the Holocaust never took place'. Perhaps the most pressing difficulty is the recognition that for many people (indeed, quite possibly for the very people with whom one is arguing) 'The Holocaust' is not so much an issue of ontological reality as one of *personal* reality – of lives touched in the most direct of ways. But to say 'the Holocaust is a discursive production' is something else entirely from suggesting that 'it never happened'. It does not deny suffering, nor does it dishonour those who were tortured and murdered.

The purpose of 'troubling' it as a concept is quite other. It is to ask disturbing questions, such as 'Why has this set of events been given prominence when, say, the model for the "The Holocaust" may well have been the earlier Turkish genocide upon the Armenians?' or 'Why do we almost automatically associate concentration camps with the Nazis when they may well have been first instigated by the British in the Boer War?'

The reason for asking questions like this is the concern that the reification of one particular set of events as 'The Holocaust', no matter how well grounded or justified, is also a particular shaping of reality. By drawing attention to the wrongs done to one group of people at one period in history, one inevitably draws attention *away* from other wrongs done to other groups at other times. Put bluntly, if Hollywood were replete with Armenians, we might have a very different understanding of 'The Holocaust'. We ourselves see critical realism, in practice, as having the effect of directed *sensitization*, which, crucially, also inexorably implies a directed *repression*. We suspect that so, too, do many critical realists, because they acknowledge that they are doing a particular politics (a working *for* which is also a working *against*). Where we may differ is in where (and how directedly) our political criticality is focused.

Critical Relativism

The oppositional to 'critical realism' is not mere 'relativism' but '*critical relativism*'. It is not a position in which 'everything goes' but one in which 'nothing goes' (Sawicki, 1991) – where all discourses must be made open to critical challenge, including our own (and others') moral and ideological readings. Thus while we *risk* a criticality which perturbates foundation, we do not read into it the same sense of *hazard* (or 'danger') that critical realists detect. Our argument is that we are quite aware of the traps of naïve relativism and the enchantments of carnivalism – and have adopted a more manifold working of concern to counter them.

Our kind of critical relativism aims to use (rather than to be used by) caution about foundational reality. It is not that we are without concern, but nor is concern somehow outwith us. To scrutinize any manifold of 'social realities' is (but is not only) also to be concerned about what each sensitizes and what each represses – what each may give and each may take, and to and from whom. It is, additionally, to open the possibilities (the not-made-real), which may or may not come to realization. Finally, it is to accept that such cost–benefit analyses of alternative readings of actions and conduct are open to double-doubt – over both the reading and the analysis.

For us it is such pervasive and perturbating doubt, inhering in a multiplex textuality, which is what we mean by – and do as – criticality. To us what is 'dangerous' is the claim that there is ever a single, foundationally proper 'ideological position' from which any set of events *must* be read. Contingent engagements are both inevitable and necessary to scrutiny. Engagement which singularizes always carries the risk of a regime of sensitization/repression which regulates the place of challenge. Right and wrong, like truth and fiction, cannot be foundationed as givens. They are discursive productions over whose regulation we set overlords (or ladies) to our peril.

In saying this we also seek to show that arguments between 'critical relativists' and 'critical realists' are only peripherally a dispute over what, if anything, can be known of 'the real' in the sense of materiality. Rather, they owe their vehemence and their persistence to the politics that are inscribed upon the knowings-of-reality debate. Critical realism is somewhat more of a project – an attempt to make the future by knowing the present and the past. Critical pluralism is somewhat more of an 'antiject' – an attempt to unmake the future we have been given by worrying our accounts of the present and the past. This is as true for their generic politics as it is for their politics of social psychology.

On Taking Oneself Seriously versus Making Mischief

Elizabeth Wilson (1985), writing on fashion and modernism, portrays the 'relativism' of the postmodern worldview as one where

> . . . no one practice or activity is valued above any other; moral and aesthetic judgements are replaced by hedonistic enjoyment of each molecular and disconnected artefact, performance or experience. Such extreme alienation 'derealizes' modern life, draining from it all notion of meaning. Everything then becomes play; nothing is serious. (p. 11)

To offer a partial 'thematic decomposition' of this extract, we will note how the metaphor shifts the ground from a *description* of epistemic doubt about knowledge claims (i.e. the analytic of not according a priori superior status to any one particular reading of a text) to the *prescriptive assertion* that this means that 'everything becomes play; nothing is serious', that 'judgements are replaced by hedonistic enjoyment', and that this drains from modern life 'all notion of meaning'.

The work/play dichotomy is, of course, one of the classic themes of modernism. We know it best in social psychology in terms of the 'need for consistency/need for variety' argument. In Wilson's description it is employed to cast the relativist as *homo ludens*, rather than *homo faber*, and thus to identify her/him with the Other (i.e. child-like; 'primitive'; living for the moment). Perhaps we should not blame Wilson totally for this – postmodernism has sometimes described itself this way as a counter-identity. Nevertheless, we would argue (along with, for example, Sampson, 1993) away from such monologics, towards dialogics.

Resisting an either/or logic, we would say that critical relativism is rather a site for both *homo faber* and *homo ludens*. For example, suggesting that we must always subject every 'truth claim' to scrutiny – that we must always question what it covers up, what it warrants, what its down-side costs may be – is nothing if not serious. It is hard work, and can often be uncomfortable – it is certainly not a recipe for hedonism. Meaning is not 'dissolved' by relativism: quite the opposite – meaning becomes precisely that whereby something has (variously) become 'an issue' and hence the prime site of scrutiny.

Nevertheless, working from the axiom that 'nothing goes' – that everything needs to be exposed to 'affirmative doubt and doubtful affirmation' (Curt, 1994) – can, and often does, bring us what Ann Game calls 'disturbing pleasure'. We can thoroughly enjoy being 'troublesome', and we can (and do) delight in mischievously subverting authority by exposing the apparatus it uses to bolster up its power games.

For example, as noted in Chapter 3, together with others we have written under the collective authorship of a fictive character, Beryl Curt (Curt, 1994). This had a serious purpose, in that it worked over some aspects of the notion of 'the death of the author'. It makes explicit that the text so written is the product not only of many hands but also of debate between us and of our reading and rewriting of the texts of others, wherein we cannot attribute any part of the text to single authorship. But we also take considerable pleasure in the way such 'deviant' authorship will cause all sorts of problems within the new systems of academic audit which have been imposed, in the UK, in order to render scholarship subject to regulation.

The text of the book itself also uses humorous devices (like irony, punning, sarcasm and parody) not just to entertain and make for readability, but also to dissolve, explicitly, the purported distinction between 'academic' and 'popular' writing. By lampooning ourselves we are, in effect, saying 'the distinction between this academic text and a comic or a TV comedy is not as great as all that'.

The result can be an object–field effect – placed against a 'field' of typical conference attenders in paper-presenting mode, the dialogics of critical relativism can indeed seem like the 'object' *homo ludens*! Transfer it into the end of conference disco and the contrast dissolves. There is a powerful sedimentation of the notion that the 'serious' needs to be seen to be done 'seriously'.

In debate it is this contrast which is often most apparent. Against the sombre, solemn (and, we have to say, at times the puritanical) tenor of the 'critical realist', the 'critical relativist' often gives off an aura of mocking, playful, pleasure-seeking mischief. It is easy to be superficially beguiled into thinking, therefore, that while the one is 'serious', the other is merely 'hedonistic' – interested *only* in having fun, and hence callously disinterested in the horrors, wrongs and harms going on all around. It is thus easy to see why such an impression can disturb 'critical realists'. Laughing as one lets go of the 'safety rail' of 'the real' can easily seem like a symptom of an inexorable letting go of one's critical faculties! The work/ play tension itself is so written into our language as a moral dimension that a 'descent' into irony, humour and having fun almost implies a leaving behind of the 'higher' faculties like criticality.

We, on the other hand, are worried that, by taking critique too seriously, without the leaven of play, one can lose sight of the entrapment this implies. We see a very short step between being convinced of the need to 'take seriously' the horrors, wrongs and harms going on all around us, and being convinced that you have an authorized, unchallengeable 'handle' on *the* horrific, *the* wrong, *the* harmful. To assume that you have access to some, extra-discursive, 'real' that can be drawn upon to determine 'right' from 'wrong' is, we would argue, too close to totalizing ethics for comfort. Of course, the criticality of critical realism is what should enable its practitioners to so 'sail close to the wind' without 'landing on the rocks' (i.e. its own foundations). However, navigation is serious, attention-demanding business, and may exclude from operations just those playful moments that may foster some passing immunity to the 'enchantments' of 'truth-making'.

Disenchantment

Rather than 'hedonistic', we see ourselves as seriously (and playfully) 'disenchanted'. The word 'enchantment' concerns the use, in magic, of songs or spells to beguile, impel or charm another into a state in which they will believe what the sorcerer wants them to believe. Equally, enchantments may be employed to prevent another person from seeing what the sorcerer wants to render invisible, in order that they shall do what the sorcerer wants them to do. Thus dis-enchantment, in this sense, is the breaking of such spells – it is about resisting being beguiled by 'realities' – whether taken-for-granted or 'critically realized' – and thereby regaining – and then retaining – the capability for critical-directed action.

Disenchantment, we would argue, is a very necessary basis from which to perturbate both the certainties of the liberal disciplines and our sense of the enduring nature and invulnerability of the social worlds that they sustain – including the social world of the academy. The 'academy' is the term used by Foucault (1970) to describe the locus of secret and exclusive – and thus prized – scholarly knowledge, which, even when those outside the academy get hold of it, cannot be fully deciphered. It is the site of 'discourse with a veil drawn over it' (p. 88). Thus disenchantment allows us to recognize that scholarly knowledge, no less than any other knowledge, is always based on 'illusion', from which we need to be able to become dis-illusioned for certain critical operations.

In saying this we are not suggesting that such 'illusions' are deliberate deceits (i.e. conspiratorial hidings or maskings) but *enchantments* which glamour pressing 'realities' into being. This is an inevitable, unavoidable consequence of the synarchy of power/knowledge (which operates in the academy just as much as it does elsewhere). It is an enchantment which fixes us as scholars (as well as ordinary, everyday people) into positions of seeming competent-knowingness. But we must always be willing to break that spell, to be dis-illusioned, to become ironical, especially about our own certainties.

Another reason why our playfulness troubles some critical social psychologists is that they think it can lead criticality to be taken as a 'joke'. A few 'clowns' can make the whole critical movement seem like a circus, goes the argument, and thereby we run the risk of giving the mainstream an easy target for marginalization. They have a point. As Tomás Ibáñez argues in this collection, we cannot ignore the vulnerability involved in being 'on the fringe'. We cannot simply act as though the mainstream does not have at its disposal all the hegemonic powers of authority which renders them 'the orthodox' and renders us 'the troublemakers'. If we do not take ourselves very seriously, the risk we run is that nobody else will take us seriously either.

We accept that we do need to take these cautions 'seriously'. For many in mainstream psychology, the 'climate of problematization' (cf. Curt, 1994; also Chapter 3 above) is seen as little more than a small and local squall, somewhere off the edge of the conceptual weather-map. It will remain so, unless and until its winds of change get to be felt – get to be taken as moving things. Impact will not come from *salon* gossip, or chat-show sound-bites dispensed by a few gurus of postmodernist theorizing, alone. There needs to be an impact across a range of sites, from the established academy to the troubles and concerns of 'the real world'. Comedy, in its classical meaning, refers to a play in which there is triumph over adversity, and that requires that we do more than simply play the joker. The trick is, we believe, to combine mischief with serious business. Indeed, the juxtaposition of teasing against 'tough text' (as we have tried to do in *Textuality and Tectonics*) is intended to be, in itself, both moving and perturbating – certainly we hope it will get Beryl noticed!

Critical Paths

We may, then, need to agree to differ over style. We hope our 'serious' friends in criticality will at least acknowledge that we are very much aware of the traps of a relativism in which 'anything goes', and that they can accept that our mischief-making has a very serious purpose. We, perhaps, may need to allow that in taking particular moral stances, they, too, are equally aware of the risks of enchantment, though we still worry about some of their positions, such as a perturbing (rather than perturbating) tendency we see in their sometimes adoption of 'the means justify the ends' arguments.

What we have in common is an agreement that much more is required of us than engagement with text solely *as* text, ignoring its consequences in 'practical reality' (where death and furniture – and much more – work *as* real). Indeed, we share a common concern with the links between what could be called discourse and action – with 'discourse work' which examines the ways that certain reality-constructions warrant certain forms of conduct. Haraway (1984), in her powerful essay about primatology being 'politics by other means', asserts that

> . . . Life and social sciences in general, and primatology in particular, are story-laden; these sciences are composed through complex, historically specific storytelling practices. Facts are theory-laden; theories are value-laden; values are story-laden. Therefore facts are meaningful within stories. (p. 79)

Haraway notes that story-telling always involves, inexorably, 'complex webs of power, including the tortured realities of race, sex and class – and including people's struggles to tell each other how we might live with each other' (p. 80). This story-quality is not a pollutant of the scientific endeavour – an unwanted intrusion of murky subjectivity into objectivity. Rather 'the struggle to construct good stories is a major part of the craft' (p. 80).

If we accept Haraway's arguments, then we can accord 'telling stories' two kinds of power. First, it is a world-making craft – tell a convincing story and you are well on the way to beguiling people into seeing 'reality' in a particular way. Moreover, those who get to tell the most credible, most persuasive (or, perhaps, most heard) stories are those whose versions of 'reality' are most likely to become 'what everybody knows'; the dominant 'commonsense' worldview, through which the 'real world' gets understood. Second, stories are never solely descriptive – they usually 'have a moral' (i.e. tell us a 'moral truth'), and often their purpose is parabolistic – to tell us what we can or should do. Hence those whose stories gain dominance gain world-making power, not only in terms of the way we 'see' the world, but also in terms of what we *do* within it.

The implication for us is that we are inexorably engaged, as persons-in-culture, in the story-making which brings the world into being. If we want to change how people understand the world around them, and the actions that they take within it, then we had better become skilful story-tellers. We need to talk and write in ways which are meaningful and have impact beyond the academy – indeed, we need to use the authority that our designation as 'academics' provides for us, and begin to engage directly in the world outside. And with no 'safety rail' of ideological 'truth' to fall back on, we must be willing to accept that taking on 'the real problems' in 'the real world' means always being willing to hold our own stories up to scrutiny. There is no 'safe passage' to the promised land, just a minefield on the way to possibilities, through which we must navigate as best we can.

There is, of course, no single way of doing this; we are a critical manifold. Some will choose the path of 'resistance', others of us will choose to play the trickster (at least some of the time). Some will work within the confines of the academy, but others of us will need to step beyond its boundaries. If playwrights can become presidents through Velvet Revolutions, why should critical social psychologists not, say, get involved in public policy-making? In what now passes for politics? In movie-making?

Scrutiny of the (Practically) Real

Perhaps the most obvious way in which we engage with 'the mundane world', but crucial in our challenge to orthodoxy from within and outwith our discipline, is through doing research. The various dialects of 'discourse work' that we do – the crafts of 'reading' and 'rewriting' textuality – are important components of the overall labour of being critical. Through it, we make our criticality manifest and operant. The reporting of disciplined inquiry is an important story-telling genre in a scientized culture in which 'research findings' are seen as the key to 'changing hearts and minds'. Mainstream psychology has used it to good effect in its missionary work (see any glossy US textbook). Through subverting that mission with our own forms of scrutiny, we can make our criticality manifest and operant (cf. Stainton Rogers, Stenner, Gleeson & Stainton Rogers, 1995).

However, early into the climate of problematization, critical psychologists were faced with the problematic of how to go about this, given that they had given up on 'objectivity' as a meaningful, workable notion. Much early critical psychological inquiry now seems little more than methodologically antithetical, the replacement of the hard and soulless with the soft and soulful. What is now becoming clear, to most of us, is that mainstream methods (even as antithesis) need to be ox-bowed from the river of critical scrutiny. At best, they can become foci of that scrutiny. Mainstream social psychology research has, by now, become yet another taken-for-granted presencing practice. The link between its goals and the means used to achieve them have become almost as automatic as reaching for a hammer to drive home a nail. Choice of method these days (as we know as reviewers) seems little more than a well-conditioned reaction born of the reinforcement schedules of 'research methods' teaching (e.g. 'got an issue, do a public opinion survey'). The mainstream has become 'methodolatrous' (see Curt, 1994, for a more detailed examination of this idea) to the point of virtual paralysis.

Clearly, we do not need 'new, improved' replacements for established methods. Rather we need (and we are generating) ways to challenge the kinds of questions and answers those methods enabled, and the means to doing something else. We are not using 'methods' at all (as they are conventionally understood, as free-standing means of canonical status) but explicitly acknowledged crafts or skills of scrutiny acquired in the doing. The first thing we ask of them is that they must be open to reflexive self-criticality – they must 'work' when applied to our own 'work'. They must also be sufficiently 'open' to alternative readings to expose the role of our own interpretative labour; yet sufficiently method-ical for that labour to stand scrutiny. They must acknowledge that

> [a]ll interpretation is fictional in the sense that it involves either the observer's or the subject's accounting of what has occurred or what something means. (Denzin, 1977, p. 137)

This cannot, for us, be achieved under either conventional qualitative or quantitative methods. Both of these are equally bound up in a melodrama of interrogation – the 'nice guy/nasty guy' interview routine beloved of police and intelligence work, designed to get at 'the truth'. The 'nasty guy' backs the target into a corner of the interview-room and demands 'just the facts ma'am' and simple 'yes or no' (quantifiable) answers. The 'nice guy' operator offers a cup of tea and a cigarette, and empathizes with the participant, even to the extent of appearing to defend her from the 'blow cold' operator and draws out qualitative information. But whichever approach to interrogation is taken, the purpose is still to break down the resistance of the subject, to get them to yield a testimony to the truth.

What we are after is not truth, but ways of 'reading' and means of interrogating textuality. The craft perhaps most commonly used by critical social psychologists is some form of 'discourse analysis'. We will leave it to others, more adept in that craft, to talk about it in its various mani-festations. Our contribution (as part of Beryl Curt) has been to offer two analytics – textuality and tectonics – as means to address text and texted-ness (these are described in Chapter 3). As for our craft skills, the collective term we have coined for them is 'critical polytextualism' (Curt, 1994; again, see also Chapter 3). How we often 'do' that is through Q methodology.

Q Methodology

One of our favourite sayings (the excuse to repeat it here) is that: Wherever data get dirty, you will find a statistician – when they get really dirty, you will find a meta-analyst. It is no accident that developments in twentieth-century statistics owe much to two 'dirty disciplines': agriculture and psychology. The problem of unpicking association amongst variation has considerably occupied both of them. Environments, whether fields used for seed trials or schools used for testing some new educational innovation (cf. Danziger, 1990), vary in complex ways, and those variabilities have a nasty habit of interacting with the very thing you are trying to test. The orthodox solution was the development of modern statistics of association amidst variation. As commonly used, these statistics reveal associations (e.g. correlations) between variables.

A craft that relies heavily on statistics might not seem, at first sight, to be the most promising possibility for critical polytextualism. Yet when we came across a procedure which intercorrelated whole structures (rather than 'measures' as in psychometrics) we felt that we had hit gold! Not all of our friends are convinced, even now, and this chapter is not the place for a detailed description of Q method (see Curt, 1994; Kitzinger, 1987; Stainton Rogers, 1991; Stainton Rogers, 1995, for different accounts).

The inventor of Q methodology, Will Stephenson, was into 'criticality' long before most of us were born, though he might well have argued with that label. For example, he suggested that psychologists should be prepared to learn from the 'brilliant and penetrating analyses of famous novelists' (1953, p. 4) if they wanted to understand an issue, rather than trying to be purely scientific. He was extremely critical of virtually all orthodox psychology, and its locus in hypothetico-deductivism. He strenuously refuted attempts to measure psychological phenomena objectively:

> . . . psychometry floods the US with pseudo testing of every conceivable kind – test intelligence, personality, skills, etc., and assess one another at work and play, as teachers assess pupils and vice versa. Everyone in the US seems bent on measuring or assessing every manner of human foible and accountability, *ad libitum*. Every strike of a baseball player is counted, and every tackle of a football player. It implies objectivity, as if it matters. . . . For myself, it is as unacceptable as the scholasticism of the early Christian philosophers: it is basically categorical only, and will one day disappear, one may hope, into a 'black hole' of grand illusions. (Stephenson, 1987, pp. 134–135)

The only reality, in his terms, is subjective reality; the only thing we can explore is 'the world in [its] subjective respects' (1987, p. 123). This was radical stuff at the time – certainly in the 1950s when he first began really pushing these ideas. Given this stance, Stephenson's Q methodology is not so strange a choice for conducting critical polytextualism.

At its simplest it consists of presenting people with a set of statements sampled from the concourse of debate about the topic in question. They are asked to sort them along a dimension, such as from 'strongest agreement' to 'strongest disagreement'. Usually around sixty to eighty statements are required to reasonably sample the different sorts of things people say about a topic. Hence sorting is usually done according to a Gaussian pattern, with just a few statements at the poles and more in the middle. The statistical part consists of a form of factor analysis which identifies statistically independent, alternative sorting patterns. Interpretation is by way of reconstituting the different patterns so identified, and making a 'reading' of them – often using open-ended comments or discussions with participants who took part in the study to help 'make sense' of the account being expressed.

Q method is certainly a craft in that a lot of careful work is required to construct the sets of statements. This may well involve several weeks or even months of work, interviewing and having conversations with people, reading academic texts and popular magazines, watching movies and TV programmes. Traditional pilot-testing is also often used, to refine the set until it 'works'.

What Q methodology has to offer, we believe, that makes it different from discourse analysis (and other forms of 'discourse work' like seeded thematics – cf. Stenner, 1993), is that it shares the task of analysis with the participants in a study. It is true that they cannot 'tell a story' unless they are provided with the statements to do so. But there are literally millions of ways in which, say, eighty statements could be ordered along an eleven-point evaluative dimension. Patterns only emerge because some participants sort in systematically similar manners, and in ways that are systematically different from the ways other participants sort. It is their sorting, not our readings, which determines the factors which emerge and hence which shape the 'stories' that are expressed.

One of the ways we use Q methodology to examine links between texts of understanding and texts of conduct is to get people to do two sorts. For example, they might sort one set of statements which have to do with explaining a 'social problem' (such as addiction, child abuse or madness); and another pertaining to conduct – what actions and policies should be adopted to tackle it. By observing the discursive links and disjunctions between these we can explore how, say, a certain policy appears to be predicated on a particular understanding of 'the problem'.

Actions Speak Louder Than Words

The results of these sorts of studies can be useful to people who are responsible for enacting public policy (e.g. professional workers dealing with 'child abuse' or the 'mentally ill'). They provide suggestions about some of the reasons why there is so much conflict about, for instance, how far children should be protected 'for their own good', and how much they should be allowed to choose for themselves what risks to take. They can offer insights into why, say, working in mainstream health care might lead to the expression of a gestalt of opinions that are completely different from those expressed by critical social psychologists!

In this sense critical polytextualist research is much like any other – it offers its 'findings' for use by people in their working and personal lives. It is different, though, in that it makes no claims to warrant its output as 'scientific support' for a particular 'Truth' (though there is obviously a danger that this is how it will be read).

More generally criticality can be used to 'work on' real-world problems through our teaching. For example, the more we can persuade our students to adopt a rigorously critical 'bull-shit detector' towards the 'truth claims' they meet in other work (or our own, when our criticality slips), the more we can inoculate them with disenchantment, and the more they can then resist being beguiled by clever stories dressed up as 'fact'.

But in neither of these cases are we really 'getting our hands dirty'. It seems to us that at this point we have to come close to the 'critical realists'. Though we may think and debate in the transitive world of 'relativism', we have to act in the substantive world *as though* it 'really is' as we construe it, and *as though* its ethical demands upon us have foundational 'truth'. In our actions we will always find ourselves working (and playing) in 'practical realities' (note the plural; we do not claim they are all the *same* reality). In this way, while keeping faith with our doubts about what may seem to be 'life-lines' of truth and certainty for the holding, we seek to avoid analysis to the point of paralysis. Like it or not, in most of the practical realities that we know, there is no escaping the risks and uncertainties involved in knowing (with all that that implies) that our actions and our inactions are more held to account than our words.

We find the idea of a 'practical reality' useful, in that while it acknowledges no 'really real' foundation, it offers a basis for the pragmatic need for action (and inaction). Our deeds no less than our words are texts, which can be held up to scrutiny. And that, of course, includes the actions that produced this text (as, we suspect, reviewers will leave us in no doubt!).

References

Bhaskar, R. (1989). *A realist theory of science*. Hemel Hempstead: Harvester Wheatsheaf.

Craib, M. (1986). Review of M. Mulkay's *The World and the Word*. *Sociology*, 20, 483–484.

Curt, B. (Pseud.). (1994). *Textuality and tectonics: Troubling social and psychological science*. Milton Keynes: Open University Press.

Danzinger, K. (1990). *Constructing the subject*. Cambridge: Cambridge University Press.

Denzin, N.K. (1977). *Childhood socialization*. San Francisco: Jossey-Bass.

Edwards, D., Ashmore, M., & Potter, J. (1995). Death and furniture: The rhetoric, politics and theology of bottom line arguments against relativism. *History of the Human Sciences*, 8, 25–49.

Foucault, M. (1970). *The order of things*. London: Tavistock.

Frow, J. (1983). Annus mirabilis: Synchrony and diachrony. In F. Barker, P. Hulme, M. Iversen & D. Loxly (Eds.), *The politics of theory* (pp. 224–239). Colchester: University of Essex.

Game, A. (1991). *Undoing the social*. Milton Keynes: Open University Press.

Haraway, D. (1984). Primatology is politics by other means. In R. Bleier (Ed.), *Feminist approaches to science* (pp. 77–118). London: Pergamon.

Kitzinger, C. (1987). *The social construction of lesbianism*. London: Sage.

Kitzinger, C., Wilkinson, S. & Perkins, R. (1992). Theorizing heterosexuality. *Feminism & Psychology*, 2(3), 293–324.

Mulkay, M. (1985). *The word and the world: Explorations in the form of sociological analysis*. London: Allen & Unwin.

Parker, I. (1989). *The crisis in modern social psychology – and how to end it*. London: Routledge.

Parker, I. (1992). *Discourse dynamics: Critical analysis for social and individual psychology*. London: Routledge.

Sampson, E.E. (1993). *Celebrating the other: A dialogic account of human nature*. Hemel Hempstead: Harvester Wheatsheaf.

Sawicki, J. (1991). *Disciplining Foucault*. New York: Routledge.

Smith, B.H. (1988). *Contingencies of value: Alternative perspectives for critical theory*. Cambridge, MA: Harvard University Press.

Stainton Rogers, R. (1995). Q methodology. In J.A. Smith, R. Harré & L.V. Langenhove (Eds.), *Rethinking methods in psychology* (pp. 178–192). London: Sage.

Stainton Rogers, R., Stenner, P., Gleeson, K., & Stainton Rogers, W. (1995). *Social psychology: A critical agenda*. Cambridge: Polity.

Stainton Rogers, W. (1991). *Explaining health and illness: An exploration of diversity*. Hemel Hempstead: Harvester Wheatsheaf.

Stenner, P. (1993). Discoursing jealousy. In I. Parker & E. Burman (Eds.), *Discourse analytic research: Repertoires and readings of texts in action* (pp. 114–133). London: Routledge.

Stephenson, W. (1953). *The study of behavior: Q-technique and its methodology*. Chicago: University of Chicago Press.

Stephenson, W. (1987). Measurement of self perception: Some reflections on the article by Knight, Fredrickson and Martin. *Operant Subjectivity, 10*(4), 125–135.

Wilson, E. (1985). *Adorned in dreams: Fashion and modernity*. London: Virago.

6

Laying the Ground for a Common Critical Psychology

Stephen Reicher

Every Sunday, the colour supplement of the *Observer* newspaper used to contain a fairly lighthearted questionnaire – the term is their own – which on 21 February 1993 was entitled 'Are you a Europhobe?' Two fairly representative questions read as follows:

How will the Maastricht Treaty affect Europe?
(a) It will establish a democratic union of Euro-citizens and increase economic growth.
(b) Italy will surrender and the French will get out all the Wilkommen to Paris signs.
(c) English sovereignty will be watered down. As will the Pimms.

The European Parliament should be situated where?
(a) Strasbourg, Brussels and Luxembourg.
(b) Westminster.
(c) In the dustbin of history.

Even early on a Sunday morning I was aware that such questions put me in a spot. For, while I like to consider myself as an internationalist, I also believe that the EU is set up to enshrine particular pro-capitalist policies as the basis for European union – the clauses which prioritize control of inflation as a primary goal and which limit both yearly and total debt as a proportion of GDP are familiar from the monetarist eighties. To claim that one is anti-European because one is anti-Maastricht is akin to claiming that one lacks a sense of humour because one fails to laugh at racist jokes. But, for this questionnaire, should I choose to reject the institutions of the EC, I am placed in one of the higher scoring categories. These label me in the following terms: either 'you despise the continentals for their extremist ways and think India was better off as part of the Empire' or, at the very top end, 'you are a Europhobe. You can't forgive the Krauts, never trusted the Frogs and can't abide foreign food'. Consequently, my engagement with the questionnaire was on restricted terms. I was forced into adopting and being defined in terms of one of two identities: either rabid nationalism or else corporate internationalism. I find neither identity particularly congenial.

All this may seem of remarkably little relevance to a critique of scientific psychology. After all, the questionnaire was in large part a joke, no-one was forced to do it, and no self-respecting psychologist would design anything vaguely comparable. However, the experience of filling it in was remarkably similar to my experience with another, and altogether more reputable, attempt to assess how people orientate towards Europe. I had agreed to complete a questionnaire, the results of which were written up in a book entitled *Understanding Attitudes to the European Community* (Hewstone, 1986). However, as I began to respond, I found, again and again, that I was being forced to address the significance of the Community in purely national terms. As an example, section G of the questionnaire was introduced as being 'interested in what you see as the gains and losses associated with EEC membership'. Of the following eight questions, seven were concerned with how the United Kingdom had fared.

Once again, the difficulty was that I do not conceptualize the EU in terms of nationality. Indeed, I consider the notion of national interest as an abstraction to cover the impact of particular economic policies on those in different economic positions – in crude terms, class. As a consequence I found it impossible to give meaningful answers. However, since I was in the relatively unusual position of being a colleague (rather than a subordinate) of the researcher, I felt confident in trying to explain my reservations, in discussing their conceptual implications and in declining to complete the questionnaire. This confidence was misplaced. Certainly my objections were not reflected in the subsequent research or book. No inkling was given that there may have been resistance to national categories. The fact that some people had refused or failed to fill in the measure was not even mentioned.

Although the newspaper quiz represents what is essentially a pastiche of the attitudinal research, there still remains an important cross-fertilization between the two. On the one hand, the *Observer* borrowed from psychology the idea that one can define the positions that individuals hold by getting them to answer a few set questions. It then popularized this notion beyond the few hundreds who read an academic text to the millions who read even such a 'quality' newspaper. On the other hand, it is probably no coincidence that Hewstone limits the positions from which subjects can respond to those that are present in the media. In other words, if mass culture delineates possible identities, psychology feeds back the process by which they come to be taken for granted.

It is this interconnection between psychology and wider social practices which gives critical social psychology its relevance and its potential force. On the one hand, a critique of present ways of doing psychology has implications for the forms of society that are deemed humanly possible. On the other, a critique of society has implications for the type of psychology that we can and should do. In acknowledging this we may possibly avoid futile debates as to whether critical psychologists are critical in the sense of the psychology they do or else in terms of the politics they seek to advance. Inevitably, we have to be both. Being a 'critical psychologist' must entail academic *and* political commitments.

Yet this is a point of departure rather than a point of conclusion. In moving beyond the facile counterposition of academia and politics, we are invariably led to inquire into the interrelationship between differing academic commitments and their political entailments. Allied to this is the question of which stance, or range of stances, marks the boundaries of a critical psychology. The aim of this chapter is to address both these issues. On the one hand, I shall sketch out a personal critique of psychology and its politics which, at least in part, represents an internal critique of other critical psychologies. On the other hand, I shall attempt to argue how, in present circumstances at least, this position can and must co-exist with such others within a common critical enterprise. These issues will be addressed by looking, in turn, at the psychological, methodological and political dimensions of the critique.

Psychology

Most critical psychologists would probably agree in challenging the way in which much psychological research treats relational acts as intra-psychic events. Whether I answer the questionnaire on the EC depends upon my position with respect to the researcher. My range of responses is dictated by the terms in which questions are posed. My actual answers are acts of communication which may therefore be affected by whom I am communicating with and the relations of power that obtain between us, However, all of these various ways in which my marks on the page depend on the social relations of investigation tend to be ignored. My answers are held to reflect my internal attitudes – representations, beliefs, attitudes or whatever.

At one level, then, critical psychology might differentiate itself from traditional psychology through an emphasis on processes of social construction. However, this only opens a new space for argument since there are various ways of conceptualizing what is constructed and how the constructive process works. Some hold that the very domain of psychology and its analytic categories – such as identity, emotion, belief – are constructed within particular historical conjunctures. Others consider both the psychological domain as well as certain analytic categories within it to have a reality independent of the constructive process, even if the substantive content of these categories is always constituted in historically specific social relations.

Yet, even if one chooses to focus on construction alone, to acknowledge that human beings depend upon humanly made understandings, and, even more, that human beings deploy such understandings to strategic ends, is to imply a fair deal about the nature of the human psychological apparatus. In the first place, it says that we are meaning-(rather than stimulus)-dependent creatures. In the second place, it says that we can maintain a reflexive distance from meaning systems in order to consider their usage. In the third place, it says that we are intentional beings who are capable of weighing up the future consequences of differing actions.

Of course, to mention nature in relation to human psychology is a rash thing amongst critical psychologists. However, it is useful to bear in mind

Rose, Lewontin and Kamin's (1984) argument that, just because deter-
minists have used the concept of human nature to portray current
inequalities as biological necessities, this does not mean that we should
abandon the concept entirely. For them, the nature of humans as opposed
to other organisms is precisely our ability to re-create our environment and
to transcend our biology. Whatever effects our genes may have, we now
have the technology to alter our genes. So, in contrast to the notion of
human nature as inferring limitation, Rose et al. conclude by stating that 'it
is our biology that makes us free' (p. 290).

Yet, again, it is worth noting that the transcendental character of human
nature is linked to the human capacity for reflexive and intentional action
upon the world. To put it slightly differently, if Rose et al. (1984) quote
Marx's dictum that human beings change their circumstances, it is also
important to invoke Marx's classic distinction between the architect and the
bee. Human beings do not just alter the world, they knowingly plan how to
undertake such transformations. We can conceptualize the consequences of
various courses of action upon the world prior to deciding on any given
course of action. I accept, as has been argued forcefully by rhetorical and
discursive psychologists, that the enterprise of conceptualization is not a
private and passive process. We predominantly act, plan and think in
public. We argue with others over the terms and when others are absent we
argue with ourselves. Moreover, we do so with the linguistic resources at
our disposal. However, I also want to suggest that the enterprise of
planning has implications for the psychological structures that need to be
so constructed.

In order to plan, individuals require an understanding of the social world
in which they are acting, where they stand within it and the ability they
have to act in and upon this world. Implicit in each of these terms is the
concept of subject position. First, a description of the social world involves
a definition of the categories of actors involved in it. Second, to define
where one stands within this world is to align oneself with one or another
of these categories. Third, to determine one's ability for action involves
knowing who counts as support and who as opposition. One implication of
this is that some form of self-concept – in the sense of a definition of one's
location and opportunities within a system of social relations – is
necessarily involved in the process of human action.

To concentrate on the definitions of identity that are allowable within a
questionnaire of the EU is therefore not simply based on textual considerations, but rather arises out of psychological considerations relating to
the relationship between identity and action. In more general terms, I am
suggesting that, important as it is to highlight constructive activity, it is
equally important to have a psychology which points to what needs to be
constructed, how it might be constructed and therefore what are the
significant features to analyse in any argument or text. However, as well as
psychology defining what is significant within a text, there is also the
possibility that psychology may point to elements beyond the text which

frame the impact of the text itself. Moreover, to argue that certain psychological structures are essential to human action suggests that there may be certain dynamics relating to the maintenance of the structures themselves.

Thus, when we look at the consequences of psychological technologies such as the questionnaire, we are directed to look at how they define identities for the individual. We may also look at how the engagement or the challenge to particular identities has consequences for the expression of passions and desires. After all, it is not simply that I note the attempt of the *Observer* and Hewstone to make of me either a little Englander or an international monetarist. I am angry at the way in which they deny my chosen identity and would define me in ways that constitute a slight to the ways in which I define myself.

The implication of all this is that a focus on the construction of psychological entities is not incompatible with a realist psychology. From such a perspective, criticizing current psychologies for ignoring the constructive process is not a critique of any possible psychology but a means of clearing the old in order to make space for a new and better psychology. Similarly, the purpose of making such criticisms is more than ideological critique. Rather, the aim is to establish a more adequate understanding of psychological process which not only provides a more congenial view of the human subject – and allows for the expression of oppositional identities – but is also a tool of considerable practical power.

To be more concrete, in criticizing attitude research for ignoring the ways in which the social relations of research impose particular identities and thereby produce particular positions, I am saying something about the contextual determination of identity and the relationship between context, identity and action. It follows that I would predict a particular pattern of variability as context (or, rather, definition of context) varies. Hence I would argue that a non-reified relational psychology can better account for the contextual specificity of responses and also provides a basis for knowing how to produce variability. These claims – indeed the very notions of a 'better' or a 'more adequate' psychology – raise questions of how one can ground such explanatory claims. It is to this issue that I will now turn.

Methodology

Critiques of cognitivism and individualism have tended to go along with critiques of the methods used to sustain these positions. This has led to attacks on the use of such technologies as the questionnaire, the survey and the laboratory experiment. The latter has been a particular focus. In general terms it is argued that the experiment serves to isolate people, to deny the ability of individuals to negotiate and contest understandings of social reality, and hence to represent relational processes as private events 'under the skull'. I would agree with the diagnosis, but not with the cure, which has been to withdraw from experimentation almost as a matter of principle.

The key step in producing de-socialized psychologies is to abstract behaviour from the relational context in which it occurs. When we, as researchers, form part of this context, then this resolves into a problem of reflexivity. That is to say, unless we are aware of the ways in which our interventions and our relationship to respondents help their response, then we will treat communications as traits, arguments as attitudes and so on. I certainly accept that most experimental research does lack such reflexivity – though not all. Some research does treat the constructive activity of the researcher as a topic, and the work of Norbert Schwarz is a good example of this (e.g. Schwarz & Strack, 1991). Characteristically, however, the role of the researcher is hidden from view. When we examine intergroup relations, we ignore the ways in which social categories are constructed and manipulated, and should subjects construe things in ways that differ from our preconceptions the work is abandoned and never published (Billig's, 1976, analysis of Sherif's 'boys' camp' studies illustrates the point well). When we put respondents in front of a questionnaire or a computer, we ignore how we give meaning to the situation, how we define what can count as a legitimate response and how the subjects might be attempting to communicate a particular view of themselves to us. Either a three-term equation is analysed with only two terms present or else a two-term equation is analysed with only one term present. In both cases it is logically impossible to provide an adequate account.

Yet the problem of non-reflexivity is not limited to experiments or questionnaires. It is possible to be non-reflexive whatever research method one utilizes. The interview or group discussion which characteristically forms the centre-piece of critical research can equally well be analysed without due regard to the place of the researcher. Indeed, many researchers do utilize interviews in such a way. By ignoring their own role, they use the method to get at what people 'really think'. However, if any research intervention can be analysed non-reflexively, it follows that, at least in some cases, it is not that methods inherently lead to de-socialized psychology but rather that this is a result of the ways in which they are interpreted. I want to argue that, while there may be a general tendency for experimentalists to eschew reflexivity, this does not mean that experiments are thereby inherently flawed and should be eschewed by any self-respecting critical psychologist. Indeed, I want to go further and argue that, properly treated, the experiment is a particularly suitable means of critical intervention.

This is not to say that experiments do not have their limitations. Like any method, the experiment can help address certain questions and is unsuitable for investigating others. It is particularly unsuited to looking at complex and shifting patterns of negotiation and argument; it is characteristically unsuitable for looking at resistance. That is to say, if any subjects wish to challenge the terms imposed by the experimenter, they rarely have the means of doing so. Resistance therefore becomes silence and the resister is excluded on the grounds of providing 'missing data'. It is therefore understandable that those who have wished to highlight such issues, and who have deplored versions of the human subject which deny all agency (e.g. Billig, 1987), have criticized the experimental method. However, to use this argument to abandon the experiment entirely is to suggest that human beings are always able to indulge in unending argumentation, that resistance is always possible, that human agency is unfettered. I accept that the conceptual space for argument is always available and that, even in the concentration camp, resistance can occur. However, in practice, many people never even get to answer back at all. Certainly, arguments are always stopped in particular places. To suppose otherwise is to ignore inequality, oppression and power in society. It is to emphasize agency to the exclusion of structure. It is here that the experiment comes into its own, for it is, in many ways, an accurate representation of our society. Some (we, the experimenters) are allowed to observe, to speak, to define the terms of argument. Others (they, the subjects) are observed, cannot argue, are forced to respond in our terms. Indeed, if one recalls Foucault's use of Bentham's panopticon as an image of how power operates in contemporary society, then the hidden experimenter to whom individualized subjects are visible but who are not visible to each other is a faithful replica. Indeed, one could argue that at a relational level there is nothing artificial about the experiment. It is precisely because the experiment replicates so accurately familiar social relations that it is so easily taken for granted.

If this argument holds water, then it follows that the experiment becomes an excellent domain within which to analyse the operation of power. In the first place, it can be used to investigate the consequences of stopping the process of argumentation and construction at particular junctures. In the second place, power relations between subject and experimenter can be made a topic of research and the consequences of changing experimental relations can be investigated. Similar arguments can be made in relation to the questionnaire. What was hitherto ignored – the role of the researcher and the questions in producing rather than measuring responses – can become the focus of research. What was a dependent variable can be treated as an independent variable. Naturally, in order to do such things it is necessary to highlight the role of the researcher in the research. We have to do precisely what the powerful wish to avoid, which is to be brought into the spotlight. If this is done, and if the experiment is subjected to reflexive analysis, then I see no reason why it should lead psychologists to continue constructing a mythical shadow world under the skull.

In order to avoid misunderstanding, let me stress that I am not suggesting that we return to a discipline dominated by the experimental method. I am simply arguing that the experiment should remain part of our toolbox. What is more, it can be used fruitfully in conjunction with other methods – interviews, studies of naturally occurring debate, and so on. However, these are secondary arguments. My main purpose is to show that conducting the argument on the level of 'yes or no to experiments', or indeed to any other methodology, is a smokescreen for the key issue. Our critique should be of *any* form of analysis in any setting which fails to give a full account of the social relations that obtain in context. The danger of such analyses is not only that they render a fully social account impossible, but also that certain participants and certain relations are more likely to remain in the shadows. If it is power that has been rendered anonymous in our society, then it is the powerful who are most likely to escape our analytic gaze. This takes me to my third and final area of concern, that of politics.

Politics

There are at least three ways in which a critique of traditional psychology as de-socialized psychology is also a political critique. First of all, by representing the response categories offered by the researcher as coming out of the respondent's head, the social process of category construction is frozen. Individuals are fixed into particular positions, change becomes hard if not impossible. Second, the positions into which people are fixed characteristically reflect dominant perceptions of society. Alternative and critical positions are excluded. Thus the European debate becomes Maastricht versus bigotry. No other voice is seen to exist. Third, the operation of power in forcing people into certain categories and excluding others becomes hidden from view.

All in all, traditional psychology is a highly conservative force. Taking the world as it is for granted, alternative worlds are excluded, continuity is guaranteed. Neville Alexander (1992), writing as a political activist who sought to overcome the ethnic divisions of apartheid and forge a new national consciousness, illustrates the implications in the following quote:

> By accepting, for example, the reality of entities such as 'ethnic groups' as part of what has been called the Cartesian order 'which is suitable for analysis of the world into separately existing parts . . ., we deprive ourselves *a priori* of the possibility of probing alternative, possibly more constructive discourses. For by doing so we reinforce the ethnic stabilization or freezing of our audience through our ideological productions. (p. 23)

Compare this with the way in which even liberal psychological research, aiming to reduce racism, takes it for granted that people will be defined in terms of 'race', and uses measures which force respondents to categorize people in such terms (cf. Reicher, 1986). Even if 'race' is not always as central as in South Africa, the choice between accepting division and challenging racialization is equally stark wherever one might be. Indeed one can argue that precisely where the categories are more liable to be more taken for granted it becomes more important that psychologists do not legitimate this through their own practices.

Taking the world as it is for granted also means a rejection of those who do not fit the dominant norms. Difference becomes a failure to be fully human. Those who contest the terms of attitude scales become missing data. Those who contest the terms of intelligence tests become stupid. Those who contest statistical assumptions underlying judgement become irrational. Those who take to the streets to express their grievances become a mad mob. A psychology which is critical of these ideas and the means by which they are produced must thereby be concerned with restoring those voices which have been either silenced or disqualified. A critical psychology is therefore intertwined with allowing a multiplicity of voices and with showing that dominant ways of being are not the only ways of being. In this sense, a critical psychology must be a radical psychology.

Of course, no-one is obliged to take up the political implications of their work. However, it would seem perverse to complain about the denial of certain voices in the abstract without addressing the substantive issue of what has been denied – for instance to complain about the process whereby certain positions on Europe are excluded from debate without insisting that such options are at least available for consideration. If it seems too ambitious to intervene at such a societal level, perhaps we could start more parochially by looking at how people have been directly silenced by psychological practices – women whose accounts of abuse have been treated as hysteria, gay people whose sexuality has been treated as a contagious aberration, anti-nuclear protesters whose judgements have been treated as ignorance . . . the list is very long indeed.

What I am suggesting, then, is that there is a level at which we, as critical psychologists, can all be in political agreement. This implies a political practice which, in consequence, it is hard to avoid. If anything is to be achieved it is important to stress this commonality. However, it is also important to recognize that there are important differences amongst us. There is, on the one hand, a radical liberalism which advocates a plurality of perspectives on the basis that no one perspective is inherently better than any other. Such perspectives are often explicitly anti- or, rather, post-Marxist in that they reject all 'essentialisms' which prioritize any particular analytic framework – apart, perhaps, from anti-essentialism itself (cf. Laclau & Mouffe, 1985, 1987). This position is therefore bound up with a form of relativism which argues that, since our understandings of the world – including scientific understandings – are always a function of humanly negotiated constructs, we can do no more than look at how things are said and the consequences of particular sayings. We certainly cannot characterize any position as better than any other.

On the other hand, there are realist radicalisms, of which Marxism is the most obvious example, which not only advocate a plurality of perspectives but which would also choose between them on the basis that some are more limited than others. This stance holds that, notwithstanding the social nature of understanding, there are grounds for declaring that some positions have more explanatory adequacy than others. The relativist and realist positions do not necessarily differ in the perspectives that they make available, nor in the perspectives that we may decide to advocate. After all, if everything is equally valid, why shouldn't the radical take the side of the oppressed or even subscribe to a class analysis? The real difference lies in the grounds on which one may settle arguments between those who advocate different perspectives.

We are therefore back, albeit in a political domain, with the same questions that I first discussed with respect to psychology. In both cases, the issue of ontology leads on to asking how to resolve disputes – whether they be political or indeed of any other sort. I have already argued for a realist psychology whereby the significant features of any text relate to the ways in which they define the location of the subject within a system of social relations. However, these forms of constructive activity were further grounded in the prerequisites of human practice as planned action. We need to construe if we are to be able to act, for our constructions organize how we act and with whom. Thus, it is not that the way in which we construe objects directly alters their nature, but rather it shapes our actions towards these objects. To call a landscape natural or else spoilt does not, in the immediate, change one jot of its make-up. It does, however, have major implications for what we do to that landscape either individually or collectively: whether we drop our crisp packets within it, whether we allow developers in to dig it up and therefore how it changes over time (cf. McNaghten, Brown & Reicher, 1992).

However, if constructions shape practice, it is also clear that they are not the only determinants of practice. In the first place, one's space for action may be limited by the actions of other individuals, groups and institutions. Second, one's ability to combine with others to overcome resistance may itself be limited by ignorance, separation in space and access to the means of communication. Third, one may lack the technology (either because only some people have it or else because it simply does not exist) to act upon other individuals or upon the physical world in certain ways. However it might have been construed, before the invention of explosives and mechanical diggers, current transformations of the landscape were (perhaps thankfully) beyond human capabilities.

If construction, and arguments over construction, occur in the process of organizing action, and certain actions are rendered impractical, then it follows that the corresponding arguments become equally useless. This has two important implications. First of all, arguments over the nature of the world are not only settled in argument. They may also be settled in the terms of the various other components of successful practice. The problem is that, if we restrict our research to one phase in which action is planned, then no one construction is self-evidently correct. Only over time will the 'practical adequacy' of different ideas be fought out. Perhaps, then, we need to move away from strategy of synchronic studies, whether experiments or interviews, and begin to look at the place of argument in the unfolding of practical struggles over a period of time as well as examining the consequences of stopping the argument in different places.

Second, the way in which we come to understand the world and our place within it, whether we define ourselves in terms of gender, race, nation, class or whatever – will be a function of our abilities to act, which in turn will depend upon our control over resources and the ways in which we are brought in relation to each other such that we can or cannot combine in action. It is the historical investigation of these factors as a function of the changing ways in which human productive activity is organized that constitutes the Marxist method and its commitment to class analysis. The use of this term in no way implies giving *experiential* priority to self-categories defined in terms of class (if that were so, there would be no need to bother with the politics). Rather, it means explicating the situated processes, the historically unfolding patterns of action and interaction within which different categories come to be used. To abandon even the attempt to address these processes means making every category adequate unto itself, ultimately unchallengeable. The more success the relativists have in propagating such a perspective, the more they undermine their individual moral commitments and the likelihood that their wit might convince anyone to join them. So the relativist may allow more voices to be heard, but possibly at the cost of making it even more certain that new voices will be rejected.

Let me stress once again, however, that is an argument for happier times. If we lived in a radical liberal world where all voices freely jostled for space, then perhaps we would have the luxury to differ. For the present, however, we can agree in fighting for openness, in agreeing to be radical without having to differentiate the term in public. The more important issue is what being radical means for what we actually do.

Conclusion

Much of what we might see as mainstream itself arose out of a critique that may be found to have many similarities to our own. If there is anything like a manifesto for recent European social psychology, it is to be found in Israel and Tajfel's edited volume *The Context of Social Psychology* (1972). As the name suggests, a series of scholars attack the way in which a predominantly American mainstream ignores the larger social relations in which exchanges between individuals are embedded. This critique is applied both to the general nature of theory and also to the way in which experimentation is designed and interpreted. However, as is so often the case, the subsequent practice has rarely lived up to the original promise. Indeed, it could be argued that the major failing of the research is a failure to apply the concern with context reflexively and hence a continued tendency towards cognitive reductionism.

The aim of this chapter has been to stress the diversity amongst those of us who accept the title 'critical' (or at least are prepared to gather together under that collective heading). In doing this, the aim has not been to foster division but rather, by openly facing our differences, to accept that which unites us. I have argued that we can agree in challenging the way that, by ignoring the role of the researcher in structuring the options open to respondents, we either deny or close off certain marginal/oppositional forms of subjectivity. If it is arrogant to suppose that we can 'give voice' to such subjectivities, we can at least try to remove the muzzle our discipline all too frequently represents.

However, as long as reflexivity is the distinguishing mark of the latest critical wave, it is important to heed our own arguments concerning the resolution of argument. If we are to be successful in being taken seriously, we must ask how critical psychology can supply not only a set of ideas but also a set of practices which make it possible to survive as a critical psychologist. The immense success of the European Association of Experimental Social Psychology and its associated journal shows that our predecessors were well aware of this issue. We, too, need to address the extent to which a critical psychology can claim space within existing institutions and whether we need to think about creating something new. We also need to ask parallel questions about being radical. Even in terms of the limited aims I discussed above: how do we challenge the ways in which current psychological practice denies people voice and how do we go about remedying the situation? Unless a major priority is given to the discussion of such issues, then, however fine our arguments, to be a critical psychologist and to be a radical psychologist will be both figuratively and literally to be redundant.

References

Alexander, N. (1992). *For a socialist Azania: An approach to the national question in South Africa*. Johannesburg: WOSA Press.

Billig, M. (1976). *Social psychology and intergroup relations*. London: Academic Press.

Billig, M. (1987). *Arguing and thinking*. Cambridge: Cambridge University Press.

Hewstone, M. (1986). *Understanding attitudes to the European Community*. Cambridge: Cambridge University Press.

Israel, J., & Tajfel, H. (1972). *The context of social psychology: A critical assessment*. London: Academic Press.

Laclau, E., & Mouffe, C. (1985). *Hegemony and socialist strategy: Towards a radical democratic politics*. London: Verso.

Laclau, E., & Mouffe, C. (1987). Post Marxism without apologies. *New Left Review*, *166*, 79–106.

Macnaghten, P., Brown, R., & Reicher, S. (1992). On the nature of nature: Experimental studies in the power of rhetoric. *Journal of Community and Applied Social Psychology*, *2*, 43–61.

Reicher, S. (1986). Contact, action and racialization: Some British evidence. In M. Hewstone & R. Brown (Eds.), *Contact and conflict in intergroup encounters*. Oxford: Blackwell.

Rose, S., Lewontin, R.C., & Kamin, L.J. (1984). *Not in our genes*. Harmondsworth: Penguin.

Schwarz, N., & Strack, F. (1991). Context effects in attitude surveys: Applying cognitive theory to social research. In W. Stroebe & M. Hewstone (Eds.), *European review of social psychology* (Vol. 2, pp. 31–50). London: Wiley.

7

Postmodernism, Postmodernity and Social Psychology

Martin Roiser

Postmodernism has gained a certain currency in recent decades, as a culture, a philosophy and a theory of society. In areas of culture, such as writing, architecture, art and photography, there has developed a tendency to mix styles, to indulge in reference and quotation, to replace progress with nostalgia, and to confound creation and criticism. Associated with these trends has been the emergence within academic circles of post-structuralist philosophies which have advanced challenging ideas about the interpretation of text, the power of discourse and the nature of subjectivity. On the basis of these and by reference to trends in Western political economy over the last twenty years, such as the decline of heavy industry, the growth of media and the end of the Cold War, it has been suggested that the modern period, lasting from the enlightenment to the recent past, has now given way to an era of new times or postmodernity. From these philosophical and sociological ideas has emerged a strenuous critique of science. According to this the social and natural sciences are merely aspects of the 'failed project of modernism', which should now be discarded in the new age. Science is seen as only one of many narratives, which may be deconstructed like any other discourse.

If more than a few of these ideas are of any substance, then they have very serious implications for social psychology. The ideas of postmodern philosophy suggest that social psychology should move its focus away from the person towards the interpreting of discourse and text. They suggest that the history and methodology of psychology are merely a product of the ideology of modernism and its 'rhetoric of truth'. Attempts to define and practise 'scientific' social psychology are therefore misguided. The use of techniques like the questionnaire and the experiment should be discarded on principle. Any attempts to underpin psychology with a coherent body of theory, whether behaviourist, cognitive, psychoanalytic feminist or even Marxist, are futile. Attempts to use social psychology to study the real world are similarly misguided as we can no longer be sure what reality is. According to this manner of thinking, the crisis in social psychology should be viewed as part of the crisis of modernism, heralding the advent of postmodernity. Postmodern approaches, suitable for a postmodern age, should be adopted in order to create a 'new paradigm' social psychology. These are indeed challenging arguments. In this chapter I will briefly examine postmodernism in its cultural, philosophical and sociological aspects. I will then address the questions it raises for social psychology.

Postmodern Culture

The term 'postmodernism' was probably first used to describe new forms of novel writing in the fifties. But its most obvious emergence was in architecture during the sixties, when the unimaginative 'international style' of post-war commercial architecture was invaded by a new willingness to mix genres and add decoration. There developed an anti-functionalism which mixed periods and styles incongruously, and consciously echoed the past. In some respects postmodern architecture resembles the eighteenth-century fashion for building follies, costly and useless pseudo-medieval architectural jokes, which still adorn the odd country estate. In comparison London's Canary Wharf was intended to have only a stylistic anti-functionalism. Its economic failure makes it a complete, but unwitting, postmodern folly. In writing, painting and music a tendency developed to mix styles and reject notions of coherence and meaning or conclusive interpretation. The novels of Milan Kundera, the musical collages of John Cage, David Lynch's film *Blue Velvet*, Cindy Sherman's self-portraits in many guises, have all been claimed as examples of postmodern culture.

But there are some problems with the category of postmodern culture. It may reasonably be described as the tail-end of modernism, of those artistic movements that arose in turn-of-the-century Europe; the Vienna secession, the Futurists, the Dadaists in the First World War, the Agit-Prop movement and the Constructivists in revolutionary Russia. The modernists articulated ideas about art and society as in Breton's *Surrealist Manifesto* in the twenties, and the *Futurist Manifesto*. These were movements associated with the huge political and economic changes of the period. They rebelled not only against the old order of the art world, but against the social order itself.

These movements lost their political energy, as did the revolutions they were associated with. The art of the 'historic avant-garde' changed to that of 'cultural modernism' (see, e.g., Callinicos, 1989). In the gradual transformation from modernism to postmodernism there was an increasing sense of superficiality of content and attitude in contrast to the seriousness of meaning and commitment so characteristic of the modernist movement. Postmodern culture is thus modernism without the politics. It catches a certain spirit of the age characteristic of a layer of intellectuals who have, by their critique, been largely responsible for creating the notion of postmodern culture. They have also created a more complex body of philosophy, to which I will now turn.

Post-structuralist Philosophy

These ideas may be traced back to Saussure's linguistics in the early years of the century, which were adopted by the structuralists of the fifties and sixties, in combination with contributions from both Marx and Freud. These were changed and elaborated in the seventies and eighties into a broad and loosely knit body of ideas called post-structuralism. These philosophies have been taken up with considerable vigour in the universities, especially, in the UK, in the new universities, or, as we might call them, the post-polytechnics. There has been a proliferation of courses in cultural and media studies and social sciences that lean heavily on them. Literary criticism, especially in America, has been very influenced. Many books have been published; textbooks introducing students to the complexities of postmodern ideas, advancing these ideas in various disciplines, and so on. They have made considerable progress in the columns of the serious press and in intellectual magazines. The body of ideas is complex and itself needs to be subdivided for easier consideration. Several related philosophical strands can be identified.

The first deals with the broad questions of language, text and meaning. This originates from the semiology, or science of signs, of Ferdinand de Saussure, set out in his *Course in General Linguistics* (1913/1974). His concepts of 'signifier', that is, words (spoken or written), 'signified', that is, concepts and images, and 'referent', that is, objects in the world, are still in use today. In Saussure's model the signifier and signified together formed the sign. Signs combined together into systems whose structure gave meaning to each sign within the system. He intended his ideas to apply beyond linguistics and indeed said that they were part of social psychology:

> A science that studies the life of signs within society is conceivable, it would be a part of social psychology and consequently of general psychology. I shall call it semiology. . . . The laws discovered by semiology will be applicable to linguistics and the latter will circumscribe a well-defined area within the mass of anthropological facts. (Saussure, 1913/1974, p. 16)

However, it was anthropologists such as Lévi-Strauss, rather than social psychologists, who were later to take up his ideas in the sixties. But then, in the seventies and eighties, post-structuralists, such as Derrida, set out to dismantle what they saw as the overly rigid systems of structuralism by 'deconstruction', a process that continually takes apart and reassembles meaning. They were reluctant to attach firm meaning to words, and argued that there was no underlying structure to meaning or indeed society. Thus any text could be reinterpreted indefinitely. No particular interpretation, even that advanced by the original author, was privileged. Meaning is thus relative, and the notion of objective reality, the 'referent' in Saussure's system, is pushed into the background.

Foucault's introduction of the concept of 'power' into this discussion seemed to reintroduce reality. But only to a degree because, for him, power was located in the discourses that defined the relationships between competing groups. Dominant discourses become the vehicles of influence, rather than physical might or ownership of property. Thus Foucault's *Discipline and Punish* (1979) opens with gruelling accounts of medieval imprisonment and execution. But his story continues by condemning the pseudo-liberalism of capitalist society which freed the body in order more effectively to imprison the mind. In *Madness and Civilization* (1973) particular criticism is levelled at the psychiatric reforms of the Quakers and at Philippe Pinel. Pinel was the founder of French psychiatry, who liberated the Paris asylums during the French Revolution, and then reorganized them as mental hospitals. The physical restraints of bars and shackles were replaced by the mental restraints of medical discourse. The book is an intense criticism of the role of reason in the age of enlightenment and, in line with its own thesis, places more emphasis on discourse than on historical accuracy. The entire first chapter concerns the 'ship of fools', a medieval tradition of consigning the mentally ill to voyaging ships. Sedgwick (1982) points out that there is no evidence for these ships; they exist only in discourse.

An important element in the postmodern critique of enlightenment is its discussion of the individual as the originator of meaning. Lacan's critique of the subject elaborated this argument and was thus a useful addition to their body of ideas. He treated the unconscious like a text, to be deconstructed like any other. He embarked on a radical rereading of Freud. It led to a critique of the ego, whose efforts to give firm meaning to unconscious thought were now impossible, and also of the id, which was rooted in a biological reductionism out of keeping with his textual approach. In consequence the Oedipus complex also fell. His approach served to 'decentre the self', and challenge the individual concept of subjectivity so central to classical Freudianism and indeed to enlightenment thinking generally.

Post-structuralist arguments have theoretical implications which go far beyond the linguistics and anthropology of the structuralists. They lead to a critique of the rationalism of Western philosophy itself and in turn a challenge to modernism as a whole. They become an assault on long-held conceptions of reason, truth and the philosophy of science. Peter Scott (1990) expresses their scope when he says, 'Postmodernism is the principal challenge to the secular scientific tradition that grew out of the 18th-century enlightenment, 19th-century industrialism, and 20th-century technology' (p. 28).

An Era of Postmodernity

Postmodern cultural ideas and post-structuralist philosophy, combined together with particular observations of society, have been used as the basis for advancing the idea that society as a whole is in the process of changing, and that the modern era is giving way to 'new times'. This thesis draws on work like Daniel Bell's *The Coming of Post-Industrial Society* (1974). He argued that material production was becoming less important compared with the production of knowledge. Francis Fukuyama's book *The End of History and the Last Man* argued that with the ending of the Cold War, the major conflict between socio-economic systems, which had driven history for many decades, had ended. The world would now have a liberal democratic future and a 'new world order'. In his book *What is Postmodernism?* Jencks (1986) outlines the characteristics of new times. He says that the industrial revolution has given way to the information revolution, mass production to segmented production, and the bourgeoisie to the cognitariat. The linear time-scale of modernism has given way to a fast-changing cyclical time-scale. History no longers moves forward; it goes round and round.

The disengagement of history is associated with a disengagement from reality. Jean Baudrillard and Jean François Lyotard argue that we are now surrounded by multiple media images so pervasive that it is difficult to tell image from reality. We live in a world of multiple realities, of computer simulations, of mediated reality, hyper-reality, virtual reality, so much so that 'reality itself' becomes just another image. The social world is saturated with, and thus comprised of, media images. We therefore live in a post-empirical world where facts have given way to images. These constitute and encompass 'reality'. There is nothing beyond these images, or, as Derrida notoriously puts it, 'there is nothing outside the text'.

Taken together these themes of the end of modernity and the end of rationality constitute a dramatic challenge to the enlightenment, and to science. We now live in a world where there are no facts, only images and their interpretations, and those interpretations cannot be conclusive. Consensus is a horizon never reached, as Lyotard put it in his essay 'The Postmodern Condition' (1990). Information is not 'data' as would have been understood in the modern era. It is not 'given', it is socially created and distributed through the media. This process of social construction does not create 'social facts', as Durkheim would have it, which can assume some force within society. The process only creates ideas and images which may be reinterpreted. Therefore knowledge is provisional. We cannot know the new world as we thought we could know the old. Facts are revealed as only images. The world is 'post-factual'. We can no longer hope to explain it rationally. The great theories, or grand narratives, of the modern period have all failed. Only the small narratives remain, the *petits récits*. As Scott (1990, p. 28) puts it, 'So out go Hegel, Marx, Freud, Smith and the rest.' Not only did they fail in the old world of modernism, they are inapplicable in the new era of postmodernity. This move away from realism involves the furthest extension of the postmodern argument as a challenge to modernist science, the rationality of the enlightenment and the whole project of modern science. If we cannot know the world, then science is impossible.

The Assault on Science

In the postmodern view science is the ideology of the modern era, its dominating rhetoric of truth. It is a discourse which has failed to understand the modern world, and moreover is now obsolete because society has changed, by moving into the era of postmodernity. There is little doubt that the postmodern argument impels its advocates towards a head-on confrontation with science. Science is, without question, the grandest of the modernist narratives – far grander than Marxism and psychoanalysis, which seek to be only part of the scientific project. It must thus be a prime target for the artillery of postmodernism.

Polkinghorne (1992) gives a political edge to this philosophical critique of science:

> Faith in the modernist programme has been eroded by the atrocities of two world wars, the awareness of environmental crises, the intractability of the problems of urban ghettoes and the continuing possibility of nuclear holocaust. Instead of building a world of prosperity, health and freedom, modernism has built a civilization fearful of the tools of destruction developed by its science. (p. 147)

This offers a credible explanation for the disillusion that many feel with science and its products. However, that disillusion might be better directed at the governments that employed the scientists, rather than them and their science. The philosophical critique similarly begins to falter when it addresses the detail of science itself. For instance, the postmodern critique of natural science has drawn on relativity theory and chaos theory. But it does so figuratively and reaches problematic conclusions. For example, it endeavours to separate Newton from Einstein and claim the latter for postmodernism. It should be noted that Einstein's theory of general relativity became widely accepted after he successfully predicted an eclipse in 1919 (Wolpert, 1992, p. 99). This triumph of the hypothetico-deductive method should give little comfort to the postmodernist.

Drawing on chaos theory, it has been argued that the flapping of a butterfly's wings in Tasmania could start a hurricane in Hawaii. This might seem to throw into doubt the principle of cause and effect so central to science. But the thrust of chaos theory is different. It argues that, underlying the apparently chaotic, random and hugely complex configurations of the natural world, there are quite simple processes at work, which are open to scientific investigation. It has to be said that the postmodern challenge to natural science is far-fetched and that postmodernism has made little progress in this field.

Postmodernism's arguments against science tend to share some features with the anti-scientific arguments of the middle ages. If science is the grandest narrative of the modern era, religion was the grandest narrative of the medieval world. In its time it provided a narrative which dealt with the whole of contemporary society: politics, science, law and education. The transition from medieval to modern was marked by, among other things, an almighty clash between science and religion. Any modern critique of science may evoke some of those old arguments. The medieval era was strenuously opposed to science. For it the source of knowledge was the Bible. Its sacred texts were interpreted by the priesthood. They distilled meaning from its numerous and often obscure pronouncements. These meanings would change from time to time, often in line with quite earthly interests. This process of interpretation is called exegesis or hermeneutics, and the latter term has, over time, found its way into postmodern writing (see, for instance Shotter, 1992, p. 60).

The political upheavals that overthrew the feudal order championed science. The French Revolution set up the modern metric system of measurement, and set to work the *philosophes* to collect and systematize knowledge. The modern encyclopedia became the cumulative storehouse of information, full of acknowledged facts made publicly available, which 'spoke for themselves' and needed no priest to tell their meaning. As a fount of wisdom it was an effective alternative to the Bible. The governments of the new order wanted from science inventions that worked, they wanted a mastery of the material world. They encouraged the scientific and experimental techniques that produced these discoveries and inventions. They were not interested in truth for its own sake, rather for the wealth that flowed from its application. Theirs was an operational criterion of truth. Galileo's model of the solar system was preferable to the notion of heavenly spheres because it made for more certain navigation of the trade routes. The application of these principles brought about ongoing revolutionary change in the worlds of science and technology.

But governments wanted the structure and hierarchy of society to remain stable, and only to change in ways that facilitated the productive process. They did not seek the same innovatory zeal from social science. They wanted to change the natural world to their advantage, but maintain the social world unchanged, which was also to their advantage. They asked of social science a lesser but still useful function, namely that it provided a legitimation for the social structure, just as the priests had done previously. They wanted truth from the natural sciences and a supportive ideology from the social 'sciences'. In fulfilling this function it is not at all surprising that social scientists came to use, or at least mimic, the methods that had proved so successful in the natural sciences. This lent authority to their pronouncements, though not necessarily truth. Social scientists varied in the ardour with which they copied natural science. Social psychology is placed in a particularly complex and ambiguous position, and is especially vulnerable to the critique of postmodernism, which I will now consider.

Implications for Social Psychology

The implications of postmodernism for social psychology may be discussed under three headings. First, the central place given by post-structuralism to questions of discourse and text has offered to social psychologists new ways of conducting their discipline, constructing what may be seen as an alternative social psychology. Second, postmodernism's onslaught on science suggests a critique of social psychology as a science, to the extent that it can be considered one. Third, the hypothesis of postmodernity as a new historical era, with a culture changed dramatically from that of modernity, invites social psychological study of the features of that culture. The first of these has been extensively explored, the second less so and the third is still at an 'experimental' stage. I will deal with them in turn.

Post-structuralism, Discourse and Text

The post-structuralist critique experienced an initial difficulty in gaining access to British and American social psychology. This was because structuralism had little influence in their intellectual tradition. There was in British social psychology only a peripheral interest in culture, linguistics and anthropology, and almost none in Marx and Freud, whose ideas were important within structuralism. Thus Michael Lane's (1970) influential reader on structuralism contained twenty articles dealing with linguistics, anthropology, literature, sociology and even mathematics. In only one chapter was social psychology mentioned. The sociologist Peter Abell wrote about '[S]ome problems in the theory of structural balance', which discussed the ideas of leading social psychologists Fritz Heider and Kurt Lewin. Although their ideas were central to the discussion it is clear that they themselves were not part of a structuralist movement.

Therefore, while the criticism of structuralism was clearly the launch-pad for post-structuralism generally and hence for the development of much of postmodernism, this was clearly not a point of access into social psychology. Social psychologists interested in post-structuralism had to begin by other means. One method was by treating social life as a series of discourses to be analysed, or texts to be deconstructed. This would develop an alternative social psychology, one sensitive to questions of discourse and power. However, it might leave the main body of social psychology largely unaddressed. Many social psychologists might regard it not as a critique, but simply as another approach to social psychology. But then social psychology can be seen as itself a series of texts. When textual analysis is turned, deconstructively, on social psychological texts themselves, the critique is much more direct. The authors could hardly fail to take note, though this might turn out to be a very internal discussion with those outside the discipline understandably showing little interest. Both of these approaches have been tried.

Potter and Wetherell argued in their book *Discourse and Social Psychology* (1987) that social psychology should take an interest in areas like discourse and semiotics. Ironically the lack of interest that British social psychology had shown in structuralist ideas made the progress of their ideas easier. They appeared as an interesting new approach which was readily taken up. Only when the wider postmodern argument was broached did it become clear that social psychology was not being augmented, it was being radically challenged.

Parker and Shotter's *Deconstructing Social Psychology* (1990) sought to sharpen the critique. It aimed to dismantle the texts of social psychology itself. Indeed to underline its subversive intent it criticized the bland nature of discourse analysis. In her chapter Burman (1990) says:

> . . . the book [*Discourse and Social Psychology*] sometimes claims that the role of discourse analysis is to comment on and critique social psychology, and at other times asserts that it is part and parcel of the proper business of social psychology. (p. 216)

But the book does not go all the way with postmodernism. In his chapter Parker (1990, p. 160) sympathetically describes postmodernism as a cultural phenomenon which is 'all around us' and advocates a 'new paradigm' social psychology based on post-structuralist ideas. But then he goes on to warn of the excesses of postmodernism, disagreeing with the tendency of new times to

> . . . come packaged with post-capitalism and post-Marxism (or worse with post-feminism and the end of ideology). We could risk buying something that will rot away our critical work on ideology and power the moment we put it to work. (p. 101)

And Shotter (1990) is similarly equivocal. He states the textualist position in order to shoot it down: 'All professional psychology and social psychology moves from text to text, usually beginning with the reading of already written texts and ending with the writing of further texts' (p. 156). This is indeed a depressingly accurate picture of much of what passes for psychology, and it is a relief when he continues:

> 'For some . . . all of psychology without exception should be seen as moving from text to text . . . but . . . there is more to a person than can ever be expressed within the confines of a text. (p. 157)

This seems to be a reassertion of humanism against textualism and contrasts sharply with Derrida. More recently, Parker (1991, p. 40) makes much more explicit his disagreements with aspects of post-structuralism and particularly with the notion of postmodernity and his commitment to a critical realism. In view of these qualifications, Parker and Shotter should perhaps count as no more than sympathizers with postmodernism.

Social Psychology as a Modernist Science

The argument that social psychology is open to criticism because it is 'a modernist science' forms the line of attack taken by Ibáñez (1990, p. 6). He calls for a 'straight postmodern commitment' in social psychology. While his arguments are derived from the general postmodernist critique of science, they are aimed specifically at social psychology. He bypasses any discussion of text and discourse and goes directly for what he sees as the jugular of social psychology, its modernist philosophy of science. He identifies the 'scientific rhetoric of truth' as a key philosophical tenet of enlightenment thinking and hence of the modernist era. He goes on to advocate the dismantling of all rhetorics of truth. We are now, he says, entering a 'post-empirical' era. This is one of the most uncompromising terms in the post-dictionary. It does not occur in Parker and Shotter's collection, despite their frequent use of post-words.

The history of social psychology thus becomes part of the modernist project and the crisis of social psychology part of the crisis of modernism now taking place as the postmodern era looms. While it is clearly the case that social psychology is a product of reasoning in the modern period, it is a relatively recent product. It stems from the late nineteenth century, as do other social sciences, rather than dating back to the enlightenment itself, like the natural sciences. And while there certainly does seem to be a crisis in social psychology, it is not clear that this can be best represented as a crisis of modernism or of modernist science. There is a danger here of misrepresenting the history of modernism and with it that of social psychology. Ibáñez (1990) says that '"modernity" is the joint outcome of the technical achievements of scientific knowledge, of the ideology of enlightenment, and of the rhetoric of scientific truth' (p. 6). This scientific truth was 'a hegemonic and engulfing logic'. Despite its association with social and technical progress it 'helped to create a new totalitarian power device, setting modern science in an almost hegemonic position' (p. 6). Modernity is thus presented as a monolithic social phenomenon whose logic of scientific rationalism dominated an entire era and engulfed the history of social psychology. It is a Kuhnian (1970) picture of 'normal science' in distinction to the scientific revolutions that marked modernism's beginning and is now, so the argument goes, marking its end.

This mistakes both science generally and social psychology in particular. Irrationalist ideas, both religious and secular, have remained powerful throughout the modern period. They acted as a real force in social life and as a barrier to scientific advance. The religious opposition to Darwin's *Origin of Species* is the most obvious example. Though psychology came later on the scene, it did not escape the opposition of religious ideology. Francis Galton published a 'Statistical Inquiry into the Efficacy of Prayer', which cast doubt on the power of prayer. It was included in *Inquiries into Human Faculty* in 1883, but discreetly removed from later editions (Hearnshaw, 1973, p. 19). Psychologists have not regarded religion as a source of anti-scientific irrationalism, rather as an aspect of human experience. One of the few psychologists to take a principled atheistic stance was Freud. Religion, particularly the established religions, have ceased to regard science, including psychology, as a threat. But other movements have developed which, while not so vehemently anti-scientific as religion was, have continued this tradition. Interest in the occult, in the supernatural, in the unexplained and the apparently unexplainable is widespread in society and present within psychology. A leading social psychologist,

Daryl Bem, has recently reviewed the findings of parapsychology and accepts that there is a psi effect (Bem & Honorton, 1994). The ideology of rationalism, which Ibáñez sees as so central to the modern era, has not been as hegemonic as he suggests, either in the world at large, or in psychology.

Nor can the crisis in social psychology be readily dated according to the postmodern calendar. The subject has been beset by a long-running series of controversies concerning psychoanalysis, introspection, group mind, humanism, the self, common sense and many others. The crisis in social psychology is thus not a recent seventies and eighties phenomenon; it has traversed the history of the discipline. Only by treating these serious theoretical disputes as internal modernist wrangles can the 'crisis of social psychology' be represented as coterminous with the 'crisis of modernity'. It is not only the long-running saga of these controversies but their content that is important. A common theme that runs through them is the status of social psychology as a science. According to conventional criteria, much of social psychology fails to make the grade, in which case the criticisms of Ibáñez are inapplicable. To this extent, then, they miss their mark. Ironically Ibáñez has to elevate social psychology to the level of a science in order to criticize it. One thing is certain here: this separates him clearly from other critics, who criticize social psychology for not being scientific enough.

Ibáñez goes on to consider the social and human aspects of social psychology. The recognition that social psychology is just another social object, says Ibáñez, will enhance the human, the social and the reflexive aspects of the subject, which are precluded by its current modernist perspective. Once we strip away all the 'rhetorics of truth', we are 'left absolutely alone with ourselves, completely deprived of any transcendental principles with from which to seek advice' (Ibáñez, 1990, p. 9). Social psychologists are asked to discard theories, models and any other truth-seeking or explanatory devices, because they stand between us and our understanding of ourselves and others. Any mediation will distract this direct human knowing. This may be a clumsy paraphrase, but the approach seems to carry mystical overtones, while its uncompromising rejection of theory has an almost positivist ring.

Social psychologists cannot impart humanity to their endeavours simply by removing the allegedly anti-human theories of modernism. This would only be sufficient if it were also argued that there is a human nature intrinsic to each one of us, which merely has to be enabled to reveal itself. This might fit with classical humanism, but is certainly too essentialist for postmodernism. For the argument to work postmodernism has to have a definitely humanistic aspect. This is difficult because postmodernism is ambiguous on this question. On the one hand, the demolition of grand theories, the recognition of 'many genres' and the encouragement of pluralism implies a certain kind of humanism. They offer a liberation from the deterministic 'grand theories' that deny human agency. But, on the other hand, the major post-structuralist thinkers have often been anti-humanist in their approach, even admitting to a 'theoretical anti-humanism'. They examined the text rather than the author, they attacked the Freudian ego and 'decentred the self', and they criticized individualism. On balance postmodernism seems to be an inappropriate philosophy for rescuing a 'truly human' social psychology.

To be fair, Ibáñez (1990) is careful to limit his argument. He says, 'I am not suggesting any ready-made device with which to construct better descriptions and explanations of social reality (p. 13). This expresses a proper scientific caution. But what is in doubt is the possibility of making such a device out of the contents of postmodernism.

New Times and Social Psychology

Ibáñez suggests that we are on the edge of the postmodern era. There are others who say that we are already in it. In his essay 'Postmodern Psychology: A Contradiction in Terms' (1992) Steiner Kvale argues that:

> The current emptiness and irrelevance of a psychological science to culture at large may be due to psychology's rootedness in modernity, in the study of an abstracted 'psyche' which is out of touch with a postmodern world. (We leave out here the issue whether modern psychology was ever adequate for understanding modern man.) (p. 52)

Kvale thus argues that the mass of humanity is already living in a postmodern culture and that psychologists have not realized this, and continue to use inappropriate and obsolete modernist psychology. He includes behaviourists, humanists, Freudians and Jungians in his indictment. But he rather blatantly side-steps the question of whether modern psychology was ever appropriate for modern man. It is an important question. It would help address the changes that are supposed to have taken place during the transition from modern to postmodern culture in the psychology of people, and the consequent changes that, says Kvale, ought to take place in academic psychology. If 'modern psychology was adequate for modern man', then another explanation is needed for the crises and debates that have beset modern psychology as it struggled to understand modern people. If it was not, then modernism was clearly not the 'engulfing logic' that postmodernists have made it out to be. It might be said that the postmodern condition precludes the answering of such a question. But that would be to presume the essential correctness of the postmodern argument. There is a way of pursuing this question, however.

If it is the case that culture has changed dramatically in a postmodern manner, then we would expect some indication of this even in the imperfect instrument of the psychology experiment. Mike Michael hints at this in his discussion of 'Postmodern Subjects: Towards a Transgressive Social Psychology' (1992):

How would the fragmented individual, say a member of the new class factions, part of whose identity is tied up with the systematic denial of group membership, self-categorize? What minimal intergroup experimental results would we find for a sample of postmoderns whose main self-category is that they belong to no category or that they are constantly shifting or transgressing categories? (p. 76)

It is consistent for the postmodernist to argue that the effects found in social psychological experiments – conformity, stereotyping, intergroup preference, brainstorming and the rest – would change, fade or even disappear in the culture of postmodern society. Whether or not such tendencies have been shown during the alleged twilight of modernity is open to empirical examination.

In a rerun of the Asch experiment, Perrin and Spencer (1980) found that Sheffield engineering students showed none of the conformity effects so apparent in US undergraduates of the early fifties. Asch himself accepted that this failure to replicate was due to cultural changes and that his effect was a 'child of its time'. But this was not a reference to the postmodern debate. The subjects of Perrin and Spencer's study were not 'new age subjects'. Their resistance to pressure could be explained by their keenness to make physical judgements accurately, or by their less deferential attitude to the psychology experimenter.

Another example is that of 'fading stereotypes' (Brown, 1986, p. 587), discussed in Roger Brown's book *Social Psychology: The Second Edition*. In 1933 Katz and Braly's study of Princeton students showed definite unfavourable stereotypes of several foreign nationalities and of American blacks. Gilbert's replication in 1951 showed a significant decline in stereotyping, hence the term 'fading stereotypes'. But by 1967, in a third run of the study, stereotypes had reasserted themselves. In the later studies, some subjects objected to the procedure, saying that traits could not apply in such a general manner. So while it cannot be concluded that stereotypes are fading, it might also be becoming more difficult to test these trends in the old way. However, indications from the real world suggest that stereotypes are not fading, and can be readily re-created, for instance stereotypes of Argentinians during the Falklands War, and of foreigners in contemporary Germany.

Stroebe, Diehl and Abakoumkin's (1992) recent researches on brainstorming challenge the long-established finding that groups are more creative than individuals. But they do not argue that this social psychological effect has faded, rather that individuals perform better than groups and that earlier research got it the wrong way round. These are a few examples of studies where it appears at first sight that social psychological effects are fading, but cannot be so concluded after further examination. So far the evidence for this postmodern hypothesis is not strong. Indeed where these effects vary across cultures, as Smith and Bond (1993) show that they do, and across time, there might be more mundane cultural explanations at hand rather than resorting to the rather sweeping explanations of postmodernity.

The Rise and Fall of Postmodernism

It is ironic that postmodernism is making its bid for social psychology when its fortunes are declining elsewhere. Postmodernism has been criticized from a number of directions for some time. On receiving the 1975 Adorno prize from the city of Frankfurt, Jürgen Habermas gave a lecture defending modernism as an incomplete project. He said, 'I fear that the ideas of anti-modernity, together with an additional touch of pre-modernity, are becoming popular in the circles of the alternative culture' (Habermas, 1990, p. 354). More recently Alex Callinicos (1989) has written a Marxist philosophical critique of postmodernism. In the field of literary criticism Malcolm Bradbury (1990) accepts that modernism is over but adds that it was a 'hard act to follow'. He concludes that postmodernism has failed the task and calls for a new 'quickening of the imagination' similar to the 1890s. Especially open to challenge is postmodernism's notion of 'new times'. This thesis is vulnerable, like any end-of-era philosophy, to the reassertion of old patterns. The idea of 'postcapitalism' is challenged by the recession, and 'post-Fordism' cannot seem credible among the dark satanic mills of the newly industrializing countries. The conditions that encouraged postmodernism, the brief boom of the eighties that created a trendy consumerism that postmodernism celebrated, is over. We now enter a period not of 'new times', but of political and economic crisis, in which the incredible lightness of postmodernism is not appropriate. The suspension of disbelief that postmodernism so often requires can no longer be allowed.

However, while I question the critical value of postmodernism, I have no doubt that its emergence within social psychology is in response to very real problems. We badly need a social psychology that is human, genuinely social and historical. But I feel that postmodernism hinders rather than helps the building of such a social psychology. Its textualism, anti-realism and opposition to science all serve as major disadvantages. I find it telling that, of the ideas that have been reviewed here, those that are more peripheral to postmodernism, such as discourse analysis, are those that have made a serious new contribution to social psychology. Those ideas which are more central to postmodernism, such as the critique of science and the concept of a new age, have had a lesser and more negative effect. By its radical appearance it has occupied part of that oppositional space from which an alternative might come, both in the sense of furnishing a coherent critique which might serve to explain the nature of social psychology and the crises that seem to dog its path, and in the sense of offering an alternative rationale for its existence and method of procedure. Ibáñez has argued that postmodernism and Marxism are partly compatible. This is not a view I happen to share but it certainly separates him from those who would deny Marxism as passé or accept it as merely another narrative. Parker and Spears (1996) have recently edited a collection on Marxism and psychology. These are hopeful signs. What is needed in the critical construction of a 'new' social psychology is the gathering together of several disparate strands of useful theory, and practice. I would include discourse analysis, psychoanalysis, social representation theory and symbolic interactionism. I am not trying to set out a definitive list, rather to suggest some ways forward. And I fully appreciate that there are serious arguments going on within these approaches. Habermas was right to say that modernism is an unfinished project. The same is true of social psychology.

References

Bell, D. (1974). *The coming of post-industrial society.* London; Heinemann.
Bem, D., & Honorton, C. (1994). Does psi exist? Replicable evidence for an anomalous process of information transfer. *Psychological Bulletin, 115*, 4–18.
Bradbury, M. (1990, 20 September). The world after the wake. *The Guardian,* p. 25.
Brown, R. (1986). *Social psychology: The second edition.* New York: The Free Press.
Burman, E. (1990). Differing with deconstruction. In I. Parker & J. Shotter (Eds.), *Deconstructing social psychology.* London: Sage.
Callinicos, A. (1989). *Against post-modernism.* Oxford: Polity.
Foucault, M. (1973). *Madness and civilization.* New York: Random House.
Foucault, M. (1979). *Discipline and punish.* New York: Random House.
Fukuyama, F. (1992). *The end of history and the last man.* London: Hamish Hamilton/New York: The Free Press.
Habermas, J. (1990). Modernity versus postmodernity. In J.C. Alexander & S. Seidman (Eds.), *Culture and society: Contemporary debates* (pp. 342–354). Cambridge: Cambridge University Press.
Hearnshaw, L. (1973). The psychology of religion. In L.E. Brown (Ed.), *Psychology and religion.* Harmondsworth: Penguin.
Ibáñez, T. (1990). Henri, Serge . . . and the next generation. *British Psychological Society Social Psychology Section Newsletter, 24*, 5–14.
Jencks, C. (1986). *What is post-modernism?* London: Academy.
Kuhn, T.S. (1970). *The structure of scientific revolutions* (2nd ed.). Chicago: University of Chicago Press.
Kvale, S. (1992). Postmodern psychology: A contradiction in terms. In S. Kvale (Ed.), *Psychology and postmodernism.* London: Sage.
Lane, M. (Ed.). (1970). *Structuralism: A reader.* London: Cape.
Lyotard, J.-F. (1990). The postmodern condition. In J.C. Alexander & S. Seidman (Eds.), *Culture and society: Contemporary debates* (pp. 330–341). Cambridge: Cambridge University Press.
Michael, M. (1992). Postmodern subjects: Towards a transgressive social psychology. In S. Kvale (Ed.), *Psychology and postmodernism* (pp. 74–87). London: Sage.
Parker, I. (1990). The abstraction and representation of social psychology. In I. Parker & J. Shotter (Eds.), *Deconstructing social psychology* (pp. 91–102). London: Routledge.
Parker, I. (1991). *Discourse dynamics: Critical analysis for social and individual psychology.* London: Routledge.
Parker, I., & Shotter, J. (Eds.). (1990). *Deconstructing social psychology.* London: Routledge.
Parker, I., & Spears, R. (Eds.). (1996). *Psychology and society: Radical theory and practice.* London: Pluto Press.
Perrin, S., & Spencer, C. (1980). The Asch effect – a child of its time? *Bulletin of the British Psychological Society, 32*, 405–406.
Polkinghorne, D.E. (1992). Postmodern epistemology of practice. In S. Kvale (Ed.), *Psychology and postmodernism* (pp. 146–165). London: Sage.
Potter, J., & Wetherell, M. (1987). *Discourse and social psychology.* London: Sage.

Saussure, F. de. (1974). *Course in general linguistics.* London: Fontana. (Original work published 1913)

Scott, P. (1990, 24 August). Reaching beyond enlightenment. *Times Higher Educational Supplement*, Issue 929, p. 28.

Sedgwick, P. (1982). *Psychopolitics.* London: Pluto Press.

Shotter, J. (1990). Social individualism versus possessive individualism: The sounds of silence. In I. Parker & J. Shotter (Eds.), *Deconstructing social psychology* (pp. 153–169). London: Sage.

Shotter, J. (1992). Getting in touch: A meta-methodology of a postmodern science of mental life. In S. Kvale (Ed.), *Psychology and postmodernism* (pp. 58–73). London: Sage.

Smith, P.B., & Bond, M.H. (1993). *Social psychology across cultures.* Hemel Hempstead: Harvester Wheatsheaf.

Stroebe, W., Diehl, M., & Abakoumkin, G. (1992). The illusion of group effectivity. *Personality and Social Psychology Bulletin, 18*(5), 643–658.

Wolpert, L. (1992). *The unnatural nature of science.* London: Faber.

8

And So Say All of Us?: Some Thoughts on 'Experiential Democratization' as an Aim for Critical Social Psychologists

Susan Condor

The Crisis of Authority in Critical Social Psychology

Writing at the time of the original 'crisis' debates, Alan Elms (1975) encouraged his readers to look back to a golden age when '[s]ocial psychologists . . . knew who they were and where they were going' (p. 967). Despite all that may have changed in the past twenty years, those of us who place ourselves at a critical distance from mainstream social psychology still experience various forms of academic identity crisis. Although we may express our identity as 'critical social psychologists' in terms of the *jouissance* of contraculture, the smug self-righteousness of the chosen people or the heady optimism and camaraderie of a social movement, at the same time we are plagued by existential doubt. The very existence of the present volume attests to our continuing self-scrutiny and attempts at ethical self-fashioning. In this chapter I shall discuss some of these issues as they relate to the problem of establishing our academic authority.[1]

Constructing Legitimacy Through Consensus

In an interesting case study of political rhetoric, Potter and Edwards (1990) point to the ways in which knowledge claims may be supported by reference to consensus. As critical social psychologists we are often concerned to submerge the variety of voices within our ranks in the interests of constructing a fictive unity: a 'we' with which to oppose the massed armies of normal social psychology. Although we are aware that our opposition draws from a variety of potentially incompatible intellectual sources, we generally prefer not to foreground any potential disputes among us. In presenting ourselves as a community of scholars, we normally refer to a series of shared constructs and common interests. These include: an attack on universalist assumptions of human nature; a critique of individualism; an interest in social context and a broad commitment to constructionism; and a concern with talk and text. Such a catalogue of common interests grants only a precarious sense of unity. We are all too aware that our ability to speak with one voice, to offer mutual support and affirmation, to inhabit the same edited text, depends largely upon preserving a lack of clarity in our use of keywords such as 'context', 'individualism', 'discourse' and 'social', in not probing the limits of each other's commitment to constructionism or relativism, in pretending not to notice when authors have quite different understandings of 'text' (is there anything beyond it?) and what may be accomplished by its analysis. Also, of course, in the interests of constructing consensus we seldom openly voice concerns as to whether various intellectual and methodological critiques of social psychology (increasingly based on broadly post-structuralist assumptions) are compatible with 'radical' or 'progressive' political critiques of current social arrangements (largely based on liberal-humanist or Marxist perspectives and on various forms of identity politics) (Burman, 1990; Parker, 1990; Roiser, this volume; Wilkinson, this volume).

In addition to constructing consensus within our ranks, we also warrant our accounts by enlisting support from academics outside critical social psychology. To use Callon & Latour's (1981) lovely phrase, we effectively 'make ourselves large' by aligning ourselves with a host of other authorities. In this way we stave off potential criticism: as Latour (1987, p. 33) notes, it is difficult for the reader to 'shrug off dozens of people'. In various contexts we mobilize support from social linguists, social theorists, anthropologists, feminists and sociologists. At times we even increase the size of our block vote by enlisting the voices of mainstream psychologists. Billig (1987), for example, in a series of splendid rhetorical flourishes, cites work by a number of mainstream cognitive and social psychologists in order to warrant his own commitment to a rhetorical approach to social psychology. A common strategy on the part of North American writers is to align their critical accounts of mainstream psychology with the American Psychological Association's own stated concern for 'promoting human welfare' (e.g. Gergen, 1989; Sampson, 1991, see below).

Disclaiming Psychological Authority

A good deal of work in critical social psychology has focused on dismantling mainstream (social) psychology's claims to authority. We have sought to expose how, behind the veneer of benign expertise, lies a reality of illegitimate 'power' exercised by psychology as a discipline and by psychologists as individuals. Unlike some of our ancestors (e.g. Adorno, Frenkel-Brunswik, Levinson & Sanford, 1950; Allport, 1954; Sherif & Sherif, 1953) who regarded their position as 'scientific' social psychologists as a powerful platform for political intervention, we point to (social) psychology's ideological grounding and its role in social regulation. Psychology, with its history of racism, sexism, heterosexism, with its insistence on the ultimate reality of the self-contained individual, with its technologies for the scrutiny and self-regulation of the individual subject, with its modernist pretensions to scientific expertise, is not a platform from which we wish to speak. Rather than speaking confidently as social psychologists, we employ a variety of strategies to manage our position on what is becoming an increasingly wobbly soap-box. One common line, associated particularly with the social identity perspective, is to argue that a properly 'social social psychology' will overcome the ideological biases of non social social psychology (Tajfel, 1972, 1978). Other theorists who claim to speak as (social?) psychologists have similarly suggested that it may be possible to recover psychology as a legitimate platform for theory and action by adding in a consideration of 'the social' (e.g. Gergen, 1989; Moscovici, 1972). Others decline to derive their authority from Psychology at all, preferring to speak as feminists (Burman, this volume), scholars (Billig, 1988) or intellectuals (Shotter, 1993). Alternatively, we may be prepared to jump on and off the (social) Psychology soap-box as the rhetorical moment requires (Kitzinger, 1990).

Our opposition to the authority of Psychology stretches to the research process itself. Critical social psychologists typically regard the micro-arena of the research setting in terms of the operation of illegitimate relations of power, documenting the ways in which the (dominant, manipulative) E exerts 'power over' the (subordinate, docile) S in the traditional social psychology experiment (e.g. Billig, 1976). In exposing power inequalities in the research process, current critical analyses tend to go further than those of the original crisis authors. We no longer assume that E's power over S can be overcome by simple variants of technique or by a concern for 'ethics' (Kelman, 1972). Rather, we tend to regard the research setting as a microcosm of more general systems of social inequality (Bhavnani, 1990). We trace these power inequalities beyond the laboratory, and point to the ways in which E also exercises 'power over' S in the process of analysing the data and reporting the research (Reicher, this volume).

To the extent that these critiques are directed at the power of science they may serve to warrant our own alternative (postmodern) academic practices. On the other hand, some aspects of these critiques may appear potentially applicable to our own practice as (critical) social psychologists. After all, in our own research we also claim the authority to define research problems, prioritize particular solutions and undertake to scrutinize and represent human beings. In the following pages I shall focus on one solution to this problem which has been articulated most clearly in the work of Edward Sampson. This strategy involves seeking the consensus to support our claims outside the academic world altogether. It suggests that we should relinquish our claims to expertise and instead listen to, and record faithfully, the voices of ordinary folk.

Forging Consensus with the People: Dialogism and the
'Democratization' of Psychology

In a paper published in *Theory and Psychology*, Sampson (1991) calls for 'the democratization' of psychology. He draws the reader's attention to the aim of conventional Psychology to develop and apply expert knowledge of human behaviour in the service of human good, or (as exemplified in Miller's 1969 APA presidential address) to give this knowledge to the people to enable their own self-regulation. Sampson argues that such accounts privilege expert psychological knowledge over the common-sense understandings of the people themselves. He claims that this expert knowledge, whilst posing as universal fact, is in reality only one account amongst many. In particular, he argues that Psychology's concern with the self-contained individual derives from, and serves the interests of, dominant social groups (cf. Rose, 1989, 1990a, 1990b). Sampson backs up this claim by pointing to the existence of different constructs of human nature articulated by 'women' (i.e. some academic Western feminists)[2] and by people from 'nonWestern' cultures.[3] This argument is outlined in more detail in his later text *Celebrating the Other* (Sampson, 1993), in which he suggests that psychology should be seen as part of the Western project to produce 'serviceable others'.

In contrast to established approaches, Sampson (1991) calls for an 'experiential democratization' of psychology. Rather than attempting to give away our (scientifically derived) expert knowledge, we should seek instead 'to democratize the bases of human self-understanding by establishing a greater equality of "voice" in setting forth the very terms by which human experience, knowledge and meaning are framed and understood' (p. 275). Academic psychology should be replaced with ethnopsychology, a discipline concerned 'with the way in which people conceptualize, monitor, and discuss their own and other's mental processes, behavior and relationships' (Lutz, 1985, p. 36). As represented by Sampson (1991), this would involve a form of relativism. Rather than judging people by 'our' (scientific, Western) standards 'we must learn about the diverse ways that human communities have rendered their lives meaningful. We cannot "give away" anything but this multiplicity we have documented by listening to the *demos* speak' (p. 284).

As a means by which to achieve the democratization of Psychology, Sampson (1991, 1993) advocates the development of dialogic theories and methods, and refers to the application of this perspective to anthropological fieldwork and the practice of ethnography (e.g. Clifford, 1986; Tedlock, 1987). On a theoretical level, dialogism would focus attention on the constructive nature of human interaction, countering mainstream psychology's concern for the self-contained individual as the focus of analysis. In terms of practice, dialogism would focus attention on the ways in which both self and other are mutually constructed in the research process, and would entail an abrogation of academic authority, including a commitment to co-author texts with the researched.

Once the democratization of inputs has been achieved, this new base of psychological knowledge should, Sampson argues, be used in the pursuit of human freedom and equality. The task for Western psychologists would no longer be to inform other people about the 'facts' of their psychology, but rather to analyse the processes by which indigenous constructions of self function in the life of the community. In the interests of 'promoting human welfare', Psychologists should 'share with the community' their insights concerning the multitude of possible constructions of human psychology, and should inform others of the relationship between local constructs of human nature and relations of dominance: 'our message to others is designed to help them gain a critical reflection of their own circumstances along with alternatives so that they can be sufficiently informed to be the *demos* that students argue is an essential element of democratic rule' (Sampson, 1991, p. 292).

As presented by Sampson (1991, 1993), this programme for the experiential democratization of psychology would appear to address many of the problems associated with our current crisis of authority. In place of scientific knowledge imperiously defining self and others in line with the self-interests of patriarchy and the West, there are a multitude of voices of equal standing. Through engaging in dialogue with those he studies, the psychologist comes to understand others in their own terms, and by the same process comes to a greater understanding of himself as a dialogic partner. In renouncing sole authorship of any written accounts of these transactions, the psychologist no longer speaks as and for himself as individual scholar or as part of the apparatus of Western hegemony. Rather, through his academic texts he speaks on behalf of ordinary folk everywhere.

People's Voices and Our Stories: Dialogism, Democracy and Academic Authority

Before proceeding with my discussion, I should like to foreground an uneasy tension in Sampson's work. On the one hand, the ideal of dialogism calls for a focus on social constructionism, particularly as it occurs in the 'space between individuals' (including the space between the psychologist and the other s/he seeks to understand). The notion of experiential democratization, on the other hand, appears to require that the psychologist stand aside in order to understand pre-existing indigenous psychologies 'in their own terms'. The implication here is that we should celebrate the other as if he, she or they existed in some ontologically prior state. I do not wish to dwell on this point here. For the time being we should note that Sampson requires that we renounce our authority in two ways. First, that we construct our accounts of human nature in concert with those whom we study. Second, that we renounce our own academic authority in the interests of allowing the Voice (or, rather, the multiple Voices) of the People to be heard and celebrated.

Critical Social Psychology Research and the Dialogic Fieldwork Ideal

In the process of making himself large Sampson on occasions locates his voice in a chorus of the morally-sanctioned. In the prologue to *Celebrating the Other*, for example, he presents his claims as little more than an echo of the words of women, African-Americans, the aged, the handicapped, members of the ecology and environmental movements. However, in subsequent chapters of this book Sampson alerts the reader to the fact that his attack on Normal Psychology is not simply supported by the rank and file of the dispossessed (or those who claim to speak for them). Far from it. In support of his mission to 'take out' Normal (Social) Psychology, Sampson has amassed a formidable squadron of Established Academic Authorities. Providing Sampson with close air support are the likes of Theodor Adorno, Mikhail Bakhtin, Pierre Bourdieu, Helene Cixous, Jacques Derrida, Clifford Geertz, Luce Irigaray, George Herbert Mead, Edward Said, Lev Vygotsky and Ludwig Wittgenstein. In addition, Sampson has also enlisted to his side a fleet of renegade social psychologists, of whom more later. And these are simply the authoritative figures whom Sampson has allowed to show up on the academic radar-screen. This great formation of visible, noisy fighters escorts more massive forces still. Although Sampson does not particularly draw the reader's attention to their presence, the looming shadows Marx and Habermas advance silently, stealthily upon the unwary Normal Psychology. This great squadron of authorities originate from academic bases which are largely beyond the firing range of Normal (Social) Psychology. Moreover, Sampson warns that, even should Normal Psychologists wish to reply to his critique, they would find their conventional weapons (objectivity, experimentation, quantification, experimental control) obsolete. They are, according to his propaganda at least, no match for the 'special weapons' of reflexivity, democracy, constructionism and dialogism.[4]

Let us now turn to consider those authors (largely critical social psychologists) whose work, Sampson suggests, exemplifies what he has in mind when proposing a 'dialogic' psychology. The textual friends (to use Shotter's, 1993, phrase) he cites include: Billig, Edwards, 'Gergen' (he does not specify whether it is Ken or Mary), Potter and Wetherell and Shotter. These authors all share a theoretical concern for what might loosely be termed the discursive construction of social reality and some (most notably Shotter and to a lesser extent Billig [e.g. 1994]) are explicitly concerned with developing dialogic accounts of social psychological phenomena. However, it is not at all clear that (as Sampson implies) these authors are in any way concerned to renounce their own academic authority by adopting the sorts of dialogical *research techniques* outlined, for example, in the work of Dwyer (1977, 1979), Clifford (1986) or Tedlock (1987).[5] Certainly, the methods that these researchers use may *appear* more dialogical than those experimental procedures 'in which college sophomores are lied to and then have a choice between alternatively strange reactions' (Billig, 1990, p. 52), or in which researchers supply their subjects[6] with closed-ended questionnaires or attitude scales (Reicher, this volume). It may well seem *to the respondents* that the interviewer is genuinely interested in hearing 'their story', in learning about their experiences, or in discussing the social or the natural world with them. In fact, it is probably the case that the researcher has led them to believe that this is the case in order to obtain their co-operation. But there the similarity with dialogic fieldwork ends. For there is no reciprocal sharing of knowledge (or, at least, the research reports do not tell us of any). Rather than engaging in a two-way debate the researcher typically poses questions and the researched dutifully respond (cf. Oakley, 1981). Moreover, in a good deal of this work it is not even the researcher who conducts the interviews! And even when the researcher is present at the scene of data gathering, she may distance herself from the discursive situation by listening in (but not personally contributing) to conversations that she has set up between other people. It is also common for social psychological studies of narrative, discourse or rhetoric to use materials such as political speeches, journal articles, TV chat shows, diaries or autobiographies, all of which pre-exist the involvement of the researcher. Potter and Wetherell (1987) regard this as a cause for celebration: 'Traditionally, one of the most important advantages of collecting naturalistic records and documents is the almost complete absence of researcher influence on the data' (p. 162).

Of course, this research could still achieve a measure of dialogical reflexivity if researchers took account of their direct or indirect involvement in the production of their data, both in the research context and at the stage of analysis. However, despite a greater tendency towards reflexivity than may be apparent in mainstream social psychological research, even critical social psychologists such as Sampson's textual friends do not seem keen to implicate themselves fully in either the data or their analysis. Certainly, it is notable that Potter and Wetherell's (1987) recommendations concerning 'How to analyse discourse' have little in common with recommendations for dialogic ethnography (e.g. Tedlock, 1987). It is often the case, for example, in social psychological research employing discourse analytic or other qualitative techniques that the 'responses' of subjects are considered apart from dialogic context. In particular, it is common practice for researchers to analyse answers apart from the questions which elicited them, treating S's words as monologue addressed apropos of nothing and nobody in particular (Condor, Íñiguez and Antaki, 1990). Even when the researcher does apparently acknowledge her place in the research conversation, she still tends to discuss the data *with respect to the respondents*, rather than dwelling deeply on her own complicity in constructing the phenomena under scrutiny.

By way of illustration, let us consider Bhavnani's (1990, 1991) accounts of her research on the ways in which young people talk about political issues. Bhavnani is not cited by Sampson as a textual friend, but I have chosen to focus on her work because it seems to me that it provides an exemplary case of the kind of work that critical social psychologists often advocate. It is clear – both from the snippets of dialogue that Bhavnani provides in her texts, and from her explicit account of the research process – that in this case the researcher was (and to some extent recognizes herself to be) centrally implicated in the talk which she recorded and analysed. For example, in her book *Talking Politics*, Bhavnani (1991) provides her readers with transcripts from interviews in which we see her painfully extorting talk about 'politics' from her reluctant young interviewees. Her respondents struggle against her questions, but Bhavnani carries on probing regardless. In the transcripts we see the respondents attempting to block the conversation by claiming ignorance ('that's got me stuck, 'cos I don't know', 'I suppose I'm not clever enough to think about it') (see Turner and Michael [1996] for an account of claims to ignorance in interviews). Heroically, Bhavnani refuses to take no for a non-answer, and continues plying her respondents with questions ('Go on, have a go', 'How do you mean?', 'Tell us why?') until they come up with a reply which satisfies her.

Bhavnani's subsequent analysis of these dialogues – and others like them – is certainly reflexive insofar as she is prepared to consider how her respondents may have been responding to her as an individual. Nevertheless, this sort of analysis (in which data are collected by means of interviews, and in which the possible 'effects' of the interviewer are considered) falls far short of 'dialogism'. First, we might note that the interviews do not take the form of a mutually-revelatory dialogue. Like most social science interviewers, Bhavnani confines herself to asking questions. Moreover, in the bulk of the analysis Bhavnani treats the words that she had so painfully extracted from her respondents as evidence of beliefs, experiences or discourses existing *prior to the interview context* in which they were uttered. Instead of presenting the interview-talk as a co-production, for which the responsibility is shared between herself and her respondents, Bhavnani treats the answers she received (her 'findings') as if they were the property of her respondents: something that they had brought with them to the interview. Finally, Bhavnani does not at any stage present her own voice – her identity, her claims, her text – as constituted dialogi-cally. Rather, in the Preface she positions herself beyond the encounters she describes and the text in which she presents them. She describes herself in terms of a set of prior identities ('a black woman in her mid thirties', 'middle class', a social psychologist, an academic) and points to her commitment to certain beliefs and activities (feminism, anti-racism) which have necessarily influenced her work.

The point of the foregoing is not to mount a critique of Bhavnani's work. On the contrary, I choose to focus on her reports of her research precisely because they seem to me to be such a good example of what critical social psychologists can achieve. But it would be a mistake to assume that all research which collects data by talking to people, and analyses it with some reflexivity, is necessarily *dialogic* in form or content. The most radical, reflexive social psychologists who conduct qualitative research using spoken or written texts rarely consider how their voice may be the subject of a negotiated construction within and beyond the context of the research interview. We are too keen on chastising ourselves for having 'power over' our subjects to ever consider how our identity claims (and 'power') may come into being by being invoked and supported by other people – our respondents, our academic colleagues, the readers of our research reports (cf. Latour, 1986; Michael, 1996). Rarely do we consider how *our* identity may be dialogically accomplished.

Authority and Authorship in Critical Social Psychology Texts

If it were the case, as Sampson suggests, that the authors he cites did conduct dialogic work, then we might expect them to produce 'polyphonic texts' (Clifford, 1986), showing evidence of co-authorship. Of course, a sceptical commentator could point to the practical impossibility of ever achieving co-authorship. Some ethnographers have argued that the inequality between researcher and researched is such that it is never really possible for the researched to speak alongside the author in an 'equal way'. Geertz (1988), in particular, has argued that anthropologists should not attempt to 'displace the burden of authorship' by appropriating the people themselves as co-workers. Moreover, Rosaldo (1989) argues that the authority of the academic becomes particularly apparent when research conversations are 'written up' in a narrative form which is alien to the people being described. Although Rosaldo's concern is for cross-cultural representation, the same almost certainly holds true for our writing practice as critical social psychologists. The genres we use when producing academic texts and research articles are clearly different to those used by the research participants in producing their own accounts. And, of course, our stories are structured to exemplify quite different points for quite different audiences.

Notwithstanding these problems, it is increasingly the case that social scientists demonstrate some concern that the texts they produce are at least acceptable to their research subjects. Some anthropologists and feminist scholars may invite their research participants to comment on early drafts of their research reports (e.g. Clifford, 1983; Lather, 1986, 1988; Mbilinyi, 1989). However, with a few notable exceptions (e.g. De Waele & Harré, 1979), current work by critical social psychologists, including Sampson's textual friends, does not demonstrate any apparent concern for co-authorship. Rather, these authors generally adopt a 'strategic location' (Said, 1978) which sets them apart from their subjects. Consider accounts such as the following:

> The modern subjects, not wishing to imagine themselves as subjects, have a gap in their imaginings of royalty. Sometimes the gap could be concealed by a reversal of conditions of inequality. This ideological reversal is to be heard in the language of jobs. . . . When applied to royalty, it has a surprising result. 'We' are imagining 'ourselves' to be in the position of command. (Billig, 1992, p. 115)

Despite the author's use of the royal 'we', it is clear that it is Billig himself that we hear 'talking of [talk about] the Royal Family'. Similarly, it is clearly Edwards and Mercer (1987) who tell us that:

> The status of certain understandings, achieved in the lessons, as 'common knowledge' was often marked overtly in the discourse by the development and repetitive use of . . . formulaic phrases, together with other devices such as simultaneous speech . . . and the teacher's use of 'we'. . . . (p. 141)

for the authors have already told us that their analysis of 'common knowledge' goes beyond the common sense of the teachers and children they studied.

When Potter and Wetherell (1987) say that:

> The 'stirrer' is an extremely useful accounting device. Political or other motivations behind violence can be dismissed or ignored since the 'stirrer' is fully explained by this kind of natural self which they possess, no other kind of account is needed. (p. 113)

this is not an example of heteroglossia. In fact, they make it clear that the white New Zealanders whose words they quote would probably not concur with their academic analyses. And, when Mary Gergen (1992) observes that:

> We all know ourselves, define our pasts, and project our futures as they fit in the acculturated story forms. But the forms for each gender are restrictive, and in many critical areas, such as achievement striving and intimate relationships, men and women are inhibited from formulating selves that would allow for a different range of expressions and actions. (p. 132)

she is not presenting a conclusion that she reached in concert with the authors whose autobiographic accounts she describes.

The authors Sampson cites, and others like them, have not simply failed in an attempt to renounce sole authorial control. On the contrary, from my reading of their texts I can find little evidence that they have any inclination to displace the burden of their authorship or, indeed, that they find authorship in any way burdensome!

Celebrating Multiple Voices: The Claim

Although there may be little evidence of dialogic research procedures or of co-authorship in the current practice of critical social psychology, Sampson's call for the valorization of common sense or folk psychology does find some echoes. As Sampson indicates, his concern for the democratization of psychology may be seen to reflect a general cultural process. This process, sometimes termed detraditionalization (*Enttraditionalisierung*), is characterized by a decline in the legitimacy of traditional authority, with 'voice' becoming displaced from pre-given authority onto the self. Of particular relevance to Sampson's critique of Psychology are current trends towards scepticism of scientific authority (Lyotard, 1979), and an ambivalence towards expertise more generally (Billig et al., 1988) reflected in academia by Marxist and feminist attempts to reformulate social science by supplanting the voice of the privileged with the 'view from below'. This process has recently attracted some attention from social theorists. The changing relationship between 'intellectuals' and 'the people' has, for example, been discussed in some detail by Bauman (1995). More specifically, Bourdieu (1984; 1990) interprets the process by which academics claim to speak on behalf of 'the people' in terms of more local identity-projects. According to Bourdieu, the current rehabilitation of 'the popular' is undertaken by particular intellectuals out of a 'desire for their own ennoblement' (1990, p. 151). By claiming an allegiance with 'the people' scholars attempt to morally outflank those of their academic competitors who stake a claim to expertise. Bourdieu argues that the use of 'the people' by an academic author is likely to vary depending upon their own current success in their academic field: 'most of the types of discourse which have been or are produced in support of the "people" come from producers occupying dominated positions in the field of production' (1990, p. 151).

Attempts to form allegiances with 'the popular' and to distance oneself from established academic authority are relatively common amongst critical social psychologists. For example, in calling for a re-evaluation of common sense, Sampson (1991) cites an ally in Billig (1990), who pointed to the way in which traditional social psychologists may legitimate their authority by juxtaposing their (scientific) knowledge with the (unsatisfactory) common sense of their subjects.[7] Similar concerns may be found in the original crisis literature. For example, Shotter (1975) suggested that 'psychology must begin, not by doing experiments to establish "the facts", but by clarifying our ordinary everyday concepts of ourselves and others as persons' (p. 35). In his original presentation of ethogenics, Harré (1979), too, to some extent valorized common-sense ('moral') constructions of human action over scientific psychological representations. In a slightly different vein, Tajfel (1978) emphasized the need to replace the outsider's ('objective') view of social groups with an insider's ('subjective') perspective.

Apparently similar concerns are also voiced in post-crisis social psychology. In this case, the call for the valorization of common sense appears to draw variously on postmodern, dialogic, Marxist and feminist intellectual sources. Parker and Shotter (1990), for example, criticize 'traditional social psychology' on the basis that its constructs (such as 'prejudice', 'attitudes' or 'learned helplessness') do not make sense to ordinary people (p. 12). They point to the existence of 'a world in which only the voice of the professional has currency, while the voices of those outside are rendered silent' (p. 9), in which people are denied the right to negotiate the meanings that academics impose upon their acts and words. They call for the 'deconstruction of the theoretical texts in social psychology, which fail to give a voice to oppressed people', linked to a 'deconstruction of the institutional apparatus of psychology' (p. 12). They argue that an attempt should be made 'to reconstruct the aim of social studies as a rhetorical enterprise in which the voices of those who are other than professional "scientists" can be heard' (p. 13). This is amplified by Shotter (1990):

> . . . no matter how benevolent a professional psychologist one may be towards those one studies, no matter how concerned with 'their' liberation, with 'their' betterment . . . the fact is that 'their' lives are not made sense of in 'their' terms.

> While what they say is treated as 'data', they themselves are not treated seriously as being able to speak the truth about their own lives. (p. 168)

He suggests that:

> instead of thinking it possible for special individuals trained in special methods simply to make 'discoveries', any further specifications of states of affairs, if they are to be considered *intelligible and legitimate* to those around us, must be negotiated in a step-by-step process with them. (pp. 159–160; emphasis in original)

This sort of perspective is particularly common amongst feminist academics. Sue Wilkinson (1986, p. 2) summarized this perspective as it is manifested in feminist social psychology, 'research is based on an exploration of women's own knowledge and experience. . . . A female perspective is to be regarded as central to the research'. This, according to Wilkinson, entails 'a critical evaluation of the research process, in terms of its adequacy in tapping women's experience'. Perhaps the most voluble advocate of this position within psychology in recent years has been Carol Gilligan (e.g. Gilligan, 1977, 1982; Brown and Gilligan, 1992).

At the European Association of Experimental Social Psychology small group meeting for which the present chapter was originally written, the critical social psychology project was often presented in these sorts of terms. The following are just a few examples of the comments that were made in the course of discussion:

> What we need to do as critical social psychologists is to let people speak about their own experiences.

> It is important to allow voices to be heard.

> The aim should be to give underprivileged people a voice.

> We must take care not to do violence to someone else's story in the name of presenting data.

> We must listen to what people have to tell us.

> In a world based on silencing we need a commitment to let different voices speak.

Thus, there seems to be some agreement that we should 'democratize the inputs' to psychological knowledge (that we should stand aside and listen while people tell us of their experience). Also, as the last quotation indicates, it is often proposed that we should appreciate a multiplicity of different voices. This is, for example, a prevalent theme in the writings of Ken Gergen (1989):

> . . . if psychology is to fulfil its avowed role of benefiting humankind, the doors should be opened to multiplicity in perspective. Rather than singing the same old refrain decade after decade . . . a premium should be placed on new songs. (pp. 79–80).

Celebrating Multiple Voices: The Practice

Notwithstanding any stated concern to 'listen to' and celebrate multiple, divergent representations of human nature and social life, critical social psychology texts normally take the form of a monovocal meta-narrative, authored by the researcher. In the process of analysing the 'stories' of the research subjects, the critical social psychologist typically fragments accounts with the consequence that the respondents' words no longer constitute proper or well-formed stories in their own right. The author then takes on the task of editing, re-packaging and re-sequencing these accounts in order to form a new narrative, the researcher's story (Squire, 1990), in which the words of the researched are not 'celebrated' in their own right, but used in a variety of ways to authorize the author's own claims. I shall explore this issue more fully in the next section. For the time being I shall focus on those (relatively rare) occasions on which the critical social psychologist does present the reader with 'voices' (transcribed conversations or accounts) which, in their own right, might appear to approximate to a well-formed narrative. I shall argue that, when we consider the ways in which these are used in the text as a whole, we can see that they are used exclusively in the service of the author's own stories. This may be accomplished in two ways: by *enlisting the other* (i.e. by using the subjects' words as confirmation of one's own), or by *constructing serviceable others*, to borrow Sampson's phrase (i.e. by quoting the subjects to exemplify positions of difference between the speaker and the writer who *reports* their account) (cf. Volossinov [1929/1973]).

I shall start by considering the less common of these two strategies: that of *enlisting the other*, that is, granting the subject's voice the status of testimonial in support for the author's own claims. Notwithstanding any stated concern for hearing a multitude of voices, we are, in fact, highly selective in which voices we allow to 'speak for themselves'. Mary Gergen (1992), for example, suggests at the beginning of her article on gender differences in popular autobiography, '[m]y voice shall be only one of many to be heard' (p. 127). She adopts a postmodern authorial style in which her own words are interspersed with quotations from others. But these others are not a cacophony of conflicting voices, but a selection of quotations from other academics which all, without exception, concur with what the author has just said, or exemplify a point that she is in the process of making. Similarly, on the rare occasions in which a researcher attempts to build a story on the basis of (relatively) direct testimony from research subjects, she is normally very careful concerning which 'others' she chooses as informants. Hollway (1989), for example, in her imaginative study of subjectivity in heterosexual relations reports having selected as participants individuals who practised 'self analysis', who would provide her with 'more than a rationalized, seamless and abstracted account of themselves' (p. 17), and that she preferred people who expressed 'a multiplicity of meanings in their subjective experience' (p. 17) so that she could, on the basis of these accounts, 'develop a theory of multiple and contradictory subjectivity' (p. 18).

One way in which we may legitimate selecting *particular* people as informants is by using the term 'people' in its exclusive rather than its inclusive sense (Burke, 1992), to refer to members of subordinate social groups rather than to the population as a whole. In effect, our concern for 'hearing multiple voices' often owes less to postmodern theoretical perspectives than to a Marxist valorization of the view from below.[8] The concern is not with multiplicity and variety per se, but to air those particular ('silenced') common senses which are construed as arising from, and challenging, experiences of oppression. So, for example, Griffin (1985) does not ironize young women's talk about factory employment and unemployment, but is prepared to contradict their employers' accounts of the 'laziness' and 'disruptiveness' of young Afro-Caribbean women. Nevertheless, it is rarely the case that even when research might be seen as granting voice to the disenfranchised, the researcher simply hands over authority to the speaking subjects. As Griffin reflects, although she took her young women's words seriously, she did not necessarily take them 'at face value in any simplistic way' (p. 5).

Not only do we select our informants carefully, we are also selective in choosing which aspects of an individual or group's testimony to hold up for celebration. Even when studying members of low-status social groups, critical social psychologists rarely give the people full rein to speak for themselves. Sampson (1991) himself is very selective in the accounts he presents from non-Western others. For example, he celebrates the 'fact' that the Ifaluk of Micronesia demonstrate a communal way of defining the person (as illustrated by their use of 'we' when a Westerner might use the singular, 'I'). It is, I would contend, no coincidence that Sampson appropriates from Lutz's (1985) account *only* those aspects of Ifaluk ethnopsychology which appear (to him) to parallel discourses of communal identity used in radical social movements in the contemporary West (cf. Moscovici, 1972; Reicher, 1987). On other matters, the Ifaluk remain doomed to silence. Sampson does not choose to inform us, for example, that there are three categories of actors among Ifaluk (as represented by Lutz). The human persons (*yaremat*), with whom Sampson is apparently solely concerned, exist alongside, and in communication with, a Catholic God and spirits (*yalus*). Even in his more detailed discussion of the various ways in which self-boundaries may be conceptualized outwith the West, Sampson (1993) does not assert the equal reality of non-Western worlds inhabited by gods and ancestors, in which spirits experience envy and compassion, or in which the physical terrain experiences emotions (Kirkpatrick & White, 1985).

Selectivity and silencing are not the only techniques we employ to ensure that our voices are heard over and above those of our subjects. We also employ various strategies to indicate our acceptance or rejection of various aspects of people's stories as we relate them. Billig (1978), for example, in his sensitive analysis of an interview with 'P', cannot celebrate this working-class fascist's story in its own terms. P *is* granted authority to speak about his biographical details and the history of his involvement with the National Front, but other aspects of his account are marked quite clearly as P's 'beliefs' or as things that P 'said'. In this way Billig marks his own authorial status as *animator* rather than *principal* (Goffman, 1981). At times the de-authorization of P's story is accomplished by placing P's words in scare quotes to separate clearly the voice of the reporter from the voice of the reported ('P's view on what is "really" happening', p. 214; 'P said he had nothing against "coloured people"', p. 221). And at one point, when reporting P's comments concerning his inability to 'have a joke with' a 'coloured fellow', Billig allows himself openly to interject: 'One might speculate about those "jokes" which blacks fail to find funny when told by a member of the National Front' (p. 222). A common example of this practice within current critical social psychology can be found in the use of the 'disclaimer' repertoire in accounts of 'racist discourse'. It is now relatively common for analysts to identify statements made by their research subjects which take the form of 'I'm not racist, but . . .'. In such cases, the respondent's gloss on their own words is rarely accepted by the authors who relay these accounts. On the contrary, the analysts typically treat such representations as 'disclaiming devices' – prefixes to the 'real' body of the message which (the authors inform us) 'really is' (functionally) racist. The respondent's claim to a (non-racist) identity, their representation of their own account as 'not prejudiced', is overruled by the analyst who grants them instead a new identity, as a person-who-is-trying-to-save-face (cf. Billig et al., 1988).

Another way in which we impose our meta-narrative over the discourse of others is by packaging quotations from research respondents in a story which overtly or covertly informs the reader what they should make of the quotations we have presented to them. For example, Wetherell and Potter (1992) inform the reader explicitly how they should interpret quotations from interviews with middle-class white New Zealanders. Furthermore, in order to access these snippets of stories, readers must first open a book with the word 'RACISM' emblazoned in large letters on the cover, and 'the legitimation of exploitation' readily visible in the subtitle.

This brings us to the second way in which critical social psychologists may use the words of their research subjects: *to construct 'serviceable others'*. This involves the presentation of fragments of accounts as a foil for our own (and our putative readers') identities and claims. I have already noted one way in which we can distance ourselves (and our readers) from our subjects by objectifying their accounts as 'beliefs' and 'statements'. Critical social psychologists can also transform their research subjects into 'serviceable others' in a rather more subtle way. We know that the processes of placing an account 'in social context' and of deconstructing or otherwise exposing the rhetorical 'tricks' of an utterance are (in terms of the common sense of our societies) conventional rhetorical means of undermining the authority of a speaker (e.g. Latour, 1988). Though we may deny that our intention in analysing accounts is to critique them (e.g. Billig, 1990), covertly we use this knowledge to our own advantage. Our concern for reflexivity would, if taken seriously, encourage us to develop symmetrical (Bloor, 1976) accounts: ones in which we applied the same rules to all discourses or claims to knowledge. Most critical social psychology which employs deconstructionist or discourse analytic methods does not do this. Rather, we apply our analytical devices to just those issues, voices or discourses which we oppose. We unpick the rhetorical tricks of Tory politicians, but not socialist ones; we scrutinize health-care literature aimed at women but not feminist texts. We map the language of racism, but not of anti-racism, the accounts of White New Zealanders, but not of Maoris. We note variability in the accounts of scientists and mainstream social psychologists, but not those of discourse analysts (cf. Ashmore, 1989).[9] In this way, whilst appearing non-judgemental, we play on the fact that our analysis has the effect of undermining the accounts we use as data.

In general, then, notwithstanding the apparent concern on the part of some critical social psychologists for a 'democratization of inputs', it is nevertheless the case that the authoritative voice of the critical social psychologist can still be heard over and above (and sometimes even shouting down!) the research subjects. Despite Sampson's suggestion of the 'democratic' nature of the current turn to language in social psychology, it is clear that the texts to which he refers, and others like them, are, in fact, decidedly autocratic. In the next section I shall go on to argue that most of the current work in critical social psychology actually rests upon a claim to academic authority. Social psychologists, such as those whom Sampson tries to enlist for his 'democracy' project, typically assume that they have a privileged representation of human nature and social behaviour (cf. Gergen, 1989). These authority claims tend not to be advertised to the same extent as the claims to democratic voice (although see Billig, 1988, for an exception). Nevertheless, it is common for critical social psychologists to emphasize that their (academic) analyses go beyond the conscious awareness of the actors themselves.

Knowing More Than They Can Tell: Constructing the View from the Panopticon

> I was frustrated in my direct inquiries seeking reasons for their food avoidances. They would never say, 'we avoid anomalous animals because in defying the categories of our universe they arouse deep feelings of disquiet'. (Douglas, 1966/ 1991, p. 173)

Claiming a Superior Point of View: The Psychological Heritage

It seems likely that current practices in critical social psychology may owe something to our academic socialization in (social) psychology. Clearly, we struggle against our intellectual roots, and we are often concerned to distance ourselves from claims to scientific authority. But I think we may have underestimated the power of these formative influences. In the quotation cited above, Mary Douglas is commenting ironically on the established practice in anthropology, and in many types of sociology (cf. Gilbert & Mulkay, 1983), which treats people as 'informants'. The assumption here is that people can report directly on the phenomena we are interested in, albeit with greater or lesser degrees of accuracy. The tradition in (social) psychology, however, has been rather different. In our training *as psychologists*, we are not simply alerted to the fact that people may, when confronted with a researcher, lie or attempt to save face. Our oral history is replete with legends concerning the power of the unconscious, of the process of denial, of the misplaced confidence and subsequent tragic fall of the introspectionists. This reluctance to take people's accounts at face value is not, I would contend, based on a simple belief in scientific method (cf. Billig, 1990). Psychologists are often concerned with issues which could not be addressed by eliciting testimonials from research subjects. They deal with populations who may conventionally be regarded as unreliable witnesses: children and the insane being amongst the most obvious. Moreover, even the most humanist of psychologists would not consider it sensible to ask people to report on their neuroanatomy ('just where did you say those synapses were firing again?') or low-level mental processes ('what will be the effects of priming on your reaction times?'). Our success in teaching apes sign-language has not been so remarkable that we can yet pose direct questions of animals, and human infants are also likely to prove unsatisfactory interviewees.[10]

Not only does a great deal of psychological subject matter not lend itself to research using personal testimony, it is also the case that as psychologists we have been raised on fables warning us against believing what our subjects say, even when they appear to be capable of reporting on their own experience. Billig (1990) suggests that psychologists' rejection of common sense has not been based on 'any alleged empirical finding'. I disagree. Lurking behind our academic consciousness are those formative experiences in the library and laboratory that demonstrated the fallibility of human memory; that informed us that we may report things we do not see (affected, for example, by the presence of others); that we may see things that do not happen (stationary dots can be perceived as moving); that we may see things without being conscious of having done so (perception may be subliminal). We have all read about studies that show that memory can be tacit, and that people may tell more than they can know, and we have all seen, captured on tired videotape, nice North American folk informing Stanley Milgram that neither they nor any other sane person would administer potentially fatal electric shocks to a sick man. Psychologists' valorization of academic accounts over folk psychology has not necessarily been warranted with reference to the power of scientific method per se. Rather, it has also been justified through detailed and convincing stories of how some privileged folk (in this case, experimental psychologists) may sometimes be, quite literally, in a position to see things which are not visible to ordinary folk (see also Reicher, this volume).

Claiming a Superior Point of View: Critical Social Psychological Perspectives

We, too, commonly construct our positions as critical social psychologists as ones which place us to 'see better' than common folk. We may berate ourselves for inhabiting ivory towers (Wilkinson, this volume) but at the same time recognize that we would be foolish to relinquish so privileged a vantage point. In our research practice we employ a series of technologies designed to render visible phenomena and processes which may not be perceived in the normal run of everyday life. In our ivory towers we amass, record, catalogue and compare samples of human behaviour. By using procedures such as video recordings and the transcription of verbal data we are able to hold time static, to replay and analyse in detail phenomena which are experienced only fleetingly if, indeed, they are consciously experienced at all. The procedure of re-presenting spoken words in written form also allows us to collapse time: to hear synchronically words which were uttered at different points in time. By bringing together in one place samples of human activity gathered from different contexts, we are able to juxtapose phenomena normally experienced in isolation. By the use of various recording and cataloguing devices we are able to regard phenomena and events synoptically, cross-reference them and note covariance between them. In these respects our 'critical' research procedures have much in common with the (normalizing) psychological gaze (Rose, 1990b) and with scientific research more generally (Latour, 1987).

The Micro-social Microscope Many critical social psychology perspectives focus on the minutiae of everyday life. This sort of concern is particularly evident in the 'turn to language', including such approaches as narrative psychology, discourse analysis, conversation analysis and rhetorical psychology. There are two things worth noting about this work. First is the fairly obvious fact that although analysts may work with people's accounts, they are not, by and large, interested in the content of people's 'stories' (cf. Sampson, 1991). Second, these academic theories and research techniques are typically directed towards phenomena of which the actors themselves are rarely deemed to have any conscious awareness. We do not assume that people can tell us the rules they use for sequencing conversation, the type of narrative convention they employ when relating their life-story, the ways in which they warrant their claims, or the extent of variability in their accounts.

In sociology, the distinction between being able to perform an act and being able to explain or describe that performance is often discussed in terms of a distinction between 'practical' and 'discursive' consciousness

(Bourdieu, 1977; Giddens, 1979). This distinction is regarded as particularly relevant to the analysis of habit, and to mundane, routine activities (cf. Edwards and Mercer's, 1987, account of ritual knowledge). In distinguishing between practical and discursive consciousness, analysts do not generally deny the existence of intentional, purposive action for which people may be able to account with reference to individual motives or social rules. However, it is argued that, although people may be able to articulate 'reasons' for action, they may none the less be unaware of their 'true' motives and of how particular social events actually came to take place (Giddens, 1991). Bourdieu (1977), in particular, in his explicitly empiricist account, has drawn theorists' attention to what he terms the implicit 'universe of the undisputed':

> The explanation agents may provide of their own practice . . . conceals, even from their own eyes, the true nature of their practical mastery, i.e. that it is *learned ignorance* . . . a mode of practical knowledge not comprising knowledge of its own principles. It follows that this learned ignorance can only give rise to the misleading discourse of a speaker himself misled, ignorant both of the objective truth about his practical mastery . . . and of the true principle of the knowledge his practical mastery contains. (p. 19; emphasis in original)

It is often suggested that it is the very taken-for-granted nature of everyday life, in which feelings may be inchoate (Shotter, 1993) and social rules incompletely discursively formulated, which necessitates academic inquiry. Harré (1993), for example, suggests that '[t]he task of social psychology is, above all, to make explicit all that is tacit in a form of life' (p. 107).

One particular set of social psychological constructs which may reach beyond the awareness of social actors are those which take place in the course of interaction between two or more co-present individuals. This is particularly the case when critical social psychologists voice a concern with dialogism and with relational acts. These sorts of concerns have, for example, been central to Shotter's (e.g. 1980, 1984, 1993) work. Shotter's aim has been to consider the way in which individual action is embedded in micro-social contexts of which the actors may be only vaguely aware, but which nevertheless shape and constrain the possibility for action on the part of any particular participant. One aspect of this work has been a concern with jointly constructed outcomes: the processes by which co-acting individuals may end up producing, through their own activity, outcomes which were not necessarily designed by any of the parties concerned. In this situation, it is often impossible for the individuals themselves to explain the outcomes of that interaction (see also Giddens, 1979, for a sociological version).

At this point it is worth noting a paradox in Sampson's work. Sampson calls both for the development of dialogism as an analytic tool for (social) psychologists, and also for a respect for people's own accounts of their action. It is difficult to see how both of these objectives could be accomplished unless it were the case that folk psychologies also draw attention to dialogic processes. Insofar as this is not the case, then it follows that the social psychologists' theoretical commitment to dialogism must be prioritized over the common sense of the folk themselves. This is a specific instance of a more general problem in Sampson's account: the tendency to confuse what social scientists 'discover' about human activity with the discursive consciousness of the actors themselves. This is apparent, in particular, in Sampson's discussion of Lave's (1988) work on everyday problem-solving. Lave takes issue with the common observation that everyday arithmetical problem-solving does not conform to normative models of good thinking. She claims that, viewed in the context of the types of decisions that people make in their real lives, their methods of problem-solving need not be seen as irrational. What is *not* apparent from Lave's work is that her subjects were themselves able to report exactly how they were going about their everyday cognitive tasks, or that they knew how their methods differed from standards of rational decision-making. Lave's analysis of everyday problem-solving rests upon her *own* constructions, not upon the meta-cognitive discursive consciousness of her subjects.

Context Lenses   A second set of concerns which characterize critical social psychological work are those relating to 'context'. Sampson (1991) suggests that psychologists should 'become adept in conducting social and historical analyses as a central element in our education and our role as psycho-logists' (p. 291), although he gives us no clues as to how this might be accomplished. Both Rex Stainton Rogers (this volume) and Wetherell and Potter (1992) have recently adopted cartography metaphors to describe their attempts to 'place' and 'trace' observed behaviour across a discursive, cultural and sociological plane. Another popular stance taken in critical social psychological work is to view current social practices through a historical lens. This may involve developing genealogies of current practices (Rose, 1990b), or interpreting people's everyday behaviour against a historical backdrop (Billig, 1988; Billig et al., 1988; Wetherell & Potter, 1992; cf. Gergen, 1973). Other critical social psychological perspectives aim for a more diachronic perspective, attempting to chart the flows of discourses or information across a social plane (e.g. Farr & Moscovici, 1984). All of these academic strategies involve contextualizing human behaviour in a historical frame which the analyst recognizes to be largely invisible to the actors who are living the historical moment. It is unlikely, for example, that any of the conversants whose behaviour is discussed in *Ideological Dilemmas* (Billig et al., 1988) were aware that the terms of their common sense derived from the ideas of the Enlightenment, any more than people in contemporary France are aware of the roots of many of their taken-for-granted constructs in psychoanalysis (Farr & Moscovici, 1984).

Our social psychological context lenses also enable us to develop a synchronic account of human behaviour *in the context of* contemporary social structural arrangements. Wetherell and Potter (1992) point to the need for studies of racism to take account of institutional practices and social structures. Griffin (1985), similarly, locates the voices of the school leavers she interviews in a wider social and political context which she constructs for the reader. It is usually tacitly assumed that this contextualization of the talk and practices we record and relay to the reader cannot be achieved simply by asking members of oppressed social groups to speak the truth about their lives. It has been well documented in sociology that people do not necessarily perceive social structure (as constructed by sociologists and economists) directly (Giddens, 1979). As Bourdieu (1977) remarked:

> Native experience of the social world never apprehends the system of objective relations other than *in profiles*, i.e. in the form of relations which present themselves only one by one . . . in the emergency situations of everyday life. (p. 18)[11]

It follows then that as critical social psychologists we are often concerned with what anthropologists often call 'experience distant' constructs (Geertz, 1983), which do not reflect the constructs that social actors use in their mundane lives.[12]

In the course of contextualizing actors' accounts and performances in a historical or sociological frame, we often rely on information about the 'social' which is based on the accumulation of statistics. The sorts of social categories and processes constructed (or 'revealed') by such statistics do not simply or necessarily reflect the lived experience of social actors (Hacking, 1982). Neither can social actors necessarily be attributed with our awareness of those correlations which point to the influence of macro-social process on everyday subjectivity and activity (Mott & Condor, in press). For example, in 1990 I took part in a conference symposium entitled 'Why Students do Psychology'. Most of the researchers had attempted to answer this question by asking students why they 'chose to do psychology'. The students' responses were certainly interesting, not least for what they omitted to mention. About 80 per cent of psychology students in the UK are female and from professional middle-class families. Not one respondent in any of these self-report studies speculated that their 'choice' of degree subject had in any way been influenced by their gender or by their social class background (Condor, 1990).

Constructing Supra-individual Actors   One of the major aims of critical social psychology is to develop constructs of social life and activity which go 'beyond' the individual social actor.[13] Sampson (1991) makes it clear that his concern with ethnopsychology lies at the level of the 'community' or 'the social world' rather than the individual. A similar concern for the supra-individual actor is evidenced in dialogical approaches such as that of Shotter already mentioned, and also in a variety of other popular critical social psychological constructs, such as interpretative repertoires (Potter & Wetherell, 1987), culture (Parker, 1988), ideology (Billig, 1991; Moscovici, 1972; Sampson, 1981; Wetherell & Potter, 1992), actor networks (Michael,

1996) and social representations (Farr & Moscovici, 1984) (see Condor, 1989, for a discussion of constructions of 'the social').

Some critical social psychology perspectives do imply that it may be possible to study a population, group or social system at the level of the individual subject. This is particularly the case, for example, in Turner's (1987) self-categorization model, which presents social systems as located in the heads of individual subjects ('the group in the individual'). In contrast, other theorists have made it plain that they conceive of the 'social' as a domain existing between, rather than within, the consciousness of individuals. They may construct 'the social' as a 'system' (Sampson, 1993), and stress the way in which social knowledge, or linguistic repertoires (Potter & Wetherell, 1987), may be distributed across individuals (Harré, 1983; Shotter, 1993). More radically still, they may conceive the world in terms of a dynamic network of social and non-human agents (Condor, 1996; Michael, 1996).

To the extent that our ability to construct these supra-individual actors depends upon a particular visual field which allows us to collapse time and space, it is unlikely that our constructs will be fully reflected in the everyday understandings of the people we study. This is not to deny a two-way flow of images between popular and social scientific arena (what Giddens terms the 'double hermeneutic'). However, we should be wary of assuming that our abstract ('critical') social scientific formulations necessarily reflect the experience near constructs of social actors. Somewhat paradoxically, it would appear that the sorts of constructs that critical social psychologists deploy are far more experience distant than are those of Normal Social Psychology. At this point I should like to argue openly with Parker and with Shotter (1990) (see p. 121). In contemporary Western societies, at least, 'ordinary people' routinely understand themselves and others with recourse to constructs such as 'personality', 'attitudes', 'prejudice' and so forth. They are far less inclined to embrace constructs such as social constructionism or dialogism, to see themselves as the conduits of disembodied 'linguistic repertoires' or 'ideologies', or to view social life in terms of networks of human and non-human agents.

At the start of this section I drew a parallel between the research activities of critical social psychology and the sorts of procedures described by Latour (1987) as taking place in 'centres of (scientific) calculation'. Latour argues that the (scientific) knowledge gained in centres of calculation is as local and context-dependent as the ethnologic of ordinary folk. Knowledge which relies upon accumulating a range of evidence, on comparing instances and on collapsing time and space cannot be constructed anywhere by anyone. At the very least, in order to be in a position to reach the same conclusions that we do from our centres of (critical social psychological) calculation, 'other' folk would require (Western?) scholarship and academic grounding (Billig, 1987), literacy, numeracy and access to hardware such as tape recorders, photocopiers, techniques of statistical analysis and so forth. In addition to the technology and other resources to acquire and interpret this evidence, the folk would, of course, need the will to knowledge. 'They' would have to want to know about human behaviour, and about social representations of human nature. 'They' would have to share our socio-logical imagination and a concern for historicity. 'They' would have to want to know about flows of information throughout the social body, about the relationship between human activity and social structure.

The View from the West: Authority, Radicalism and the Missionary Position

> Someone, an authoritative, elegant, learned voice, speaks and analyses, amasses evidence, theorizes, speculates, about everything – except itself. (Said, 1978, p. 212)

> Of course, the 'I' who writes . . . must also be thought of as, itself, 'enunciated'. We all write and speak from a particular place and time, from a history and a culture which is specific. What we say is always 'in context', *positioned*. (Hall, 1990, p. 222)

Up to this point I have considered two ways in which critical social psy-chologists may warrant their academic accounts. The first, advocated by Sampson and by many feminist authors (see Mott and Condor, in press), involves the writer adopting the guise of a neutral spokesperson, claiming authority to speak on behalf of others (cf. Leudar and Antaki, this volume; Goffman, 1981). The second (and more usual) way in which we warrant our accounts is by laying claim to particular, expert knowledge. In this final section of the chapter I shall return to consider the question of how critical social psychologists may authorize their accounts by glossing their claims as 'democracy', but this time in a more critical vein. Clearly, it is the case that all social actors need to employ a variety of rhetorical devices to authorize their accounts, and (critical) social psychologists are no different. I do not intend to question the use of this rhetorical strategy because it *is* a rhetorical strategy, nor do I criticize it simply on the grounds that (as we have already seen) it misrepresents much current critical social psychological practice. Rather, my objection to 'democratization' – the claim to speak on behalf of 'the people' – is based on the fact that it exemplifies (and is underpinned by) an assumption that, as critical social psychologists, we speak universal truths. In the following pages I shall outline some of the ways in which we (critical) social psychologists may fail to take account of our positions of enunciation, and I shall finally go on to consider Sampson's proposal for the 'democratization of psychology' as essentially *positioned*.

Escape from Context: The Dream of Zion

> . . . if indeed psychology's subject is a sociohistorical, sociocultural product . . . then it must necessarily 'belong' to its particular time and place. In this sense, 'belong to' means to fit the ongoing structures and arrangements of current Western society. (Sampson, 1989, pp. 2–3)

For all our commitment to social constructionism and our concern with ideology, critical social psychologists nevertheless often imply that it is theoretically possible to find a place outside or on the margins of context, a position from which our voices are not contaminated by the same discourses or ideological forces as are those of our subjects. Often we construct ourselves in the image of Mannheim's 'free floating intellectual'. This attempt to escape context is apparent in our common (though often implicit) assumption that whereas the psi-sciences (to use Foucault's term) are 'the child of modernity' (Kvale, 1992), in concert with 'the Western project' (Sampson, 1990, 1991), a lynch-pin in the machinery of disciplinary society (Rose, 1990b), the same is not equally true of other academic disciplines. Sampson's suggestion that psychologists renounce their discipline in favour of social anthropology is but one example of numerous emigration fantasies which have been proposed as solutions for our academic dysphoria.[14] But to what extent is it possible to see other disciplines as located outside the ongoing structures and arrangements of current Western society? Sociology, with its concern to map the social body, arose at the same historical juncture as did the psi-sciences with their complementary interests in identifying individuals from the social array (Nisbet, 1976). Sociologists, like social psychologists, have suffered crises of confidence, recognizing the ways in which their discipline may contribute to social surveillance:

> Sociologists stand guard in the garrison and report to their masters on the movements of the occupied populace. The more adventurous sociologists don the disguise of the people and go out to mix with the peasants in the 'field', returning with books and articles that break the protective secrecy in which a subjected population wraps itself, and make it more accessible to manipulation and control. (Nicolaus, 1969, p. 155)

Anthropology also is an intellectual product of the modern West (Scholte, 1978). Although Sampson apparently regards it as an antidote to Psychology, we should note that anthropology's past is no less murky than our own, originating as it did as the intellectual arm of nineteenth-century Western imperialism (Asad, 1973; Dwyer, 1977; Gough, 1967; Hymes, 1974). Even cartography, which developed in its present form in the expansionist atmosphere of early modern Europe, cannot provide an ideologically neutral metaphor for our activity.

The fantasy of a 'place outside' culture is partly fuelled by images of hegemonic or dominant ideologies (cf. Abercrombie, Hill & Turner, 1980), all-embracing systems of thought and practice. When cultural practices are viewed in this light, it follows that critiques and challenges can only originate from spaces 'outside' or 'on the margins'. In contrast, however, there has been a recent trend amongst Western scholars to point to ways in which challenges to the existing structures and arrangements of Western society may originate from *inside* the system itself. This issue has been discussed at some length by Young (1990), who, in criticizing Said's assumption that intellectuals may be 'distanced' from mainstream culture, argues that 'resistance, like power, is part of culture itself' (p. 133). Similar viewpoints have also begun to infiltrate critical social psychology (e.g. Billig et al., 1988; Wetherell & Potter, 1992). If this is the case, it follows that the social sciences themselves may be used as a power base from which to subvert as well as sustain the status quo (Rose, 1990a, 1990b). I do not wish to overstate this point. I do not deny, as Walkerdine and Lucey (1989) so eloquently point out, the possibility of opposition to colonialism and patriarchy arising from the experiences of oppression, that '[t]here *are* other stories, other accounts, there is resistance and fighting that all the covert regulation in the world cannot completely keep down' (1989, p. 151). But I would contend that even these fantasies of opposition, of other possible worlds, are fashioned from available cultural resources. The other possible worlds that we critical social psychologists visualize (whether or not based on personal experience of oppression) do not, by and large, encompass personal escape through opportune marriage, of social transformation through magic, cosmic forces or divine intervention. Our fantasies of the collective refashioning of society, of the overturn of relations of domination through human action, draw from Enlightenment fantasies of human self-determination, freedom and equality. The fact that we may construct ourselves as 'critical' need not imply that our own perspectives are not as contingent as the discourses and ideological forces we oppose.

Our 'View from Nowhere': The Decontextualization of Critical
Social Psychology

Critical social psychologists do not only suggest that they might (potentially) lay claim to an acontextual, universal voice. Very often we imply that we already do so. Bruno Latour (1993), amongst others, has pointed to the way in which the sanctioned sciences 'tear themselves away from all context, from any traces of contamination by history'. It seems that, notwithstanding a general commitment to reflexivity, critical social psychology often does the same. We, too, fail to articulate our own positions of enunciation, presenting our ideas as a 'view from nowhere' (Nagel, 1986) in a manner not dissimilar to that displayed in the scientific psychological texts which have attracted so much ridicule from more reflexive social psychologists and feminist critics.[15] Sampson, for example, uses what Gilbert and Mulkay (e.g. 1984) call a 'contingent repertoire' to delegitimate the claims of cognitive psychologists (he suggests that their constructs are not universal but part of the 'Western project'). Moreover, he claims that these cognitive constructs are empirically false: 'There is no such creature as the self-contained individual, meaningfully abstracted from others' (Sampson, 1993, p. 166). In contrast, he presents dialogism as a universal, transhistoric truth: 'a correct view of how human nature is formed and sustained' (p. 171).[16] Sampson, of course, is not alone in this. It is common for critical social psychologists to present their own constructs ('variability', 'history' and, most ironically, 'social constructionism') as indisputable, universally true 'facts'.[17]

More generally, we critical social psychologists tend to universalize our own concerns with 'culture' and with knowing and changing the social body (cf. Latour, 1993; Michael, this volume). We fail to articulate the positions of enunciation which enable us to value ('recognize') fluidity and multiplicity and to appreciate (in both senses) open-ended interpretation and argumentation. We seldom consider how our vision of fragmented and inessential selves, our self-reflexivity and concern with ethical self-fashioning are themselves historically and socially located in late modernity (Berman, 1982) or postmodernity (Lyotard, 1979) (see Friedman, 1992, for a discussion of this point with respect to the adoption of dialogic models in anthropology, and Lemaire, 1991, for a discussion of cultural criticism as an 'occidental obsession'). This neglect is particularly apparent when we enlist evidence from 'the past' or from 'other' cultures to warrant our claims about contemporary Western social life. This is the case, for example, in Sampson's (1988, 1991, 1993) and Gergen's (1973) use of anthropological examples of personhood in 'simple', 'cold' societies as models for the ethical reformulation of people in late twentieth-century North America.[18]

At this point it becomes pertinent to question the use to which Sampson is putting the 'non-Western others' he constructs in his texts. In place of constructing 'serviceable others' (repositories of characteristics and values we deny in ourselves (Said, 1978)), Sampson constructs a romantic, idealized image of 'women' and of 'non-Western' people in an attempt to construct models for the reconstitution of dominant Western selves. The problem is, of course, that in so doing, Sampson is also enlisting the Other into a Western project (the modernist project of critical reflexivity and concern with social transformation through human agency).

In this respect Sampson's treatment of the exotic Other reflects a long tradition within Western scholarship (Barkan, 1992; Rousseau and Porter, 1990). Self-celebratory accounts, in which intellectuals of the Enlightenment constructed the Other as a foil for the West, have always been accompanied by the converse rhetorical move: the use of travellers' tales of non-Western Others to destabilize and to question the taken-for-granted assumptions of the writers' own societies (Porter, 1990).

Sampson himself seems unaware of this, partly because he fails to see his own mission (to reformulate the self and thereby reorganize the social body in the interests of human emancipation) as in any way culturally or historically positioned. At various points in his texts, Sampson (1991, 1993) criticizes the 'values of the Enlightenment', by which he means the construct of universal human nature and the value of the self-contained individual. He does not reflect on the fact that many of the values he himself expresses might themselves be regarded as components of enlightenment thought. In fact, it is quite easy to see the preoccupations of the enlightenment mirrored in Sampson's work, as well as in the writings of most other critical social psychologists. This is apparent, for example, in our prioritization of the interests of the collectivity over the 'law of the fathers'. It is apparent in our sociologism: our secular vision of society as an object for rational study and as a domain for moral judgement and action (Porter, 1990). It is reflected in our self-positioning as intellectuals with a responsibility – an obligation – for the monitoring of society (Bauman, 1995), and in our belief that by the application of rationality we may free human beings from inherited inequalities. Sampson's (1991, p. 292) project for (social) psychology – to help people to 'gain a critical reflection of their own circumstances along with the alternatives so that they can be sufficiently informed to be the *demos*' – vividly reflects the enlightenment assumption that 'the education of the individual must . . . expose him to rational knowledge and prepare him to be part of a society which organizes the action of reason' (Touraine, 1995, p. 12). The very foundations on which Sampson's argument rests – cultural relativism, a concern for human equality and emancipation, for 'rights', 'tolerance' and 'democracy' – are all key features of classic enlightenment thought. Sampson (1991) regards it as 'paradoxical' that it will be the more 'democratic' countries which will welcome his definition of 'the problem' and the solution he offers. But this is no paradox. As Sampson himself acknowledges, the ideals which he sets up as (and, no doubt, assumes to be) cross-cultural and transhistoric universals are, in fact, the positioned truths of contemporary Western societies.

Democracy as Western Ethno-logic

Despite Sampson's attempts at descriptive relativism (the recognition of cultural variability), he subscribes only to a limited sense of normative or 'moral' relativism (which would suggest that cultures should be judged by their own standards – Spiro, 1986). There is, as far as Sampson (like most critical social psychologists) is concerned, a single, pancultural standard by which cultures may be judged: the Western standard of 'democracy'. Sampson is not alone in this. Potter (this volume) and Wetherell and Potter (1992) also suggest that a commitment to (descriptive) relativism need not preclude an adherence to (enlightenment) ideals of equality and an opposition to exploitation. In fact, it might be noted that, paradoxically, the notion of descriptive relativism might itself be seen to derive from enlightenment values of tolerance (Lemaire, 1991).

Through the procedure of associating dialogic social psychology with the value of 'democracy', and implicitly assuming the universality of the (or rather, a *particular form* of the) value of democracy, Sampson enlists as allies the whole of humanity. His proposals for the reformulation of academic psychology are thereby re-presented as what everyone (politically right or left, cognitive psychologist or psychoanalyst, scientist, scholar or citizen, man or woman, McDonald's employee from Kansas, Ifaluk taro cultivator or Islamic fundamentalist) wants. His claims are thereby presented as universal truths which nobody could deny. To appreciate the positioned nature of the value of democracy would lend quite a different reading of Sampson's work than that suggested by the author himself. Sampson (rather immodestly to my mind) suggests that his aim in proposing dialogism and ethnopsychology is to contribute to the downfall of Western civilization. In contrast, it could also be suggested that the 'democratization of psychology' could be viewed as part of the Western project. Not only does Sampson's work (unwittingly) universalize Western ideals and critical practices, it is also clear from Sampson's 1991 paper that he regards his goal of the democratization of society through the application of dialogical psychology to warrant the intervention of Western academics into the lives of others. Sampson's rejection of enlightenment thought does not prevent him from subscribing to a firm and unquestioned belief in the liberatory power of academic knowledge.[19] Despite Sampson's apparent concern for a 'democratization' of the inputs to Psychology, there is still a clear role for 'us' –one which is tacitly warranted in terms of 'our' superior expertise. 'We' are granted the role of educators. It is 'our' task to tell 'them' about the various exotic constructions of human nature that we have encountered and catalogued on our academic travels. 'We' also take on the task of telling 'them' how their current social constructions of human nature relate to the life of their community in order to equip 'them' as active citizens to implement the social change which we perceive to be necessary.

Paradoxically, a major function of Sampson's model of 'democratic psychology' is that it maintains *our* power, *as psychologists* and, in particular, *as Western academics*, inviolate. Sampson may claim to 'give away' psychology, but let us be clear about it: in his account it is still 'we' who are the psychologists. 'Others' play a role only insofar as they provide 'us' with information about 'them' (and, incidentally, about ourselves). But it is still 'we' who are the researchers and the harbingers of the new world order. It is up to 'us' to do the crucial work which will lead to our (human) Independence Day. At no stage does Sampson suggest that 'women' or the inhabitants of Micronesia, whose ethnopsychologies may be so informative, should 'be' psychologists. 'We' (like US foreign policy-makers?) take on the mantle of the global guardians and – if necessary – enforcers of democracy. In effect, dialogic social psychology is the White Man's Burden.

So what is the solution? To align our interests with the value of 'democracy' is an immensely powerful warrant. It creates an illusion of consensus, and thereby obscures the existence of disagreement and forecloses the possibility of debate. To the extent that we ourselves believe that our ideals are universal, this also forecloses on the critical reflexivity that we value so highly. Should we keep our critical social psychology project 'for us, among us', to borrow Mauss's famous words? Even when, in a situation of globalization, it may become increasingly difficult to ascertain who 'we' are? Maybe we should just come clean, and stop hiding behind the claim to represent the universal voice of human experience. Maybe we should be aware of, and make explicit, the grounding of our own claims in a particular cultural heritage and set of academic practices. Maybe we should be prepared to engage in argument: to make explicit our claim to a privileged and particular (Western, academic, politically left-wing) understanding of the human condition? Maybe we should also make explicit that we reject normative relativism and assert the absolute value of critical reflexivity, human equality and self-determination (cf. Kolakowski, 1983). If we are genuinely concerned to adopt democratic academic practice, maybe we should allow others the chance to refuse the critical social psychology (and with it the model of human being and social structure) which we are offering them.

Notes

Although I am happy to accept responsibility for authorship of this chapter, I could not have written it without the stimulation and support of my colleagues at Lancaster, many of whose ideas I have seen fit to plagiarize. I should also like to express particular thanks to Mick Billig and Mike Michael for their comments on an earlier draft of this chapter. Special thanks also to Richard Mobray for his technical advice and to Alan Collins for his presence in this text.

1. The reader will, of course, note my own use of the first person plural. The texts and authors alluded to here do, of course, vary in the extent to which they exemplify the various processes that I shall be outlining below. In particular, I anticipate that the reader may wish to distance her or his own work from some of the charges I make. My use of the terms 'us' and 'we' in this chapter concerned with the construction of supportive consensus in critical social psychological texts should, of course, be read ironically. However, it also has a serious purpose insofar as, for the purposes of this chapter, I am not concerned to attack individual authors, nor generally to prioritize one particular sort of account over another. Rather, my concern is with a series of processes which, I believe, concern us all (albeit in different ways), myself included.

2. The penetration (*sic*) of academic feminist accounts into Sampson's work, and other literature in this vein, is remarkable. However, it is interesting to recognize that only certain aspects of this work are used: in particular those accounts which argue for there being a particular feminine 'standpoint' or 'experience'. On a cynical note, it is worth raising the possibility that the popularity of this (particular, and by no means consensual, sub-theme in) feminist scholarship is due to the fact that it is one of the few examples within the critical social psychological literature in which the author can with some legitimacy herself speak *as* the 'other'. There are far fewer cases of researchers claiming authority to speak 'as' the working class (Walkerdine, this volume) or 'as' people of colour (Bhavnani, 1990) rather than as enlightened white middle-class academics who choose to 'side with', and help in constructing more positive representations of, these 'others'.

3. The category of 'the West', constructing Europe and the USA as a homogeneous social space, is clearly problematic. In my subsequent use of the term I shall be following Sampson, although I should be grateful if the reader would read the term as if placed in scare quotes.

4. If one wished to extend this ludicrous metaphor still further, one could point to the dangerous possibility that the deployment of this armoury (reflexivity, constructionism, dialogism etc.) could wipe out 'us' at the same time that it disposes once and for all with 'them'. This consideration has been voiced by many commentators – including several contributors to this volume – and I shall be alluding to some of these arguments later in this chapter.

5. The critical social psychologist whose work most clearly involves dialogic perspectives is Shotter. However, his 'dialogism' is evidenced almost entirely on the level of theory.

6. Although the term 'subject' has received much criticism in the critical social psychology literature, this has been based on a rather narrow understanding of the ways in which the term has actually been deployed in mainstream psychology (cf. Danziger, 1990). I shall be retaining the term as an allusion to the ambiguities of identity and 'power' in the research and authorial processes.

7. In his account Billig (1990) is actually careful to emphasize that this account of rhetorical strategies in social psychological texts need not be read as a critique.

8. Of course, not all Marxist scholars have valorized the 'view from below' over the views of intellectuals (e.g. Gramsci, 1971; Lenin, 1947).

9. More generally, it is interesting to note how we subtly use the claim that everyday accounts are 'variable' to warrant our own academic authority. Discourse analysis is often advertised on the basis of its ability to reveal consistency (at the level of the functions of the linguistic repertoire) which would not be apparent if we were to take ordinary people's words at face value (e.g. Ashmore, 1989; Potter & Wetherell, 1987).

10. So deep-rooted is our mistrust of human testimony that even when (social) psychologists apparently conduct research by asking people questions, they rarely do so in the belief that they can learn directly from the answers. Rather questions often take the form of (empirically derived) 'tests', diagnostic devices which allow the analyst to classify individuals according to their replies without concern for their ultimate veracity.

11. The taken-for-granted nature of social life may pose problems for researchers wishing to elicit information from informants, since informants may omit to tell the researcher what s/he assumes 'everyone' 'already knows' (Bloch, 1992; Rosaldo, 1989).

12. It should be noted here that my reading of Geertz differs from Sampson's. Sampson reads Geertz as advocating adopting the 'native's point of view' in the place of our own 'experience-distanced' ways of understanding. My reading of Geertz is that he is saying that Western academics can never in fact take the 'native's point of view', and that their constructs are necessarily 'experience-distanced'.

13. In fact, social psychologists rarely do construct models of human functioning which focus on the individual social actor (Condor, 1996). Moreover, as Danziger (1990) has argued, even when psychologists do claim to speak of individuals, in the process of their research they typically focus on a fictive collective subject (the 'experimental group') rather than on individuals. To the extent that *social* psychology contributes to the surveillance, identification and comparison of individuals (Rose, 1990a, 1990b) it does so by contributing to an awareness of population norms rather than providing technologies for the identification of individuals from a social array. In fact, social psychologists are often critical of their own reluctance to employ methods which allow for description at the level of the individual.

14. For most of us, however, this is no more than a pipe-dream. Even if we felt confident of our ability to pass as social linguists or as anthropologists, we would surely encounter immigration restrictions from disciplines which already regard themselves as over-populated. Moreover, those of us who have enjoyed interdisciplinary contact will probably have realized that, to the extent that historians, social anthropologists, feminists, linguists or social theorists want 'us' as collaborators, they want 'us' *as psychologists*. For they also look beyond the bounds of their disciplines for the solution to their own theoretical stalemates and disciplinary crises of authority. Ironically, the constructs they grasp at as potential solutions (e.g. 'cognition', 'personality') are often just those aspects of Psychology which we are committed to rejecting.

15. This again points to a distinction between contemporary critical social psychology practice and the dialogic ideal. Dialogism, according to Clifford (1986), should encourage academics to recognize the contingent nature of their knowledge of others.

16. It is common for 'dialogism' to be presented as acontextual amongst social psychologists. Recently, Hermans, Kempen and van Loon (1992) went as far as to suggest that dialogism would 'transcend the cultural limits of individualism and rationalism' (p. 23).

17. This point also relates to a number of other tensions running through social construc- tionist work, some of which Sampson (1993) mentions in passing. For example, analysts may attempt to claim both that the psi-sciences construct actors in modern societies, but at the

same time these constructions are not 'true' (cf. Henriques, Hollway, Urwin, Venn & Walkerdine, 1984; Rose, 1990b). It is commonly implied that psychological constructions are a form of oppressive ideology which merely masks (rather than constructs) the true identities and experiences of human beings. So, for example, it may be suggested that people will, if asked, tell us on the basis of their lives or experiences (which have apparently escaped social construction) that current social (including psychological) constructions of human nature are not true.

18. Of course, in the processes of warranting our claims we often point to the dawn of a postmodern era, implying that our new perspectives represent a 'timely' advance on old modernist social psychological models.

19. His suggestion that informing people about how their indigenous constructs of human nature function in the lives of their communities will necessarily bring in its wake the downfall of Western civilization might, of course, be met with some scepticism (cf. Ibáñez, this volume). After all, Western academics and politicians have 'known' for a long time about the implication of individualism in capitalist systems (Macfarlane, 1978), even if it took a while for social psychologists to catch on. This knowledge does not seem to have contributed one jot to the downfall of Western civilization. If anything it has been valorized and utilized in the pursuit of 'enterprise society' (Heelas & Morris, 1991; Keat & Abercrombie, 1991). Sampson's account also assumes that, once 'told' about the empirical relationship between constructs of human nature and social structure, people both would wish to utilize this knowledge, and also would know how to translate this information into successful technologies for social transformation. Even in advanced Western democracies, in which human agents are used to critical self-reflection and are concerned to 'make their own history', attempts at fashioning the social body rarely work out in practice in the way in which they were imagined (Condor, 1990).

References

Abercrombie, N., Hill, S., & Turner, B. (1980). *The dominant ideology thesis*. London: George Allen and Unwin.

Adorno, T., Frenkel-Brunswik, E., Levinson, D., & Sanford, R. (1950). *The authoritarian personality*. New York: Harper & Row.

Allport, G. (1954). *The nature of prejudice*. Reading, MA: Addison Wesley.

Asad, T., (Ed.). (1973). *Anthropology and the colonial encounter*. London: Ithaca.

Ashmore, M. (1989). Analysts' variability talk. In *The reflexive thesis: Wrighting the sociology of scientific knowledge*. (pp. 139–165). Chicago: University of Chicago Press.

Barkan, E. (1992). Rethinking orientalism: Representations of 'primitives' in western culture at the turn of the century. *History of European Ideas*, *15*, 759–765.

Bauman, Z. (1995). *Life in fragments: Essays in postmodern morality*. Oxford: Blackwell.

Berman, M. (1982). *All that is solid melts into air: The experience of modernity*. London: Verso.

Bhavnani, K.-K. (1990). What's power got to do with it? Empowerment and social research. In I. Parker & J. Shotter (Eds.), *Deconstructing social psychology* (pp. 141–152). London: Routledge.

Bhavnani, K.-K. (1991). *Talking politics: A psychological framing for views from youth in Britain*. Cambridge: Cambridge University Press.

Billig, M. (1976). *Social psychology and intergroup relations*. London: Academic Press.

Billig, M. (1978). *Fascists: A social psychological view of the National Front*. London: Harcourt Brace Jovanovich.

Billig, M. (1987). *Arguing and thinking: A rhetorical approach to social psychology*. Cambridge: Cambridge University Press.

Billig, M. (1988). Methodology and scholarship in understanding ideological explanation. In C. Antaki (Ed.), *Analysing everyday explanation: A casebook of methods* (pp. 199–215). London: Sage.

Billig, M. (1990). Rhetoric of social psychology. In I. Parker & J. Shotter (Eds.), *Deconstructing social psychology* (pp. 47–59). London: Routledge.

Billig, M. (1991). *Ideology and opinions: Studies in rhetorical social psychology*. London: Sage.

Billig, M. (1992). *Talking of the Royal Family*. London: Routledge.

Billig, M. (1994). Celebrating argument within psychology: Dialogue, negation and feminist critique. *Argumentation, 8*, 49–61.

Billig, M., Condor, S., Edwards, D., Gane, M., Middleton, D., & Radley, A. (1988). *Ideological dilemmas*. London: Sage.

Bloch, M. (1992) What goes without saying: The conceptualization of Zafimaniry society. In A. Kuper (Ed.), *Conceptualizing society* (pp. 127–146). London: Routledge.

Bloor, D. (1976). *Knowledge and social imagery*. Chicago: University of Chicago Press.

Bourdieu, P. (1977). *Outline of a theory of practice*. Cambridge: Cambridge University Press.

Bourdieu, P. (1984). *Distinction: A social critique of the judgement of taste*. London: Routledge.

Bourdieu, P. (1990). *In other words: Essays towards a reflexive sociology*. Cambridge: Polity Press.

Brown, L., & Gilligan, C. (1992). *Meeting at the crossroads: Women's psychology and girls' development*. Cambridge, MA: Harvard University Press.

Burke, P. (1992). We, the people: Popular culture and popular identity in modern Europe. In S. Lash & J. Friedman (Eds.), *Modernity and identity* (pp. 293–308). Oxford: Blackwell.

Burman, E. (1990). Differing with deconstruction: A feminist critique. In I. Parker & J. Shotter (Eds.), *Deconstructing social psychology* (pp. 208–220). London: Routledge.

Callon, M. (1986). Some elements of a sociology of translation. In J. Law (Ed.), *Power, action and belief*. Boston: Routledge & Kegan Paul.

Callon, M., & Latour, B. (1981). Unscrewing the big Leviathan: How actors macro-structure reality and how sociologists help them to do so. In K. Knorr Cetina and A. Cicourel (Eds.), *Advances in social theory and methodology*. Boston: Routledge & Kegan Paul.

Clifford, J. (1983). On ethnographic authority. *Representations, 1*, 118–146.

Clifford, J. (1986). Introduction. In J. Clifford & G. Marcus (Eds.), *Writing culture: The poetics and politics of ethnography* (pp. 1–24). Berkeley: University of California Press.

Condor, S. (1989). 'Biting into the future': social change and the social identity of women. In S. Skevington & D. Baker (Eds.), *The social identity of women* (pp. 15–39). London: Sage.

Condor, S. (1990, November). *Why students choose to do psychology: Some methodological and analytic problems*. BPS annual conference, London.

Condor, S. (1996). Social identity and time. In P. Robinson (Ed.), *Social groups and identities* (pp. 284–315). London: Heineman.

Condor, S., Íñiguez, L., & Antaki, C. (1990, July). *The crisis and the notion of 'context' in social psychology*. Paper presented at the International Sociological Association XIIth World Congress, Madrid.

Danziger, K. (1990). *Constructing the subject: Historical origins of psychological research*. Cambridge: Cambridge University Press.

De Waele, J., & Harré, R. (1979). Autobiography as a psychological method. In G. Ginsburg (Ed.), *Emerging strategies in social psychological research* (pp. 177–209). Chichester: Wiley.

Douglas, M. (1966/1991). *Purity and danger: An analysis of the concept of pollution and taboo*. London: Routledge.

Dwyer, K. (1977). On the dialogic of fieldwork. *Dialectical Anthropology, 2*, 143–151.

Dwyer, K. (1979). The dialogic of ethnography. *Dialectical Anthropology, 4*, 205–224.

Edwards, D., & Mercer, N. (1987). *Common knowledge: The development of understanding in the classroom*. London: Methuen.

Elms, A. (1975). The crisis of confidence in social psychology. *American Psychologist, 30*, 967–976.

Farr, R., & Moscovici, S. (1984). *Social representations*. Cambridge: Cambridge University Press.

Foucault, M. (1977). *Discipline and punish: The birth of the prison*. Harmondsworth: Penguin.

Friedman, J. (1992). Narcissism, roots and postmodernity: The constitution of selfhood in the global crisis. In S. Lash & J. Friedman (Eds.), *Modernity and identity* (pp. 331–366). Oxford: Blackwell.

Geertz, C. (1983). *Local knowledge*. New York: Basic Books.

Geertz, C. (1986). Making experiences, authoring selves. In V. Turner & E. Bruner (Eds.), *The anthropology of experience* (pp. 373–380). Urbana: University of Illinois Press.

Geertz, C. (1988). *Works and lives*. Cambridge: Polity.

Gergen, K. (1973). Social psychology as history. *Journal of Personality and Social Psychology*, *26*, 309–320.

Gergen, K. (1989). Warranting voice and the elaboration of the self. In J. Shotter & K. Gergen (Eds.), *Texts of identity* (pp. 70–81). London: Sage.

Gergen, M. (1992). Life stories: Pieces of a dream. In G. Rosenwald & R. Ochberg (Eds.), *Storied lives: The cultural politics of self-understanding* (pp. 127–144). New Haven, CT: Yale University Press.

Giddens, A. (1979). *Central problems in social theory*. London: Macmillan.

Giddens, A. (1991). *Modernity and self-identity: Self and society in the late modern age*. Cambridge: Polity.

Gilbert, G., & Mulkay, M. (1983). In search of the action. In G.N. Gilbert & P. Abell (Eds.), *Accounts and action* (pp. 8–34). Aldershot: Gower.

Gilbert, G., & Mulkay, M. (1984). *Opening Pandora's box: A sociological analysis of scientists' discourse*. Cambridge: Cambridge University Press.

Gilligan, C. (1977). In a different voice: Women's conceptions of self and morality. *Harvard Educational Review*, *47*, 481–517.

Gilligan, C. (1982). *In a different voice*. Cambridge, MA: Harvard University Press.

Goffman, E. (1981). *Forms of talk*. Oxford: Blackwell.

Gough, A. (1967). *Anthropology and imperialism*. Radical Education Project Ann Arbor, Michigan: Mimeo.

Gramsci, A. (1971). *Selections from the prison notebooks* (Q. Hoare and G. Smith, Eds.). London: Lawrence & Wishart.

Griffin, C. (1985). *Typical girls? Young women from school to the job market*. London: Routledge.

Hacking, I. (1982). Biopower and the avalanche of printed numbers. *Humanities in Society*, *5*, 279–295.

Hall, S. (1990). Cultural identity and diaspora. In J. Rutherford (Ed.), *Identity: Community, culture, difference* (pp. 222–237). London: Lawrence & Wishart.

Harré, R. (1979). *Social being*. Oxford: Blackwell.

Harré, R. (1983). *Personal being: A theory for individual psychology*. Oxford: Blackwell.

Harré, R. (1993). *Social being* (2nd ed.). Oxford: Blackwell.

Heelas, P., & Morris, P. (1991). *The value of enterprise culture*. London: Routledge.

Henriques, J., Hollway, W., Urwin, C., Venn, C., & Walkerdine, V. (1984). *Changing the subject: Psychology, social regulation and subjectivity*. London: Methuen.

Hermans, H., Kempen, H., & van Loon, R. (1992). The dialogic self: Beyond individualism and rationalism. *American Psychologist*, *47*, 23–33.

Hollway, W. (1989). *Subjectivity and method in psychology: Gender, meaning and science*. London: Sage.

Hymes, D. (1974). *Reinventing anthropology*. New York: Vintage Books.

Keat, R., & Abercrombie, N. (1991). *Enterprise culture*. London: Routledge.

Kelman, H. (1972). The rights of the subject in social research: An analysis in terms of relative power and legitimacy. *American Psychologist*, *72*, 989–1016.

Kirkpatrick, J., & White, G. (1985). Exploring ethnopsychologies. In G. White & J. Kirkpatrick (Eds.), *Person, self and experience: Exploring Pacific ethnopsychologies*. Berkeley: University of California Press.

Kitzinger, C. (1990). Resisting the discipline. In E. Burman (Ed.), *Feminists and psychological practice* (pp. 119–138). London: Sage.

Kolakowski, L. (1983). Op zoek naar de barbaar, de illusie van een cultureel universalisme. In *Essays van L. Kowlakowski* (pp. 7–30). Utrecht: Aula/Spectrum.

Kvale, S. (1992). *Psychology and postmodernism*. London: Sage.

Lather, P. (1986). Research as praxis. *Harvard Educational Review, 56*, 257–277.

Lather, P. (1988). Feminist research perspectives on empowering research methodologies. *Women's Studies International Forum, 11*, 569–582.

Latour, B. (1986). The powers of association. In J. Law (Ed.), *Power, action and belief.* London: Routledge and Kegan Paul.

Latour, B. (1987). *Science in action: How to follow scientists and engineers through society.* Cambridge, MA: Harvard University Press.

Latour, B. (1988). The politics of explanation: An alternative. In S. Woolgar (Ed.), *Knowledge and reflexivity: New frontiers in the sociology of knowledge* (pp. 155–176). London: Sage.

Latour, B. (1993). *We have never been modern*. New York: Harvester Wheatsheaf.

Lave, J. (1988). *Cognition in practice: Mind, mathematics and practice in everyday life.* New York: Cambridge University Press.

Lemaire, T. (1991). Anthropological doubt. In L. Nencel & P. Pels (Eds.), *Constructing knowledge: Authority and critique in social science.* London: Sage.

Lenin, V. (1947/1902). *What is to be done?* Moscow.

Lutz, C. (1985). Ethnopsychology compared to what? Explaining behavior and consciousness among the Ifaluk. In G. White & J. Kirkpatrick (Eds.), *Person, self and experience* (pp. 35–79). Berkeley: University of California Press.

Lyotard, J.-F. (1979). *The postmodern condition: A report on knowledge.* Minneapolis: University of Minnesota Press.

Macfarlane, A. (1978). *The origins of English individualism: The family, property and social transition.* Oxford: Blackwell.

Mbilinyi, M. (1989) 'I'd have been a man': Politics and the labour process in producing personal narratives. In Personal Narratives Group, *Interpreting women's lives: Feminist theory and personal narratives.* Bloomington: Indiana University Press.

Michael, M. (1996). *Constructing identities: The social, the nonhuman and change.* London: Sage.

Miller, G. (1969). Psychology as a means of promoting human welfare. *American Psychologist, 24*, 1063–1075.

Moscovici, S. (1972). Society and theory in social psychology. In J. Israel & H. Tajfel (Eds.), *The context of social psychology: A critical assessment* (pp. 17–682). London: Academic Press.

Mott, H., & Condor, S. (in press). Sexual harassment and the working lives of secretaries. In C. Kitzinger & A. Thomas (Eds.), *Sexual harassment: Contemporary feminist perspectives* (pp. 69–112). Buckingham: Open University Press.

Nagel, T. (1986). *The view from nowhere.* New York: Oxford University Press.

Nicolaus, M. (1969). Remarks at ASA Convention. *American Sociologist, 4*, 155.

Nisbet, R. (1976). *The sociological tradition* (2nd ed.). London: Heinemann.

Oakley, A. (1981) Interviewing women: A contradiction in terms. In H. Roberts (Ed.), *Doing feminist research* (pp. 30–61). London: Routledge & Kegan Paul.

Parker, I. (1988). Deconstructing accounts. In C. Antaki (Ed.), *Analysing everyday explanation: A casebook of methods* (pp. 184–198). London: Sage.

Parker, I. (1990). The abstraction and representation of social psychology. In I. Parker & J. Shotter (Eds.), *Deconstructing social psychology* (pp. 91–101). London: Routledge.

Parker, I, & Shotter, J. (1990). Introduction. In I. Parker & J. Shotter (Eds.), *Deconstructing social psychology* (pp. 1–14). London: Routledge.

Porter, R. (1990). *The Enlightenment.* London: Macmillan.

Potter, J., & Edwards, D. (1990). Nigel Lawson's tent: Discourse analysis, attribution theory and the social psychology of fact. *European Journal of Social Psychology, 20*, 24–40.

Potter, J., & Wetherell, M. (1987). *Discourse and social psychology: Beyond attitudes and behaviour.* London: Sage.

Reicher, S. (1987). Crowd behaviour as social action. In J. Turner, M. Hogg, P. Oakes, S. Reicher & M. Wetherell (1987). *Rediscovering the social group: A self-categorization theory* Oxford: Blackwell.

Rosaldo, R. (1989). *Culture and truth: The remaking of social analysis.* Boston: Beacon Press.

Rose, N. (1989). Individualizing psychology. In J. Shotter & K. Gergen (Eds.), *Texts of identity* (pp. 117–132). London: Sage.

Rose, N. (1990a). Psychology as a 'social' science. In I. Parker & J. Shotter (Eds.), *Deconstructing social psychology* (pp. 103–115). London: Routledge.

Rose, N. (1990b). *Governing the soul: The shaping of the private self.* London: Routledge & Kegan Paul.

Rousseau, G., & Porter, R. (1990). *Exoticism in the Enlightenment.* Manchester: Manchester University Press.

Said, E. (1978). *Orientalism: Western concepts of the Orient.* New York: Pantheon.

Sampson, E.E. (1981). Cognitive psychology as ideology. *American Psychologist, 36,* 730–743.

Sampson, E.E. (1988). The dialogue on individualism: Indigenous psychologies of the individual and their role in personal and societal functioning. *American Psychologist, 43,* 15–22.

Sampson, E.E. (1989). The deconstruction of the self. In J. Shotter & K. Gergen (Eds.), *Texts of Identity* (pp. 1–19). London: Sage.

Sampson, E.E. (1990). Social psychology and social control. In I. Parker & J. Shotter (Eds.), *Deconstructing social psychology* (pp. 117–126). London: Routledge.

Sampson, E.E. (1991). The democratization of psychology. *Theory & Psychology, 1,* 275–298.

Sampson, E.E. (1993). *Celebrating the other: A dialogic account of human nature.* New York: Harvester Wheatsheaf.

Scholte, B. (1978). On the ethnocentricity of scientistic logic. *Dialectical Anthropology, 3,* 177–189.

Sherif, M., & Sherif, C. (1953). *Groups in harmony and tension.* New York: Harper.

Shotter, J. (1975). *Images of man in psychological research.* London: Methuen.

Shotter, J. (1980). Action, joint action and intentionality. In M. Brenner (Ed.), *The structure of action.* Oxford: Blackwell.

Shotter, J. (1984). *Social accountability and selfhood.* Oxford: Blackwell.

Shotter, J. (1990). Social individuality versus possessive individualism: The sounds of silence. In I. Parker & J. Shotter (Eds.), *Deconstructing social psychology* (pp. 155–168). London: Routledge.

Shotter, J. (1993). *Cultural politics of everyday life.* Milton Keynes: Open University Press.

Spiro, M. (1986). Cultural relativism and the future of anthropology. *Cultural Anthropology, 1,* 259–286.

Squire, C. (1990). Crisis what crisis?: Discourses and narratives of the 'social' in social psychology. In I. Parker & J. Shotter (Eds.), *Deconstructing social psychology* (pp. 33–45). London: Routledge.

Tajfel, H. (1972). Experiments in a vacuum. In J. Israel & H. Tajfel (Eds.), *The context of social psychology: A critical assessment* (pp. 69–119). London: Academic Press.

Tajfel, H. (1978). *Differentiation between social groups.* London: Academic Press.

Tedlock, D. (1987). Questions concerning dialogical anthropology. *Journal of Anthropological Research, 43,* 325–337.

Touraine, A. (1995). *Critique of modernity.* Oxford: Blackwell.

Turner, J. (1987). Introducing the problem: Individual and group. In J. Turner, M. Hogg, P. Oakes, S. Reicher & M. Wetherell (1987). *Rediscovering the social group: A self-categorization theory.* Oxford: Blackwell.

Turner, J., & Michael, M. (1996). What do we know about Don't Knows? Or, contexts of 'ignorance'. *Social Science Information, 35,* 15–37.

Volosinov (1929/1973). *Marxism and the philosophy of language.* Cambridge, MA: Harvard University Press.

Walkerdine, V., & Lucey, H. (1989). *Democracy in the kitchen: Regulating mothers and socializing daughters.* London: Virago.

Wetherell, M., & Potter, J. (1988). Discourse analysis and the identification of interpretative repertoires. In C. Antaki (Ed.), *Analysing everyday explanation: A casebook of methods* (pp. 168–183). London: Sage.

Wetherell, M., & Potter, J. (1992). *Mapping the language of racism: Discourse and the legitimation of exploitation.* Hemel Hempstead: Harvester Wheatsheaf.

White, H. (1981). The value of narrativity in the representation of reality. In W. Mitchell (Ed.), *On narrative* (pp. 1–25). Chicago: University of Chicago Press.

Wilkinson, S. (1986). *Feminist social psychology.* Milton Keynes: Open University Press.

Young, R. (1990). *White mythologies: Writing, history and the West.* London: Routledge.

9

Discourses, Structures and Analysis: What Practices? In Which Contexts?

Lupicinio Íñiguez

Social psychology, and the social sciences in general, have changed enormously in the last few years. There is no doubt that we can talk about a new 'atmosphere' in social psychology which manifests itself through a plurality of perspectives, practices and directions. Some dissident positions are heeded now more than they were some years ago. This is particularly appreciable in the empirical analysis of social processes, where, for example, there is a progressive abandonment of experimental and correlational quantitative methods. The extensive presence of the 'discourse' of discourse analysis, of discursive and similar psychologies (*palabreros*, as they are called pejoratively in Castilian), supports this diagnosis.

Of course, this has its advantages for those who work in the same direction, which I am deliberately going to keep vague and call 'discursivist' by convention. The advantages are progressive disciplinary and academic recognition, the attention paid to this speciality by previously inaccessible journals, specific collections from major publishing houses, and so on.

However, criticisms have not ceased from the mainstream position. In fact, from the position of hegemonic social psychology, 'this type of work' is attributed with a series of traits, a position in the panorama of scientific orientations which is often inaccurate if not erroneous but above all stereotyped (subjectivity, invalidity, triviality, relativism, etc.), which is typical of cases where a target is aimed at without seeing its whole. The clarification of the different 'places' of debate, the definition of the discussion coordinates, and above all a more attacking than defensive attitude will give rise to a creative and fruitful space for discussion.

The lines of any debate must be defined. In the academic context of this book, the framework for discussion could be that of a lecturer/researcher within a university system who is 'obliged' or 'impelled' to do research and therefore researches into discourse using a special analytical tool, discourse analysis (DA). This gives rise to a discussion of the notion of discourse in use and of the kind of practices which fall within this semantic area.

There are a great variety of motivations for this type of practice: from those who hope to achieve something by doing DA, to the fulfilment of the the rules of competitivity set out by the university itself, or the secret passion of a voyeur to see and observe everything that affects the people with whom we share our surroundings. Such motivations might also include, though perhaps less emphatically, the need to obtain the recognition of colleagues in the profession.

While this suggestion is possible, it would lead us to an excessively psychologistic debate. The alternative would be to present the practice of DA as a rational one in its own right, and in this way feed a minimally coherent discourse. A debate in this direction might be based on the answers to the classic questions about what we aim to achieve: an explanation? A description? An understanding? An interpretation? All these activities generate knowledge and make knowledge possible; however, not all are pertinent in work such as that suggested by a 'critical social psychology', which is the reason behind this book. My final suggestion would be to turn the notions of discourse and DA and some of the consequences of the various positions into *problems*.

Conceptions of the Discourse/s

Discourse is such a polysemic term that saying 'I am going to make the notion of discourse problematic' is equivalent to saying nothing at all. I am therefore going to limit this exposé to the consideration of some notions of discourse that are used most commonly and appear in the disciplinary framework of social psychology, considering their characteristic disciplinary or theoretical traditions and avoiding the consideration of other notions of discourse which fall outside these limits. In particular, I am going to consider the notions of discourse founded mainly on the following three traditions: first, the linguistic philosophy associated with the Oxford School; second, the work of Michel Foucault; and, finally, French pragmatics and discourse analysis. This simplification only answers the need to make an equivalent interpretation of the terms possible in the discussion. I am not going to present an exhaustive revision but simply one from the additional viewpoint we could call the 'Spanish School of DA' (Delgado & Gutiérrez, 1994; Ibáñez, 1979, 1991; Lozano, Peña-Marín & Abril, 1989).

Depending on the notion of discourse we work with, DA will mean very different things. Therefore, if we want to avoid a de facto definition such as 'discourse is what analysts analyse' or something similar, the exact definition of this term is a very pertinent task.

Without attempting a complete classification, the following brief typology summarizes some of the most usual conceptions of discourse, at least as they are expressed in common analytical practices in social psychology:

- any statement or set of statements produced by a speaker;
- a set of statements which construct an object;

- a set of statements produced in a context of interaction, with special relevance given to the power of action of the discourse on the other person/s (subject speaking, moment, space, history . . .);
- a set of statements in a conversational (therefore normative) context;
- a set of constrictions that explain the production of a set of statements from a certain social or ideological position;
- a set of statements the production conditions of which can be defined.

The final conception can be clearly recognized in the French School of discourse analysis (Maingueneau, 1984, 1987, 1991). This movement has been profoundly influenced by Foucault's work and it considers the distinction between statement and discourse. Statement is defined as the succession of phrases set out between two semantic blanks and discourse is the statement considered from the perspective of the conditioning discursive device. The term 'statement' is regarded in this context as a result, as something with memory.

Of these conceptions of discourse the most appropriate, from my point of view, is the last. This does not intend to discredit other common conceptions of social psychology; they are not, in fact, incompatible but can be superimposed. One first superimposition consists of the different levels of analysis, from the purely inter-individual to the clearly structural. In fact, they reproduce the sequence going from the more typical naïve definition to the consequences of speech act theory, passing through the ethnomethodological tradition – which is the closest to conversation analysis – and the common ones in the post-structural tradition. They are not mutually exclusive either; we often find aspects of several of them in notions or in practices of discourse analysis (e.g. Antaki, Parker, Potter or Walkerdine, to name but contributors to this book, wholly or partially combine aspects of these conceptions).

My preference for the last conception is because I believe it allows three essential operations: the differentiation between text and discourse, the distinction between announcer and enunciator, and the operationalization of the corpus.

The Text

The first problem we find once we define discourse is the type of texts which comprise it. The main difference is in the consideration of the text as a set of transcribed statements, irrespective of their origin, or as a wider specification of what texts really are. In other words: is any text a discourse?

From our position the answer is *no*. For a text to be a discourse, a set of conditions should be fulfilled. Statements can be considered discourse if they are produced in an institutional framework which restricts the statement itself, in other words, those statements enunciated from defined positions, registered in a specific inter-discursive context and revealing historical, social and intellectual conditions.

Not every set of statements fulfils these conditions, only those which carry a specific value for a collective unit, which imply shared beliefs and convictions, that is, texts which have a clear position in a discursive network. In Foucauldian terms (1978), text is considered not in isolation, but as a part of a recognized institution which 'defines for a given social, economic, geographical or linguistic area the conditions for the fulfilment of the enunciative function' (p. 198). The relationship with the place of enunciation enables what Foucault defines as discursive formation to be identified:

> . . . a complex series of relationships working as rules; it prescribes what has had to be related in a discursive practice in order that it might refer to this or that object, bring this or that statement into play, use this or that set, organize this or that strategy. The definition of a system of formation in its singular individuality is therefore the characterization of a discourse or set of statements by the regularity of a practice.

Briefly, what transforms a specific text into a discourse is the fact that it defines the social space of an identity or enunciating identity with a spatial and historical circumscription.

Subject (Enunciator)

From this perspective there is another important consequence, which is what kind of subject is created. The origin of the statement, who enounces, is not necessarily considered a form of subjectivity but rather as a *place* where the enunciators are replaceable and interchangeable. In Foucault's (1978) words again

> describing a formulation from the viewpoint of statement does not consist of analysing the relations between the author [*sic*] and what he says (or wanted to say, or said unconsciously), but rather the identification of what the *position* is that any individual can and must occupy to become the subject.

The subject assumes the status of enunciator that defines the discursive formation where he or she is located. Nevertheless, each discursive formation has more than a single enunciative position; in fact, different sets of statements referring to the same position can be distributed over many discursive genres. The genre heterogeneity of a discursive formation contributes to the definition of its identity.

There is a distinction between the speaker (locutor) – material source – and enunciator – textual author. The former is logically different from the latter as it is an empirical reality, while the latter is a construction; he or she is the logical author and is responsible for the text, but, simultaneously, he or she is constructed by it, and both aspects are inseparable.

Enunciative locations imply the existence of certain institutions involved in the production and diffusion of specific discourses. Nevertheless, the term 'institution' should not only suggest formal structures like, for example, the church, justice, education, and so on. We should consider as an institution any device that limits the production of enunciative functions, the status of enunciators and receivers, acceptable content type and the legitimate enunciative circumstances for such positioning. The so-called 'Spanish School' claims that the understanding of this aspect enormously facilitates the analysis of the social processes of construction and intersubjectivity, of power, social order and social transformation.

'Materialization' of the Text: The Corpus

As the French School has emphasized, a corpus can be constructed from any discursive production, even if different practices stress different aspects. There is the possibility, considering the means of transmission, that any graphic or transcribed statement may be constructed, even though it has not been graphically produced. Productions may be more or less context-dependent; in other words, the statements can be directed at a subject present in the enunciative situation or at other subjects located in other contexts. Finally, the statements can also be embedded in a specific structure. For example, standardized, ritualized discourse requires a specific institutional context, with a strong thematic restriction and great formulaic stability, and so on.

This description can include, therefore, transcribed interviews and institutional conversations, that is, both oral statements and previously written texts such as articles, documents, reports, declarations, studies, forms, and so on.

Some Implications for Discourse Analysis as Analytics

Discourse Analysis as Practice

Until now we have been given an image of the discourse, the discursive practice and discourse analysis. This vision is intended not to replace others but rather, as has already been said, to define the boundaries of the position from which the debate is supposed to be established. One of the most important consequences of the vision is precisely the role of the analyst. As Michael and Condor (1990) say:

> The idea that we wish to emphasize is that there are numerous contexts which are suitable for a certain piece of discourse, and how one gives sense to a discursive function is a reflex of context or a configuration of contexts already analytically (and politically) presupposed. (pp. 389–390)

We are no longer afraid to recognize that any scientific practice is influenced by the social conditions under which it occurs, such as the social, political or ideological context. One relevant concern here is how to adapt my political commitment to my professional activity as a social scientist.

This preoccupation was difficult to resolve within the scientific ideology in which many social scientists were instructed, the modern ideology. The 'crisis' of social psychology opened the way for a critical social psychology to be constituted which now seems to be consolidating itself. Referring once more especially to Foucault, other processes in parallel disciplines have also had emancipatory effects in this sense.

Discourses are social practices. If we follow Foucault, we should talk more about discursive practices than about discourses. Discursive practices are anonymous, historical rules, always determined in time and space, which define the conditions for any enunciation for a specific period and for a specific community. Nevertheless, analysis is also a practice, not only used to reveal or identify other discursive practices but also and especially to transform them.

Context

By the historical character of the statement, any discourse analysis must consider the analysis of enunciation (the process the subject applies to convert certain language into discourse). The enunciation is the immanent context of enunciation. As is proposed in the discourse analysis of the Spanish tradition (Ibáñez, 1991), the analysis of enunciation allows us to relate language structures with social structures and make social understanding possible from the analysis and interpretation of discourse. At this point, however, we have an unanswered question: what is the role of linguistic analysis in discourse analysis? There is no lack of people who see this analysis as a way to apprehend what is social, but a similar number of analysts do not consider linguistic analysis to provide a sufficient basis for such work.

On Discourse and Social Structure

It is possible to agree that if discourse and/or discourse analysis are unable to connect theoretically in some way with the social structure, they lack importance, or, in somewhat stronger terms, they are trivial actions. This is the last topic I would like to discuss.

Any practice, including discourse analysis, would be drab if we accepted a conception of social structure in only institutional/political or institutional/economic terms, or if we took any other reified version in which discursive, linguistic and meaningful aspects are external to social structure. This is because discourse analysis would have rid itself of any ability to produce social transformation. For this it is essential to lay the exclusive grounds for what an intention and a desire primarily are, even though they are still somewhat unclear and provisional.

To be able to establish any relation between discourse and social structure, it is necessary to define, in the same way as with discourse, a provisional notion of the structure in use.

Within the framework of an interesting polemical issue (Turner, 1988), Porpora (1989) refers to at least four traditions in the notion of 'social structure':

- as patterns of behaviour grouped in periods of time (from Homans);
- as human relation systems between social positions (Marxist);
- as regularities that govern social behaviour (structural sociology);
- as collective rules that structure behaviour (ethnomethodology, symbolic interactionism, etc.).

No doubt we could talk about more traditions, even within the four we have indicated. Even if it seems simplistic, I consider it appropriate at this point to assume, even if only strategically and 'theatrically', a position comprising all these topics: structure, social practice and discourse. This position seems to relate best to the last tradition, as we can tentatively add certain of Giddens's and Foucault's contributions with connotations from Wittgenstein to – why not? – certain Marxists. The initial approach could be more or less the following:

I think Giddens appropriately distinguishes between structure, system and structuring. *Structure* refers to the rules and/or the set of transformative relationships organized as properties of social systems. *System* refers to relations reproduced by actors or collectives organized as regular social practices. *Structuring* refers to the conditions governing the continuity or transmutation of structures and the reproduction of social systems.

It is not easy to place discourse in this plan. It is easier to locate language but only if we use the concept of *agency*. It is essential, therefore, to accept the contributions I referred to above in order to locate discourse adequately. The work of Fairclough (1989, 1992) shed much light on this work when he analysed the connection between discourse and macro-social variables.

We should, in the first place, distinguish acceptably between *language* and *discourse*. Discourse is language as social practice determined by social structures (rules and/or sets of transformative relationships organized as properties of social systems). Thus, the social structure determines the productive conditions of the discourse. On the other hand, socially constructed discursive orders constrain discourse. I understand by discursive orders, sets of conventions associated with social institutions (discursive orders, for example, are ideologically formed by power relations in social institutions and in society as a whole).

By virtue of the *duality of structure*, in Giddens's terms, discourse has effects on social structures and is determined by them. Therefore, discourse contributes simultaneously to the maintenance and transformation of the social order. The analysis of discourse and of discursive practice thus informs us of the construction and reconstruction of social structure, as well as of the forming of subjects (where structural duality also operates).

To consider this proposal positively it is necessary to define certain limitations. In the first place, the fact that discourse is language as a social practice caused by social structures means that: first, language is a part of society and not something outside it; second, language is a social process;

and, finally, language is a socially and historically conditioned process in the same way as other parts of society or non-linguistic processes. Actually, there is no external relationship 'between' language and society but an internal one of structural duality. Language is one part of society; linguistic phenomena are social phenomena and social phenomena are to a large extent linguistic phenomena.

The second limitation is more direct. By sustaining that social structure is a set of rules and relations, we do not necessarily share the descriptive hypothesis of methodological situationism (it is possible to obtain adequate descriptive explanations for large-scale social phenomena from the analysis of social practices in specific situations).

As different authors (e.g. Knorr Cetina, 1988), have indicated, we could place another hypothesis in opposition to this one: that the macro-social order is, first, an order of representation. In other words, macro-social order is a sum of present references extracted from micro-situations.

The difference may seem trivial and could be disputed. However, in this context it is not, as it enables the differentiation of discourse analysts from linguistic analysts and analysts of immediate interaction. The difference also allows us to connect with constructionist positions, at least with a compromised socio-constructionism.

Epilogue

The assertive style that I adopt here is not indicative of a security in my position or the intention of being more provocative or persuasive. It is but a rhetoric device to reinforce my weak conviction.

I have proposed projects and problems and traces of solutions which result more from the consideration of the practices in which different analysts have been involved than from a rigorous study of the 'State of the art' as imposed by academic regulations. In fact, it is a position that I am trying to characterize. If we are involved, for example, in a highly problematic and/or conflictive social situation, the question from this position would be as follows: 'what is our position and how can we intervene in it?', rather than, 'what is the best way to study this process?' 'How do we counter the power discourse?', rather than, 'has the process of analysis been the right one?' If, returning to what has been said before, the analysis of a particular discourse is to be no more than an academic exercise, the subject loses its interest and falls into Byzantine argument. The fact that the opposition talk/do – which confronts talking with doing – has dominated, does not mean that talking must be rejected as a privileged form of social transformation (García Calvo, 1989). In this context, as I have argued, discourse analysis in itself is, at one and the same time, a tool for understanding and a tool for transforming. Let me finish with a long quotation from Foucault (1978):

I fear you are twice mistaken: on the discursive practices I defined and on the part you yourself reserve for human freedom. The positivity I have tried to establish must not be understood as a set of determinations imposed by the exterior on the thoughts of individuals or as living in the interior and as in advance. They rather constitute the set of conditions by which a practice is exercised producing partially or totally new statements by which they can be modified. This is less about the initiative than about the field in which the subject's initiative is articulated (without being its centre). This is about the rules used (without them being invented or explicit); about the relations which support them (without being the last result nor their point of convergence). This is about showing the discursive practices in their complexity and thickness, about showing that talking is doing something, something different from expressing one's own thoughts, from translating one's own knowledge, from using language structures. This is about showing that adding a statement to a pre-existent series of statements is a complex and costly act with certain conditions implicated (and not only a situation, a context, reasons) and with certain rules (different from the logical and linguistic rules of construction). This is about showing that a change in the discourse order does not mean 'new ideas', a new mentality through invention or creativity but rather some transformations in a practice, in those which are approaching and in their common articulation. I have not rejected the possibility of changing discourse, far from it. I have removed from it the instant and exclusive right of subject sovereignty. (pp. 350–351)

Finally, there is one feature I would like to highlight – discourse analysis as a social praxis can be nothing more than an act of communication. Scientific activity, and discourse analysis, as a contemplative exercise, as a provocative activity, deprives social science of a privileged means for action.

References

Delgado, J.M., & Gutiérrez, J. (Eds.). (1994). *Métodos y técnicas de investigación en ciencias sociales.* Madrid: Síntesis.

Fairclough, N. (1989). *Language and power.* London: Longman.

Fairclough, N. (1992). *Discourse and social change.* Oxford: Polity.

Foucault, M. (1978). *Las palabras y las cosas: Una arqueología de las ciencias humanas.* Madrid, Siglo XXI.

García Calvo, A. (1989). *Hablando de lo que habla: Estudios del lenguaje.* Zamora: Editorial Lucina.

Ibáñez, J. (1979). *Más allá de la sociología. El grupo de discusión: teoría y crítica.* Madrid, Siglo XXI.

Ibáñez, J. (1990). La investigación social de segundo orden. *Suplementos, 22,* 178–187.

Ibáñez, J. (1991). *El regreso del sujeto. La investigación social de segundo orden.* Madrid: Siglo XXI.

Knorr Cetina, K. (1988). The micro-social order. In N.G. Fielding (Ed.), *Actions and structure* (pp. 20–53). London: Sage.

Lozano, J., Peña-Marín, C., & Abril, G. (1989). *Análisis del discurso: Hacia una semiótica de la interacción textual.* Madrid, Cátedra.

Maingueneau, D. (1984). *Genèses du discours.* Liège: Mardaga.

Maingueneau, D. (1987). *Nouvelles tendences en analyse du discours.* Paris: Hachette.

Maingueneau, D. (1991). *L'analyse du discours: Introduction aux lectures de l'archive.* Paris: Hachette.

Michael, M., & Condor, S. (1990). Conceptos de estructura social en una psicología social construccionista. In *Libro de simposios. III Congreso Nacional de Psicología Social* (pp. 389–394). Santiago de Compostela.

Porpora, D.V. (1989). Four concepts of social structure. *Journal for the Theory of Social Behaviour, 19*(2), 195–211.

Turner, J.H. (1988). A behavioral theory of social structure. *Journal for the Theory of Social Behaviour, 18*(4), 355–372.

10

The Unconscious State
of Social Psychology

Ian Parker

The project of critical social psychology necessarily entails a reflection upon our place in the body of the discipline and its associated practices, in the network of ideas and institutions that have as their centre the professional associations that define what 'psychology' is. This dense network is the psy-complex (Ingleby, 1985; Rose, 1985). How can we take forward a reflection on the activities and mentalities of uncritical psychologists, and comprehend the trajectory of our colleagues through the bureaucratic layers of this grid? This chapter is about economies of desire in the ego of psychology considered as a state apparatus, and the ways in which psychoanalytic debates over the nature of desire and the rise of conformist ego-psychology may be brought to bear on our discipline and self-discipline as 'critical social psychologists'.

Problems and Questions

The many tiny opposition movements which emerged through our various scientific 'crises' (Armistead, 1974; Harré & Secord, 1972; Israel & Tajfel, 1972; Wilkinson, 1986) have failed to capture key institutional sites in the discipline, and radical work is still marginalized. More extravagant appeals in recent years to supposed postmodern transformations in culture (Gergen, 1991; Kvale, 1992) are symptoms less of the power of alternative ideas than of their isolation. Some critics may think that there has been a qualitative change in psychology and that they now have the opportunity to pilot the ship through new times, but this delusion is part of the problem. Some radicals down the years have always had that view of psychology, and that has not prevented the psy-complex from growing apace and churning its way through the popular imagination, continuing the project of the policing of subjectivity that was its original impulse. Four problems which were identified in the crisis literature twenty years ago are still apparent.

Individualism in psychology was a key target of early critique (Billig, 1976; Israel & Tajfel, 1972), and the task of constructing explanations which focus on social processes has long preoccupied radicals. The issue is still on the agenda in accounts of the social and cultural location of mental phenomena, but there is often a conceptual slippage, in which an individual explanation is called for to supplement the social story, and psychology enters the picture again with an even stronger mandate. Individualism still needs to be tackled as a problem in psychology, and as much as an ideological formation that masks collective phenomena (of class, gender, sexuality and race, for example) as simply a mistake.

Positivism was subjected to thorough critique, as was the mistaken image of investigative procedures in the natural sciences that bewitch social psychologists and the failure to appreciate the distinctive tasks that the phenomenon of consciousness set the researcher (Gauld & Shotter, 1977; Harré & Secord, 1972). The quantification of social phenomena is, for many, now, unreasonable, and qualitative research methods have grown in popularity. This critical impulse still needs a further push, however, to highlight how positivist research is dangerous in the very way it conceals moral–political values.

Politics came onto the scene as it became clear that social psychology was not an objective or neutral value-free enterprise, but carried with it political assumptions, and could not but encourage a demeaning view of the person and the collective (Armistead, 1974; Parker, 1989). Social psychology's conception of the relation between the individual and the social was and is free enterprise incarnate. Even so, it is still tempting to defend the distinctive expertise and knowledge that psychology offers, and it is important to resist this temptation and insist instead that there are no such things as 'facts' independent of political perspectives. Psychology inhabits ideology, and ideology feeds on power.

Gender has moved more slowly to centre stage as an exemplar of political resistance in psychology. The position of women in psychology, as researchers and as objects of inquiry, is a distinct aspect of the political imbrication of gender and culture in the discipline (Burman, 1990; Wilkinson, 1986). But the questions raised by feminists outside and then inside the discipline, in social psychology and then in psychology as a whole, as to the masculine character of this fake science are themselves part of a deeper problem. Feminism's critique of the male control and gendered description of psychological processes has necessarily extended to an account of the sexual dynamics of research. And now, theoretical and methodological reflection needs to focus on how particular configurations of sexual desire constitute what psychology does, and who psychologists think they are.

In sum, we still urgently need: a thoroughly social account of subjectivity that does not fall foul of individual–social dualism; qualitative research methods that look back into the process of study; a 'psychology' that is explicitly permeated with political argument; and research that embeds that argument in an account of the production of sexual contradiction.

Reflexive Analytic Critique

Self-reflexive critique must, then, be constituted with reference to processes of oppression and opposition, of repression and resistance. Such critique has to be grounded so that it does not simply go round in circles but deepens our understanding of how the psy-complex operates to suppress certain forms of self-understanding and to produce particular subject positions; theories and positions which disempower those on whom psychological knowledge is practised and empower those who are invited to step into the machinery and keep the academic and professional institutions rolling along. The critique also has to ground psychology in a culture that is deeply 'psychological', in which people absorb and display theories of self and other that confirm the truth of psychological investigation. But the irony is that the culture that succours the psy-complex does not run so much on behaviourist, cognitivist or humanist lines as on psychodynamic principles. We live in psychoanalytic culture, and it is as much a precondition for psychology that it expresses and legitimizes psychoanalytic thought as it expels and refuses home to psychoanalytic theorists.

Psychoanalysis, Psychology and Culture

The paradoxical double operation which psychology compulsively repeats is to draw upon psychoanalytic notions, and to deny their truth. It must also do this whenever it touches on everyday reasoning, and the appeals to common sense in psychology are characterized by a routine and ruthless cleansing of psychodynamic notions from accounts reckoned to be ordinary enough to be taken on good coin. The history of psychology is a repression of psychoanalysis, and a repression of its own past ties with psychoanalytic ideas (including an efficient amnesia about the psychoanalytic allegiances of figures ranging from A.R. Luria to Jean Piaget to E.G. Boring). To say that psychoanalysis is the 'repressed other' (Burman, 1994) of psychology must also, in this context, where we are examining the fate of critical ideas at times of crisis, include an awareness of the political repression that has facilitated and accompanied the suffusion of psychoanalytic theory through the webs of Western culture (Berger, 1965; Bocock, 1976; Foucault, 1981; Moscovici, 1976).

This is important if psychoanalysis is not to be seen here as the alternative or the only solution to the problems that beset social psychology. It is not the alternative. We should not do psychoanalysis instead of psychology. I want to be clear that I do not think either that psychoanalysis in general is a true explanation, and can thus be simply counterposed to the falsities of psychology, or that the particular psychoanalytic approaches I am concerned with here are correct (Parker, in press). Psychoanalytic theories are fictions, but powerful fictions that structure subjectivity and contain within them the very contradictions of those material political and economic structures that give them life, the very contradictions in which we experience the oppressive aspects of this culture and through which we might imagine better lives.

To say that psychoanalysis is the repressed other of psychology is also, in this case, because culture is psychoanalytic, to highlight that peculiar way in which psychology represses culture. Culture is also the repressed other of psychology, its Other, and that culture is threaded together on psychoanalytic narratives, held in place by 'discursive complexes'. But culture is not straightforwardly nor transparently storied. The accounts of individual and collective action that are passed from mouth to mouth, and the theories of experience and identity that circulate across the social order, conceal as much as they tell, and they must mask as much as they explain for ideology and power to link together, and for class exploitation, among other kinds of oppression, to work. And if this is a psychoanalytic culture, then the reproduction of ideology is also the repression and transformation of stories that were once told or that could be told. This is the culture that contains within it repression as a condition of its oppression, and a version of psychoanalysis as a theoretical framework which operates as much as does psychology in the service of power.

To understand what is happening when psychology reproduces itself in the machinery of the psy-complex must also be to understand what happened in psychoanalysis as the other, the threat and the guarantor of our discipline. As psychoanalysis passed into Western culture it fragmented, and, not surprisingly perhaps, the fragments function as homologues to psychology. But more than that, and this is why we need to take it seriously, not only did the fragments embed themselves more thoroughly in culture than did orthodox psychological theories, but also the relationship between the fragments carried with it a history of contradiction, a history of reflection and resistance that can be of use to 'critical social psychologists'. And more than simply being homologues, the fragments *organize* 'psychology' as common sense in the archive of the contemporary social imaginary and 'social psychology' as a discipline in the centres of the psy-complex.

Repression in Psychoanalysis

Three phases in the repression are important; for our purposes here, the third most so. The repression of psychoanalysis was first accomplished in Central Europe in the 1930s through self-censorship as the International Psychoanalytic Association, in a misguided attempt to placate the fascists, excluded radicals from its ranks (Kovel, 1988). The expulsion of Reich and the sanctions against Langer are significant moments here, and the lesson that other psychological organizations could learn, but refuse to learn, is that political caution will not persuade conservative forces to treat you politely. Already, in this first phase, the radical elements were being slewed off from the psychoanalytic mainstream. (It is worth noting, incidentally, that orthodox professional psychology associations in Germany collaborated enthusiastically with the fascists, and with thoroughly social conceptions of the person in relation to their community to boot.) Then, second, the repression proper started as the psychoanalytic movement was crushed, books were burned, and analysts who were fortunate enough not be taken to the camps fled, many of them to America. Not many fled eastwards, for psychoanalysis there, too, was under threat, and Stalinism also claimed the lives of radical analysts. But the migration of psychoanalysis to the US did not provide a safe haven for radicals, and the immediate fear of expulsion back to Europe and certain death combined with McCarthyism after the war led to the censorship and suppression of social critique. The secret communiqués of Fenichel and the cryptic aesthetic productions of Adorno exemplify this active silence (Jacoby, 1977, 1983).

The third phase commences with the incorporation of analysts and analytic writers into professional institutions and the refusal of American medics to relax restrictions on the practice of psychoanalysis to doctors, the insistence on the nature of psychoanalysis as a natural science and as a process of 'cure' that would satisfy insurance companies, and the production of a form of psychoanalysis best adapted to the American way of life, an 'ego-psychology' concerned with the adaptation of the individual to society. Ego-psychology, and American object-relations theory which succeeded it (Greenberg & Mitchell, 1983), have provided a fund of observations and models that our discipline of 'scientific psychology' could connect with, and the convergence between mainstream psychology and American psychoanalysis can be seen in the American textbooks which include a run through 'Freudjungandadler' to Harry Stack Sullivan and Karen Horney et al., together with a good deal of misrepresentation of each (Richards, 1989), and more recently in attempts to connect psychoanalysis with developmental psychology in the work, for example, of Daniel Stern (Cushman, 1991). Critiques from within French psychoanalysis have stressed the adaptationist tendencies in ego-psychology (Roudinesco, 1990), but more important for us is the way the arguments *then* as to how we might respond to ego-psychology have trickled into popular culture and *now* into 'our' psychology.

The Integrity of the Psychological Sciences

The debate between Herbert Marcuse and Erich Fromm is particularly telling (Rickert, 1986). They tell stories that structure the unconscious investments of both conservative psychologists and radical anti-psychologists. Not only do we have a radical attack on conformity in psychoanalysis in Marcuse's (1955) work, but also a refusal to conform by one of the objects of his attack, Erich Fromm (1941). Fromm's refusal, from a humanist standpoint, carries with it dangers and possibilities of its own; dangers and possibilities we may attend to and learn from as we consider our place in a sister discipline. I will take up themes in the debate as they touch upon the problems we have encountered in social psychology, and use those themes to elaborate an analysis of the self-images and practices of psychology. The analytic framework I use is derived from discourse analysis and psychoanalysis (Hollway, 1989; Parker, 1992), and structures my reading of social psychology around 'discursive complexes'.

Discursive complexes are sets of statements which constitute particular varieties of objects and subjects and also, simultaneously, are patterns of subjective investment which structure the experience of those who understand themselves in relation to the texts. They are psychoanalytic themes. Self-characterizations by psychology and social psychology of their aims and objects carry with them allusions to approaches that they find unacceptable, and the projects of radicals are implicitly framed no less than those of conservatives, in a kind of mirror image, by the fear of what they may become should they fail. A reading of a text which attends to the silences and absences, to the alternatives to the statements, is already, in a sense, a psychoanalytic reading. But which psychoanalytic reading? In this case, I am suggesting that we are committed to a double reading, and that this derives from the arguments between Marcuse and Fromm, and this double reading can help us subvert the state as ego in modern psychology. As I describe this reading, I will be running back through the four enduring problems in social psychology I outlined above.

Sexuality

The foundation stone of psychoanalysis for Freud (1953) was the Oedipal form, but the identification of this structure as a 'complex' only appeared in his writings in 1910, and under the influence of Jung. Until that point, Freud's description was of relationships that were organized by forms of family prevalent in Europe at the time, and what is important in this description is the notion of infantile and unconscious sexuality. Sensual and erotic ties that bind the infant to the first love object govern the shape of all later relationships. For Freud, in addition, the infant had to learn gender identity through a painful and humiliating process of repression, repression of erotic feelings which were not directly genital, and repression of erotic feelings about members of the same sex.

These most radical aspects of psychoanalytic theory, and a theory of the self as a deeply sensual being, which Marcuse defended, were first casualties in the rise of ego-psychology, and Fromm, for good humanist and not reactionary reasons, did collude with two major revisions of psychoanalytic theory at this point. For ego-psychology and for Fromm, other drives were more important than the sexual drives. For Fromm, the ideal sexual state that an individual should attain was of genital sexuality, of heterosexuality. Marcuse's notion of polymorphous perversity, on the other hand, retained and accentuated the radical dynamic of Freud's work, and was concerned with uncovering how the focus on genital sexuality was a repressive component of a particular type of reality principle locked into place by the performance principle. But the stakes are higher than that if we consider how different conceptions of sexuality underpin a discipline like psychology, considered as an ego which is structured around the performance principle.

Two psychoanalytic themes function as discursive arrangements in psychology's texts, those of 'stages of development' and 'polymorphous perversity'. The discursive complex 'stages of development' is a powerful one in psychology; it structures the way psychologists understand Freud, Piaget, Vygotsky, and so on, and the way those who suffer psychology read the progress of their child through normative developmental milestones. It also presents a myth of the development of a young science from affiliation with philosophy to mature self-governance. The discursive complex 'polymorphous perversity' narrates the past as state of untutored sensual being that should be left behind and as a warning to radicals and perverts of all kinds who may regress too far. It is important to note how a radical gesture by Fromm led him from one side of the equation ('polymorphous perversity') to the other ('stages of development'), just as humanists in psychology now sometimes appear to be resisting psychology at one moment only to end up celebrating it the next. For all the value of humanism, its conception of individual growth fits with psychology's subject, a subject Marcuse can still help undermine.

Marxism

It is also important to note that both Marcuse and Fromm identified themselves, in different ways, with Marxism, and so their debate is underpinned by an attempt to understand the political and economic structures and functions of power and ideology (Jay, 1973). But an adherence to Marxism is no less an invulnerable talisman than is an adherence to feminism. And, though the tide is hardly turning in favour of Marxist academics at the moment (cf. Parker & Spears, 1996), the self-discipline of radicals who think they have better secret agendas and learn to keep them to themselves to protect the small gains made so far is still a temptation and a tangle which enmeshes even the most critical social psychologists in the psy-complex. The critique of ego-psychology was developed by both Marcuse and Fromm. Although Marcuse lumped Fromm together with other ego-psychologists (in particular with Harry Stack Sullivan and Karen Horney), Fromm himself was adamant that the attempt to adapt an individual to social circumstances as part of the 'cure' was deeply conformist and at odds with the critical reflexive spirit of psychoanalysis. The questions posed are always, for both writers, as much political issues as analytic ones.

Two discursive complexes mark an opposition within psychology which effectively delegitimizes politics. The complexes of 'working through' and 'acting out' are derived from clinical work, but function as specifications of boundaries and proper arenas in which certain issues can be explored and changed. To 'work through' is to carry forward the therapeutic work in its proper place, to reflect upon and feel the implications and changes that an interpretation provokes (Freud, 1957). To 'act out' is to do more than speak, and, usually, to do it outside the therapeutic arena. Things in their place, and only in speech. This puts incredible obstacles in the way of effective and committed action research. But also important is the way this seals the inside from the outside such that criteria set by the institution are applied by some good radicals working within it in the name of 'taking responsibility'. Here, the radical humanist intentions of Fromm came to grief on the issue of clinical practice, just as radicals in social psychology now get mired most in the psy-complex when they move from academic to applied work. Fromm insisted that Marcuse did not understand Freudian theory because he did not practise as a psychoanalyst, and used this argument to discredit Marcuse's academic but politically committed critique. Now, the solution is not to say, as Marcuse did, that Fromm was *necessarily* compromised because he did practise, but to insist that professional boundaries are not always inviolable and that we do often need to 'act out', to act politically.

Dialectics

Questions of method are also questions of aims, and researchers attempt to produce an account which is plausible enough to be taken as true. Traditional psychology both fetishizes and is deeply uncomfortable with claims to truth. The true theory is warded off in rituals of hypothesis testing and falsification, and the Popperian fantasy about a realm of being which one touches without knowing it, along with procedures which ensure that the account is robust and provisional enough to stand between guesswork and reality, function to suffocate radical approaches. Radical approaches should, and Marxist approaches must, claim to reveal the structural economic and political preconditions for the mutable truths psychologists will feel happy enough entertaining. The more recent relativist fetish in social psychology simultaneously transforms and reproduces, celebrates and laments the impossibility of truth and the fragility of analysis. Relativism appears to be radical, but mirrors empiricism in traditional psychology.

As discursive complexes, forms which produce and repress what we feel we can know, these notions crystallize as cultural–psychoanalytic themes around the figures of 'construction' and 'the traumatic event' (Freud, 1964). These two forms are conceptually interconnected in Freud's writings such that the formulation of a 'construction' is designed to bring the patient closer to the memory of the event and the memory is always a deferred action which *reconstructs* what the patient imagines, and invests with meaning what *has* happened. But, as artificially discrete complexes in the contemporary social imaginary, they often feel as if they must be opposites: either the past is a story, narrated into being, and so has no referent, or the account is an accurate rendition of the facts of the case. The relativist obsession with the dangers of realism, in which it is imagined that the past, and preconditions for ideology and power, must either be entirely present or not there at all, reproduces this split between the two complexes.

In the case of Fromm, stages of development effectively replace the work of memory in reworking the past in the present, and we are then invited to construct ourselves anew through loving relationships in the present day. Again, while this appears to be a radical position, opening room for movement in the present-day, just as present-day relativists would wish, the denial of the structuring power of memory, and the power of material collective memories of society as they bear on the minds of the living, leads to a foolishly optimistic and liberal picture of social relationships. In Marcuse's work, in contrast, the reality of the (life and death) drives carries the past, and the task of change in a connection with what lies hidden, as entangled within the text of the life of the individual and of the collective but tangible at the moment of liberation as a revelation of the truth. Although at first glance this appears to be a conservative position, an insistence on real and enduring conditions for action actually helps secure the wider political project of emancipation as simultaneously the retrieval and production of truth. Against the either/or stance of orthodox empiricism and radical relativism is a position which works for both a real and a reconstruction of the real as we comprehend it.

Collective Action

A common starting point for both Marcuse and Fromm as one-time adherents of the tradition of critical theory is a notion of psychoanalysis as pertaining as much to the social order as to the individual, as much as an approach to state institutions as to the structure of the ego. Here we move to the core, or a fantasy of a core, of rational and sensible thought which monitors and directs the body and the body politic. For Freud (1961), the ego could be conceptualized as if it were the garrison in a conquered city, and the development of civilization is through the development of police institutions which function in the garrison as surveillance mechanisms. What is frightening to those charged to maintain the garrison is as much the perception by other city states that there are uncontrollable forces that may triumph and flood out, perceptions that may lead rival cities to attack first, as the internal forces themselves. A fantasy of what lies *inside*, then, is produced as a relation with other bodies, as a precondition for the fantasy of control and unity. When radicals are charged with responsibility for the garrison, they, too, are frightened by those inside who are disorderly.

Discursive complexes of 'ego' and 'id', of the mental apparatus and its network of 'defences', structure the institutions of psychology and social psychology here. The mutual reflection of the self in the social structures that contain it also draws attention to processes of identification in the practice of the self as an individual, as a discrete and undivided self. The trap Fromm seemed to fall into was to treat humanism as the property of the individual. It is important to remember that the conception he had of humanism was as a hope, as potential which is realizable only in social relations, social relations in which forms of freedom are distorted or expressed. However, what is at issue here is the way an appeal to individual potential was quickly and easily recuperated, despite Fromm's intentions, into bourgeois individualism. Marcuse's attempt to distance himself from the individualist illusions of humanism was to produce a sense of liberation as deriving only from what lay outside the self, in the 'id'.

The production of the 'id' as an 'it' is itself the work of repression, and in like form the inability of mainstream psychology to adequately comprehend irrationality and the unconscious precisely *produces* irrationality and the unconscious as things which seem to lie outside the individual self, and outside the discipline, as forces which then, quite understandably, feel dangerous. The sense that the social is dangerous follows the contours of the discursive complex of an 'id' as incomprehensible, and bears about as much relation to reality as do popular characterizations of 'anarchy' as being a state of violent disorder. We should take care not to get caught in the ego of psychology, and in the sense that there are dangers within and without that need to be predicted and controlled. Marcuse's critique of Fromm is valuable in this respect, for while it caricatures Fromm's own position, it does touch on a danger, on the way humanism can fold quickly into individualism, and then into an individual identifying with what feels like secure social institutions.

Questions and Conclusions

I have moved from the level of the individual to a conception of the ego as an institutional apparatus which ties together particular senses of self and social organization, senses which warrant and reinforce the state. Psychology and social psychology are forms of state apparatus which can only be comprehended with a properly collective analysis of subjectivity. That attack upon, and location of, individualism was supported by a type of analysis which focuses on the place of subjectivity in objective social processes. This is a variety of qualitative research which uses, works with instead of suppressing, what psychoanalytic writers call the counter-transferential investments of the researcher in the phenomena under investigation. This method, which psychology would like to write off as merely subjective, is a political method. The inclusion of subjectivity in psychology is, at present, a political matter. Any demand which touches upon the state, and which threatens the state, is a political demand. A reflection upon the subjective investments of researchers in psychology is a threat to the ego of psychology, and is necessarily a political enterprise. The tracing of networks of desire, and the construction of sexual identity, as classed, gendered and racialized is an imperative of method here. I have tried to provide an analysis which opens up the text of psychology to show how it is riven by economies of desire.

The debates over the rise of ego-psychology in psychoanalysis inform and underlie the way we are positioned in the present state of social psychology, and the deconstruction of the opposition between the objective and the subjective also then entails a deconstruction of the opposition between the individual and the collective. For, just as our individual identity is rooted in the collective, so we can only grasp that identity through the collective. In the critical theory tradition, a conception of the collective becoming conscious as a 'for itself' treats subjective and objective factors as co-determinants of action. A reflection upon conditions of existence produces a qualitatively different relationship to those conditions, and it does so through collective action (Lukács, 1971). And here humanism reappears, this time in radical political form. The analysis of potent discursive complexes brings into sight the fault-lines in the ego of the discipline, in its reflective and rational core. It does not, and psychoanalysis in general does not, display clearly what lies in the unconscious, but rather the shape of the defences that hold unconscious material in place. How psychology excludes its other is more important than what it excludes. For what it excludes, in this case psychoanalytic material, is as much a production of the exclusion as the solution. Psychoanalysis is not a solution as such, but opens up the cracks in the ego of psychology and in the political economic state of affairs it inhabits and supports.

References

Armistead, N. (Ed.). (1974). *Reconstructing social psychology*. Harmondsworth: Penguin.

Berger, P.L. (1965). Towards a sociological understanding of psychoanalysis. *Social Research, 32*, 26–41.

Billig, M. (1976). *Social psychology and intergroup relations*. London: Academic Press.

Bocock, R. (1976). *Freud and modern society*. London: Van Nostrand Reinhold.

Burman, E. (Ed.). (1990). *Feminists and psychological practice*. London: Sage.

Burman, E. (1994). *Deconstructing developmental psychology*. London: Routledge.

Cushman, P. (1991). Ideology obscured: Political uses of the self in Daniel Stern's infant. *American Psychologist, 46*(3), 206–219.

Foucault, M. (1981). *The history of sexuality. Vol. I: An introduction*. Harmondsworth: Penguin.

Freud, S. (1953). Three essays on the theory of sexuality. In *The standard edition of the complete psychological works of Sigmund Freud* (Vol. 7). London: Hogarth Press. (Original work published 1905)

Freud, S. (1957). Remembering, repeating and working-through. In *The standard edition of the complete psychological works of Sigmund Freud* (Vol. 14). London: Hogarth Press. (Original work published 1914)

Freud, S. (1961). Civilization and its discontents. In *The standard edition of the complete psychological works of Sigmund Freud* (Vol. 21). London: Hogarth Press. (Original work published 1930)

Freud, S. (1964). Constructions in analysis. In *The standard edition of the complete psychological works of Sigmund Freud* (Vol. 23). London: Hogarth Press. (Original work published 1937)

Fromm, E. (1941). *Escape from freedom*. New York: Holt, Rinehart & Winston.

Gauld, A.O., & Shotter, J. (1977). *Human action and its psychological investigation*. London: Routledge & Kegan Paul.

Gergen, K.J. (1991). *The saturated self: Dilemmas of identity in contemporary life*. New York: Basic Books.

Greenberg, J., & Mitchell, S. (1983). *Object relations in psychoanalytic theory*. Cambridge, MA: Harvard University Press.

Harré, R., & Secord, P.F. (1972). *The explanation of social behaviour*. Oxford: Blackwell.

Hollway, W. (1989). *Subjectivity and method in psychology: Gender, meaning and science*. London: Methuen.

Ingleby, D. (1985). Professionals and socializers: The 'psy complex'. *Research in Law, Deviance and Social Control, 7*, 79–109.

Israel, J., & Tajfel, H. (Eds.). (1972). *The context of social psychology: A critical assessment*. London: Academic Press.

Jacoby, R. (1977). *Social amnesia: Conformist psychology from Adler to Laing*. Hassocks: Harvester.

Jacoby, R. (1983). *The repression of psychoanalysis*. New York: Basic Books.

Jay, M. (1973). *The dialectical imagination: A history of the Frankfurt School and the Institute of Social Research*. London: Heinemann.

Kovel, J. (1988). *The radical spirit: Essays on psychoanalysis and society*. London: Free Association Books.

Kvale, S. (Ed.). (1992). *Psychology and postmodernism*. London: Sage.

Lukács, G. (1971). *History and class consciousness*. Cambridge, MA: MIT Press.

Marcuse, H. (1955). *Eros and civilization: A philosophical inquiry into Freud*. Boston: Beacon Press.

Moscovici, S. (1976). *La psychoanalyse: Son image et son public* (2nd ed.). Paris: Presses Universitaires de France.

Parker, I. (1989). *The crisis in modern social psychology – and how to end it*. London; Routledge.

Parker, I. (1992). *Discourse dynamics: Critical analysis for social and individual psychology*. London: Routledge.

Parker, I. (in press). *Psychoanalytic discourse*. London: Sage.

Parker, I., & Spears, R. (Eds.). (1996). *Psychology and society: Radical theory and practice*. London: Pluto Press.

Richards, B. (1989). *Images of Freud: Cultural responses to psychoanalysis*. London: Hutchinson.

Rickert, J. (1986). The Fromm–Marcuse debate revisited. *Theory and Society, 15*, 351–400.

Rose, N. (1985). *The psychological complex: Psychology, politics and society in England 1869–1939*. London: Routledge & Kegan Paul.

Roudinesco, E. (1990). *Jacques Lacan & co.: A history of psychoanalysis in France 1925–1985*. London: Free Association Books.

Wilkinson, S. (Ed.). (1986). *Feminist social psychology: developing theory and practice*. Milton Keynes: Open University Press.

11

Postmodernity, Subjectivity and the Media

Valerie Walkerdine

Recently the *Guardian* newspaper carried an editorial about the day-long strike by rail workers. One of the things that interested me about the editorial was the suggestion that the rail workers would have been more effective putting a day's pay into a media campaign about their position than losing it on a strike, which it described as a 1960s tactic. Whether their political judgement was wise or not is not the issue that I want to address here. Rather, it is what it signals about the relation of 'mass', 'mass action', subjectivity and the media.

What I would like to do in this short chapter is to sketch out the possibility for a new psychological engagement with the media. I do so because various writers on the postmodern have pointed to the media as the site of considerable importance in the production of subjectivity. Not only have writers like Baudrillard and Jameson put forward a thesis of split-off and psychically distressed subject, but in each case the writers are making a point about modernity and the place of grand meta-narratives, the narratives which have been so clearly criticized within the new social psychologies. However, while many proponents of discourse theory battle on with sterile debates about realism and relativity, psychology fails to engage critically with debates relevant to the present political conjuncture.

Thus, while the trajectory of my work might usefully be signalled with reference to Henriques, Hollway, Urwin, Venn and Walkerdine's *Changing the Subject* (1984) and to the use of post-structuralism and psychoanalysis for feminism and left thinking in psychology, I do not want to rehearse that trajectory here. Rather, I want to sketch out some of the relevant issues for a critical psychology in the age of electronic reproduction.

I want to explore what some of the recent pronouncements about post-modernity might have to say to us at this moment. Most of the work comes from outside psychology, but I think that it is vital that we address it. It seems to me especially relevant because it addresses the power and import-ance of the media in an age of information. I want to look at what all this might mean for approaches to subjectivity. I use the term 'subjectivity' advisedly. My interest derives from the position developed in *Changing the Subject*. My particular interest has always been how to understand the relationship between subjectification and subjectivity. If the subject is created as a textual relation, positioned in apparatuses of power/knowledge and regulation, it is not co-terminous with lived subjectivity. However, hardly any post-structuralist work addresses this question: it simply neatly sidesteps it. Indeed, most work has turned to psychoanalysis to fill this gap, though the relation between post-structuralism and psychoanalysis is uneasy. I have explored ways in which it might be possible to understand ourselves as formed within apparatuses of social regulation but also to be able to move, to shift and change. If there is no underlying person to be set free as in humanism, what is the status both of the inquiry and of the stories that can be told about ourselves? If, when we try to say something different, we are not setting free some suppressed inner voice, what are we doing? This work has led me to examine, among other things, my own subjectification and to use it as a point of questioning. I have tried to focus on the relation between regulation and the gaps and silences, the places in which material/discursive relations can be spoken another way, so that another story of our subjectivity may be told. While this kind of work has been important for feminism and is common in the humanities, it has certainly placed me at the very margins of what could be considered acceptable psychology, with its scientific narratives, and at times I shift uneasily between the kinds of stories that I tell. However, I do feel strongly that it is important for us to be able to address these issues at this time: a time in which we are already post-crisis but in which the regulative power of normative stories continues unabated.

Postmodernity and the Media

The lessons of the 'postmodern' for psychology seem important to consider because, in various ways, psychology has been implicated in the production of the postmodern condition and a number of writers have argued for a transformation not only of forms of the subject, but in social organization, arguing that both grand meta-narratives and grand social movements are phenomena that rightly belong to modernity.

I want to sketch out some of the issues that we might address, bearing in mind that the boom of the 1980s has turned to bust and that we are witnessing not only a huge rise in nationalism in Europe, for example, but a level of poverty and oppression in Britain and elsewhere that has brought with it a resurgence of the diseases of poverty: TB, typhoid, scabies, etc. What do we do as critical psychologists in a world in which change seems tied to the grand movements and grand narratives that have been so roundly criticized and which rely so wholeheartedly on psychological models, especially in relation to the twin poles of ideology and consciousness?

In an article in the magazine *Wired*, entitled 'Virtual War', the journalist Bruce Sterling (1993) points out a number of links between the development of virtual systems and American war technology. In particular he points to a link between the defeat of the US in Vietnam (referred to as South-East Asia) and strategies deployed in the Gulf (referred to as South-West Asia). He sees the development of virtual war systems as an attempt to gain absolute certainty of military superiority and victory, to make certain that South-West Asia cannot become like South-East Asia. He details the way in which areas of the world such as the Gulf are digitally mapped in great detail, so that simulated battles can be fought. His claim is that virtual technology creates not only a cheaper, virtual military (i.e. one that may be part-time, scaled down) but also one which is elaborately prepared and trained in simulated battles which would be bound to ensure massive superiority in actual ones. Taken to its limits his arguments relate to important psychological concomitants of the military machine that he sketches out. Basically, I suggest that it can be understood in terms of an extension of the desire for the kind of omnipotent control that I sketched out in *The Mastery of Reason* (1988). Here Reason's Dream was that things once proved stayed proved for ever. But in this military scenario we are confronted with the mastery of a super-rationality, a virtual system whose goal is the total and omnipotent control of war, of complete dominance and military superiority. The 'real' is not evacuated in this scenario but rather the aim is total knowledge and mastery of the real through its virtual simulation. In this sense, then, the postmodernist turn implies a move to far greater levels of regulation and surveillance and very particular kinds of megalomaniac f/phantasies. Thus, the fears and fantasies underpinning the *Cogito* are not weakened but strengthened by this move. In addition to this the distinction between fantasy and 'reality' becomes blurred and, in actual battles, the distinction between simulated object and material object becomes increasingly unclear.

> War has become a phenomenon America witnesses through screens. And it is a simple matter to wire those screens to present any image desired. Fake threats can show up on real radar screens, and real threats on fake screens. While the crews in real machines can no longer tell live from Memorex, the simulators themselves will move closer to the 'scratch and sniff; level of realism. . . .
>
> It is intense and horrific violence at headlong speed, a savage event of grotesque explosive precision and terrible mechanized impacts. The flesh of real young men was there inside those flaming tank-shaped polygons, and that flesh was burning. . . . That is what one knows and not what one sees. What one really sees . . . is something new and very strange: a complete and utter triumph of chilling, analytic, cybernetic rationality over chaotic, real-life human desperation. . . . The omniscient eye of computer surveillance can now dwell on the extremes of battle like a CAT scan detailing a tumour in a human skull. This is virtual reality as a new way of knowledge: a new and terrible kind of transcendent military power. (Sterling, 1993)

What I am trying to point to here is the way in which that 'new way of knowledge' builds upon the surveillance of modernity so well detailed by Foucault, but the new knowledge, the new mastery, has some components which suggest the production of new forms of the subject and subjectivity. In this case, we are talking about a virtual knowledge as omnipotent control over a real which can no longer be adequately and easily separated from virtuality and in which 'chaotic, real-life human desperation' is controlled, surveilled, monitored, dealt with, but yet also occluded. Something to be seen by the observer, only fleetingly, out of the corner of an eye and then maybe as a dream, just as we have only ever barely seen and in horror turned away from the chilling reality of the charred Iraqi bodies, the huge numbers of Iraqi dead, the decimation of the Iraqi infrastructure.

I believe that this is something like what Baudrillard (1983) was getting at when he talked about 'cool fascism': it is characterized not by the hyperactivity of modernity, but by a melancholic fascism, drained of drive and energy. It is silent, it longs nostalgically only for some other space, some other place, the lost belongingness that attracts a melancholy and not a mourning.

While this may seem unsupported and a little far-fetched, I want to argue that we urgently need to address the issues raised, because they suggest to me the necessity of rethinking the subject/social relation especially in a political conjuncture in which so much has broken down and so little in terms of radical political organization has sprung up in its place.

It would seem to me that, for example, children's playing of computer games could then be looked at in two ways: the way in which they present us with a mode of learning which has nothing to do with realist models of development and the ways in which they suggest super-rationality, with its dreams of power and ambivalent relation to destruction and violence – destruction as a game, protected by a screen from any material pain and destruction. Pain, oppression and destruction have to be split off from a disconnected rationality. I suggest that this might be similar to the drug-induced hypnotic state in which two teenage girls savagely humiliated and killed an elderly woman neighbour on a Welsh housing estate or the recently well-publicized cases in which children and adults tortured and murdered their helpless victims. It was Frederic Jameson (1984) who suggested that the new subjectivity was 'schizophrenic'. I think that idea is much too general, but it is suggestive of states of being in which a virtual state splits the subject off from and disavows the consequences of material action.

This is further amplified by the concept put forward by several writers (notably Baudrillard, 1983; Hebdige, 1989) of the breakdown of traditional communities and solidarities (of class for example) being accompanied for Baudrillard not by an alienation but by an autistic silence (an absence of depth, of unconscious) and for Hebdige by what he calls the development of communities of affect, imagined communities of *Neighbours* watchers, for example, in which the community is not geographical, but in virtual space, yet a place in which affective ties can be formed in the absence of classic community ties (weakened or destroyed by the apparatuses of social regulation of modernity, of the modern form of the individual). This latter claim does have some support from studies of fans of soap operas (e.g. Ien Ang's, 1985, study of *Dallas*). It also touches on issues raised in an important paper written by two American anthropologists, Horton and Wohl (1956), where they inaugurate both the idea of simulation and a mode of simulated or para-social interaction, in which they suggest that TV viewers can form imagined relationships and interactions with TV stars and in which the television set in the corner of the living room brings simulated relationships for the lonely.

I am here particularly concerned with the relationship between materiality, pain, oppression and their occlusion by virtual systems. If this relationship is not a simple one of ideological representations obscuring materiality, then how can we understand it? I am suggesting that the relationship is far more complex than previous models of ideology would allow. I say this because I am suggesting that postmodernity is characterized by horrendous pain and oppression but exists within a governmentality and civil society that produces as its object an individual, isolated, Robinson Crusoe on the desert island, in a space in which cybernetic rationality works by attempting to master materiality without ever having to confront it. In this scenario oppression doesn't leave the stage, but it is harder and harder to see, to talk about. Are we then increasingly in an age in which virtuality, veridicality and the real get so mixed up that ordinary people, just like the soldiers in the Gulf War, cannot really tell which one they are operating with? In addition to this, the oppressed increasingly become the dispossessed: they are not seen, addressed. They are isolated and cannot cling to old solidarities, such as those of class. Did Baudrillard's apparently wacky comments about silence and autism have something to offer after all?

The Masses

Baudrillard certainly shares modernity's obsession with the masses, but what interests me here is the move from the nineteenth-century obsession with the classification of the masses through, on the one hand, Le Bon's lawless rabble to the individuated moral subject, and, on the other, Marx's mass, which has to become The Working Class through its conscious realization of its place in history and the power of its agency. Baudrillard turns the mass into a silent majority, with no consciousness and no agency. If theories of ideology and of consciousness belong to modernity, to grand meta-narratives of classes and forces and History, what are we to make of those narratives in a moment of post Cold War, of the breakdown of the Eastern bloc, of the fall of a Berlin Wall in which East Berliners got their view of the plenty of the West from West Berlin television? Theories of ideology and models of consciousness derived from Marx (as in false consciousness) assume a depth model, a materiality to be seen, the real relations, when not obscured by clouds of ideology. But at a conjuncture in which 'fictions can function in truth', real effects can be produced out of fictions and the real, veridical and virtual get hopelessly mixed up, accounts of the relations of ideology to un/consciousness seem hopelessly crude. I am therefore proposing that it is important to begin to examine how we might understand the production of subjectivity outside such grand totalizing narratives and what effect this might have for our understanding of change and transformation, given that Marxist and Marxian models have relied so heavily on concepts of the subject. I would argue that critical social psychologists are well placed to address such issues. They are vital, because most of the work which has gone on comes from sociology, cultural studies and literary theory, which disciplines and fields of study have often stated too crudely the psychological issues that I am attempting to raise here.

The Masses and the Mass Media

One of the central tropes of modernity is the concern with the emergence of the urban population in towns and cities. Foucault (1979) has well described the strategies of disciplining this population through techniques of management which relied upon a knowledge of the population to be managed. The endless description of the masses, from the human and social sciences, charted both the problems and the potential of the masses and was central to the emergence of certain aspects of social psychology. It is this figure of the masses which has been so central to modernity, in sociology, in politics.

Judith Butler (1990) suggested that

> . . .what is commonly that called an introject is . . . a fantasied figure within a fantasied locale, a double imagining that produces the effect of the empirical other fixed in an interior topos. As figurative productions, these identifications constitute impossible desires that figure the body, active principles of incorporation, modes of signifying the enactment of the lived body in social space. Hence, the gender fantasies constitutive of identifications are not part of the set of properties that a subject might be said to have, but they constitute the genealogy of that embodied psychic entity, the mechanism of its construction. One does not have fantasies, and neither is there a one who lives them, but the fantasies condition and construct the specificity of the gendered subject with the enormously important qualification that these fantasies are themselves disciplinary productions of grounding cultural sanctions and taboos. (p. 334)

In her analysis, fantasy becomes a central trope for understanding the social and the psychic, but while her account uses psychoanalytic concepts, it does so in a different way, not assuming the primacy of a universalized set of unconscious phantasies. I suggest that working on these issues is important for any kind of critical approach to the psychological in the present conjuncture.

What, then, is the relationship of the veridicality and fantasies through which the tropes of the masses have been constructed? It is my argument that the production of a scientific truth about the masses has been a central aspect of their regulation and that the pleasures and fantasies of the masses have also been the target of considerable concern right across the political spectrum. What I propose to do here is to sketch out the trajectory of concern in relation to the relationship between the mass mind and the mass media in order to demonstrate how we might approach that concern today. I shall then briefly discuss how we might understand the relation of subjectification to subjectivity, in order to sketch out a project for a critical social psychology.

The dubious pleasures of the masses have been the object of concern as outlined by volumes such as Nicolas Rose's *The Psychological Complex* (1985) and *Governing the Soul* (1992). Getting the masses off the streets, away from crime, vagrancy and disease, were key attributes of a nineteenth- and early twentieth-century project of disciplining and governing. But alongside that was a psychological project of training, reform, from the inculcation of habits of industriousness in schools to a process of individuation, in which the threats posed by mass action were to be transformed into the production of the bourgeois individual.

I am arguing therefore that concern about the psychology of the masses and the relation to mass pleasures was around long before the introduction of film, radio and television. Indeed, concern about the mass media built upon these already existing concerns. The whole of the work in this area of the Frankfurt School, for example, relies upon certain ideas about the mass psyche taken from remarks made by Freud in his 1927 paper 'The Future of an Illusion'. In this he prefigures work on fascism by pointing to the way in which the masses are both stupid and gullible, too easily gratified by the satisfaction of infantile pleasures. Good leadership was essential, he argued, to lead the masses to give up such pleasure for the pain of struggle to reach higher goals: the mature personality that has not been crushed by depriva-tion, but has worked through privation to reach a strong and bounded ego. The work of the Frankfurt School built upon this idea by assuming that the mass media contained the seeds of that too easy gratification. The political project became therefore also quite centrally a psychological project. Indeed, I would argue that much of the social psychology of the media has been concerned with uses and gratifications, with effects of the media and with the continuation of the project of constant surveillance of the mass psyche (Walkerdine, 1993a, 1993b).

Statements by Baudrillard and Jameson, for example, need therefore to be understood in the light of the trajectory I have signalled. That trajectory comes not only from the right and centre, but from a left for whom the necessity of production of a revolutionary consciousness, unclouded by obfuscating ideology, was a central goal. When Jameson and Baudrillard put forward their fears about a mass schizophrenic psyche, cool fascism, they are building upon the history of fears about and hopes for the masses. Their despair is a despair which indeed sees the masses in Europe, for example, further and further away from anything that might be called a revolutionary consciousness and, it is assumed, living in increasing isolation in which media and imagined communities replace the ties of traditional community.

Yet, clearly, we are a long way from being able to understand the production of actual subjectivities in the present. The grand psychological meta-narratives endlessly describe the mass psyche and behaviour, to the point, as in Jameson, of mass pathologization. Schizophrenia has moved from the product of dysfunctional families, as in Laing, to a general psychological concomitant of the postmodern condition.

If the project of governmentality attempts to produce subjects who can be all the better monitored through the networks of virtuality, how do those subjects live in a world in which virtuality and veridicality are hopelessly intertwined?

The 1970s and 1980s projects in media and cultural studies all tended to cohere around the problems of pleasure and the need to take apart, to deconstruct and move beyond those mass arenas of subjectification. But what if subjectivity is produced in the practices which make up daily life, not according to some meta-psychological narrative? Judith Butler (1990) argues for a basic personality structure not produced out of a universal process of phantasizing which inaugurates the unconscious, but as an aspect of the regulation of the social itself. Thus, any subject is produced in practices regulated through the twin poles of fantasy and reality (science, truth). But those stories, truthful or fictional narratives do not have the whole measure of the subject. As I have argued elsewhere (Walkerdine, 1997), both the fictional and factual discourses have their gaps and absences, things that they simply do not speak about. Subjects, then, struggle to find their own stories through which they might articulate other kinds of stories to understand their own formation and transformation.

Conclusion

I believe that the work of understanding the production of subjectivity in the present conjuncture is a politically important one. The failure of grand narratives in the so-called 'developed world' has left a profound pessimism, which is to be countered not by a nostalgia or a denial but by the work of building afresh some new stories. In this short piece all that I have been able to do is to signal that this work needs to be done, but I hope that I have also signalled that the political moment of simply deconstructing the modern has passed. To be politically effective, this must be joined together with the work of building new narrative frameworks, which do not have as their basis the grand meta-narratives that have been and still are so central to our regulation. Understanding and taking these apart is clearly a central part of the project that I am outlining, but I am stressing that this is not enough to understand how subjectivity is lived today and how it might be lived tomorrow.

References

Ang, I. (1985). *Watching Dallas*. London: Methuen.
Baudrillard, J. (1993). *In the shadow of the silent majorities*. New York: Semiotext(e).

Butler, J. (1990). Gender trouble. In L. Nicholson (Ed.), *Feminism/postmodernism* (pp. 324–340). New York: Routledge.

Foucault, M. (1979). *Discipline and punish*. Harmondsworth: Penguin.

Freud, S. (1927). The future of illusion, *Standard Edition, Vol. 21*, 3.

Hebdige, D. (1989). After the masses. In S. Hall & M. Jacques (Eds.), *New times* (pp. 77–93). London: Lawrence and Wishart.

Henriques, J., Hollway, W., Urwin, C., Venn, C., & Walkerdine, V. (1984). *Changing the subject: Psychology, social regulation and subjectivity*. London: Methuen.

Horton, D., and Wohl, R. (1956). Mass communication and para-social interaction. *Psychiatry, 19*, 19–35.

Jameson, F. (1984). The postmodern condition. *New Left Review, 146*, 33–64.

Rose, N. (1985). *The psychological complex*. London: Routledge.

Rose, N. (1992). *Governing the soul*. London: Routledge.

Sterling, B. (1993). Virtual war. *Wired*.

Walkerdine, V. (1988). *The mastery of reason: Cognitive development and the production of rationality*. London: Routledge.

Walkerdine, V. (1993a). *Subject to change without notice: Psychology, postmodernity and the popular*. Inaugural Lecture Series, Goldsmiths' College, University of London.

Walkerdine, V. (1993b). Daddy's gonna buy you a dream to cling to (and mummy's gonna love you just as much as she can): Young girls and popular television. In D. Buckingham (Ed.), *Reading audiences*, Manchester: Manchester University Press.

Walkerdine, V. (1997). Working class women: Social and psychological aspects of survival. In S. Wilkinson (Ed.), *Feminism and social psychology: International perspectives*. Milton Keynes: Open University Press.

12

Prioritizing the Political:
Feminist Psychology

Sue Wilkinson

Feminist psychology is explicitly informed by the political objectives of the feminist movement: centrally, to end the oppression of women. Feminist psychology is a key ally of critical social psychology, in that it – like critical social psychology more generally – is deeply critical of mainstream psychology and of the damages wrought in its name. One might expect critical social psychology, likewise, to be an ally of feminism. However, this chapter points to some important divergences between critical social psychology and feminist psychology, which make the relationship between them less comfortable than it might at first appear.

Critical social psychology emerged out of the 'crisis' in social psychology (cf. Parker, 1989) and from the resultant attempts of those who defined themselves as critical of the mainstream to 'deconstruct' (e.g. Parker & Shotter, 1990) and to 'reconstruct' (e.g. Armistead, 1974; Morawski, 1994) its practices and institutions in a more humanistic, liberatory or radical way. Critical social psychology is an umbrella term constituted by such diverse, but related, areas as: discourse analysis and discursive psychology (e.g. Burman & Parker, 1993; Edwards & Potter, 1992; Parker, 1992; Potter & Wetherell, 1987; Wilkinson & Kitzinger, 1995); the study of rhetoric and ideology (e.g. Billig, 1987, 1991); deconstruction (e.g. Parker & Shotter, 1990); social constructionism (e.g. Gergen, 1985, 1993; Kitzinger, 1987); post-structuralism and postmodernism (e.g. Gergen, 1992; Hollway, 1989; Walkerdine, 1996); and the analysis of textuality, polyvocal (e.g. Curt, 1994) or otherwise (e.g. Shotter & Gergen, 1989). Many of these areas are represented by the work of contributors to this book, and by those whose work they cite, or include in their own edited collections. Critical social psychology, then, is characterized by a range of epistemological, theoretical and methodological positions at variance with the mainstream of the discipline, which relies on conventional realist models and positivist-empiricist methodologies.

As is apparent, then, critical social psychology encompasses feminist psychology, including (as cited above) the work of Burman, Hollway, Kitzinger, Walkerdine, Wetherell and Wilkinson. Moreover, critical social psychologists often cite the work of feminist psychologists. Many routinely include chapters by feminists in their anthologies (e.g. Parker & Shotter, 1990; Shotter & Gergen, 1989). It is common for critical social psychologists routinely to cite feminist work as contributing to their own perspectives (e.g. Curt, 1994; Gergen, 1985, 1992; Parker, 1992; Sampson, 1989, 1993). In other words, critical social psychologists typically represent feminist psychology as a subset of their own broader project.

Some feminist psychologists welcome this inclusivity as providing them with an intellectual 'home', and it is common for feminist psychologists also to identify themselves as critical social psychologists, using terms such as 'social constructionist' (Kitzinger, 1987), 'discursive' (Kitzinger & Thomas, 1995), a 'poststructuralist discourse analysis' (Hepworth & Griffin, 1995) or a 'commitment to poststructuralist deconstruction' (Heenan, 1996, p. 21) to describe their approaches. However, my central argument in this chapter is that in the process of subsuming feminist psychology under the banner of critical social psychology in this way, feminist psychology is fundamentally misrepresented. To characterize feminist psychology as no more than a type of critical social psychology is to obliterate feminist psychology's passionate driving force: its central – and overt – political goals.

I develop my argument in four sections. In the first, I outline feminist psychology and some of the features it shares with critical social psychology. In the second, I highlight the many varieties of feminist psychology which clearly do *not* fall within the remit of critical social psychology as it is usually defined. Then, in the third section, I consider some of the criticisms feminist psychologists have levelled at some of the key tenets of critical social psychology. Finally, in the last section, I argue that the political force of feminist psychology is rarely recognized or acknowledged by critical social psychologists.

What is Feminist Psychology – and Why Might It Be Considered 'Critical'?

Feminist psychology is – and always has been – critical of mainstream psychology, and the harms it has inflicted on women. Back at the turn of the century, feminist psychologist Helen Thompson Wooley (1910) commented searingly on the contemporary research purportedly demonstrating women's mental inferiorities: 'There is perhaps no field aspiring to be scientific where flagrant personal bias, logic martyred in the cause of supporting a prejudice, unfounded assertions, and even sentimental rot and drivel, have run riot to such an extent as here' (p. 340). More than half a century later, as second-wave feminism gathered momentum, feminist activist and psychologist Naomi Weisstein (1968/1993a) asserted that '[p]sychology has nothing to say about what women are really like, what they need and what they want . . . because psychology does not know' (p. 197). Feminists have been amongst the most insistent and vociferous voices critical of psychology.

What distinguishes *feminist* psychology from other kinds of critical social psychology, however, is that feminist psychology is explicitly informed by the political goals of the feminist movement. Within the plurality of definitions and viewpoints embraced by feminism, two themes are common (Unger & Crawford, 1992, pp. 8–9). First, feminism places a high value on women, considering us as worthy of study in our own right, not just in comparison with men. Second, feminism recognizes the need for social change on behalf of women – feminist psychology is avowedly political.

The terms 'feminist psychology' and 'psychology of women' are sometimes used interchangeably, particularly in mainstream North American psychology (e.g. Worrell, 1990). However, critical social psychologists do not generally align themselves with 'psychology of women' – although it is true that much of the research conducted under the label of 'psychology of women' is explicitly or implicitly feminist in intent. Across at least five English-speaking countries (the UK, USA, Canada, Australia and New Zealand), the national organizations for academic and professional psychologists – for example, the British Psychological Society (BPS), the American Psychological Association (APA) – have strenuously opposed the formation of internal groupings (Sections, Divisions, Interest Groups) clearly identified as feminist (Wilkinson, 1990a, 1990b). Consequently, psychologists with explicitly feminist commitments have found themselves instrumental in forming groupings within their national professional bodies which avoid the term 'feminist'. Instead the label 'Psychology of Women' (or even 'Psychology of Gender') has become the (sometimes euphemistic) title of the field. The cost of entry into mainstream institutions has been loss of the label 'feminist'.

This has arisen because of mainstream psychology's opposition to any kind of overt politics. Mainstream psychology has polarized 'science' (pure, objective scholarship) against 'politics' (ideologically biased advocacy), and has actively resisted feminist psychology with its clear political basis (Unger, 1982; Wilkinson, 1989). Critical psychologies do not develop in a vacuum, simply on the basis of the theories, methods and politics of their advocates. The mainstream defines the context within which sub-fields are allowed (or refused) entry and uses its institutional power to shape and control the field as a whole. Incorporation into national psychological organizations necessarily involves feminists in attending to the business of these organizations, rather than in setting our own agenda as feminists (Wilkinson, 1991a, 1997).

There is a great deal of relatively mainstream work conducted under the title 'psychology of women'. A recent survey of the members of the BPS 'Psychology of Women' Section reported concerns about the 'stigma of feminism' (Walker, 1994, p. 8), and in its ten-year history the Section has held at least two formal discussions on 'Should Psychology of Women be Political?' – implying that the answer 'no' might be a reasonable and plausible outcome. Similarly critical social psychologists are unlikely to find in *Psychology of Women Quarterly*, the official journal of the APA Division for the 'Psychology of Women', the kind of radical political analysis or sweeping critique of mainstream psychology with which they might align themselves.

By contrast, the key driving force of *feminist* psychology is political. Those of us who call ourselves 'feminist psychologists' often set out explicitly to differentiate ourselves from the (relatively) acceptable face of 'psychology of women'. We use the term 'feminist' to highlight the political and critical aspects of our work. Feminist psychology challenges the discipline of psychology for its inadequate and damaging theories about women, and for its failure to see power relations as central to social life. The international journal *Feminism & Psychology* was founded in 1991, and, unlike *Psychology of Women Quarterly*, is deliberately not affiliated with any national psychological association. As its inaugural editorial makes clear: 'Our title is a statement of intent: the journal is about the conjunction between feminism (not women, or gender, or sex roles) and psychology; and feminism comes first in our order of priority' (Wilkinson, 1991b, pp. 9–10).

'As feminists within psychology,' says the Editorial Group in the launch issue of the journal *Feminism & Psychology*, 'we share major dissatisfactions with our discipline's failure to engage with the lives of the majority of women, and the distortion and damage often produced when it does engage' (Wilkinson, 1991b, p. 5). The purpose of feminist research within psychology 'cannot rest with the transformation of the discipline', they continue – rather, 'we must constantly evaluate its effectiveness in dismantling social inequalities and transforming women's lives' (Wilkinson, 1991b, p. 9). With feminism (rather than psychology) as the primary referent, feminist psychologists can 'give priority to setting our own agendas and developing our own work, with the primary objective of social change, rather than being primarily accountable to psychology' (Wilkinson, 1991b, p. 16). When feminist psychologists address feminist questions in feminist terms, we can begin to expose psychology's role in women's oppression; to challenge its – sometimes attractive – ideologies; and to undermine its structures.

So, feminist psychology and critical social psychology are united in that they both offer critiques of the mainstream of the discipline. However, unlike critical social psychology more generally, the motivating force behind the *feminist* critique of psychology is unashamedly *political*: feminist psychology aims to end the social and political oppression of women. In the remainder of this chapter, I explore three key consequences for critical social psychology of feminist psychology's fundamental political engagement.

First, I consider the way in which their overriding political objectives may lead feminist psychologists to develop analyses and to use strategies *not* in favour among critical social psychologists more generally. Because feminist psychology is principally *political* in intent, it may sometimes not be 'critical' in the sense in which critical psychologists typically use that term. Most feminist psychologists today do *not* favour the constructionist, discursive or postmodern approaches in vogue among most critical social psychologists. Indeed, many feminist psychologists continue to use the tools of positivist empiricism, and argue for these passionately (Unger, 1996). Rather then embracing, or eschewing, critical perspectives per se, feminist psychologists adopt particular epistemological, theoretical or methodological frameworks in order most effectively to advance feminist political objectives.

Second, many feminist psychologists question the value for the feminist political project of constructionist, discursive or postmodern approaches – and, indeed, may actively oppose their use. They challenge, for example, the relativism of such approaches, their self-referentiality, their intellectual gloss over power relations, and their refusal to recognize the material effects of oppression (cf. Wilkinson & Kitzinger, 1995).

Third, many of those feminist psychologists who are cited by critical social psychologists as contributing to their own constructionist, discursive or postmodern approaches are crucially distinguished by specifically *feminist* political engagements. This feminist commitment is often ignored or written out of the accounts of feminist psychologists' work produced by critical social psychologists. Although sometimes seen (and sometimes choosing to be seen) as critical social psychologists, feminist psychologists use the tools of contemporary critical social psychology specifically in pursuit of *feminist* goals. By the same token, their commitment to and engagement with feminist politics may lead them, on occasion, to *repudiate* the theoretical and methodological tools of contemporary critical social psychology as inappropriate to, or inadequate for, feminist political ends. The key point here is that the decision to align oneself (or not) with critical social psychology, and the decision to use (or not to use) its tools, is made primarily for – feminist – political reasons.

Feminist Psychology Which is *not* Critical Social Psychology

Many feminist psychologists acknowledge a debt to the constructionist, discursive or postmodern approaches which constitute critical social psychology and/or use these approaches in their work (e.g. Hare-Mustin & Marecek, 1990; Hollway, 1995; Kitzinger, 1987; Morawski, 1994; Walkerdine, 1996; Wetherell, 1995). However, there are also many contemporary strands of feminist psychology which are apparently antithetical to such critical frameworks. Most feminist research in psychology continues to be governed by representational realism, and to use positivist empiricist frameworks and methods of inquiry. Examples include essentialist concepts of women's 'different voice' and 'relational knowledge' (e.g. Brown & Gilligan, 1993; Taylor, Gilligan & Sullivan, 1996); the continuing refinement of standpoint epistemologies (e.g. Henwood & Pidgeon, 1995; Smith, 1991) and, especially, the emphasis on empirical methods, such as laboratory experiments, questionnaires, tests and scales, the use of which is vigorously defended by many feminists (e.g. Shaw-Barnes & Eagly, 1996; Shields & Crowley, 1996; Unger, 1992, 1996; Weisstein, 1968/1993a).

It is the political engagement of feminism which accounts for this epistemological, theoretical and methodological divergence between many critical social psychologists and feminist psychologists. In the fight against oppression, feminist psychologists need to fight on all fronts, using any and every tactic which will advance our cause. There are good reasons to include traditional empiricist approaches: when arguing that women are oppressed within the home, it is useful to have available statistics about the relative number of hours of housework done by men and women (cf. Croghan, 1991); when arguing that women are oppressed by male violence, it is useful to have documented the frequency and types of 'dating violence' (cf. Mahlstedt & Keeny, 1993). As feminist psychologist Alice Eagly (1996) argues, 'evidence of women's oppression (e.g. statistics showing victimization and discrimination) can be deployed to attract attention to women's plight and to galvanize people into action to raise women's status' (p. 159).

In researching sexual harassment, many feminists welcome as politically advantageous the kinds of clear definitions offered by positivist researchers, because such definitions enable accurate answers to questions such as 'How many women have experienced harassment?' and provide the courts and policy-makers with clear and concise information (Kitzinger & Thomas, 1995). Feminist experimental work on the menstrual cycle goes back to Leta Hollingworth at the turn of the century (see Shields, 1982), attempting to counter arguments that education for young women would damage their reproductive systems (Ehrenreich & English, 1979). It is continued today by feminist psychologists such as Barbara Sommer, a self-confessed 'quanto-maniac' (Sommer, in Kitzinger, 1989, p. 197), who aims to replace stereotype with scientific fact in her studies of the effects of the menstrual cycle on complex cognition (e.g. Sommer, 1983).

Working within a positivist-empiricist framework, feminists have also been able to mount a successful institutional challenge to the diagnostic categories of the US mental health system. Reviewing the evidence for the category 'Self-Defeating Personality Disorder' (or 'masochistic personality'), which is disproportionately applied to women, feminist psychologists Paula Caplan and Maureen Gans show that the existence of the category is not supported by empirical data, that research in the field is seriously flawed methodologically, and that the category has poor diagnostic power. They conclude that the idea that 'suffering people – and especially women – consciously or unconsciously bring their suffering on themselves' is the result not of objective scientific investigation but of the ideological bias of white male psychiatrists (Caplan & Gans, 1991, p. 263). More generally, feminists working within the field of sex differences have exposed its traditional empirical studies as riddled with technical flaws, such as experimental biases, inadequate sampling techniques, lack of control groups, insufficiently sensitive measurement techniques, unreplicated findings and unspecified effect sizes (e.g. Eagly, 1994; Hyde, 1994; Tavris, 1992, 1993). In sum, they argue, weak data are used to support sexist practices. Naomi Weisstein (1968/1993a), castigating sex differences research as 'Theory Without Evidence', indicts the practice of sexist researchers: '[They] simply refuse to look at the evidence against their theory and practice. And they support their theory and practice with stuff so transparently biased as to have no standing as empirical evidence' (p. 197).

The critique of patriarchal 'science' on its own terms (i.e. as methodologically inadequate or ideologically biased), and the implication that feminist analyses can lead to better science, is an important strategy for feminist psychologists in our fight against oppression. Acknowledging recent challenges to empiricism, not least from 'postmodernist theory', feminist psychologist Rhoda Unger (1996) asserts: 'I believe, however, that feminist psychologists should not willingly discard one of the most powerful tools at our disposal' (p. 166). Many feminist psychologists see the continuing use of traditional psychological frameworks as key to the feminist struggle, and so their work cannot be regarded as part of the project of critical social psychology.

Feminist Psychology's Criticisms of Critical Social Psychology

A second sense in which feminist psychology is at variance with critical social psychology is that many feminist psychologists criticize – or refuse – constructionist, discursive or postmodern frameworks. The typical approaches of critical social psychology are seen as problematic (at best), or destructive (at worst), for the feminist *political* project. As Margaret Wetherell (1995) notes: 'It has frequently been suggested that discourse analysis is antithetical to and even explodes the possibility of political action' (p. 141). Similarly, Erica Burman (1990) is 'wary' of and 'even hostile' toward 'deconstruction and associated post-structuralist ideas' (p. 208), because 'the main danger deconstruction holds for feminists is that of depoliticization' (p. 213). She identifies the approach's 'inability to ally itself with any explicit political position' and 'deliberate distancing and "deconstruction" of any progressive political program', pointing out that '[f]or deconstruction to join forces with feminism and socialism would be to prioritize particular textual readings in a way that is utterly antithetical to its intent' (pp. 210–211). Elsewhere, Burman (with Parker) has identified 'four political problems' with discourse analysis: relativism, liberal pluralism, individualized notions of resistance, and reflexivity (Burman & Parker, 1993, pp. 166–168).

For feminists attempting to bring about social change, the relativism and reflexivity of constructionist, discursive and postmodern approaches poses some serious problems. If there is nothing outside the text, then there is no means to assert the existence of even the starkest material realities: war, genocide, slavery, poverty, physical and sexual abuse. Feminist psychologist Carol Gilligan says of postmodernism:

I think it's a kind of nihilism. . . . To me it's very important to say the Holocaust happened, and the Middle Passage – you know, the slave trade – happened; and an incestuous act happened. And it wasn't just someone's interpretation. I mean, I think it's *extremely* dangerous when women are talking about what happened – 'He hit me'; 'He beat me up'; 'He raped me'. It's very dangerous to say, 'Oh well, there's no external reality, there's only stories, nothing really happens'. . . . That's not to say that there aren't different interpretations, but it can get to a point where nothing's real, nothing happened, nothing matters, and nobody knows – and I think that's a dangerous thing for feminists to be saying. (Gilligan, in Kitzinger, 1994, p. 412)

The exercise of textual relativity (favoured by many critical social psychologists) ignores the exercise of power and the material realities of women's lives: 'Relativistic assumptions of a free play of meaning that denies power relations are of little use for those struggling to free themselves from normalizing bounds and categories' (Lather, 1992, p. 99).

Many feminists – and other critics of critical social psychology's main approaches – also doubt that social change can be effected merely through textual change: 'we very much doubt that . . . racism can be reduced substantially by challenging discourse. The social conditions which give rise to racism will not go away just because the language has been altered' (Abrams & Hogg, 1990, p. 224). Others question even the rhetorical efficacy of critical approaches: 'Increasingly, research from a [social constructionist] perspective points reflexively to its own socially constructed nature and thus loses the potential rhetorical impact of "empirically verified facts"' (Kitzinger, 1995, p. 156). An approach which continually undermines itself ('like a magician who shows you how the trick is done, but still hopes you'll believe in the magic' – Kitzinger, 1992a, p. 245) is unlikely to be *politically* useful.

If, within critical frameworks, all truth claims are to be read as provisional, and all as equally valid, such frameworks do not permit us to prioritize *feminist* truth claims. If no one set of meanings is more valid than any other, there is no basis (for example) for distinguishing between the rape victim's account of sexual coercion and the rapist's account of pleasurable seduction (Jackson, 1992). If the meaning of discourse is never fixed, but always open to multiple interpretations, feminists have no warrant to disprove *others*' truth claims. There is no basis for rejecting any version, however absurd, bizarre or offensive it may be – for example, Derrida's defence of de Man's infamous *La Soir* article as a denunciation of anti-Semitism (cf. Lehman, 1991).

It is the *moral* relativism of critical approaches which generates most passion – and perhaps the greatest difficulty for feminists, and other critics. In reviewing Kenneth Gergen's latest book, critic Leslie Baxter (1996) says: 'Perhaps the most intense criticism that has been advanced against social constructionism is that of relativism. Those with deep ethical convictions accuse the orientation of tolerating everything and standing for nothing' (p. 457). 'What worries me about the position [of certain discursive psychologists],' says feminist psychologist Ros Gill (in an article which is, in part, an impassioned response to Edwards, Ashmore & Potter's, 1995, analysis of 'bottom line arguments against relativism'), 'is that it offers no principled alternative to realism by means of which we might make *political interventions*. They deconstruct realism's claim to offer ontological guarantees . . . but do not have anything to substitute with which we could challenge oppression in all its monotony and all its variety' (Gill, 1995, pp. 171–172; emphasis in original).

Relativists' refusal to engage with questions of value has also led to political paralysis. There is no principled way in which the thoroughgoing relativist can intervene for political ends. Referring to the 'tentativeness', 'anxiety' and 'paralysis' of postmodern, post-structuralist counter-enlightenment forms of *feminism*, feminist psychologist Naomi Weisstein (1993b) cautions:

> *Of course* there is paralysis: once knowledge is reduced to insurmountable personal subjectivity, there is no place to go; we are in a swamp of self-referential passivity. Sometimes I think that, when the fashion passes, we will find many bodies, drowned in their own wordy words, like the Druids in the bogs. Meanwhile, the patriarchy continues to prosper. (pp. 243–244; emphasis in original)

She contrasts such stasis with 'times of dynamism, change and movement': in which 'the fact of movement gives us a clearer picture of what is really out there – what we are fighting against, and what we are fighting for', and she calls for the continuing collective resistance of 'an activist, challenging, badass feminist psychology' (Weisstein, 1993b, p. 244). Many feminist psychologists simply do not see the epistemological, theoretical or methodological frameworks of contemporary critical social psychology as providing the basis for such collective resistance.

Critical Social Psychology's Failure to Acknowledge Feminist Politics

Despite the many feminist criticisms of social constructionist, discursive and postmodern approaches, certain feminist psychologists are routinely cited by critical social psychologists as contributing to 'a social constructionist movement' (Gergen, 1985), to 'the discourse tradition' (Parker, 1992) and to 'a postmodern turn' (Gergen, 1992). It is true that feminist psychologists (e.g. Burman et al., 1996; Fine, 1992; Hollway, 1989; Kitzinger, 1987; Morawski, 1994; Wilkinson & Kitzinger, 1993, 1996a) have been in the forefront of such critical work, and that feminism has made important contributions to social constructionist, discursive and postmodern psychologies. What is often missing in such citations, however, is any sense of the *political* imperative informing the development of feminist theory. As such, critical social psychology may seem sometimes to be appropriating and assimilating the theoretical advances of feminist psychology without due recognition of the political visions which inform and energize it.

One major contribution of feminist psychology to critical social psychology more generally is the feminist challenge to psychology's dominant ethnocategories, including the Western 'individuated' self, sex/gender, 'race'/ethnicity, and sexual/political identity. Feminist work in this area is not merely an intellectual exercise – rather, it is driven by the political imperative of social and political change to improve women's lives. It is subordinated groups who are now swinging the spotlight from the 'deviant' to the normative and demanding that the oppressors deconstruct their own oppressive identities or discourses. So, for example, women are requiring men to theorize masculinity (Griffin & Wetherell, 1992; Wetherell & Griffin, 1991); black women are requiring white women to theorize whiteness ([charles], 1992; Frye, 1992); and lesbians are requiring heterosexual women to theorize their heterosexuality (Kitzinger, Wilkinson & Perkins, 1992; Wilkinson & Kitzinger, 1993). It is the political necessities which energize this work that are routinely ignored by critical social psychology.

For example, Sampson (1989, pp. 1–2) cites six 'discernible challenges' to the notion of the individual as the subject of psychology's inquiry, one of which is 'feminist reconceptualizations of the patriarchal version of social, historical and psychological life'. Nowhere is the political purpose of this feminist work acknowledged or discussed. Moreover, the feminists Sampson cites in support of his claim are Chodorow (1978), Gilligan (1982) and Lykes (1985). This seems a strangely limited appropriation of feminist work, and, moreover, one which overlooks key debates *within* feminism itself: Carol Gilligan, in particular, has routinely been criticized by feminists for her essentialism (cf. Wilkinson, 1994), and, particularly, for unwittingly incorporating into her theory much of the individualism she purports to reject (e.g. Lykes, 1985).

Similarly, many contemporary feminist analyses problematize sex and gender as categorical imperatives; and deconstruct 'woman' as a unitary category. Feminist psychologists working within the frameworks of social constructionism and postmodernism (e.g. Hare-Mustin & Marecek, 1994; Hollway, 1994) have argued that sex/gender should no longer be theorized as 'difference', but reconceptualized as a principle of social organization, structuring power relations between the sexes. In this tradition of feminist psychology, as within postmodern varieties of feminism more generally, sex/gender is seen as a relatively flexible (albeit politically driven) *process*, rather than as a relatively fixed set of attributes; and as highly historically, culturally and socially contingent (Bohan, 1992). Maleness or femaleness is not a core identity; rather, men and women are engaged in 'doing gender' (West & Zimmerman, 1987), which is 'performative' (Butler, 1990), a 'temporary positioning' (Gergen, 1993, p. 4). This is not mere intellectual playfulness, however, – it has a serious political objective: to 'deprive the naturalizing narratives of compulsory heterosexuality of their central protagonists: "man" and "woman"' (Butler, 1990, p. 146) and to illustrate the social constructedness of 'sex' in all its multiple meanings. It embodies a hope for the future abolition of these divisive patriarchal binarisms, a vision of a brave new world where sex/gender would be irrelevant, and so could not be used as a basis for oppression. There are, of course, passionate debates within feminism about the use of such approaches, but, crucially, it is their effectiveness in achieving feminist goals – that is, their *political* value – which is in question (e.g. Jackson, 1992; Wilkinson & Kitzinger, 1996b). In seeking to dispel the hegemony of white Western, heterosexual worldviews, feminists are not simply proliferating discursive positions, nor merely recognizing the multiple, conflicting subjectivities of identities in flux. These are the interests of critical social psychologists: feminists, by contrast, are doing politics.

The extent to which feminists are driven by political goals (rather than by the principles of critical social psychology) can be illustrated by the fact that feminists have argued just as vigorously, on political grounds, *against* the deconstruction of ethnocategories. Margaret Wetherell (typically identified as a discourse analyst), for example, asks: 'How can feminism . . . be based on a deconstruction of the category "female"?', and answers:

> . . . feminist psychology must also be about taking stands and fighting, probably and usually other psychologists and their control of women's lives. And for this we have to mobilize around some identities and some, rather than other, senses of community. (Wetherell, 1995, p. 141)

Feminist psychologist Sandra Bem argues, even more forcefully:

> I think right now, here in the real world, the last thing that women need to do is to forget about being female. . . . We have to use these cultural constructions for purposes of liberation and protest. . . . I think we do need organized social movements that are built around being a woman, being black, being lesbian or gay. The culture says 'we are going to oppress you on that basis' so it doesn't seem problematic to turn around and say, 'well, we are going to take this category and transform its meaning and fight for being privileged or at least not discriminated against', even while at the same time we are saying, 'this category doesn't need to last for ever, and by the time we get to Utopia it won't exist any more, but we can't get from here to there without taking your category, damn you, and transforming its meaning and using it for our own politics. (Bem, in Kitzinger, 1992b, p. 225)

Feminist debates about the value of deconstructing ethnocategories, and when to (or not to) do so, are primarily about the most effective means of getting 'from here to there' – that is, about political strategy.

Similarly, the deconstruction of the category 'homosexual' has sometimes been seen to run counter to the political interests of lesbians and gay men – even on occasion, by social constructionist researchers themselves. When Mary McIntosh was writing her germinal article 'The Homosexual Role' (which opposed the notion of the transcultural and transhistorical existence of the homosexual) in the late 1960s, male homosexuality was still illegal in the United Kingdom, and the Homosexual Law Reform Society was campaigning for law reform on a thoroughly essentialist basis. She has said:

'I felt very diffident about actually publishing anything, because . . . this was not the moment to be going round talking about it. It would not contribute to the political developments of the time to say that sort of thing' (McIntosh, 1981, p. 45).

Of course, any given approach or tactic needs to be used self-consciously and critically, with a clear awareness of the costs and benefits entailed. Essentialist ('born that way') arguments have indeed (tactically) been deployed by erstwhile social constructionists campaigning for lesbian and gay rights. Such arguments are intended to suggest that homosexuality is 'natural', the assumption being that what is natural is both ethically acceptable and politically unchangeable. However, there are clearly import- ant political costs associated with such a move, not least that 'arguing about the proper definition of nature only evades and obscures the political context defining the terms of the debate' (Kitzinger, 1995, p. 153; see also Hall, Kitzinger, Loulan & Perkins, 1991). It is a rare acknowledgement by critical social psychologists that 'some psychologists well-versed in the language of textuality . . . nevertheless adopt a "realist" perspective for *strategic* critical purposes'; moreover, that 'realism is not, in this context to be read as some "trap" into which such authors have gullibly fallen, but a deliberate choice they have made for purposes they argue explicitly' (Curt, 1994, p. 20). The explicit purpose of *feminism* is to achieve women's liberation.

Feminist political goals, then, underpin the epistemological, theoretical and methodological choices made by feminist psychologists in particular contexts. Moves to deconstruct ethnocategories, for example – or, con- versely, to reinforce such categories, by organizing around them or by protesting their 'naturalness' – are made on the basis of advancing feminist struggles against oppression. Such explicit political objectives are generally obliterated in critical social psychologists' citations, and representations, of feminist writing. Critical social psychologists routinely assimilate feminist work to their own intellectual agendas without regard for the crucial role of feminist politics.

Conclusion: Prioritizing the Political

In sum, feminist psychology is key to critical social psychology, shares many of its critiques of mainstream psychology, and has made some important contributions to its key debates, particularly (as I have indicated) in the area of deconstructing psychology's ethnocategories. However, there is an uneasy relationship between the two. Unlike critical social psychology more generally, feminist psychology is driven primarily by political impera- tives, rather than by purely theoretical or intellectual goals. Its primary commitment is to ending the social and political oppression of women, and it uses any and every means available towards this end. This often makes the work of feminist psychologists appear theoretically and methodologi- cally eclectic, even chaotic at times. The frameworks feminists use range from empiricism to postmodernism, and our methodological choices are concomitantly diverse (Wilkinson, 1996).

Despite the best efforts of some critical social psychologists, it is difficult to see how feminist psychology can readily be subsumed under the banner of critical social psychology. The majority of feminist psychologists do not use constructionist, discursive or postmodern approaches. Rather, they select their approaches on the grounds of political expediency or likely effectiveness. Positivist empiricist work is common – and vigorously defended. Further, many feminist psychologists – including those who *do* use such critical frameworks – are highly sceptical about their value for the feminist political project. They have produced trenchant critiques of constructionist, discursive and postmodern approaches, particularly in relation to the ethical relativism of these approaches. Finally, feminist psychologists adopt critical approaches (or not) for primarily *political* reasons. This is rarely recognized or made explicit by the critical social psychologists who cite feminist work.

In one sense, of course, it could be argued that feminist psychology is even *more* relativistic than critical social psychology (which *never* uses essentialist theories and methods). Feminist psychologists put feminism first, and will choose to align themselves either with essentialism or with social constructionism, or with neither, according to their specific political purposes. 'My own solution is to be a radical lesbian feminist first, a social constructionist (or essentialist) when it suits my radical feminist purposes, and a "psychologist", as conventionally defined, virtually never' (Kitzinger, 1995, p. 155). Feminist psychologists will utilize whatever tools seem politically expedient at the time, or most likely to be effective in creating social and political change to benefit women. However, it is rare for critical social psychologists to acknowledge – much less to support or promote – the passionate driving force of feminist politics.

Acknowledgement

With thanks to Celia Kitzinger.

Note

This paper has been somewhat revised and updated since its presentation at the Barcelona Critical Social Psychology Conference in 1993. At that time the author was based at the University of Hull.

References

Abrams, D., & Hogg, M.A. (1990). The context of discourse: Let's not throw out the baby with the bath water. *Philosophical Psychology*, *3*(2), 219–225.
Armistead, N. (Ed.). (1974). *Reconstructing social psychology*. Harmondsworth: Penguin.

Baxter, L.A. (1996). Constructing 'social constructionism' (review of Kenneth J. Gergen's *Realities and relationships: Soundings in social construction*). *Contemporary Psychology*, *41*(5), 457–458.

Billig, M. (1987). *Arguing and thinking: A rhetorical approach to social psychology*. Cambridge: Cambridge University Press.

Billig, M. (1991). *Ideology and opinions: Studies in rhetorical psychology*. London: Sage.

Bohan, J.S. (Ed.). (1992). *Seldom seen, rarely heard: Women's place in psychology*. Boulder, CO: Westview Press.

Brown, L.M., and Gilligan, C. (1993). Meeting at the crossroads: Women's psychology and girls' development. *Feminism & Psychology*, *3*(1), 11–35.

Burman, E. (1990). Differing with deconstruction: A feminist critique. In I. Parker & J. Shotter (Eds.), *Deconstructing social psychology* (pp. 208–220). London: Routledge.

Burman, E., Alldred, P., Bewley, C., Goldberg, B., Heenan, C., Marks, D., Marshall, J., Taylor, K., Ullah, R., & Warner, S. (1996). *Challenging women: Psychology's exclusions, feminist possibilities*. Buckingham and Bristol, PA: Open University Press.

Burman, E., & Parker, I. (Eds.). (1993). *Discourse analytic research: Repertoires and readings of texts in action*. London: Routledge.

Butler, J. (1990). *Gender trouble: Feminism and the subversion of identity*. New York: Routledge.

Caplan, P., & Gans, M. (1991). Is there empirical justification for the category of 'Self-Defeating Personality Disorder'? *Feminism & Psychology*, *2*(1), 27–44.

[charles], H. (1992). Whiteness: The relevance of politically colouring the 'non'. In H. Hinds, A. Phoenix & J. Stacey (Eds.), *Working out: New directions for women's studies* (pp. 29–35). London: Falmer Press.

Chodorow, N. (1978). *The reproduction of mothering*. Berkeley: University of California Press.

Croghan, R. (1991). First-time mothers' accounts of inequality in the division of labour. *Feminism & Psychology*, *1*(2), 221–246.

Curt, B. (Pseud.). (1994). *Textuality and tectonics: Troubling social and psychological science*. Buckingham: Open University Press.

Eagly, A.H. (1994). On comparing women and men. *Feminism & Psychology*, *4*(4), 513–522.

Eagly, A. (1996). Differences between women and men: Their magnitude, practical importance and political meaning. *American Psychologist*, *51*(2), 158–159.

Edwards, D., Ashmore, M., & Potter, J. (1995). Death and furniture: The rhetoric, politics and theology of bottom line arguments against relativism. *History of the Human Sciences*, *8*(2), 25–49.

Edwards, D., & Potter, J. (1992). *Discursive psychology*. London: Sage.

Ehrenreich, B., & English, D. (1979). *For her own good: 150 years of the experts' advice to women*. London: Pluto Press.

Fine, M. (1992). *Disruptive voices: The possibilities of feminist research*, Ann Arbor: University of Michigan Press.

Frye, M. (1992). White woman feminist. In *Willful virgin: Essays in feminism 1976–1992* (pp. 147–169). Freedom, CA: The Crossing Press.

Gergen, K.J. (1985). The social constructionist movement in modern psychology. *American Psychologist*, *40*, 266–275.

Gergen, K.J. (1992). Toward a postmodern psychology. In S. Kvale (Ed.), *Psychology and postmodernism* (pp. 17–30). London: Sage.

Gergen, M. (1993). Unbundling our binaries. In S. Wilkinson & C. Kitzinger (Eds.), *Heterosexuality: A 'Feminism & Psychology' reader* (pp. 62–64). London: Sage.

Gill, R. (1995). Relativism, reflexivity and politics: Interrogating discourse analysis from a feminist perspective. In S. Wilkinson & C. Kitzinger (Eds.), *Feminism and discourse: Psychological perspectives* (pp. 165–186). London: Sage.

Gilligan, C. (1982). *In a different voice: Psychological theory and women's development*. Cambridge: MA: Harvard University Press.

Griffin, C., & Wetherell, M. (Eds.). (1992). Open forum: Feminist psychology and the study of men and masculinity – Part II: Politics and practices. *Feminism & Psychology*, 2(2), 133–168.

Hall, M., Kitzinger, C., Loulan, J., & Perkins, R. (1991). Lesbian psychology, lesbian politics. *Feminism & Psychology*, 2(1), 7–25.

Hare-Mustin, R.T., & Marecek, J. (Eds.). (1990). *Making a difference: Psychology and the construction of gender*. New Haven, CT: Yale University Press.

Hare-Mustin, R.T., & Marecek, J. (1994). Asking the right questions: Feminist psychology and sex differences. *Feminism & Psychology*, 4(4), 531–537.

Heenan, C. (1996). Women, food and fat: Too many cooks in the kitchen? In E. Burman, P. Alldred, C. Bewley, B. Goldberg, C. Heenan, D. Marks, J. Marshall, K. Taylor, R. Ullah & S. Warner, *Challenging women: Psychology's exclusions, feminist possibilities* (pp. 19–35). Buckingham and Bristol, PA: Open University Press.

Henwood, K., & Pidgeon, N. (1995). Remaking the link: Qualitative research and feminist standpoint theory. *Feminism & Psychology*, 5(1), 7–30.

Hepworth, J., & Griffin, C. (1995). Conflicting opinions? Anorexia nervosa, medicine and feminism. In S. Wilkinson & C. Kitzinger (Eds.), *Feminism and discourse: Psychological perspectives* (pp. 68–85). London: Sage.

Hollway, W. (1989). *Subjectivity and method in psychology: Gender, meaning and science.* London: Sage.

Hollway, W. (1994). Beyond sex differences: A project for feminist psychology. *Feminism & Psychology*, 4(4), 538–546.

Hollway, W. (1995). Feminist discourses and women's heterosexual desire. In S. Wilkinson & C. Kitzinger (Eds.), *Feminism and discourse: Psychological perspectives* (pp. 86–105). London: Sage.

Hyde, J.S. (1994). Should psychologists study sex differences? Yes, with some guidelines. *Feminism & Psychology*, 4(4), 507–512.

Jackson, S. (1992). The amazing deconstructing woman. *Trouble and Strife*, 25, 25–31.

Kitzinger, C. (1987). *The social construction of lesbianism.* London: Sage.

Kitzinger, C. (1989). Barbara Sommer: Lifting the curse. *The Psychologist*, 2(7), 297.

Kitzinger, C. (1992a). The individuated self concept: A critical analysis of social-constructionist writing on individualism. In G. Breakwell (Ed.), *The social psychology of identity and the self concept*. Guildford: Surrey University Press.

Kitzinger, C. (1992b). Sandra Bem: Feminist psychologist. *The Psychologist*, 5(5), 222–224.

Kitzinger, C. (1994). The spoken word: Listening to a different voice: Celia Kitzinger interviews Carol Gilligan. *Feminism & Psychology*, 4(3), 408–419.

Kitzinger, C. (1995). Social constructionism: Implications for lesbian and gay psychology. In A. D'Augelli and C. Patterson (Eds.), *Lesbian, gay and bisexual identities over the lifespan: Psychological perspectives* (pp. 136–161). New York: Oxford University Press.

Kitzinger, C., & Thomas, A. (1995). Sexual harassment: A discursive approach. In S. Wilkinson and C. Kitzinger (Eds.), *Feminism and discourse: Psychological perspectives* (pp. 32–48). London: Sage.

Kitzinger, C., Wilkinson, S., & Perkins, R. (Eds.). (1992). Heterosexuality [Special Issue]. *Feminism & Psychology*, 2(3).

Lather, P. (1992). Postmodernism and the human sciences. In S. Kvale (Ed.), *Psychology and postmodernity* (pp. 88–109). London: Sage.

Lehman, D. (1991, April). Oh no, (de) man again! *Lingua Franca*, pp. 26–32.

Lykes, M.B. (1985). Gender and individualistic versus collectivist bases for notions about the self. *Journal of Personality*, 53, 356–383.

Mahlstedt, D., & Keeny, L. (1993). Female survivors of dating violence and their social networks. *Feminism & Psychology*, 3(3), pp. 319–333.

McIntosh, M. (1981). Interview. In K. Plummer (Ed.), *The making of the modern homosexual.* London: Hutchinson.

Morawski, J.G. (1994). *Practicing feminisms, reconstructing psychology: Notes on a liminal science.* Ann Arbor: University of Michigan Press.

Parker, I. (1989). *The crisis in modern social psychology – and how to end it.* London: Routledge.

Parker, I. (1992). *Discourse dynamics: Critical analysis for social and individual psychology.* London: Routledge.

Parker, I., & Shotter, J. (Eds.). (1990). *Deconstructing social psychology.* London: Routledge.

Potter, J., & Wetherell, M. (1987). *Discourse and social psychology: Beyond attitudes and behaviour.* London: Sage.

Sampson, E.E. (1989). The deconstruction of the self. In J. Shotter and K.J. Gergen (Eds.), *Texts of identity* (pp. 1–19). London: Sage.

Sampson, E.E. (1993). *Celebrating the other: A dialogic account of human nature.* Hemel Hempstead: Harvester Wheatsheaf.

Shaw-Barnes, K., & Eagly, A.H. (1996). Meta-analysis and feminist psychology. In S. Wilkinson (Ed.), *Feminist social psychologies: International perspectives* (pp. 258–274). Buckingham: Open University Press.

Shields, S.A. (1982). The variability hypothesis: The history of a biological model of sex differences in intelligence. *Signs, 7,* 769–797.

Shields, S.A., & Crowley, J.J. (1996). Appropriating questionnaires and rating scales for a feminist psychology: A multi-method approach to gender and emotion. In S. Wilkinson (Ed.), *Feminist social psychologies: International perspectives* (pp. 218–232). Buckingham: Open University Press.

Shotter, J., & Gergen, K.J. (Eds.). (1989). *Texts of identity.* London: Sage.

Smith, D.E. (1991). Writing women's experience into social science. *Feminism & Psychology 1*(1), 155–169.

Sommer, B. (1983). How does menstruation affect cognitive competence and psychophysiological response? *Women and Health, 8,* 53–90.

Tavris, C. (1992). *The mismeasure of woman.* New York: Touchstone/Simon & Schuster.

Tavris, C. (1993). The mismeasure of woman. *Feminism & Psychology, 3*(2), 149–168.

Taylor, J.M., Gilligan, C., & Sullivan, A.M. (1996). Missing voices, changing meanings: Developing a voice-centred, relational method and creating an interpretive community. In S. Wilkinson (Ed.), *Feminist social psychologies: International perspectives* (pp. 233–257). Buckingham: Open University Press.

Unger, R.K. (1982). Advocacy versus scholarship revisited: Issues in the psychology of women. *Psychology of Women Quarterly, 7*(1), 5–17.

Unger, R.K. (1992). Will the real sex difference please stand up? *Feminism & Psychology, 2*(2), 231–238.

Unger, R.K. (1996). Using the master's tools: Epistemology and empiricism. In S. Wilkinson (Ed.), *Feminist social psychologies: International perspectives* (pp. 165–181). Buckingham: Open University Press.

Unger, R.K., & Crawford, M. (1992). *Women and gender: A feminist psychology.* New York: McGraw-Hill.

Walker, A. (1994, Spring). Psychology of women publications survey. *British Psychological Society Psychology of Women Section Newsletter, 13,* 4–12.

Walkerdine, V. (1996). Working class women: Psychological and social aspects of survival. In S. Wilkinson (Ed.), *Feminist social psychologies: International perspectives* (pp. 145–162). Buckingham: Open University Press.

Weisstein, N. (1993a). Psychology constructs the female; or, the fantasy life of the male psychologist (with some attention to the fantasies of his friends, the male biologist and the male anthropologist). *Feminism & Psychology, 3*(2), 195–210. (Original work published 1968)

Weisstein, N. (1993b). Power, resistance and science: A call for a revitalized feminist psychology. *Feminism & Psychology, 3*(2), 239–245.

West, C., & Zimmerman, D.H. (1987). Doing gender. *Gender and Society, 1,* 125–151.

Wetherell, M. (1995). Romantic discourse and feminist analysis: Interrogating investment, power and desire. In S. Wilkinson & C. Kitzinger (Eds.), *Feminism and discourse: Psychological perspectives* (pp. 128–144). London: Sage.

Wetherell, M., & Griffin, C. (Eds.). (1991). Open forum: Feminist psychology and the study of men and masculinity – Part I: Assumptions and perspectives. *Feminism & Psychology, 1*(3), 361–392.

Wilkinson, S. (1989). The impact of feminist research: Issues of legitimacy. *Philosophical Psychology, 2*(3), 261–269.

Wilkinson, S. (1990a). Women's organizations in psychology: Institutional constraints on disciplinary change. *Australian Psychologist, 25*(3), 256–269.

Wilkinson, S. (1990b). Women organizing within psychology. In E. Burman (Ed.), *Feminists and psychological practice* (pp. 141–151). London: Sage.

Wilkinson, S. (1991a). Why psychology (badly) needs feminism. In J. Aaron and S. Walby (Eds.), *Out of the margins: Women's studies in the nineties* (pp. 191–203). London: Falmer Press.

Wilkinson, S. (aided and abetted by Condor, S., Griffin, C., Wetherell, M., & Williams, J.) (1991b). *Feminism & Psychology*: From critique to reconstruction. *Feminism & Psychology, 1*(1), 5–18.

Wilkinson, S. (Ed.). (1994). Special feature: Critical connections: The Harvard Project on Women's Psychology and Girls' Development. *Feminism & Psychology, 4*(3), 343–424.

Wilkinson, S. (Ed.). (1996). *Feminist social psychologies: International perspectives*. Buckingham: Open University Press.

Wilkinson, S. (1997). Still seeking transformation: Feminist challenges to psychology. In L. Stanley (Ed.), *Knowing feminisms: On academic borders, territories and tribes* (pp. 97–108). London: Sage.

Wilkinson, S., & Kitzinger, C. (Eds.). (1993). *Heterosexuality: A 'Feminism & Psychology' reader*. London: Sage.

Wilkinson, S., & Kitzinger, C. (Eds.). (1995). *Feminism and discourse: Psychological perspectives*. London: Sage.

Wilkinson, S., & Kitzinger, C. (Eds.). (1996a). *Representing the other: A 'Feminism & Psychology' reader*. London: Sage.

Wilkinson, S., & Kitzinger, C. (1996b). The queer backlash. In D. Bell & R. Klein (Eds.), *Radically speaking: Feminism reclaimed* (pp. 375–382). Melbourne: Spinifex/London: Zed Books.

Wooley, H.T. (1910). Psychological literature: A review of the recent literature on the psychology of sex. *Psychological Bulletin, 7*, 335–342.

Worrell, J. (1990). Feminist frameworks: Retrospect and prospect. *Psychology of Women Quarterly, 14*(1), 1–5.

13

Reflexively Recycling Social Psychology: A Critical Autobiographical Account of an Evolving Critical Social Psychological Analysis of Social Psychology

Ian Lubek

Critical Autobiography: The Sincerest Form of Reflexivity?

This chapter, when previously presented as a paper to a conference on 'Critical Social Psychology', somehow summoned up for me the spectre of a public affirmation at a meeting of 'Social Psychologics Anonymous': 'I admit I am a social psychologic. I've been on the wagon now for over two decades; I haven't done a laboratory experiment since my PhD thesis in 1971.' A supportive network with empathic tendencies provides an important context for both the critical autobiographical revelation itself, and the will to move forward and not regress. The critical autobiographical genre, part of a broader critical historiographical approach, attempts to retrospectively and reflexively question career and life history events within their broader socio-political contexts, and can therefore, at times, be somewhat less self-promoting than standard celebratory, presentist self-presentations.[1] For an audience interested in critical social psychology, it is possible to summarize the evolution of one critical, reflexive stance towards social psychology; the end result becomes, in essence, a contextualized account of 'what I've been doing for a living' since I walked away from experimental social psychology at the very moment when Israel and Tajfel's (1972) critique was being prepared for publication.[2] But in addition, critical autobiography may be able to remove some of the hidden ideological agenda items which pervade both positivist and critical writings.[3] Because conferences on critical social psychology have framed the development of my own critical thought, let us first examine the context for organizing such critical events.

Contextualizing the History of Critical Social Psychology

Modernist and Postmodernist Critiques

The critique of social psychology is not of course an exclusively post-modernist innovation, but has long been a feature of the earlier positivist and modernist perspectives, although not always placed at the sub-discipline's centre-stage nor under its publication spotlight. Such criticism, always co-existing with the sub-discipline's mainstream activities, has challenged it at three different levels, with a varying volume of 'voice', and differing degrees of persuasive success. At the *scientific level*, critical analysis offered competing paradigmatic, theoretical, methodological or research ethics formulations. At the *meta-scientific level*, we find intellectual tensions between competing root metaphors or models of (hu)man(kind), between rival philosophy-of-science or disciplinary perspectives, and between contending meta-theoretical, meta-methodological and epistemological research strategies. Finally, at the broader, *extra-scientific level*, contextual concerns involve the politics and economics of organizing the material arrangements, and institutional structures, for the conduct of science; these, in turn, often reflect additional differences among underlying values and ideological positions (Lubek, 1995a).

Critical voices can emerge at each of these levels within public debates even during formative, proto-disciplinary periods of research activity (Apfelbaum, 1986), as well as during 'normal science' periods of sub-disciplinary expansion. Critiques, when generated from marginal/minority perspectives, can at any time be relegated by scientific decision-makers to non-mainstream channels, and thus be eclipsed by established science. They also can suddenly become brightly highlighted during periods when research strays from normal science into a state of disciplinary or paradigmatic crisis, or, as in the case of the late 1960s, when various extra-scientific protest movements in a number of countries led to increased interest in a broader range of alternative intellectual formulations to explain the evolving phenomena of socio-political conflict, upheaval and change.[4] Once critical floodgates are opened, questions may surface anywhere, at scientific, meta-scientific and extra-scientific levels.

Elsewhere, I have attempted to show how these debates and divergences have affected, at all three levels and over time, both psychological research on the pressing social problem of aggression, and the dissemination of the public image of that research (Lubek, 1993a, 1995a). Similarly, historical examples of the critical–mainstream tension may be cited during a pre-formative period in social psychology's development, as in the attempts by Augustin Hamon in France to create in the 1890s a series of social psychological studies at a time when the label 'social psychology' had not been clearly delineated. His highlighting of anti-militarist and pro-anarchist ideas (Hamon, 1893, 1895) about social interaction, socialization, solidarity, and so on, met resistance and rejection from mainstream journal editors and publishers, including Gabriel Tarde, who was at the same time trying to forge an interactive view of social psychology (Lubek, 1990, 1995b, 1995c; Lubek and Apfelbaum, 1989), and who himself met stiff resistance from Durkheim's sociological perspective.[5]

Still other examples might include the paradigmatic switch from McDougall's instinct position to Floyd Allport's behaviourism in the

1920s, which was met with debate and resistance (Collier, Minton & Reynolds, 1991); the critical debates among social psychologists when they organized their first professional association, the Society for the Psychological Study of Social Issues (SPSSI), about whether it should be more research- or activist-oriented (Finison, 1986; Harris, 1986); the pendulum-like swings over time described by Apfelbaum (1986) between a social psychology which had a political or a non-political content, a scientific or non-scientific allure, and a social versus individualistic centring; changing root metaphors within social psychology (Minton, 1992); and interdisciplinary differences between sociological and psychological academic branches and perspectives (cf. Good & Still, 1992; Karpf, 1932; Lubek, 1992). There has thus been a constant critical counter-current in social psychology, which becomes even more salient when a conference focuses its attention directly upon what is usually a marginal activity.

A Tale of Three Cities: Elsinore, Ottawa and Barcelona

The Barcelona conference on 'Critical Social Psychology', where some of the ideas in this chapter were initially presented, specifically focused on critical trends in social psychology arising with the accelerating renewal of criticism in the 1970s, especially after the publication of Israel and Tajfel's (1972) collection of articles by ten European authors from the Elsinore conference in 1970. (cf. Ibáñez's, 1990, assessment of the after-effects of some of these pioneering critical volleys.) These criticisms of the predominant North American definition of the sub-discipline,[6] and the 'received' models for both experimentation and theorization, provided glimpses of alternative approaches and questions from critical theory, Marxism, social constructionism, ethology, ethogeny, cognitivism, linguistics and hermeneutics; these critical ideas seemed to cross disciplinary boundaries quite freely.[7]

For European readers, these articles served to legitimate a variety of fields of inquiry not given priority in the North American-dominated sub-discipline, and to suggest redrawing social psychology's demarcated boundaries to give new voices to the definition of its contents. For the North American reader, they offered, for those able to see beyond the confines of their restrained, pragmatic, paradigmatic research focus, a new perspective on social psychological issues, containing a much deeper philosophical and epistemological analysis than was common in mainstream discussions. The contextual differences surrounding North American and European social psychologies were made most explicit in this volume.[8] Many of the threads from the Elsinore conference would be eventually woven together and 'retranslated' for a North American audience in what would become social psychology's 'crisis' literature (Collier et al., 1991; Elms, 1975; Jackson, 1988; Rosnow, 1981).[9]

While the transatlantic confrontation of ideas may have been given indirect impetus with the publication of the Israel and Tajfel (1972) volume

– wherein European scholars criticized the North American-dominated mainstream – a more direct confrontation followed in 1974, when Lloyd Strickland and Henri Tajfel organized a conference in Ottawa on 'Research Paradigms and Priorities in Social Psychology', bringing together, face-to-face, North Americans and Europeans.[10] The book emanating from this conference (Strickland, Aboud & Gergen, 1976) still reverberates with the tensions and stimulating exchanges of an experiment in living, and daily confronting, the crisis of social psychology. There was the excitement of the discovery of tempting new alternatives, such as 'the social construction of reality', 'social psychology as history', ethogenics, ethnomethodology, critical theory and emancipatory social psychology; as well, there was the anticipation of a threatened unscheduled intervention/disruption by a Marxist group juxtaposed against both the predictable territorial defensiveness of established scholars and the sometimes spirited suggestions for boundary renegotiations and new perspectives from less ensconced researchers. It certainly was not dull![11] The Barcelona meeting, almost two and a half decades after the Elsinore conference, picked up the critical torch and examined both the progress made, and new critical pathways for social psychology, largely 'pushing the envelope' from a European perspective.[12]

Well, It's a Living! Evolving Critical Historical Social Psychological Analyses of Social Psychology

Some Notes on the Relativity of Outsiders and Insiders, or the Recurrent Flow of 'Marginals' into 'Mainstream'

One of my first lessons in the relativity of marginality occurred at the Ottawa conference, where a number of those critical of social psychology felt themselves marginalized with labels such as 'radical', 'critical' or paradigmatic darkness cursers (Gergen & Gergen, 1994; Lubek, 1995c).[13] However, in the conference proceedings, prominent space was given to some of these critical marginal voices, and their disagreements with the mainstream (Strickland et al., 1976). For example, when the issue of 'the power structure in social psychology' was raised, concerns were expressed about how new paradigms could evolve and young researchers be given a voice, when established social psychologists in fact controlled all the disciplinary resources, as well as the definition of the mainstream paradigm. This discussion was quickly co-opted by the more prominent participants. Although at the time a window of opportunity for a mutually reflective, respective and reflexive collective self-inquiry was bypassed, the contents of that discussion appeared in the published volume and in a journal, with critical analysis attached.[14]

This discussion, in fact, proved doubly rewarding for the extension of my evolving critical analysis of social psychology. The socially hierarchic dynamics demonstrated in the discussion – 'visibles' dominating 'less-visibles' – seemed to me the very exemplar of more general disciplinary concerns involving the influence of unequal power in the production of knowledge, as well as the resistance to new ideas, paradigmatic challenges and social and scientific change. At the same time, two published analyses (Lubek, 1976a, 1976b) of the difficulties that certain ideas and voices faced within social psychology helped tip the balance towards a favourable tenure decision, which in turn supported the continuation of critical research concerning social factors in science.

To the extent that marginal positions can garner some institutional support or visibility, such critical views can become available for main-stream discussion and, in particular, may vie for the attention of persons with flexible worldviews, or not yet irrevocably committed to a paradig-matic perspective or a fixed theoretical allegiance.[15] Marginalized, minority or token voices, when given access to regular dissemination channels, may have persuasive or rhetorical impact on others facing similar intellectual problematics and institutional problems. Eventually, through informal or formal networking, marginal workers in an area can be given a structural presence, being brought together for a conference and/or included in a collective volume or speciality journal.[16]

Finally, over the years a 'marginal' paradigmatic position may actually come to attract the majority of workers in an area.[17] Access to apprentice doctoral students may be another indicator of marginality's relativity. Many of the Barcelona participants, while blazing alternative trails, may perhaps be described as 'quasi-marginals', in that they have had success in the dissemination of their critical ideas about social psychology, although not always easily nor through the discipline's front door. However, their articles are represented in scholarly publications, find their way onto graduate reading lists, and are cited by other authors. Do the relative changes in visibility and (quasi-)marginality occurring during a career lead to one's becoming 'ex-marginal', or 'post-marginal'?[18]

As critical dissident perspectives find *some* success in obtaining an outlet or voice, we must none the less not lose sight of those who are not yet being heard formally. Continued efforts are needed to provide 'marginal' ideas, and their authors, with support and diffusion resources. Ultimately, then, much that starts out marginally may finish in the mainstream, as boundaries are pushed further and a fascination with novelty outpaces entrenched traditionalism.

Multiple Hats, Disciplinary Boundary Disrespect, Consorting with Positivists, and Stretching for a Systematic Synthesis

The incomplete critical social psychological analyses which I first began to describe after the 1974 Ottawa conference stressed the connection of social psychological issues to their real-world socio-political context, and the probing of power relations and domination. My goals involved: (a) evaluating critically what mainstream social psychology was then *currently doing* (and *omitting to do*); (b) tracing and seeking to understand the institutional and research strategy *choices previously made* which somehow guided the sub-discipline to its current state; and (c) eventually making impertinent suggestions about what it *ought to be doing*!

The evolving analyses blended elements of critical contextual historiography, epistemology and a reflexive social psychological analysis of the social aspects of scientific activities. There was also shameless borrowing from history, philosophy and sociology of science. Use of ideas from outside the 'specialty area' of experimental social psychology must also be situated within the context of the general criticism of the social sciences in the 1970s, a specific 'crisis of confidence' within social psychology (cf. Collier et al., 1991; Elms, 1975; Jackson, 1988; Rosnow, 1981), and a renewed interest in social and historical studies of science, technology, progress and paradigms, all propelled by a variety of philosophers, epistemologists, sociologists and historians (e.g. Cole & Cole, 1973; Kuhn, 1970; Feyerabend, 1975; Lakatos & Musgrave, 1970; Merton, 1977; Popper, 1959). At the same time, others offered internalist, disciplinary critical analyses (e.g. Gergen, 1973; Ring, 1967; Samelson, 1974/1986).

One of the hats I began wearing was that of a 'critical historian of social psychology'.[19] My particular brand of historical analysis has often made use of quantified data, which offered a useful rhetorical interface for critical discussions of sub-disciplinary historical trends with mainstream, empirical, positivist social psychologists.[20] The critical historical analyses generally re-examined, within their contexts, certain 'lost', 'hidden' or 'marginal' social psychological formulations which had been rejected or ignored by mainstream science and its appointed gatekeepers (cf. Lubek, 1981, 1995b; Lubek & Apfelbaum, 1987, 1989).

Other hats were also donned. The epistemological analyses focused more on uncovering the underlying values and ideological stances within evolving mainstream paradigms (Apfelbaum & Lubek, 1976; Lubek, 1979, 1986, 1995b). Finally, with a critical, reflexive eye on research directions taken by the sub-discipline in the 1970s, I began the more detailed examination of a series of social psychological influence processes at work in my own sub-discipline's scientific practice and entourage (Lubek, 1976a, 1980, 1993a, 1995c).

This multi-hat, cross-disciplinary, critical approach still left open the possibility of dialogue with mainstream researchers and sought to create a systematic synthesis between critical historical and social contextual analyses, with the latter borrowing heavily from the tools and concepts of traditional social psychology. Thus far, this has resulted in a more complex, 'multi-faceted' critical historiographical approach detailed elsewhere (Lubek, 1993b), and the preliminary delineations (Lubek, 1993c, 1995c) of a 'social psychology of science' approach for critical analyses of our own sub-discipline (or others). We shall briefly examine this second approach, which stresses the importance of inter-personal and small-group interactions upon scientific outcomes, especially those involving a series of unequal power relations (Febbraro, Lubek, Bauer, Ross, Thoms, Brown & Hartt (1996); Lubek, 1976a, 1980, 1990, 1993c).

Asymmetric Power Relations: Elements Towards a Definition of a Social Psychology of Science[21]

Critical, Reflexive Recycling: Old Social Psychology for New

The 'social psychology of science' approach recycled standard concepts and observational methods from the 'old' mainstream social psychology, augmented with historiographical archival methods when needed, in order to trace scientific decision-making processes 'behind-the-scenes'. Some novelty perhaps lay in its grafting critical, epistemological and reflexive analyses onto historical and social psychological questions and focusing these specifically on the social processes involved in the generation and transmission of scientific knowledge, in general, and one's own scientific output, in particular. By centring on social negotiations involved in generating scientific knowledge and supporting scientific careers, attention was fixed upon institutional (student) recruitment, apprenticeship and mentoring, research dissemination and support, career advancement (and/or exclusion), as well as the social relations between experimenter and subject, within the confines of data-generating experimental research practice (cf. Danziger, 1990).

Specific notions of hierarchy and asymmetric power were examined, as they impinged upon dyadic or small-group interactions, making science a quite *inter*-personal, rather than *im*-personal activity. Mainstream social psychologists should not have been much surprised with this 'new critical' analysis of social interactions within science, since much of the terminology, and the social psychological level of analysis itself, were already familiar. Both 'gatekeeping' and 'consensus-formation' have long been part of the sub-discipline's conceptual repertoire.[22] However, it is their *reflexive* application to social psychologists' own scientific behaviour which may prove problematic for some.[23]

This new analysis suggested that each time a potential scientific contribution or candidacy is submitted for judgement to the (s)elected representatives of the scientific community, gatekeeping mechanisms are invoked, involving consensual quality-control criteria. These latter agreements about what constitutes good, bad or marginal science are negotiated within the confines of scientific communities which are rather relatively restricted – according to historical moment, discipline, culture, socio-political context and/or ideology. The social processes of gatekeeping and consensus-formation can in fact readily be observed by the social psychologist in a variety of scientific arenas.

Gatekeeping and Consensus-formation in Science: Six Asymmetric Power Relationships

Six sets of scientific relationships involving asymmetric power interactions have been identified, which involve:

(a) publishing (authors and journal editors);
(b) funding (grant applicants and funding panels);
(c) research mentoring (PhD apprentices and research mentors or supervisory committees);
(d) undergraduate teaching/recruitment (undergraduate students recruited as disciplinary majors and professors screening with texts, tests, course requirements and grades);
(e) career progress (academics and research scientists seek career stability and various administrative, promotion and hiring committees decide on their candidacies); and
(f) research practices of experimentation/data-generating (Subjects and Experimenters controlling experiments/studies).

These interactive situations often involve unidirectional communications, where scientific decisions may be final, and without appeal. (See Figure 13.1.)

In addition, following van Strien (1993), the analysis takes account of a series of 'contextual' (systemic, categorical, group and personal) influences, for the most part meta- or extra-scientific, which impinge upon the social negotiations of science. Included in the list might be: meta-theoretical commitment; allegiance to a scientific discipline or profession; bureaucratic or group (dys)functioning; adherence to a political ideology or religious doctrine; membership in a (socio-economic) class; sharing an 'ethnic identity', 'cultural heritage' or 'racial origin'; language use or language grouping; presence of a personal challenge, disability or pathology; groupings according to age, gender or sexual preference; and so forth.[24]

The traditional social psychologist may have trouble both with the *reflexivity* of the analysis of social behaviour turned inward upon her/his *own* scientific practices, and with the more general *social relativity* of science per se. If one accepts that scientific outcomes, like other creative and work activities, are more or less affected by a series of social influence processes, can science still then be portrayed as an objective system of logical decision-making rules which lead to the discovery of universal scientific laws, principles, facts and/or truths? Or has the 'social psychology of science' approach somehow robbed science of its 'special' status, and made it quite relative to human, social and perhaps, at times, even irrational activity involving negotiations and power? Does the application of a critical, reflexive scientific social psychology subvert and undermine science itself? Certainly one of the functions of a critical social psychology is to make visible hidden social processes, especially when they involve

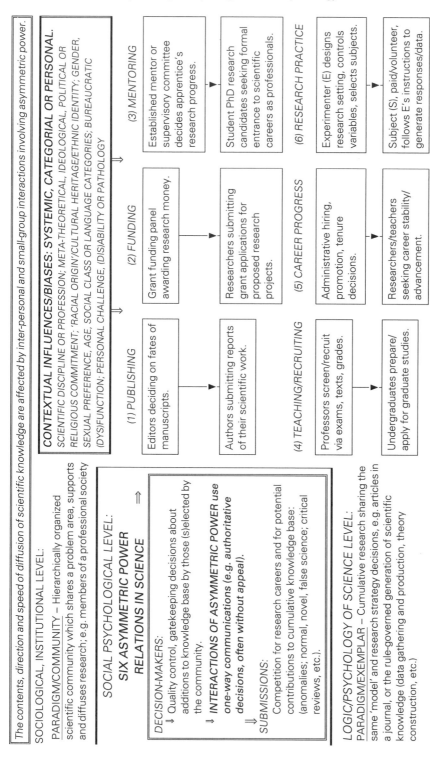

Figure 13.1   The 'social psychology of science' approach

abuse of power and inequitable treatment. As an example of such unmasking, one brief illustrative example of dynamics in the publishing relationship is presented.[25]

John Garcia versus Mainstream Psychology Editors: A Tale of Research, Rejection, Resistance and Reward

The case of John Garcia's challenge to neo-behaviourist learning theory (Lubek & Apfelbaum, 1987) dramatically illustrates the asymmetric power interactions involved in contemporary, professional editorial gatekeeping. We therefore detour temporarily away from our sub-discipline of social psychology to enter the wider avenues of mainstream psychology.[26]

Garcia began to rebel publicly against the dominant paradigm in 1965 (at roughly the same time as a secure career position was obtained at Harvard). His experimental results had, in fact, been contradicting established wisdom ever since 1955. His discourse, however, had remained 'scientifically polite' throughout the decade and the discussions of his anomalous findings did not take an overly combative tone towards the mainstream ideas they increasingly, and cumulatively, called into question.

In 1979, Garcia was professionally recognized with the highest honour of the American Psychological Association (APA) – its Distinguished Scientific Contribution Award. His work had been increasingly acknowledged, and cited, by colleagues working in the same specialty area, and his professional career had advanced through a series of prestigious appointments. Yet, as Lubek and Apfelbaum (1987) noted, during the immediate period leading up to this award, *none of his senior-authored articles (and only one of his students' articles, with Garcia as junior author) had been published in any APA journal.* Bisecting his pre-award publication record, it was noted that the second half (1966–79) had in fact seen a dramatic decline in professional visibility. Garcia's articles in prestigious, mainstream journals relevant to learning theory declined 34 per cent from 52 per cent of his output during the first half, to 18 per cent in the second (see Figure 13.2).[27] The plunge in published articles in the APA's own journals, from 22 per cent to 2 per cent, seems particularly more striking considering that 20 per cent of all citations of his learning research originated in articles in those same mainstream APA journals. Thus during the period 1966–79, Garcia's work was increasingly discussed by his colleagues within the APA journals, but his own input was absent.[28]

This seeming puzzle was partially solved when we examined the correspondence between Garcia, various editors and referees during this period (as part of the 'social psychology of science' concern with the asymmetric 'publishing' relationship).[29] As detailed elsewhere (Lubek & Apfelbaum, 1987), we found Garcia being subjected to *ad hominem* attacks and often extra-scientific criticism for having abandoned the then-dominant Hull–Spence neo-behaviourist perspective in 1965, in favour of an alternative, cognitivist position more in keeping with Berkeley neo-Tolmanism. From

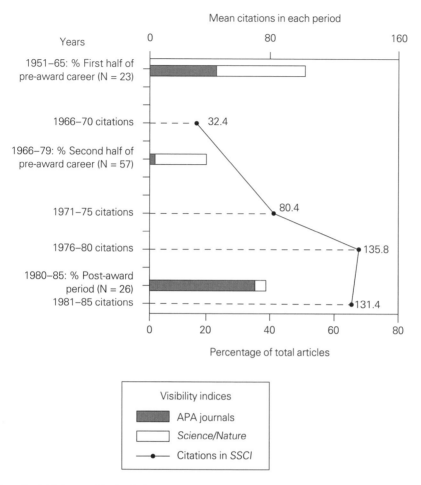

From *Social Sciences Citation Index*
five-year cumulative volumes

Figure 13.2 *Percentage of John Garcia's total articles in APA journals,
Science, Nature (1951–85) and mean annual citations (from Social
Sciences Citation Index, five-year cumulative volumes)*

this point onward, having openly declared a paradigm shift, editors and
referees became suddenly highly critical of his methods, his theory, his
research design, his use of control groups, and even the clarity of his
graphs.

In some of the reviews, referees may have stepped beyond the bounds of
their task of evaluating the soundness of a submitted article; in one evaluative sequence, we found evidence of another motivation in the gatekeeping
and/or scientific marginalization process – the settling of old scores. Garcia
had submitted to *Science* an article which described a novel set of findings

contradicting another long-held belief, the classical conditioning concept of overshadowing. Two short reviews, one positive and one neutral, were followed by a longer, negative one. In June 1977, following the editor's suggestion, the manuscript was revised by Garcia and resubmitted, taking special care to answer the negative reviewer's comments about clarity and procedure. But in July, the editor wrote back that the original negative reviewer now demanded still more revisions. Again, Garcia revised the manuscript and this time included an accompanying point-by-point description of all requested changes made, citing chapter and verse. When the negative reviewer *still* refused these changes, the editor brought in a fourth referee to read the manuscript, who now criticized the figures as obscuring information and judged the article as 'technically deficient' and portions of the research as 'clumsily designed'. The editor now rejected the paper, based upon two negative reviews. Garcia persisted, however, with the editor, who then sent Garcia *additional* arguments from one of the negative reviewers:

> The reviewer argued for highest standards of rigor in the case of novel and unique findings, because of the amount of follow-up work that will be stimulated. If the original work is not 'an excellent description of and [*sic*] obviously well-designed and executed study . . . then a great deal of time and effort on the part of other investigators will be lost in pursuing false criticisms'. Then, referring to work *more than a decade old*, the reviewer continues, 'I do not mean to be unkind, but that other work on toxicosis, particularly on the cue-to-consequence feature of it, was seriously flawed both in design and execution.' Such research had wasted 'the time of many competent and careful investigators trying to evaluate these flaws'. (Lubek & Apfelbaum, 1987, p. 78)

The article, delayed by a year, eventually appeared in a non-psychology journal. None the less, the episode is quite instructive in that it shows that Garcia, unlike most authors receiving a negative editorial decision, resisted the uni-directional decision-making process and during the negotiated revision process challenged the editor and referees on several occasions.[30] Much additional time was spent by Garcia in such 'social renegotiations' after negative decisions, and much time was lost getting novel findings into print ahead of colleagues who were working in the same area, but who had easier access to mainstream journals.[31]

Finally, in the course of interviewing persons knowledgeable about the inner workings of the neo-behaviourist community, there appeared spontaneous anecdotal accounts pointing to prejudicial or racist treatment, which we did not quote in our analysis, because we had not 'systematically' probed for this. In retrospect, and with the recent incorporation of extra-scientific 'contextual' influences such as sexism and racism into the 'social psychology of science' analysis, perhaps we should have paid closer heed to reports of research colleagues and editorial decision-makers making negative and prejudicial comments about Garcia's Hispanic origins. (See Winston's discussions (1996a, 1996b) of anti-semitism, for example, within psychology.)

Overall, Garcia's ideas were, perhaps somewhat tardily, recognized by his profession, by his colleagues in his specialty research area, and by textbook writers, although he was required to exhaust additional energies and develop new, creative, work-around research dissemination strategies simply because his anomalous ideas challenged the mainstream. At a most productive moment in Garcia's career, and for almost eighteen years, the APA editors proved highly effective gatekeepers.[32] But rather than have his ideas languish in a file drawer of rejected manuscripts, Garcia resisted and adopted an activist, confrontational approach, which ultimately ensured alternative publication outlets.[33] Although this made it somewhat harder for psychologists to follow his work, his ideas at least maintained a certain visibility level; this alternative is not always available for other marginalized or anomalous ideas.

Garcia was also quite fortunate in that although his new ideas met a stone wall of resistance from mainstream *editors*, he had no reported problems with any other asymmetric scientific interactions. Thus, for example, he received increasingly prestigious academic appointments (Harvard, Stony Brook, Utah, UCLA), attracted excellent graduate students, became the first chairperson of Hispanic descent in an American psychology department, and received adequate funding (perhaps because of the potential applicability of his work for addiction research, predator control among farmers and ranchers, and medical consequences of radiation).

Garcia's anomalous findings over a long career opened various chinks in the armour of neo-behaviourist learning theory and paved the way, along with several other research currents, for a paradigmatic shift towards neo-cognitivism, which accelerated in the late 1970s; the fruits of the cognitive approach have also permeated mainstream social psychology during the 1980s. None the less, one wonders how the field of psychology – its knowledge base, its 'recruitment' textbooks, and its pathways towards cognitivism – would have otherwise evolved if mainstream editorial decision-making had not so strongly protected an earlier research consensus, and been so doggedly resistant to early calls for paradigmatic change.

Social Psychology and Its Own Sub-disciplinary Asymmetric Power Relations: What's to be (Un)Done?

Other case histories, more directly attached to social psychology's development, shed light on various asymmetric power relations in different contexts and at different historical moments: compare the French turn-of-the-century publication difficulties of Gabriel Tarde and Augustin Hamon (Lubek, 1981, 1990, 1995b, 1995c; Lubek & Apfelbaum, 1989); Rockefeller Foundation funding problems in the 1930s in French social sciences; and American administrative, publishing and mentoring problems for Carl Murchison (1923–36) at Clark University (Lubek, 1995c); undergraduate textbooks and experimental social psychology methodology texts as tools of recruitment (Lubek, 1993a; Lubek & Stam, 1995; Stam & Lubek, 1992);

mentoring of social psychologists at the University of Michigan (Febbraro et al., 1996; Ross, Febbraro, Thoms-Chesley, Bauer & Lubek, 1996); and the funding relationship (Bauer, Thoms & Lubek, 1995).

The 'social psychology of science' approach helps unmask any inequitable consequences of abuse of power in the social transactions within a scientific community. Many of these 'scientific injustices' – receiving an arbitrary or unmerited negative evaluation or rejection letter – have been commonly experienced, at some time or other, by researchers and students, and by positivist and critical social psychologists alike.[34] Such an analysis may therefore be understood because it makes intuitive sense and overlaps with everyday experience. But *as a critical analytical device*, its primary task is not to propagate large systematic research efforts resembling the classic positivist programmes of social psychological lore of yore (beyond, of course, the few case histories needed for a convincing overall argument or at least a telling tale). The analysis should be *critical, reflexive and unveiling*, offering systemic insights while carefully weighing any overly self-indulgent scholastic whining about minor career progress inconveniences, which affect relatively few privileged academics, researchers and/ or apprentices.

Rather, a more general task is suggested for social psychologists: as sensitized observers, especially adept as detectors of structural, social-contextual or inter-personal inequities or more general processes of oppression, they might employ analytical tools available from critical perspectives (supplemented by others salvaged from positivist research) for emancipatory actions, whistle-blowing, resistance or change (cf. Minton, 1986, 1993a, 1993b; Rappoport, 1986).

Positivist and Critical Social Psychologists Unite – You Have Nothing to Lose But Your Navels

An intellectual enterprise such as social psychology, in either its more traditional, positivistic versions or any of its alternative, 'critical' incarnations (e.g. Armistead, 1974; Billig, 1982; Larsen, 1980; Wexler, 1983; Wilkinson, 1986) always runs the risk of navel-gazing, of turning inward upon itself and losing sight of the external world supplying its problematics; it may then concentrate excessively on building and transmitting a narrowing, within-house, consensus or intertanglement of ideas, concepts and exclusive discourse. Any social psychological research object can become 'overworked' – either by parametrically pushing a specialized positivist research paradigm/exemplar to a point of experimental non-return, or by promoting deeper, but increasingly abstract and convoluted, critical insights from an alternative formulation. In both cases, after initial and usually innovative productive runs of research, discovery, insight and/or understanding, there follows a period of 'hardening of the artistry', with routines of normal (critical) science busy-work, accumulation of increasingly smaller 'advances' or self-reinforcing details/minutiae/trivia; all of this may be accompanied by a full range of self-absorbed, intellectual navel-gazing.[35]

Consensus-formation, 'Turning Inward' and Trends Towards Trivialization in Positivist Social Psychology

For positivist research, this inward-turning nature can be demonstrated for the case of renewed empirical work in the 1960s using a neo-frustration–aggression formulation; after little more than a decade of research, most studies in the leading social psychology journals had come to adopt just one methodology (using the Buss 'aggression machine').[36] By 1971, as well, the majority of references in these journal articles were to either a small group of pioneers, or to the researchers' own work.[37] This tendency towards research conformism and an increasing over-reliance on a narrow range of 'expert' sources as the base of paradigmatic knowledge also occurred outside the primary, professional literature; it was reflected within textbooks used as part of the recruitment process for future social psychologists. Lubek (1993a, 1995a) has described, quantitatively, the changes over three decades in the image of aggression research given to readers of undergraduate textbooks; there is an increasingly more homogeneous, and conservative, portrayal of aggression on a number of scientific, meta-scientific and extra-scientific dimensions.[38]

The continuous reworking of the dominant 'Berkowitz' model of neo-frustration–aggression research in social psychology, and the 'variables' affecting violent behaviour, continued to follow previously successful laboratory practices. This created a certain homogeneity in the journal literature, where one might have an instant feeling of *déjà vu* after reading just a study's title and the names of its authors.[39]

Aggression research was one of the few areas of social psychology which regularly excluded the use of women subjects, after several early studies in the 1960s found them too 'co-operative'. Laboratory experiments were almost exclusively modelled after what we may call a 'two guys fighting' model of human aggressive interaction, although the original frustration–aggression hypothesis (Dollard, Doob, Miller, Mowrer & Sears, 1939) was much less parochial in outlook and was formulated on a much broader set of psychological, social psychological, sociological and anthropological concerns about aggression (Lubek, 1986). The narrower 1960s laboratory operationalization, and its theoretical linkage between anger or frustration and aggressive outbursts, somehow made sense intuitively to the (almost always male) experimenters who designed the research, as well as to the (mainly male) social psychologists being trained in the 1950s, 1960s and 1970s to read about the research, extend it, and teach it to student apprentices.[40]

But Lubek (1995a) questioned the generative flexibility of such a proto-typical scientific focus, so strongly embedded in the validated social psychological research consensuses about theory and methodology *of the 1960s*, and also grounded in the *Realpolitik* of that same period. Would specialized paradigmatic success not lead to a diminished sensitivity or understanding about other manifestations of violence based on dramatically different dynamics, which either existed in other settings, or were evolving with events of the 1970s and 1980s? Does the evolution of a successful paradigmatic model for aggression (see also Apfelbaum & Lubek, 1976, on conflict research) give licence to a researcher to become a productive experimental hermit, isolated in the laboratory in order to perfect a paradigm 'that works' scientifically, while ignoring changes in the real-world manifestations of the phenomenon under study which 'don't fit'?[41] To what extent, however, could such a 'two guys fighting' metaphor or exemplar of violence, locked in a cycle of narrowing, specialized parametric exploration, be expected, without dramatic restructuring and requestioning of its underlying assumptions, to *generate new knowledge* relevant to the understanding of assault or rape (by date, acquaintance or spouse), where *women* are the primary victims, and a very different set of violent interaction dynamics seem to be operating?[42]

Will these same narrowly focused, highly specialized, male laboratory researchers, using the accepted 'two guys fighting' aggression paradigm/ exemplar, also show interest about, and sensitivity towards, a much broader range of manifestations of international, inter-group, inter-personal and/or self-directed violence? These have greatly evolved since the 1960s, and men are no longer necessarily the principal victims of such. Thus torture, military massacres, ethnic cleansing and genocide have been occurring in ex-Yugoslavia and elsewhere. Although women have always been subject to mass rapes, especially in times of war (Brownmiller, 1976), the reports of the programmed mass rape of an estimated 20,000 Bosnian women in less than a year (Drozdiak, 1993) have changed women victims from individual 'objects of assault' to systemic 'political targets'. And how do modern researchers of violence react to clitoridectomy, practised in many countries at the insistence of men, and misogynist violence against women and children which has now 'progressed' from abuse to murder, to mass murder (Brickman, 1992; Cherry, 1995)?[43]

Specialized research, for positivist paradigms, may consist of repeating a research design 'that works' and tacking on additional variables, either because they have worked elsewhere, or because they can be connected to the theoretical formulation, *post hoc* if necessary.[44] One sign of extreme inward-turning or a 'trend towards trivialization' of a paradigm occurs when variables lose their connectedness to the real-world phenomena originally under study, and researchers instead begin to explore the intricacies of the artificial, experimental situation itself – for example, a study which tests whether more aggressive behaviour is demonstrated when the colours of the buttons on the Buss shock box are varied. Such parametric twiddling, while directly prolonging a productive paradigmatic research line and claiming the legitimating aura of scientific sophistication, may be, in fact, the ultimate in *experimental navel-gazing*.[45]

*On Political and Anatomical Correctness: Can Critical Social
Psychologists Have Navels Too?*

The reflexive mode adopted by critical social psychologists may, in combination with their sensitization to social contexts and interactive sequences
involving power inequities, insulate much of their work from various
faddish debates about political correctness; at the same time, this same
reflexivity may highlight the anatomical correctness of critical psychologists, who also have navels susceptible to contemplation. To date, I have
not, however, targeted any critical, alternative social psychological perspectives for a case study seeking signs of such inward turning.[46]

For lack of any 'concrete evidence', therefore, the analysis of critical
social psychological work must rest, for the moment, with each author's
auto-critical reflexive spirit. Several potential warning signs can be listed for
a self-examination in the privacy of one's own writing-place:

(1) *Hello, what planet are you from?*: Can an uninitiated reader, or the
proverbial 'observer from another planet', coming across your critical
formulation for the first time, immediately see a connection between the
words, language and argument of the account and some social event,
structure, interaction or problem in the real world? Or does excess gravity
imprison the work in your own world?

(2) *Yes, you'll need a dictionary:* On page 1 of your article, are there
more than three key terms which have technical significance to you and
your co-workers, but are not yet in the standard vocabulary of social
psychologists, of either critical or positivist stripe?

(3) *They told me this film had subtitles!:* To understand the arguments
and analysis, do we have to 'speak your language'? Or if the leap has been
made across an incommensurable paradigmatic gap, can new paradigm
subtitles be supplied?

(4) *I cite, therefore I am:* In the bibliography, do a majority of the
references come from just a handful of pioneers in the area and your own
(team's) work?[47]

(5) *To boldly go where no person has gone before:* When work begins on a
broad new area such as the bringing back of rhetoric, discourse, argument
and texts into social psychology, how soon is it before specialization
produces increasingly narrowed studies of the sort: 'The importance of the
preposition "of" in social negotiations of identity'?[48]

(6) *Is this the theatre of the absurd?:* When pushing the envelope of a new
meta-theory for social psychologists, how much scholarly care must be
taken with basic philosophical groundings, to avoid loosely argued, potentially 'absurd' positions? In recent conversations with those stretching the
limits of relativism and social constructivism, and in the chapter by Potter
(in this volume), which alludes to, in passing, the 'death and furniture'
reality debate (Edwards, Ashmore & Potter, 1995), there may be reached a
slippery point where the arguments about rhetoric concerning reality blur
with those denying the 'reality' of events such as the Holocaust, and

discourse analysts, relativists and/or constructionists may (inadvertently) enter the intellectual playing field alongside 'historical revisionists' and 'negationists' with a different political agenda. A quite different scholarly critical social psychological perspective is offered by Kren and Rappoport (1994), who use their inquiry of the Holocaust to raise volatile and deeply existential questions concerning our basic assumptions about human behaviour, social and political life.

(7) *Pardon me, your agenda is showing:* Do critical writings contain the same sorts of hidden ideological agendas and value assumptions as have been noted to lurk just under the textual surface of positivist writings? Or have all the philosophical and, when necessary, critical autobiographical declarations – for example, feminist, phenomenologist and anarcho-epistemologist – been placed prominently up front and rendered transparent?[49]

(8) *Blueprint for action or just more bla-bla-bla?:* Has the analysis stayed solely at the abstract level (even if brilliantly), or are there connective bridges shown to the world of social action and strategies for change, emancipation, resistance and alleviation of injustices?

The Descent from the Ivory Tower to the Street

With these sorts of questions in mind, both positivist and critical social psychologists might manage to avoid some of the pitfalls and convolutions of hyper-specialization and the concomitant turning-inwards upon themselves. If so, then a final stage in a critical social psychology may yet require an additional step: the return from the academic researcher's 'ivory tower' to the everyday social problems of 'the street'. This would lead to renewed interest in: (a) the dynamics of interactions and the problems – be they real, constructed or imagined – of daily subjectivity and social lives (Burman, 1993; Henriques, Hollway, Urwin, Venn & Walkerdine, 1984; Walkerdine, 1986); (b) power inequities shaping the broader socio-political contexts for these social lives (Minton, 1986); and (c) strategies for any needed, or requested, interventions or emancipatory actions (Minton, 1993a, 1993b; Prilleltensky, 1989, 1990).

Critical Social Psychology and the Outside Social World

Conferences as Safe Havens: Elsinore, Ottawa, Barcelona, not Belfast, Beirut or Sarajevo, Mogadishu, Soweto, Hebron . . .

The 'social psychology of science' analysis, offered as a critical analytic tool for social psychology, is a rather 'safe' offering for a 'safe' conference. It offers insights into various practices that may affect the comfort and careers of several hundred 'marginalized' critical researchers and practitioners of social psychology; as such, it is a relatively safe, if not slightly subversive, topic, and there will be relatively little disruptive effect on the social world outside of the conference or of academia, more generally. The critical conferences themselves, not unlike their positivist counterparts, are designed to bring otherwise dispersed social psychologists – in this case 'marginal' and/or critical – together to form a socially 'critical mass', with sufficient time for mutual discussion and/or supportive networking. Although there are some intellectual sparks and academic fencing, generally such conferences are rather safe, congenial affairs, held in attractive, relatively conflict-free venues.[50] Such conferences would not generally occur where the host city was in turmoil, involving real-world, and real-war, conflicts; Elsinore was therefore preferred over Belfast in 1970, Ottawa over Beirut in 1974, and Barcelona, in 1993, over Sarajevo, Mogadishu, Soweto, Hebron, and so on.[51]

Internecine paradigmatic conflict among either positivist or critical social psychologists generally leads, at these conferences, to predictable, intra-disciplinary, academic battles of words, complete with the discursive firing of critiques and rejoinders; this pales in comparison with the social and ideological disputes that lead to real-war, inter-group battles of bullets, complete with the deadly artillery firing of mortar rounds and anti-personnel shells. The ideas and the abstract world of a conference of 'quasi-marginals' critically looking at social psychology would lose much of their interest if conference participants were faced with greater challenges than those at Barcelona – presenting a coherent twenty-minute talk, speaking at all times into recording microphones, and struggling to translate the lunch menu.

If such a conference had instead been held in a location such as Sarajevo, whose environment between 1993 and 1996 included random sniper bullets and deadly mortar rounds, unpredictable supplies of electricity, heating and water, and food shortages linked to airport closures, it would not have proceeded as smoothly in such a place. Our Sarajevan hosts, facing potential victimhood daily, themselves would have a hierarchy of social and personal concerns more linked to a basic struggle for daily survival against the terrors of a social world run amok. As such, the outcomes of a conference on critical social psychology would have little import, and might seem, in that context, to be a superfluous luxury.[52]

Reconnecting Critical Social Psychology with the World

The consequences of 'scientific decision-making' as described above in the 'social psychology of science' approach can be seen, relatively and reflexively, to be 'small potatoes'; much of it possesses, despite some inequities for marginal players, at least the surface aura of civility and perhaps reflects an aspect of Moscovici's (1972) 'social psychology of the nice person'. But from the early beginnings of social psychology, writers such as Tarde, Hamon, Le Bon and others also explored themes of social pathology. Critical social psychology, sensitized to iniquitous situations, may need to look social atrocities squarely in the face, a task, for the moment, largely relegated to the occasional grouping of Nobel Laureates, documentary or occasionally Hollywood film-makers, or the whims of journalists and their employers' overarching mediatic concerns for dramatic conflicts (generally referred to as 'bang-bang' footage); social psychology's problem focus, and gatherings, still retain the safety of the 'tower' over the dangers of the 'street'.

Many of the collective outrages and much social suffering may be directly traced to decisions made by scientific, military and/or political small groups or committees. Such decision-making could easily fall under the purview of social psychology. Group decisions and negotiations involving scientists and others occurred before constructing the first atomic bomb, designing 'Star Wars', testing effects of radioactivity on unknowing US 'volunteers', building the Chernobyl reactor or testing contraceptives and AIDS-related pharmaceuticals on Third-World subjects, and they have helped define what constitutes the treatment of prisoners of war, genocide, torture, the use of chemical, biological and nuclear weapons, and so forth.[53]

The lives of many people can simultaneously be affected by dyadic and small-group negotiated decisions outside of the scientific arena as well, especially in the economic and political spheres.[54] A group of decision-makers at Wannsee, Germany, in January 1942 agreed on a 'final solution' for European Jews, and millions subsequently perished; in August 1945 the US government decided to drop atomic bombs on Hiroshima and Nagasaki; a series of US cabinet decisions in the 1960s led to escalated warfare in Viet Nam, followed closely in the 1970s by decisions of the Khmer Rouge leadership under Pol Pot, which resulted in genocide in Cambodia. Such decisions, especially when transmitted asymmetrically through obedient military organizations, can lead to mass destructiveness, with little critical questioning of orders or decisions, even when apparently inequitable.[55] Such small-group negotiating and decision-making can also lead to both positive and negative long-term socio-economic consequences for much of the world (as with the OPEC oil-producers' price change in 1973, or with recent European Union, NAFTA and GATT trade agreements). Small groups and powerful individuals both can lead the world to political brinkmanship (as in the Cuban missile crisis, cf. Janis, 1968) or can seek pathways for peace (Janis, 1986).[56]

A critical 'social psychology of science' offers a blueprint for analysis of power inequities in, and possible resistance and change strategies against, social interactions determining important outcomes for us as scientists; a broader critical *social psychology*, more generally – especially if it focused on political decision-making – might use parallel analyses. Such a critical social psychology may offer an additional analytical tool and legitimating voice for guiding socio-political and moral action as an extension of the earlier Lewinian vision of action research (Lewin, 1946). The narrower 'social psychology of science' may thus be seen as a starting point for a broader emancipatory, committed, action-oriented critical social psychology which engages itself in the detection of inequities, the 'bearing of witness' to various public and hidden social behaviours and pathologies, and the suggestion of systematic strategies for intervention, resistance and change.

Notes

Portions of this chapter were prepared while the author was visiting the Groupe d'Études sur les Divisions sociales et sexuelles du Travail (GEDISST) and the Institut de Recherche sur les Sociétés Contemporaines (IRESCO), CNRS, Paris, France. Portions of this research have been supported by the Social Sciences and Humanities Research Council of Canada (SSHRC).

1. Compare the standard autobiographical accounts in mainstream series such as the *History of Psychology in Autobiography*, begun by Murchison (1930, 1932, 1936), with three dramatically divergent types of critical-reflexive reporting by Rappoport (1994), Gergen & Gergen (1994) and Cherry (1995). For discussion of varieties of historiography and celebratory versus critical histories, cf. Hilgard, Leary & McGuire (1991), Lubek (1993b), Lubek, Innis, Kroger, McGuire, Stam & Herrmann (1995).

2. The tendency for 'older critical voices' to use a form of justifactory career accounting for 'what I've done, step by step, over the past twenty-five years, and what I'm doing today' overlaps with, and shares important elements with, the common 'research talk' practice of mainstream social psychologists. The latter often summarize for their audiences their empirical research accomplishments, using somewhat different rhetorical devices (experimental methodologies and statistics), and with a more assured conviction that Science, Reality and Truth are all firmly in their corner.

3. This additional element of critical autobiography involves making transparent, from the outset, some of the guiding ideological and value commitments of the author. Thus I can indicate that during the rise of various social movements in the 1960s, I sided with the activist protesters; in the debates between left and right, I sided with the left; I favoured Paul Feyerabend's (1975) anarchic epistemology over Sir Karl Popper's (1959) approach to science; I shamelessly borrowed elements of Klaus Riegel's dialectical approach in the 1970s, and attended Foucault's lectures on power at the Collège de France, while pretending not to understand some of the complex ideas of other French writers; I sided with critical historians against 'antiquarians'; I left Stony Brook just as the seeds of a Marxist social psychology were being planted, but I never inhaled; feminist thought provided an important awakening, although I still sometimes inadvertently cat-nap; for a while, I trusted no-one over thirty, although now I trust no-one who has worked on the same paradigm for more than thirty years.

4. They may also become more salient at times of a broader intellectual shift, such as that between modern and postmodern periods in the social sciences, humanities and arts. For elements of the change in sociology, social psychology and psychology, cf. Collier, Minton & Reynolds (1991: chap. 13); Gergen (1991); Touraine (1995); Wagner (1994). Various authors suggest key works or events signalling a transition to a more self-reflective, deconstructive mode. While films by diverse French New Wave directors, David Lynch or Woody Allen are mentioned, no-one has yet noted the ironic anti-scholasticism of Jeff Kanew's 1985 *Revenge of the Nerds*. And it is perhaps prudent to refrain from entering the debate about whether Amy Heckerling's 1995 film *Clueless* is really a postmodern Valley Girls and Beverly Hills meets Jane Austen's *Emma* or can be so constructed . . . whatever!

5. Even Durkheim was not completely immune to a critical social psychological current. Correspondence among the early Durkheimian sociologists shows that while Durkheim was against the use of the term 'social psychology' and effectively kept it out of his journal *Année Sociologique*, a number of his collaborators secretly discussed their 'marginal' social psychological ideas behind his back (Apfelbaum, 1981; Besnard, 1979; Documents, 1979). There were minimal opportunities to explore social psychology openly, prior to Durkheim's death in 1917. Dominique Parodi, an *Année Sociologique* collaborator, however, seems to have signed a contract with the publisher Doin around 1905 for a textbook on social psychology (after Augustin Hamon failed to fulfil his contract with the same publisher signed in 1900). Although Parodi published articles and other books during this time, after fourteen years of non-delivery his name was removed from the list of forthcoming works in 1919, and G.-L. Duprat (who had taken a clear social psychological stand at the turn of the century and was

not welcomed among the Durkheimians) wrote the book (Duprat, 1920). Durkheim's nephew and successor, Marcel Mauss, was later elected president in 1924 of the French *Psychological Society* and he strove to build a bridge between psychology and sociology (Mauss, 1924; cf. Lubek, 1995b, 1995c).

6. Gordon Allport (1954) had defined the discipline from a narrow, individualist perspective as 'an attempt to understand and explain how the thought, feeling and behavior of individuals are influenced by the actual, imagined or implied presence of other human beings' (p. 5); this psychological definition was echoed thereafter in many English-language textbooks, and in reprintings of this *Handbook* chapter in 1968 and 1985.

7. At the initiative of Henri Tajfel, Joachim Israel and Serge Moscovici, the conference was held in Elsinore, Denmark, in April 1970, after earlier concerns had been expressed at a spring 1969 meeting of the European Association of Experimental Social Psychology, in Louvain, Belgium. At that meeting, while some papers followed mainstream ideas,

> [o]thers expressed dissatisfaction or searched for new avenues of theorizing and research. The discussions [demonstrated] . . . a complex and conflicted collective state of mind . . . many felt that an unquestioned acceptance of the assumptions – social, scientific and philosophical – underlying much of this research was a heavy price to pay for achieving a modicum of 'scientific respectability' and even for making *some* gains in knowledge. (Tajfel, 1972, p. 2)

Tajfel suggested that certain long-standing issues included

> . . . the nature of theory in social psychology; the adequacy of the methods used for the analysis of 'natural' social phenomena; the nature of the unstated assumptions, values and presuppositions about Man and society determining theories and methods of research; the relevance and significance of the results of science; the relations of theories, problems and methods of research in social psychology to those in the physical and in the natural sciences. (p. 3)

8. Moscovici was most direct in confronting the work of American social psychologists.

> As we read them and try to understand and assimilate the principles that guide them we must often conclude that they are strangers to us, that our experience does not tally with theirs, that our views of man, of reality and of history are different. . . . This 'social psychology of the nice person' was to me then – as it still is today – offensive in many ways; it had little relevance to what I knew or had experienced. . . . But I also concluded that, in Europe, we must turn towards our own reality, towards our own maxims from which we must derive our own 'scientific' consequences. (Moscovici, 1972, pp. 18–19)

For a retrospective account two decades later, see Moscovici (1993).

9. See especially Gergen's (1982a) socio-rational alternative meta-theory, Minton's (1986) summary and Parker's later (1989) perspective.

10. Sixty persons were invited, including 'the most prominent social psychologists in Europe, Britain, and North America', in addition to 'relatively unknown graduate students or recent Ph.D.'s, either in (or from) Canadian graduate programs or studying outside Canada' (Strickland, 1976, p. 5). Of fifty-nine listed participants plus the three editors, thirteen were women (21 per cent), twelve (19 per cent) came from European universities and twenty-seven (44 per cent) were estimated, at the time, to be 'visible' or prominent social psychologists. It is interesting to note differences in emphasis and interpretation in descriptions of the 'context' for the conference by one of the organizers (Strickland, 1976), and one of the (then) young, critical social psychologists (Lubek, 1976a, pp. 317–320).

11. One direct aftereffect of this meeting was the forming of the Society for the Advancement of Social Psychology, which soon rivalled in size the APA's Division 8 (Personality and Social Psychology) and which provided, in its newsletter, outlets for critical comments. Some of this criticism was siphoned off by the founding of the *Personality and Social Psychology Bulletin* in 1975, which, in its early days, was an important voice for issues in the crisis of social psychology. Five years later, however, the articles had become largely indistinguishable from those of the mainstream *Journal of Personality and Social Psychology*, at about the same time as Leon Festinger (1980) was suggesting: 'The malaise is probably over' (p. 253).

12. I was very pleased to be invited to a conference for European, critical voices as a lone North American participant. However, for over two decades, I have worked part-time each year in France, and consequently now use much more complex sentence structures than my compatriots. I somehow felt implicitly beckoned to offer a prototypical North American-style critical paper. I trust the reader will find included many of the requisite ingredients: offering a slick, superficial and/or arrogant allure; using catchy, pretentious titles reminiscent of the zenith of the 'fun-and-games' period of experimental social psychology (Ring, 1967; Lubek & Stam, 1995); relying heavily on rhetorical gimmicks, over-extended or mixed metaphors, flashy graphics and the constant enumerating of ideas in point form, as if in preparation for a multiple-choice exam; seeking epistemological naïveté or philosophical shallowness by (a) avoiding any mention of Locke, Hegel, Wittgenstein, Habermas or Charles Taylor; (b) abstaining from any temptation to translate Foucault or Derrida; while (c) tolerating several references to Kuhn, providing they are strictly focused on the word 'paradigm'; (d) avoiding overt political or ideological commitment, or language possibly offensive to any category of ten or more members. While the terms 'critical' and 'positivist' may be sparingly used without additional bibliographlation, the addition of seven to fifteen extra references is still recommended to compensate for light-handed treatment of the terms 'realist', 'constructivist' and its profusion of prefixes, 'subjectivity', 'discursive' or 'discourse analysis', 'post-modern', any word beginning with 'cyber-' and, alas, 'social-contextual'. Avoid inclusion of any technical discourse introduced by other conference participants: because of all the work entailed in mastering newly coined concepts or the extensive literature of the wordsmiths involved – coupled with the dubious status of the concept of 'meaning' itself – embarrassment can be avoided by awaiting the appearance of such concepts in a proper textbook with a legitimizing glossary of short, memorizable definitions at the back. Provide no clear definition of critical social psychology; you may then be reinvited to the next conference to express yourself on this matter. When it is discovered that the wrong package of illustrative figures has been included with the text, use them anyway (after all, they're just rhetorical devices and both you and your audience may be pleasantly surprised by such nova-constructivism); in critical social psychology, as in Hollywood, the account must go on.

13. After a paper critical of conflict research (Apfelbaum & Lubek, 1976), Morton Deutsch (1976) reacted by saying 'it is time for those who profess in radical change to go beyond cursing the darkness and to help light a few candles' (p. 101). Apfelbaum (1991) recalled that shortly after that conference session

> . . . a highly visible mainstream researcher, this time a woman, actually advised me, for my own sake, to refrain from further unseemly critical outbursts. She indicated that it would certainly be wiser to behave from now on 'like a good girl' and go back to normal science activities. I still remember her words: 'After all, you are so very young; you certainly do not wish to jeopardize your career.' (p. 6)

Gergen and Gergen (1994, p. 72) also describe quite openly the tensions between 'radical' marginals and the more senior mainstream individuals at that conference. They also discuss other tensions during this period of crisis, including transcultural tensions in 'supercharged' discussions, argument and the 'dialogic process' discovered in Europe (p. 76), and earlier troubles in getting critical ideas on 'social psychology as history' published (p. 70; see also Gergen, 1982b, for a more 'critical' description of these same difficulties).

14. Contextual historical information and the quantitative analyses of the transcripts of this discussion (Lubek, 1976a, 1976b) suggested that prestigious, 'visible', mainstream social psychologists disproportionately dominated the discussion initiated by the younger, less visible social psychologists.

15. While 'classic' critical articles by Ring (1967) and Gergen (1973) gained tenuous footholds in mainstream social psychology journals, each was followed by a strong rebuttal article; no rejoinders were then permitted by the respective editors.

16. Examples include the Elsinore, Ottawa and Barcelona conferences for critical social psychology, the Paris International Conference on the History of Social Psychology in 1991 (Lubek, Apfelbaum & Paicheler, 1993; Lubek, Minton & Apfelbaum, 1992); or the biennial

meetings of the International Society for Theoretical Psychology (see e.g., Lubek, van Hezewijk, Pheterson & Tolman, 1995; Stam, Mos, Thorngate & Kaplan 1993; Tolman, Cherry, van Hezewijk & Lubek, 1996, and issues of the journal *Theory & Psychology*).

17. The interdisciplinary Cheiron Society (the International Society for the History of the Behavioral and Social Sciences) had a small group of 'critical historians' who met informally in discussions in 1976 and 1977, and decided to plan a small workshop a day in advance of the next meeting; between 1978 and 1985, the workshops attracted increasingly more of the regular members, who also came a day early to participate. The 'critical history workshop' eventually became incorporated into the formal programme; by 1986 almost all the members of the Society's executive came from the critical group, and I found myself the programme co-chair that year. A majority of papers accepted to the most recent programmes, especially by younger society members, now contain elements of critical historiography (see Lubek, 1993b). Some of this work can also be seen in two issues of the *Journal of Social Issues* in 1986 devoted to the history of SPSSI (Volume 42, Issues 1 and 4).

18. Perhaps a separate category for *vieux marginal* would also be useful for someone such as myself: at the Barcelona conference, a graduate student wanted to interview me as a 'historical figure' (although at this time I was not yet fifty!) as one of only two conference members present who had also been at the Ottawa conference as a 'critical' or 'marginal' social psychologist.

19. The reversion to 'history' perhaps recapitulates an earlier branching or choice-point in the evolution of social psychology. At the turn of the century, Gabriel Tarde suggested building sociological and social psychological inquiry on an historical model; the debate was won, however, by Émile Durkheim, who offered a Comtean positivist scientific perspective. During the recent 'crisis in social psychology', Gergen (1973) re-raised the question of whether or not 'history' offered a better vehicle than science for understanding social psychological phenomena.

20. As a former 'social psychologic', I admit to the continuing use of numbers and charts as communicative devices, although I gave up almost all statistical manipulations and inferences some years ago ($p < .01$).

21. A fuller description of the 'social psychology of science' perspective appears in Lubek (1993c, 1995c).

22. These terms were revitalized from their earlier usages in social psychology, political science and communications studies by sociologists of science specifically dealing with scientific journals and publication practices. See, for example, Crane (1967); Mulkay (1972, p. 16).

23. Consider the dilemma of traditional social psychologists whose research demonstrates the parameters of such social phenomena as obedience to authority, conformity and attitude change. As consultants, they may apply their scientific knowledge and give advice about building chains of command in the workplace, or about the dynamics of selecting or swaying a jury. But would there still not be a tendency, even among the most ardent 'universalists' or positivists, to exempt oneself from the influence press of these social factors, and to declare that all *one's own* decisions are objective and independent? Therefore, sitting on a courtroom jury or scientific promotion and tenure committee, they might still be convinced that their own judgemental faculties were beyond all social influence. They might not, however, be so sure about the other jury/committee members, even if they also happened to be social psychologists.

24. Lubek (1995c) suggests imagining the additional difficulty of getting a PhD if supervisory interactions involved additional 'contextual influences' such as: being at meta-theoretical, religious and ideological loggerheads over positivist versus hermeneutic, and Marxist versus Islamic, analyses; discriminatory treatment of a foreign student, through overt racism or non-constructive evaluations of 'language difficulties' in written drafts; sexist harassment.

25. Case materials involving five of the six asymmetric power relations are summarized in Lubek (1995c, Febbraro et al., 1996). The S–E relationship has been left in the capable critical hands of Kurt Danziger (1990); see also Stam, Lubek & Radtke (in press).

26. Learning theory is not completely foreign to the contents of social psychology, and some may recall a time when 'learning' was an indispensable, if not required, part of graduate

education, as well as of the textbooks and handbooks of social psychology. So central were deemed the mechanisms of habit, conditioning and reinforcement, that earlier social psychologists such as Lewin and Festinger addressed these issues directly. Many discussions of social behaviour, socialization, modelling, attitude formation, frustration–aggression, and so forth, built upon learning theory concepts and research, considering it but a small price to pay for the added scientific legitimacy received. Garcia arrived at Berkeley after World War II and received his MA in 1949. He briefly explored the world of social psychological research and his very first publication was in this area (Christie & Garcia, 1951). He then gravitated towards the eclectic, cognitivist learning formulations of Tolman, Krech, Ritchie and others.

27. All APA journals have been scanned, although research on taste-aversion was most likely to be reported in four major APA journals relevant for mainstream learning theorists (*Journal of Comparative and Physiological Psychology*, *Psychological Bulletin*, *Psychological Review* and *Journal of Experimental Psychology*) and Garcia had already published in the first three prior to 1965. As well, this research area was also represented in two respected, general scientific journals, *Science* and *Nature*. In discussing 'prestigious' mainstream publishing outlets, APA journals, *Science* and *Nature* are combined. Garcia's decline is more accentuated than for fifteen other winners of the same award, who declined only 16 per cent – from 46 per cent to 30 per cent (Lubek & Apfelbaum, 1987).

28. Nor was Garcia, as a pioneer in the field, being asked to participate in editorial reviewing as a consultant for these same APA journals.

29. About the same time as it was announced that he would receive the award from the APA, he received the following review from a mainstream journal (which, one might surmise, was almost a generic 'negative review', easily adaptable to almost any article one might wish to reject):

> My impression of this manuscript is unfavourable. The paper suffers from a lack of operational definitions that allow one to distinguish between key concepts . . . it also suffers from an excessive use of subjective terms and phrases. . . . The failure to operationalize the concepts under investigation resulted in the problem being ill-defined. Ill-definition of the problem led, in turn, to a poor experimental design, procedural inadequacies, and inappropriate, as well as insufficient, statistical analyses, all of which disallow any meaningful interpretation of the results. As a consequence, the experiment contributes little that is of theoretical or empirical value, and, in my opinion, does not merit publication. (cited in Lubek & Apfelbaum, 1987, p. 79)

Eventually, this paper was published in a *biology* journal, thus being diverted from its primary intended audience of psychologists.

30. On one occasion, another prominent researcher in the area, reading one of the negative reviews Garcia had received, himself wrote to a prestigious editor and former mentor, protesting the unfair treatment. Years later, the editor wrote to Garcia admitting he had mistakenly rejected his study, which would later become 'a classic' (Lubek & Apfelbaum, 1987, p. 89, fn. 57).

31. In trying to understand why the mainstream publication channel was suddenly closed, we may look at the makeup of the editorial boards during the time of Garcia's challenges to the mainstream (Lubek & Apfelbaum, 1987, Table 3.1); in fact, in the four mainstream APA journals, there was a stronger presence of first-generation neo-behaviourists (students of Hull or Spence) than of students from the two major competing formulations of Tolman (one of Garcia's mentors) and Skinner (whose students eventually formed their own journals, when they encountered mainstream publication difficulties).

32. See Garcia's (1981) good-humoured account of his campaign to decondition the neo-phobic editorial consultants to accept his manuscripts. It was the policy of the *American Psychologist* to publish the acceptance talks of all APA award winners, and this article marked Garcia's re-entrance to APA journals after a long absence. In the article, Garcia not only movingly evokes his Hispanic origins, but also good-naturedly satirizes the psychological establishment which had been giving him a relatively hard time, using nine illustrations related to the tale of Don Quixote; the APA editors, however, at the last moment, decided to remove several of the most trenchant drawings, but did not censor his text.

33. Some articles were published as short, technical reports (as in the two-page format in the [then] 'anti-mainstream' journal *Psychonomic Science*), in other non-APA journals, as chapters in edited books, and in journals in either highly specialized areas (e.g. *Radiation Research*) or in neighbouring disciplines, especially biology.

34. The enhancement of such awareness about research inequities may be illustrated anecdotally. Several years ago, when I gave a talk about publishing gatekeeping, one listener, during the discussion period, related how his career had resembled John Garcia's, and that his novel work had been blocked unjustly by the establishment's editors. When he shortly thereafter left the room, others in the audience then added that the previous speaker, as current editor of an important journal, had arbitrarily blocked *their* publications!

35. This tendency towards an inward-turning trivialization may be even more acute when research objects eponymously become attached to a researcher or research group. For positivist research, this may be relatively easy to spot and track through several decades of research, as in Bandura's modelling approach, the Milgram obedience paradigm, the Deutsch and Kraus Acme-Bolt trucking game and the Buss machine for the study of aggression. For critical, alternative formulations, which are generally more recent and do not have as lengthy a research history attached, we might wish to monitor, for example, Gergen's social construc-tionism, Harré and Secord's ethogenics, Potter and Wetherell's discourse analysis or, for that matter, Lubek's 'social psychology of science' perspective.

36. Lubek (1995a) suggests that the use of the false shock-delivery response as a laboratory measure of aggressiveness was introduced around 1960 almost simultaneously by Arnold Buss, Leonard Berkowitz and Stanley Milgram, with Richard Walters also an early user. For aggression articles published in three major social psychology journals – *Journal of Abnormal and Social Psychology/Journal of Personality and Social Psychology* (*JASPI/JPSP*); *Journal of Experimental Social Psychology* (*JESP*); and *Personality and Social Psychology Bulletin* (*PSPB*) – there was 0 per cent usage during the period 1956–9; 30.8 per cent use in the 1960s; 66.7 per cent use during the 1970s, declining back to 32.4 per cent for the period 1980–7. Peak usage occurred in 1970–1, with 87 per cent of sixteen articles using this method.

37. Lubek (1979) reported that the era of increasing mutual citation or 'turning inward' of the literature had peaked in 1971, when 62 per cent of the citations in aggression articles published in *JESP* and *JPSP* were either self-citations or citations to a small group of ten pioneers (and their students and co-workers). Self- and ingroup-citation fell to 34 per cent by 1977, as new researchers became active. For the period 1980–7, with data added from *PSPB*, self- and expert-citation averaged 29 per cent (Lubek, 1995a).

38. This may be part of the wider proselytizing for an experimental laboratory social psychology which would become the dominant research mode in the 1960s, and which continued to be promoted well past its prime (when its effectiveness, validity, ethical appro-priateness and relevance were all critically evaluated during the crisis of social psychology (Lubek & Stam, 1995; Stam & Lubek, 1992).

39. Such recognition experiences may occur for any 'well-worn' paradigm, whenever research practices have, by consensus, become near-universal. The prototypical study by Berkowitz and associates involved a confrontation between two males: the 'experimental confederate' angers or frustrates the subject, who may then respond aggressively by delivering (bogus) electric shocks, often with a violent or non-violent film interposed. Such a laboratory interaction sequence may seem an appropriate simulation of aggressive behaviours, evoking the 'familiar boyhood school-yard altercation: male-gets-angry-and-hits-male' (Lubek, 1995a).

40. In an ongoing study of social psychology PhDs granted between 1949 and 1974 at the University of Michigan – probably the most active centre of American social psychological training – preliminary analyses show that only 15.7 per cent of the 338 PhD students were women, and only 4.3 per cent of the 70 thesis supervisors were women mentors (Febbraro et al., 1996).

41. Laboratory aggression researchers did make attempts to extrapolate beyond their own personal experiences, laboratory data and liberal, middle-class, white backgrounds. They attempted to explain, for example, 'riot' violence occurring in black ghettos. A retrospective reading of these accounts gives some indication of the great distance separating the successful

laboratory work from real-world events. Berkowitz (1972), for example, suggested that 'impulsive reactions undoubtedly occur in urban riots, and evidently play an important role in the initial stages of these violent occurrences' (p. 78). He then goes on (pp. 80–85) to elucidate a series of variables impinging on individuals which might lead to rioting including: one's personal sense of control about expected gratifications, social comparisons, sexual arousal, loud noise, victory or loss of the home team, and 'clammy heat' experienced by ghetto residents.

42. The question extends beyond science, as men and women from the 1960s onwards sought to redefine gender relations. But in the originally male-dominated sub-discipline of social psychology, one may still ask today whether male designers of laboratory studies of aggression empathize with many women's shared sense of danger or vulnerability when walking alone at night across the very university campuses where their experimental data are generated during the day. And although men may well know the statistics about high rates of (often unreported) sexual assaults or near-rape experiences of women, they do not share the ever-present worry of being potential victims. They may also not be as deeply or as personally affected by pervasive effects of coercive, sexist social dynamics, harassment or pornography, and any consequent feelings of humiliation and/or debasement.

43. In addition, the methodological consensus that aggression be operationalized as the delivery of painful or noxious 'stimuli' may constrain scientists from considering more subtle forms of violence involving the harmful abuse of power (such as harassment and discriminatory practices involving racism, sexism, ageism or homophobia), the degrading effects of pornography, and self-destructive behaviours such as substance abuse, dangerous driving, anorexia nervosa and suicide.

44. Seasoned social psychological observers can usually predict when, in the development of a paradigm, journal articles will begin to 'tack on' the standard panoply of 'variables': gender, race, cross-cultural location, socio-economic status, age cohort, educational level or ordinal position of birth; consumption of various substances – tobacco, alcohol, coffee, etc.; or extreme score groupings on any one of several hundred scales of aptitudes, personality or social characteristics, etc.

45. This should not be confused with 'experimental *naval*-gazing' from the time when social psychologists turned their gaze to the US Office of Naval Research (ONR) for grants to establish experimental laboratories, as well as for funding individual projects. In the 1950s and 1960s, the US government began switching more funding to non-military agencies and departments (e.g. the National Institute of Mental Health [NIMH], the National Science Foundation [NSF] and the US Government Department of Health, Education and Welfare [HEW]); the growing protests against military intervention in South East Asia in the 1960s brought additional criticism of 'military' research funding. Most social psychologists switched to other sources, although Bauer, Thoms & Lubek (1995) have found that one highly productive group of experimental social psychologists trained by Leon Festinger, in comparison with all other social psychologists trained at the University of Michigan during the same period (1949–53), had relied on military funding for 55 per cent of their studies in the 1950s, 42 per cent in the 1960s and 32 per cent, still, in the 1970s, while fellow Michigan-trained social psychologists and their mentors had military research support respectively of 33 per cent, 15 per cent and 4 per cent in the same three decades. Febbraro et al. (1996) found male social psychologists relying more heavily on government and military sources than did females.

46. Perhaps some of the discussions and quarrels among, for example, various recent versions of the treatment of discourse and language in social psychology between Loughborough and Manchester proponents may offer one such starting point. See Kroger & Wood (1992) for a brief historic overview of social psychology's varied bridges to language. In addition, several of the contributors to this book may shed further light on this debate.

47. In this chapter approximately 23 per cent of the author's (and co-workers') own work; the chapter's subtitle does, however, specifically warn the reader in advance of the 'auto-biographical' nature of the work.

48. On reflexive re-examination, the example may be culturally insensitive, since the equivalent word in French, 'de' serves to distinguish aristocratic titles: while Gabriel Tarde

refused to use his family's 'de', his sons reinstated its use (e.g. Guillaume de Tarde, Alfred de Tarde). The German 'von' and the Dutch 'van' may also play some identificatory roles.

49. In two autobiographical accounts of social psychologists going through, and contributing to, the crisis in social psychology and the offering of alternative views, Gergen & Gergen (1994) and Rappoport (1994) each discuss how various anti-war, student and protest movements coloured their visions of social psychology. Cherry (1995) shows also the impact of feminism and her reactions to sexism within psychology in her personalized account of social psychology's development. The running of my own PhD thesis, a laboratory study simulating conditions of police–student confrontation, was delayed on several occasions when both experimenter and student subjects participated in real-life confrontations linked to the Viet Nam War. Despite pressure from colleagues during the untenured portion of my career, the thesis was never published because, at the time, I felt that the artificial laboratory results, even with their statistical significance, did not speak to the very real-world problems of violence they sought to simulate; in addition, there was a possibility of 'misuse' or mystification of the conclusions by social control agents, who had more power and resources for implementation than students, who were also part of the conflict scenarios.

50. The Ottawa conference was not touched by ideas from the separationist movement in Québec (just across the Ottawa River), although a delegation from a Progressive Labour group did interrupt a session, denouncing the research of 'Nazi doctors' and the partial military funding of the conference from NATO. Barcelona, host for the Olympic Games and then our critical conference, was in a period of expression of strong Catalan, nationalist sentiments. As with the Ottawa conference made up of 'visibles' and 'less-visibles', the Barcelona conference took care of the expenses for the invited 'critical social psychologists', who prepared papers, while the local faculty and graduate students attending played a more low-key, observer role. For many, English was not their second (or even third) language; near the end of the conference, several papers were delivered in French (including an abbreviated version of this paper), at their request. However, of all cities in Spain, Barcelona's past – its courageous anti-fascism, defence of free thought, movements of anarchism and political independence – offers an important contextual intellectual aura.

51. Colleagues have described anecdotally the tensions of going ahead, as scheduled, with an East–West meeting of social psychologists (planned by Henri Tajfel) in Prague, shortly after Soviet tanks had invaded in 1968.

52. Jasna K. (her former translator) managed, during a period of daily shelling by Serbian guns, to get a letter out of Sarajevo to the author Sandra Cisneros:

> Everything is so humiliating that I sometimes wonder how much longer I shall be able to stand all these difficulties and the terror of our everyday life, this ever-present feeling of the closeness of death, this hunger for normality, peace, freedom, civilized life. I haven't taken a proper bath for months. We haven't had a single proper normal meal since the beginning of the war. . . . I'm lucky because I live so close to the place where I work, so, statistically, my changes to survive are a little bit greater. Still, I walk around the city a lot, I move a lot and I believe that is how I am managing to remain normal. . . . I know that the old faces can never return, what is done cannot be undone, not here, not ever again, but I wish at least that the killings, rapes, torture would be halted so we can try to go on with our ruined lives. (Jasna K., 1993)

53. The president of the International Committee of the Red Cross recently described seminars held on the problem of the estimated 85–100 million mines buried in sixty-two countries: 'one for military experts and another last year for war surgeons, mine manufacturers, legal experts and the media'. He has urged, in the absence of a ban, that mine manufacturers build in 'reliable self-neutralizing mechanisms so that mines do not go on exploding years after hostilities cease'. In addition, the Red Cross is seeking a ban on 'blinding weapons. Using hand held laser rifles, these could blind a person up to 1 kilometer (0.6 mile) away. The beams are invisible and cannot be protected against. For the damage they inflict, there is no cure' (Sommaruga, 1994). The negotiations about these weapons took place in March 1994 in Geneva concerning the 1980 'Convention on Prohibitions or Restrictions on the

Use of Certain Conventional Weapons Which May Be Deemed to Be Excessively Injurious or to Have Indiscriminate Effects'.

54. In focusing more on the roles of leaders in such decision-making, Elms (1986) shows the role of US Secretaries of State, while Kelman (1983) seemed prescient, by a decade, with his analysis that PLO leader Yasser Arafat was ready for peace with Israel.

55. In the aftermath of the massacre of thirty Muslim worshippers in a mosque in Hebron during Ramadan prayers by a Jewish settler on 25 February 1994, an inquiry was told that the Israeli military had given orders not to fire on Jewish settlers, but rather to seek shelter until the gunman had emptied his ammunition clip, and then try to detain him. One general, in explaining the differential response to Jews or Arabs firing a weapon, said 'For us, the basic interpretation is clear: A Jew who carries a weapon, does so for self-defence; an Arab who has one, this is a terrorist' (Claude, 1994, p. 3). It is ironic to note that almost one year earlier, also during Ramadan prayers, Serb artillery targeted the Sarajevo mosque.

56. Hoffman (1993) details the role of Norwegian social scientist Terje Rod Larsen as an important facilitator for the secret 'back-channel' talks between Palestinians and Israelis during 1993 that produced a formal peace-accord agreement.

References

Allport, G.W. (1954). The historical background of modern social psychology. In G. Lindzey (Ed.), *Handbook of social psychology* (Vol. 1, pp. 3–56). Reading, MA: Addison Wesley.

Apfelbaum, E. (1981). Origines de la psychologie sociale en France: Développements souterrains et discipline méconnue. *Revue française de Sociologie, 22*(3), 397–407.

Apfelbaum, E. (1986). Prolegomena for a history of social psychology: Some hypotheses concerning its emergence in the 20th century and its raison d'être. In K. Larsen (Ed.), *Dialectics and ideology in psychology* (pp. 3–13). Norwood, NJ: Ablex.

Apfelbaum, E. (1991, 13 June). *Social psychology, feminist research and theory: Past, present and future.* Paper presented at the annual meetings of the Canadian Psychological Association, Calgary, Alberta.

Apfelbaum, E., & Lubek, I. (1976). Resolution versus revolution? The theory of conflicts in question. In L. Strickland, F. Aboud & K. Gergen (Eds.), *Social psychology in transition* (pp. 71–94). New York: Plenum.

Armistead, N. (Ed.). (1974). *Reconstructing social psychology.* Baltimore, MD: Penguin.

Bauer, N., Thoms, H., & Lubek, I. (1995). Social influences on scientific development: Funding patterns for a cohort of University of Michigan social psychologists. In R. Stachowski & A. Pankalla (Eds.), *Studies in the history of psychology and the social sciences. Proceedings of the 12th Conference of Cheiron-Europe, August 31st–September 4th, 1993* (pp. 20–31). Poznań, Poland: 'Impressions' Publishing Agency.

Berkowitz, L. (1972). Frustrations, comparisons, and other sources of emotional arousal as contributors to social unrest. *Journal of Social Issues, 28*(1), 77–91.

Besnard, P. (1979). La formation de l'équipe de l'*Année Sociologique. Revue française de Sociologie, 20*(1), 7–31.

Billig, M. (1982). *Ideology and social psychology: Extremism, moderation and contradiction.* Oxford: Blackwell.

Brickman, J. (1992). Female lives, feminist deaths: The relationship of the Montreal massacre to dissociation, incest, and violence against women. *Canadian Psychology/Psychologie canadienne, 33*(2), 128–143.

Brownmiller, S. (1976). *Against our will: Men, women and rape.* New York: Bantam Books.

Burman, E. (1993). Beyond discursive relativism: Power and subjectivity in developmental psychology. In H.J. Stam, L.P. Mos, W. Thorngate & B. Kaplan (Eds.), *Recent trends in theoretical psychology* (Vol. 3, pp. 433–440). New York: Springer-Verlag.

Cherry, F. (1995). *The 'stubborn particulars' of social psychology.* London: Routledge, Chapman & Hall.

Christie, R., & Garcia, J. (1951). Subcultural variation in authoritarian personality. *Journal of Abnormal and Social Psychology, 46*, 457–469.

Claude, P. (1994, 12 March). L'enquête sur le massacre d'Hébron: Les soldats israéliens avaient l'ordre de ne 'pas tirer sur les juifs'. *Le Monde*, p. 3.

Cole, J.R., & Cole, S. (1973). The sociology of science. In *Social stratification in science* (pp. 1–20). Chicago: University of Chicago Press.

Collier, G., Minton, H.L., & Reynolds, G. (1991). *Currents of thought in American social psychology*. New York: Oxford University Press.

Crane, D. (1967). The gatekeepers of science: Some factors affecting the selection of articles for scientific journals. *American Sociologist, 2*, 195–201.

Danziger, K. (1990). *Constructing the subject: Historical origins of psychological research*. New York: Cambridge University Press.

Deutsch, M. (1976). Critique: On cursing the darkness versus lighting a candle. In L. Strickland, F. Aboud & K. Gergen (Eds.), *Social psychology in transition* (pp. 95–101). New York: Plenum.

Documents. (1979). Correspondance reçu par Celestin Bouglé. *Revue française de Sociologie, 20*(1), 32–44.

Dollard, J., Doob, L.W., Miller, N.E., Mowrer, O.H., & Sears, R.R., with the collaboration of Ford, C.S., Hovland, C.I., & Sollenberger, R.T. (1939). *Frustration and aggression*. New Haven, CT: Yale University Press.

Drozdiak, W. (1993, 9–10 January). EC study puts Bosnia rapes at 20,000. *International Herald Tribune*, pp. 1, 4.

Duprat, G.-L. (1920). *La psychologie sociale, sa nature et ses principales lois*. Paris: Doin.

Edwards, D., Ashmore, M., & Potter, J. (1995). Death and furniture: The rhetoric, politics and theology of bottom line arguments against relativism. *History of the Human Sciences, 8*(2), 25–49.

Elms, A. (1975). The crisis of confidence in social psychology. *American Psychologist, 30*, 967–975.

Elms, A. (1986). From house to Haig: Private life and public style in American foreign policy advisors. *Journal of Social Issues, 42*(2), 33–53.

Febbraro, A., Lubek, I., Bauer, N., Ross, B., Thoms, H., Brown, S., & Hartt, M.A. (1996). Incidence du genre et du mentor sur la production scientifique et la carrière des psychologues: La perspective de la psychosociologie de la science. *Cahiers du GEDISST, 16*, 123–160.

Festinger, L. (1980). Looking backward. In L. Festinger (Ed.), *Retrospections on social psychology* (pp. 236–254). New York: Oxford University Press.

Feyerabend, P.K. (1975). *Against method*. New York: Humanities Press.

Finison, L. (1986). The psychological insurgency, 1936–1945. *Journal of Social Issues, 42*(1), 21–33.

Garcia, J. (1981). Tilting at the papermills of academe. *American Psychologist, 36*, 149–158.

Gergen, K.J. (1973). Social psychology as history. *Journal of Personality and Social Psychology, 26*, 309–320.

Gergen, K.J. (1982a). *Toward transformation in social knowledge*. New York: Springer-Verlag.

Gergen, K.J. (1982b). This week's citation classic. *Current Contents, 14*(47), 18.

Gergen, K.J. (1991). *The saturated self: Dilemmas of identity in contemporary life*. New York: Basic Books.

Gergen, M., & Gergen, K.J. (1994). Let's pretend: A duography. In D.J. Lee (Ed.), *Life and story: Autobiographies for a narrative psychology* (pp. 61–86). Westport, CT: Praeger.

Good, J., & Still, A. (1992). The idea of an interdisciplinary social psychology: An historical and rhetorical analysis. *Canadian Psychology/Psychologie canadienne, 33*(3), 563–568.

Hamon, A.F. (1893). *Études de psychologie sociale: Psychologie du militaire professionnel*. Brussels: C. Rosez.

Hamon, A.F. (1895). *Psychologie de l'anarchiste-socialiste. Étude de psychologie sociale* (2nd ed.). Paris: P.V. Stock.

Harris, B.J. (1986). Reviewing 50 years of the psychology of social issues. *Journal of Social Issues, 42*(1), 1–20.

Henriques, J., Hollway, W., Urwin, C., Venn, C., & Walkerdine, V. (1984). *Changing the subject: Psychology, social regulation and subjectivity*. London: Methuen.

Hilgard, E.R., Leary, D.E., & McGuire, G.R. (1991). The history of psychology: A survey and critical assessment. *Annual Review of Psychology, 42*, 79–107.

Hoffman, D. (1993, 1 September). Norwegians played a discreet role in facilitating talks. *International Herald Tribune*, p. 5.

Ibáñez, T. (1990). Henry, Serge . . . and the next generation. *British Psychological Society, Social Psychology Section Newsletter, 24*, 5–14.

Israel, J., & Tajfel, H. (Eds.). (1972). *The context of social psychology: A critical assessment*. London: Academic Press.

Jackson, J.M. (1988). *Social psychology, past and present: An integrative orientation*. Hillsdale, NJ: Erlbaum.

Janis, I. (1968). *Victims of groupthink*. New York: Harcourt, Brace & Jovanovich.

Janis, I. (1986). Problems of international crisis management in the nuclear age. *Journal of Social Issues, 42*(2), 201–222.

Jasna K. (1993, 9 April). Note from my Sarajevo friend: 'There is no good news here'. *International Herald Tribune*, p. 6. (Letter to Sandra Cisneros originally written 22 Jan. 1993.)

Karpf, F.B. (1932). *American social psychology*. New York: McGraw-Hill.

Kelman, H.C. (1983). Conversations with Arafat. *American Psychologist, 38*, 203–214.

Kren, G.M., & Rappoport, L.H. (1994). *The Holocaust and the crisis of human behavior* (rev. ed.). New York: Holmes & Meier.

Kroger, R.O., & Wood, L. (1992). Whatever happened to language in social psychology? *Canadian Psychology/Psychologie canadienne, 33*(3), 584–594.

Kuhn, T.S. (1970). *The structure of scientific revolutions*. (2nd ed.). Chicago: University of Chicago Press.

Lakatos, I., & Musgrave, A. (Eds.). (1970). *Criticism and the growth of knowledge*. Cambridge: Cambridge University Press.

Larsen, K. (Ed.). (1980). *Social psychology: Crisis or failure?* Monmouth, OR: Institute for Theoretical History.

Lewin, K. (1946). Action research and minority problems. *Journal of Social Issues, 2*(4), 34–46.

Lubek, I. (1976a). Some tentative suggestions for analyzing and neutralizing the power structure in social psychology. In L. Strickland, F. Aboud & K. Gergen (Eds.), *Social psychology in transition* (pp. 317–333). New York: Plenum.

Lubek, I. (1976b). A note on the power structure in social psychology. *Representative Research in Social Psychology, 7*, 87–88.

Lubek, I. (1979). A brief social psychological analysis of research on aggression in social psychology. In A. Buss (Ed.), *Psychology in social context* (pp. 259–306). New York: Irvington.

Lubek, I. (1980). The psychological establishment: Pressures to preserve paradigms, publish rather than perish, win funds and influence students. In K. Larsen (Ed.), *Social psychology: Crisis or failure?* (pp. 129–157). Monmouth, OR: Institute for Theoretical History.

Lubek, I. (1981). Histoire des psychologies sociales perdues: Le cas de Gabriel Tarde. *Revue française de Sociologie, 22*(3), 361–395.

Lubek, I. (1986). Fifty years of frustration and aggression: Some historical notes on a long-lived hypothesis. In K. Larsen (Ed.), *Dialectics and ideology in psychology* (pp. 30–84). Norwood, NJ: Ablex.

Lubek, I. (1990). Interactionist theory and disciplinary interactions: Psychology, sociology, and social psychology in France. In W.J. Baker, M.E. Hyland, R. van Hezewijk & S. Terwee (Eds.), *Recent trends in theoretical psychology* (Vol. 2, pp. 347–358). New York: Springer-Verlag.

Lubek, I. (1992). The histor(y/ies) of social psycholog(y/ies). *Canadian Psychology/Psychologie canadienne, 33*(3), 657–661.

Lubek, I. (1993a). Social psychology textbooks: An historical and social psychological analysis of conceptual filtering, consensus formation, career gatekeeping and conservatism in science. In H.J. Stam, L.P. Mos, W. Thorngate & B. Kaplan (Eds.), *Recent trends in theoretical psychology* (Vol. 3, pp. 359–378). New York: Springer-Verlag.

Lubek, I. (1993b). Some reflections on various social psychologies, their histories and historiographies. *Sociétés contemporaines, 13*, 33–68.

Lubek, I. (1993c). The view from 'Social psychology of science'. In H. van Rappard, P. van Strien, L. Mos & W. Baker (Eds.), *Annals of theoretical psychology: History and theory* (Vol. 8, pp. 249–260). New York: Plenum Press.

Lubek, I. (1995a). Individualism and aggression: A multi-layered contextualist view. *Theory & Psychology, 5*(1), 99–129.

Lubek, I. (1995b). Towards an interactive 'inter-psychology': The successive, but relatively unsuccessful, social psychological perspectives of Gabriel Tarde (and sons). In M. Donzelli (Ed.), *Folle e politica: Cultura filosofica, ideologia, scienze sociali in Italia e Francia a fine Ottocento* (pp. 129–156). Naples: Ed. Liguori.

Lubek, I. (1995c). A 'social psychology of science' approach: Towards an inter-personal history of social psychology. In S. Jaeger, I. Staeuble, L. Sprung & H.-P. Brauns (Eds.), *Psychologie im soziokulturellen Wandel-Kontinuitäten und Diskontinuitäten* (pp. 98–114). Frankfurt: Peter Lang.

Lubek, I., & Apfelbaum, E. (1987). Neo-behaviorism and the Garcia effect: A social psychology of science approach to the history of a paradigm clash. In M. Ash & W. Woodward (Eds.), *Psychology in twentieth century thought and society* (pp. 59–91). Cambridge: Cambridge University Press. (Reprinted, 1989, paperback.)

Lubek, I., & Apfelbaum, E. (1989). Les études de psychologie sociale de Augustin Hamon. *Hermès: Cognition, communication, politique, 5–6*, 67–94.

Lubek, I., Apfelbaum, E., & Paicheler, H. (1993). Numéro Spécial/Special Issue: La psychologie sociale et ses histoires/Social psychology and its histories. *Sociétés contemporaines, 33*, 1–220.

Lubek, I., Hezewijk, R. van, Pheterson, G., & Tolman, C. (Eds.). (1995). *Trends and issues in theoretical psychology*. New York: Springer Publishing Co.

Lubek, I., Innis, N.K., Kroger, R.O., McGuire, G.R., Stam, H.J., & Herrmann, T. (1995). Faculty genealogies in five Canadian universities: Historiographical versus pedagogical concerns. *Journal for the History of the Behavioral Sciences, 33*(1), 52–72.

Lubek, I., Minton, H.L., & Apfelbaum, E. (Eds.). (1992). Special Issue/Numéro Spécial: Social Psychology and its History/La psychologie sociale et son histoire. *Canadian Psychology/Psychologie canadienne, 33*(3), 519–661.

Lubek, I., & Stam, H.J. (1995). Ludicro-experimentation in social psychology: Sober scientific versus playful prescriptions. In I. Lubek, R. van Hezewijk, G. Pheterson & C. Tolman (Eds.), *Trends and issues in theoretical psychology* (pp. 171–180). New York: Springer Publishing Co.

Mauss, M. (1924). Rapports réels et pratiques de la psychologie et de la sociologie. *Journal de Psychologie normale et pathologique, 21*, 892–922.

Merton, R.K. (1977). The sociology of science: An episodic memoir. In R.K. Merton & J. Gaston (Eds.), *The sociology of science in Europe* (pp. 3–141). Carbondale: Southern Illinois University Press.

Minton, H.L. (1986). Emancipatory social psychology as a paradigm for the study of minority groups. In K.S. Larsen (Ed.), *Dialectics and ideology in psychology* (pp. 257–277). Norwood, NJ: Ablex.

Minton, H.L. (1992). Root metaphors and the evolution of American social psychology. *Canadian Psychology/Psychologie canadienne, 33*(3), 547–553.

Minton, H.L. (1993a, 7–8 May). Toward an emancipatory psychology: Lessons from the construction of sexual identities. Invited address presented to the Symposium: 'Psychology in the 21st Century', York University, Toronto.

Minton, H.L. (1993b). Social psychology and its commitment. *Sociétés Contemporaines, 13,* 121–127.

Moscovici, S. (1972). Society and theory in social psychology. In J. Israel & H. Tajfel (Eds.), *The context of social psychology: A critical assessment* (pp. 17–68). London: Academic Press.

Moscovici, S. (1993). Which histories to write? What stories to tell! *Sociétés Contemporaines, 13,* 25–32.

Mulkay, M.J. (1972). Conformity and innovation in science. *Sociological Review Monograph, 18,* 5–23.

Murchison, C. (Ed.). (1930). *A history of psychology in autobiography* (Vol. 1). New York: Russell & Russell. (Reprinted 1961.)

Murchison, C. (Ed.). (1932). *A history of psychology in autobiography* (Vol. 2). New York: Russell & Russell. (Reprinted 1961.)

Murchison, C. (Ed.). (1936). *A history of psychology in autobiography* (Vol. 3). New York: Russell & Russell. (Reprinted 1961.)

Parker, I. (1989). *The crisis in modern social psychology – and how to end it.* London: Routledge.

Popper, K.R. (1959). *The logic of scientific discovery.* New York: Harper & Row.

Prilleltensky, I. (1989). Psychology and the status quo. *American Psychologist, 44*(5), 795–802.

Prilleltensky, I. (1990). Enhancing the social ethics of psychology: Toward a psychology at the service of social change. *Canadian Psychology/Psychologie canadienne, 31*(4), 310–319.

Rappoport, L. (1986). Renaming the world: On psychology and the decline of positive science. In K.S. Larsen (Ed.), *Dialectics and ideology in psychology* (pp. 167–195). Norwood, NJ: Ablex.

Rappoport, L. (1994). Playing in the rough. In D.J. Lee (Ed.), *Life and story: Autobiographies for a narrative psychology* (pp. 87–107). Westport, CT: Praeger.

Ring, K. (1967). Experimental social psychology: Some sober questions about some frivolous values. *Journal of Experimental Social Psychology, 3,* 113–123.

Rosnow, R.L. (1981). *Paradigms in transition.* New York: Oxford University Press.

Ross, B., Febbraro, A., Thoms, H., Bauer, N., & Lubek, I. (1996). Is there a season for theory? Patterns of theoretical, methodological and empirical writings of a sample of men and women social psychologists over the lengths of their careers. In C. Tolman, F. Cherry, R. van Hezewijk & I. Lubek (Eds.), *Problems of theoretical psychology* (pp. 228–241). Toronto: Captus Press.

Samelson, F. (1974). History, origin myth and ideology: Comte's 'discovery' of social psychology. *Journal for the Theory of Social Behavior, 4,* 217–231. Revised and updated in K.S. Larsen (Ed.). (1986), *Dialectics and ideology in psychology* (pp. 14–29). Norwood, NJ: Ablex.

Sommaruga, C. (1994, 24 February). To contain war's new horrors. *International Herald Tribune,* p. 6.

Stam, H.J., & Lubek, I. (1992, 21 June). *A textual development of experimentation in social psychology.* Paper presented at the 24th annual meetings of the Cheiron Society, Windsor, Ont.

Stam, H.J., Lubek, I., & Radtke, L. (in press). Repopulating texts: Disembodied subjects and embodied subjectivity. In B. Bayer & J. Shotter (Eds.), *Material transcriptions: Disciplinary practices and the making of subjects.* London: Sage.

Stam, H.J., Mos, L.P., Thorngate, W., & Kaplan, B. (Eds.). (1993). *Recent trends in theoretical psychology* (Vol. 3). New York: Springer-Verlag.

Strickland, L. (1976). Priorities and paradigms: The conference and the book. In L. Strickland, F. Aboud & K. Gergen (Eds.), *Social psychology in transition* (pp. 3–11). New York: Plenum.

Strickland, L., Aboud, F., & Gergen, K. (Eds.). (1976). *Social psychology in transition.* New York: Plenum.

Tajfel, H. (1972). Introduction. In J. Israel & H. Tajfel (Eds.), *The context of social psychology: A critical assessment* (pp. 1–13). London: Academic Press.

Tolman, C.W., Cherry, F., Hezewijk, R. van, & Lubek, I. (Eds.) (1996). *Problems of theoretical psychology*. Toronto: Captus Press.

Touraine, A. (1995). *The critique of modernity*. Oxford: Basil Blackwell.

van Strien, P. (1993). The historical practice of theory construction. In H. van Rappard, P. van Strien, L. Mos and W. Baker (Eds.), *Annals of theoretical psychology: History and theory* (Vol. 8, pp. 149–228). New York: Plenum Press.

Wagner, P. (1994). *A sociology of modernity: Liberty and discipline*. London: Routledge.

Walkerdine, V. (1986). Post-structuralist theory and everyday social practices: The family and the school. In S. Wilkinson (Ed.), *Feminist social psychology: Developing theory and practice* (pp. 57–76). Milton Keynes: Open University Press.

Wexler, P. (1983). *Critical social psychology*. Boston: Routledge & Kegan Paul.

Wilkinson, S. (Ed.). (1986). Sighting possibilities: Diversity and commonality in feminist research. In S. Wilkinson (Ed.), *Feminist social psychology: Developing theory and practice* (pp. 7–24). Milton Keynes: Open University Press.

Winston, A.S. (1996a). 'As his name indicates . . .' R.S. Woodworth's letters of reference and employment for Jewish psychologists in the 1930s. *Journal for the History of the Behavioral Sciences, 32*, 30–43.

Winston, A.S. (1996b). The context of correctness: A comment on Rushton. *Journal of Social Distress and the Homeless, 5*(2), 231–250.

14

Differentiating and De-developing Critical Social Psychology

Erica Burman

In this chapter I want to problematize the project of 'critical social psychology' by exploring the terms by which we envisage and debate it. My account here was generated by the task of writing a 'position paper' mapping out my view of the landscape and directions of 'post-crisis' psychologies, and my place(s) within those. I want to topicalize some of my unease with this task, thereby treating this process as a scaled-down version of the larger questions that exercise those of us engaged in the various enterprises subsumed under 'critical social psychology'. These questions include: is, and, if so, how is, 'critical social psychology' different from psychology? What traditions and trajectories does it call upon, make possible, map out? In addressing these questions I will be drawing upon discussions of the theoretical adequacy of notions of difference and development currently in circulation in cultural politics. In particular, an attention to critiques in developmental psychology will help us question the development of something called 'critical social psychology'. Such accounts can inform analyses of the politics of psychology, and of the political interventions of 'critical psychologists'.

Positions and Identities

The notion of position underlies the call to formulate joint projects or a common programme. Within this, the prospect of formulating a 'position paper' is theoretically anomalous as well as daunting. The connotations of stable fixity associated with the notion of a single 'position' is at variance with the fragile, fractured and shifting identifications I slide between in my relationships to psychology. These identifications speak both of strategic interventions and of institutional locations. To be sure, I am not so fascinated with the brilliant surfaces of postmodernism as to sacrifice political agency for mere multiple subjectivities. But the confident stance of a unitary position cannot be formulated except in relation to (fantasized) others, and I am concerned that the dynamic of misrecognition this sets up is not only reminiscent of a particularly culturally masculine style of argument, but is one which also reproduces some of the debates about 'identity politics' that have so exercised feminists of late.

There are lessons for how we 'critical social psychologists' conduct our debates. Parallel questions are: what does it mean to identify as 'a critical social psychologist'? Do those who do identify in this way share a common enterprise? What kinds of relationships does this imply between those who espouse this identity? What (if anything) lies beyond the 'crisis'? Is a 'post-crisis psychology' a contradiction in terms? Does designating the rest of psychology 'old paradigm' imply the false impression that it is over? Is there a danger that the drive towards a 'critical psychology' retrospectively confers a spurious homogeneity on the rest of psychology, which is thereby designated as 'non-critical' (eclipsing precisely those histories of debate from which current 'radical' approaches have emerged)? Does the epithet 'critical psychologist' threaten to impose uniformity on disparate and conflicting sets of tendencies? Finally, is critical (social) psychology critical of psychology? or social psychology? How does 'critical social psychology' (if such there is) fit with other movements, other politics, other positions and identifications we bring to it, and should bring it to?

The exhortation to a 'position' invites a differentiation, an activity of demarcation, of splitting to maintain some fragile integrity. The process of elaborating a 'position' locks into the modern discourse of identity and difference which, in political terms, can function destructively rather than constructively. It becomes tempting to chart and compare degrees of distance from mainstream psychology, with displacements from the centre functioning as hierarchies of (an implicitly quantifiable) measure of 'criticality'. There are two problems here: first, this imposes a uniform understanding of 'critical', and, second, this privileges positionings in relation to psychology rather than other commitments and perspectives we bring to those positions. Just as we are not singly positioned, so (drawing on debates in feminism) we should reconceptualize the project of 'critical social psychology' to turn its phallic trajectory into provisional networks, coalitions and alliances (what Squire, 1989, calls 'associative psychologies' or Haraway, 1991, 'affinity groups'). Otherwise it will be recuperated within the progressivist narrative of psychology, robbing it of its 'critical' edge and incorporating it within its march onward to true science. I am suggesting that attention to differences between 'critical social psychologists' can ward off that dynamic of unwitting co-option into psychology's developmental grand narrative.

'Critical Social Psychology' and Its Objects

I could point out that I am not a 'social psychologist', let alone a 'critical social psychologist'. Or am I? What is interesting here is how the domain of 'critical psychology' has been attached to the sub-discipline of social psychology, as if it is irrelevant to the rest of (supposedly non-social) psychology. There are whole histories here of the suppression of 'the social' in psychology. This strategy of confinement is equivalent to the way discourse analysis has been assimilated as a new tool for social psychological research rather than a framework whose conceptual apparatus challenges the very foundations of psychology (Burman, 1990; Burman & Parker, 1993; Parker & Burman, 1993). Hence, it is with some bemusement that I often find myself treated as a 'social psychologist' as soon as I start to make political critiques of developmental psychology. If 'social psychology' has carried the burden (or banner?) of theorizing 'the social' within psychology, then it is by some curious – but by no means necessary – chain of associations that 'the social' codes for 'critical' within psychology.

It is up to 'critical psychologists' to refuse to be contained within existing frameworks and categorizations. Critique is more than social, it is political, and allowing 'social psychology' to signify 'critical psychology' is to collude in maintaining the depoliticization of psychology. This book focuses on what lies beyond 'the crisis'. But we should refute the temporal positioning of 'beyond', and instead take up its spatial meaning to locate ourselves at least partially outside psychology. It is political commitment rather than any alternative psychological theory that marks us as 'critical': 'critical (social) psychology' only stands in relation to its converse, the psychology it qualifies rather than supplements. To designate it as part of the 'post-' scene, then, is to accept that 'the crisis' is over, and that psychology has survived intact – for us to be positioned as mere historical successors. I have a postcard on my wall which says 'I'll be a post-feminist in post-patriarchy'; I'll be a post-psychologist when psychology is no more.

Positions Revisited: Home and Away

Hence there is a politics as well as a psychology of space that is structured within the notion of 'position', and which is, interestingly, reproduced within the production of this book. These chapters speculate about the demise of psychology, or the crisis, or both. But a key question is who 'we' are, and are not. It seems that 'critical (social) psychology' is composed primarily of elements within British and European psychology, presumably drawn up in contradistinction to US psychology. (But even this is to impose a spurious uniformity with the French-Canadian contingent occupying an ambiguous position, and, beyond this, multiple points of positioning and intervention in terms of age, class, sexuality, culture, gender, and so on.) Like the subject of psychology (both as discipline and as disciplined subject) we are fond of critiquing, we are dispersed, differentially placed in space and time.

But the other 'others' are, of course, post-colonial critiques which have figured so little within psychology. European social psychology has been taken as the resource by which to critique Anglo-US positivism. Like an old master tiring of indulgence and overcome by irritation, Europe disowns its crass offspring and strives to restore a more glorious and complex tradition. To make a relevant connection, Fortress Europe rises to counter US domination of the psychology market (and thus pretends a greater independence from it than it actually has). But we should not overstate the differences between Europe and the US, as perhaps we in Britain must be especially aware. Moreover, to treat Europe as both the original site of resistance to, or the newly emerging alternative to, the colonizing impetus of US psychology is to omit and rewrite a significant chunk of history, a history of active or complicit colonization. On this score we should recall that the interpretative, hermeneutic, psychoanalytic or post-structuralist resources we draw upon in this struggle are located within practices which are themselves structured by North–South oppositions and power relations. As Spivak (1988) points out, the critiques we draw upon in commenting on the wrongs and limitations of (Anglo-US psychological) theory are, like those they are employed to deconstruct, rooted in philosophical frameworks and representations of subjectivity of the northern hemisphere (nor do they claim to be more than this). So while we use them to reveal the yawning (philosophical and existential) chasm (of solipsism, self-delusion and alienation) that lies beyond psychology's confident exterior of the rational unitary subject, the critiques themselves have constituted, and continue to constitute, the colonial domains that Anglo-US psychology has gone on to export further.

The point is that the free space for the debate that this volume aims to provide is not free at all. All space is occupied, and this no less than any other. The places, the spaces from which we speak, are meaningful, and 'critical social psychology' as it is currently formulated necessarily addresses dominant northern psychological perspectives, *and also is part of those*. This means how we engage in this debate is structured by our varying positions, histories of struggle and compromise. On whose terms, then, does the debate take place? The language we speak in occludes and privileges particular positions, as feminist and post-colonial critiques have pointed out (Weed, 1990). To put it bluntly, this book may be published in Castilian and English, but the majority of us writing here are pretty monolingually Anglophone. What of the voices that are absent or have been silenced through the desire to intervene in, and thus participate in, the dominant Anglo-US arena? We should draw on post-colonial critiques both to tackle the Anglo-US cultural hegemony of psychological models, and to provide some intimation of the limits of these perspectives and other strategies of resistance. Let me make clear that I am not advocating some kind of exoticizing study of 'indigenous psychologies', for in these 'postmodern times' the search for the authentic cultural voice untouched by the West not only has been rendered impossible through the ravages of imperialism, but is also an instance of that very colonizing impulse.

Moving Metaphors

At this point it is instructive to note how discussions of space and place have spawned an attention to metaphors of travel. In cultural studies, maps, nomads and migrations are all the rage. There is a celebration of flexibility and mobility in what post-Marxists call 'new times' that masks how the 'choice' to exercise these qualities is restricted to the privileged. Discussions of crossing borders or boundaries, for example, while so evident in accounts of androgyny and 'queer politics', advocate a sharing of the pleasures of femininity but offer no such reciprocal access to the powers and privileges associated with masculinity (see e.g. Moore, 1988). Correspondingly, it seems at best bizarre that at a time when ever greater restrictions are being imposed on the movement of people between states, cultural criticism is preoccupied with distributed and unbounded subjectivities. In one such account Star (1992) correctly points out '[p]ower is about *whose* metaphor brings worlds together, and holds them there' (p. 52). Wolff (1993) sees more mileage in metaphors of 'exile' and 'marginality', but points out that while nevertheless acknowledging histories and geographies of oppression, these can still serve to essentialize, reproducing the rhetorical opposition of periphery and centre they seek to problematize.

In terms of the constitution of 'critical social psychology' it is clear that we will not solve our intellectual and political problems by migrating to other disciplines (or from Manchester to Barcelona) (tempting though this sometimes is), since these are in the throes of debates equivalent to those that form our focus here. Rather, notwithstanding the impact they have made on the resources we bring to critique psychology, the attraction of more hospitable and exciting domains outside psychology (whether sociology, anthropology or women's studies) itself betrays something of the dynamic of cultural tourism.

Emerging from the debates within feminism on 'identity politics' it has been suggested that 'who we are has replaced what we do' (Bourne, 1987), and that place currently threatens to re-place an essentialism based on some notion of fixed and unmediated identity (Fuss, 1989). But the concept of subject position provided within post-structuralist frameworks can be read as offering a notion of place and identification that is strategic rather than ontological. I am suggesting that we should use this as part of the project to maintain the critical impulse of 'critical (social) psychology', and that multiple positionings can be crucial (and 'critical') within this. Taking up my position as a mis/dis-placed 'critical (social) psychologist', I will briefly elaborate these issues through the identifications and interventions implied in shifting the focus and definition of developmental psychology. Attending to the metaphors of development that creep into 'critical social psychology' may, paradoxically, be important in structuring the ways we prefigure its development.

Developmental Investments

The tensions of who the subject of psychology is are vividly played out in developmental psychology. The Cartesian legacy of the rational unitary subject deeply structures developmental psychology so that accounts focus on the abstracted epistemic subject which is then treated as equivalent to 'the child'. As a feminist teacher not only of women's studies, but also of that contradictory arena called the 'psychology of women' *and* of developmental psychology, I have found it difficult to clarify the aims and scope of my interventions. In challenging the naturalized and normalized child-centred apparatus of 'what the child does, and does next' as functioning to evaluate and regulate women and families through the project to produce self-governing citizens (Burman, 1994a; Walkerdine & Lucey, 1989), it seems that the prospect of a woman-centred (or even women-centred) psychology dissolves too. Moving from a child-centred account fractures any notion of unitary development into varieties of historico-political conditions, but along with this tumble some central tenets of feminism and psychotherapy. Alice Miller's work (e.g. 1985) has been enormously influential in drawing attention to the limits of psychoanalysis and its collusion in the denial of the abuse, including the sexual abuse, of children. Yet despite her protests, her emphasis on the child as innocent victim lapses into mother-blaming (although this is not to say that mothers are blameless, but that more than this needs to be said).

To develop her ideas further within this arena, we could perhaps analyse how we are drawn into the story of child development because our identification with the child functions as a protection against the repetition of the narcissistic assault and abuse we felt as children: we relive our development as sanitized and romanticized by the reassuringly progressivist ages and stages of developmental psychological models. The appeal to 'the child within' in various brands of therapy (feminist therapy included – cf. Orbach & Eichenbaum, 1982) reproduces aspects of the developmental models they claim to critique. Similarly, our propensity to rush to rescue children is a key structuring (and constraining) factor in designing aid appeals. This consequently abstracts children from culture and history, and in appealing to their 'innocence', families and cultures are thereby positioned as responsible for their distress (Burman, 1994b; Holland, 1992). Within developmental psychology, the resistance to moving beyond a focus on the child seems to indicate that this constitutes something of another narcissistic assault on the psyche of the psychologist, who, notwithstanding the gaping holes that are emerging within its fabric, hangs onto the developmental apparatus to provide a sense of security of past origins and future trajectories.

A similar issue arises for the 'family romance' of 'critical social psychology'. A shared history of devaluation may constitute a narrative of origins, but we should be clear that this is a narrative structured by corresponding suppressions, subordinations and productions. Hence the conventions of narrative form (of goals, synthesis, resolution – development even) may come to govern the ways we conceptualize the interventions made by 'critical social psychology'. When I read in (bad) student practical work of how the 'new paradigm' in psychology has championed over the 'old', I realize how powerful that developmental narrative is, and how hard it is to maintain a sense of history that is more than merely progressivist.

Development and De-development

Staying with my example, it would be foolish and dangerous to overstate the demise of old-style developmental psychology. Whatever its status in the discipline, its practices live on, and, like the scandal of medicines peddled to Third World countries that are beyond their expiry date, obsolete psychological models flourish in neo-colonial contexts (constituted as markets). Hence it is most irresponsible to proclaim the end of psychology, since the models have acquired a new rhetorical force through their inscription in aid and development policies. Hierarchies of need fit in nicely with quantifiable measures of human development employed by the UN (see Burman, 1995a, 1995b). We should not be surprised at the mesh between the apparatuses used to describe individual and societal development. Just as the US now dominates the psychological scene, so it, too, created the more general discourse, with Truman's inaugural speech in 1949, such that 'development' became an 'emblem, a euphemism, used ever since to allude either discreetly or inadvertently to the era of American hegemony' (Esteva, 1992, p. 7). History becomes destiny; economics has replaced God; and urban industrial development is the evangelical mission for all: the project of development enjoins everyone, but alludes to the homogenizing and linear steps toward the Western middle-class male (US) model.

The discourse of 'helping' (facilitating, accelerating, promoting, etc.) development common both to psychology and to international aid programmes has a history that speaks of the conditional basis of giving, and presumes that the recipient is lacking: 'help is not help in need but help in the overcoming of a deficit' (Gronemeyer, 1992, p. 65). Gronemeyer distinguishes between 'need' and 'neediness', so that helping those suffering need is an act of restoration to a self-defined state, but in contrast those deemed needy are subjected to a diagnosis of normality that is a bureaucratic creation (as both tool and commodity) of economic and cultural imperialism. And it was psychologists (such as Maslow) who supplied the human (as opposed to the market) element for this needs discourse, with needs ordered hierarchically, and administered by experts to control the 'needy'.

Just as the end of history is an illusion propagated by some in the US State Department in 1990 to herald their 'victory over communism', so, too, is development far from over. Rather it 'serves the purpose of self-defence against an exaggerated sense of generational envy' (Gronemeyer, 1992, p. 63). Is it infantile omnipotence, some wild wish-fulfilment writ globally to declare the end of development? Or, more parochially, the end of developmental psychology? Or the end of psychology? We should be wary of prematurely hailing our death sentences for psychology as functioning as speech acts. Nor should we hurry to install our own developmental narrative. Teleological models inscribe their own end within them: they foretell their own death (and nothing more). But the way current analyses aim to thwart this implosion is not to deny history but to spatialize it. And (given the critical discussion above on metaphors of space) that means elaborating different forms of organizing and organization that not only recognize varieties of positioning and experience, but also address these as structured by power inequalities. This is not a call for some liberal (or radical) pluralism, but an attempt to build an association of 'critical (social) psychologists' premised on, rather than simply tolerating, diversity. This will necessarily be provisional and transient. For whom or what does social psychology 'help', facilitate or promote? And how do our politics shape whom and how we 'help'? How can we do more than 'help'?

Gendered Agendas: Women or Children First?

In times of crisis women and children are the first targets for aid (in rhetoric at least). Where do they figure in 'post-crisis psychology'? We are faced with the question of how to order and allocate our interventions: in developmental psychology, both women and children have been deeply oppressed by developmental discourse, but all too often the empowerment of each seems to be at the expense of the other. This highlights the inadequacy and the individualism of the liberal discourse of human rights, which, as we know, is inscribed within our psychological models. The issue is not one of competing priorities, but this is the way the issues are often presented. Upholders of children's rights insist that children's interests do not necessarily correspond to those of their parents or families – as widespread child abuse and child slavery makes manifest (Ennew, 1988). Equally, women have been defined in terms of their relations to others, and in the context of the development (in both senses) of their relationships to children. Even the imputation of the rational separable self-governing subjects (consumers) underlying rights discourses can be seen as reflecting an economically fuelled global psy-complex.

While there are important areas of commonality between women's studies and children's studies (as both previously devalued areas of study, and both devalued groups), one asymmetry is that the arena of women's studies is based on a politics of experience whereas children's studies is conducted (up till now) by academics and activists working on behalf of children (Oakley, 1992). This may be one reason why the call for children, like development, can be recruited for a host of other (including anti-feminist) purposes. And while children provide the rallying cry for aid to 'developing' countries ('a hungry child has no politics' was the disingenuous slogan for US aid to the 1984–5 Ethiopia famine, which was patently reduced because of its status as a socialist country – Gill, 1986), women become the means by which this aid is administered. Not surprisingly this gives rise to protests, both from children's rights activists who highlight how many children are psychologically and economically separated from their families (and who therefore lose out) (e.g. Aptekar, 1991), and from feminists who dispute the instrumental and conditional rather than absolute respect for women (e.g. Elson, 1992).

The current focus on 'Women in Development' can be understood as the latest move in developmental colonialism: with the formal economy now saturated/exhausted, it is time to incorporate the informal one (Antrobus, 1989). There are parallels in psychology too. The 'psychology of women' offers a new market for the recycling and consumption of more or less structurally adjusted psychological models to apply to women. The British Psychological Society, at least on paper, welcomes more courses on the 'psychology of women' (Scientific Affairs Board, 1988), but proscribes the self-organization of disadvantaged groups within its apparatus. Divisions and Sections within its bureaucracy are set in competition against each other so that until recently the Psychology of Women Section was used as a key gatekeeper preventing the setting up of a Psychology of Lesbianism Section (Beloff, 1993; Comely, Kitzinger & Perkins, 1992; Sayers, 1992). The metaphors of splitting (Divisions, Sections) that structure the institutional forms that the discipline of psychology takes on are apt.

Developmental psychology portrays not only a northern but also a masculine developmental trajectory: from attachment to detachment, from the concrete to the abstract and detached. Development is structured as the repudiation of femininity; and since the developing child is masculine, the state of childhood is rendered feminine (Burman, 1995c; Walkerdine, 1988). Part of what drives on Piaget's budding scientist, the active pioneer, to chart new territories may well be the resolution of contradictions; but these can be soothed and smoothed away by disembodiment and abstraction. The dynamic is one of structural disengagement from what in psychology is called 'context', or politico-historical conditions. The parallels between women and children, the feminization and infantilization of those designated 'underdeveloped', and the ecological devastation that follows in the wake of 'development' speak to the resonances between psychology and the globalization of patriarchy and capitalism. In this context the general problem of the shape the project of a 'critical (social) psychology' might take can be restated in a particular form. In terms of my preoccupations it becomes: what would it mean to do a feminist (developmental) psychology (that is, in a critical and social way)? There can be no setting out of an alternative body of theory without reproducing an equivalent set of problems. There is no body of knowledge, but there are (embodied) sets of interventions, of activities.

Differentiating and De-developing 'Critical Social Psychology'

It seems that there is very little that differentiates the frameworks currently under review within 'critical social psychology'. Rather they reflect in microcosm broader debates on the proliferating models and metaphors born of the 'deconstructive turn'. But the attention to difference itself demands attention to how the call to 'difference' functions: in other words, differentiating between differences. For, contrary to postmodern fantasies, there is no free play of difference, and some differences are more important than others. In this chapter I have argued for the need to theorize the political consequences of the historical constructions of the places from which we as 'critical social psychologists' (claim to) speak, and whom we speak for, subjecting the metaphors of place and development to some scrutiny.

No doubt the opposition between inside and outside is not absolute, and here discussions of the politics of women's studies may be instructive (Cixous & Clément, 1985; Lorde, 1984). These suggest that feminist theory should be conceived of as intervention rather than domain. It does not provide a rival account, since this would be to compete for authority over the same ground rather than question how this has been constituted as territory in the first place. As such there can be no quintessential feminist theory, since there is no theoretical purity or absolute separation between an intervention and that which it critiques: in order to intervene, we have to participate in that which we seek to change (Gross, 1992). It follows from this that we cannot determine in advance what precise form an autonomous theory takes, since this runs counter to the notion of autonomy. Hence utopian and strategic tendencies both complement and co-exist in tension. Similarly, it is hard to specify an autonomous 'critical social psychology', since this is constituted as a strategic intervention in relation to dominant oppressive forms of psychology. Metaphors of progress, of the development of 'critical social psychology', therefore can function only in strategic and local contexts – in relation to the particular project or intervention currently undertaken.

'Critical social psychology' (if it exists, or will come to exist) is therefore necessarily a tense and fragmentary affair. The key question for those of us who want to work towards this motley alliance is whether we can sufficiently distinguish our own and others' strategies from our and their goals to find ways of working – if not together, then alongside each other. What unites us is not a common position, a common language, but a willingness to juxtapose our activities, to fashion a new landscape of interventionist and transformative enterprises, 'a powerful infidel hetero-glossia' (Haraway, 1991, p. 181). Irrespective of whether it was ever whole, psychology is now fragmenting (along with its expansion), and the diversity of 'critical (social) psychologists' can be understood as an index of this (albeit potentially also a measure of its amenability to co-option). The cracks in the edifice of psychology can function in a variety of ways – from the misconceived empire-building of 'postmodern psychologies' to the deconstruction of a discipline. This book explores the textures and topologies of these fissures, but it is important that our investments in these surfaces do not beguile us into thinking this is all we are doing. Psychological models produce and generate (some of) us as subjects and (others as) objects. It should come as no surprise if we inadvertently reproduce those disciplinary divisions when we collectively consider such activities. But it should be helpful to know that they arise from, and in part reflect, the dynamic instability of the enterprise.

References

Antrobus, P. (1989, April). *Women in development.* Paper presented at the XVth General Assembly of Development Non-Governmental Organizations, Brussels.

Aptekar, L. (1991). Are Columbian street children neglected? The contributions of ethnographic and ethnohistorical approaches to the study of children. *Anthropology and Education Quarterly, 22,* 326–349.

Beloff, H. (1993). Progress on the BPS Psychology of Lesbianism front. *Feminism & Psychology, 3*(2), pp. 282–283.

Bourne, J. (1987). Homelands of the mind: Jewish feminism and identity politics. *Race & Class, 29,* pp. 1–24.

Burman, E. (1990). What discourse is not. *Philosophical Psychology, 4,* 325–342.

Burman, E. (1994a). *Deconstructing developmental psychology.* London: Routledge.

Burman, E. (1994b). Poor children: Charity appeals and ideologies of childhood. *Changes: International Journal of Psychology and Psychotherapy, 12*(1), 29–36.

Burman, E. (1995a). The natural rights of the child. In I. Lubek, R. van Hezewijk, G. Pheterson & C. Tolman (Eds.), *Trends and issues in theoretical psychology* (pp. 88–94). New York: Springer.

Burman, E. (1995b). The abnormal distribution of development: Policies for Southern women and girls. *Gender, Place and Culture, 2*(1), 21–36.

Burman, E. (1995c). What is it? Masculinity and femininity in the cultural representation of childhood. In S. Wilkinson & C. Kitzinger (Eds.), *Feminism and discourse* (pp. 49–67). London: Sage.

Burman, E., & Parker, I. (1993). Introduction: discourse analysis: The turn to the text. In E. Burman & I. Parker (Eds.), *Discourse analytic research: Repertoires and readings of texts in action* (pp. 1–16). London: Routledge.

Cixous, H., & Clément, C. (1985). *The newly born woman.* Manchester: Manchester University Press.

Comely, L., Kitzinger, C., & Perkins, R. (1992). Lesbian psychology in Britain. *Feminism & Psychology, 2*(2), 265–268.

Elson, D. (1992, November). *Public action, poverty and development: A gender aware analysis.*

Paper prepared for seminar on 'Women in extreme poverty: Integration of women's concerns in national development planning', Division for Advancement of Women, United Nations Office at Vienna.

Ennew, J. (1988). *The sexual exploitation of children*, Oxford: Polity.

Esteva, G. (1992). Development. In W. Sachs (Ed.), *The development dictionary* (pp. 6–25). London: Zed Press.

Fuss, D. (1989). *Essentially speaking*. London: Routledge.

Gill, P. (1986). *A year in the death of Africa*. London: Paladin.

Gronemeyer, M. (1992). Helping. In W. Sachs (Ed.), *The development dictionary* (pp. 53–69). London: Zed Press.

Grosz, E. (1992). What is feminist theory? In H. Crowley & S. Himmelweit (Eds.), *Knowing women: Feminism and knowledge* (pp. 355–369). Oxford: Polity.

Haraway, D. (1991). *Simians, cyborgs and women: The reinvention of nature*. London: Verso.

Holland, P. (1992). *What is a child?* London: Virago.

Lorde, A. (1984). *Sister outsider: Essays and speeches*. Freedom, CA: The Crossing Press.

Miller, A. (1985). *Thou shalt not be aware: Society's betrayal of the child*. London: Pluto Press.

Moore, S. (1988). Getting a bit of the Other: The pimps of postmodernism. In R. Chapman & J. Rutherford (Eds.), *Male order: Unwrapping masculinity* (pp. 165–192). London: Verso.

Oakley, A. (1992, 14 October). *Children's and women's studies: Parallels and differences*. Childhood Study Group workshop, London.

Orbach, S., & Eichenbaum, H. (1982). *Understanding women*. London: Penguin.

Parker, I., & Burman, E. (1993). Against discursive imperialism, empiricism and constructionism: Thirty-two problems with discourse analysis. In E. Burman & I. Parker (Eds.), *Discourse analytic research: Repertoires and readings of texts in action* (pp. 155–172). London: Routledge.

Sayers, J. (1992). A POWS reply, *Feminism & Psychology*, 2(2), 269–270.

Scientific Affairs Board. (1988). *The future of the psychological sciences: Horizons and opportunities for British psychology*. Leicester: British Psychological Society.

Spivak, G.C. (1988). Can the subaltern speak? In C. Nelson & L. Grossberg (Eds.), *Marxism and the interpretation of culture* (pp. 271–313). London: Macmillan.

Squire, C. (1989). *Significant differences: Feminism and psychology*. London: Routledge.

Star, S.L. (1992). Power, technology and the phenomenology of conventions: On being allergic to onions. In J. Law (Ed.), *A sociology of monsters* (pp. 26–56). London: Routledge.

Walkerdine, V. (1988). *The mastery of reason: Cognitive development and the production of rationality*. London: Routledge.

Walkerdine, V., & Lucey, H. (1989). *Democracy in the kitchen: Regulating mothers and socializing daughters*. London: Virago.

Weed, C. (Ed.). (1990). *Coming to terms: Feminism, theory, politics*. New York and London: Routledge.

Wolff, J. (1993). On the road again: Metaphors of travel in cultural criticism. *Cultural Studies*, 7(2), 224–239.

15

Critical Social Psychology: Identity and De-prioritization of the Social

Mike Michael

Since the publication of *The Context of Social Psychology* (Israel & Tajfel, 1972), social psychology has developed in numerous directions. There are those efforts, most notably intergroup theory/self-categorization theory, which continue to toil in the experimental tradition while aspiring to the political high ground (e.g. Turner, 1987). There are hybrid perspectives, specifically social representation theory, which has sustained cordial relations with the experimental tradition but which nevertheless finds roots in the Durkheimian school (e.g. Moscovici, 1981, 1984). Above all, there is social constructionism, with its profound eclecticism (discourse, rhetoric, semiotics, Foucault, social theory, ethnomethodology) and its admirable commitment to trouble-making (whatever the long-term political value of this might be). This chapter would like to indulge these qualities too: the eclecticism concerns both disciplines and 'objects of study'; the trouble comes when we begin to take the 'non-social' seriously.

So, this chapter is a brief reflection on some of the stories we might tell about one of the potential avenues that (social) constructionist social psychology might take. Elsewhere, (Michael, 1992) I have argued that, if we take social constructionism as a moment in postmodern social psychology, and if we stress the dimension of transgression, as opposed to that of the linguistic turn, it is possible to ask how we might break down the disciplinary and conceptual boundaries that shape the analytic objects and practices of social psychology: In particular, we might consider how to incorporate the 'natural' – as autonomous actor rather than social construct – in the construction of such social psychological staples as identity. Even if we dispense with the postmodern problematic, this question remains pertinent in light of current developments in a number of fields which directly address the introduction of 'nature' (albeit as a highly ambiguous entity) into social theorizing.

In what follows, I first briefly outline some of the disciplinary dynamics that are beginning to problematize the social/natural (sciences) divides that have traditionally characterized the (critical) social sciences. I will then consider how some of these might find expression in critical social psychology. This will be elaborated with the aid of an important, if ambivalent, strand in the sociology of scientific knowledge (SSK), namely actor-network theory, especially as it applies to the construction of identity. In the process, I will use two examples of the impact of 'natural actors' on the construction of identity: the local environment and animals.[1]

The (Possible) Return of 'Nature'

'Nature', in its various guises, has been a topic of social inquiry for some time now. In recent times it has been apprehended as a socially constructed (broadly construed) entity or phenomenon. For example, Collingwood (1960) describes the conceptions of 'nature' that have developed from the period of the ancient Greeks to the rise of modern science. According to Collingwood, the Greeks conceived of 'nature' as a rational, mindful organism: it was saturated with mind which orchestrated the ceaseless movement of bodies and elements to yield orderliness and regularity, and hence the possibility of science. By the Renaissance period, the order of 'nature' was thought to be imposed from without: 'nature' was conceived as a machine – a configuration of parts designed, wrought, assembled and animated by an intelligent mind – God. By the end of the eighteenth century, derived from the study of human affairs, 'nature' was no longer seen to be cyclical, but evolving.

If Collingwood provides us with a broad outline of the cosmological construction of 'natural', other authors have studied historically more nuanced changes in our conception of 'natural'. Thus, Williams (1980) notes the transition from the Elizabethan and early Jacobean representation of 'nature' as singular, abstracted and personified as God's minister and deputy instructing humankind as to its duties (this was preceded by a 'natural' and absolute monarch) into a sort of constitutional lawyer from the seventeenth to the nineteenth century, where attention effectively moves from the law-giver to the details of the laws and their interpretation. Other scholars (e.g. Berman, 1981; Merchant, 1980) have reconstructed the changing conception of 'nature' with the aim of recovering a more environmentally friendly formulation or of mapping out the historically variable valuation of various 'natural entities' such as animals and wilderness (e.g. Tester, 1991; Thomas, 1984). Beck (1992) has considered the emergent contradictory reconceptualization of 'nature' under the conditions of what he calls the 'Risk Society'. 'Nature' is no longer the antithesis of society – where once a 'pure nature' was directly accessed by the layperson, now it is mediated by experts who inform us of the risks that lurk in every part of a thoroughly 'corrupted nature'. On a less epochal level, some writers have considered the social construction of (aspects of) 'nature' as a rhetorical device to defend a particular picture of society/science relations (Michael, 1991) or to deflate relativist arguments (Edwards, Ashmore & Potter, 1992).

However, all these approaches have constituted 'nature' as a construction, as opposed to some external given. The analytic purpose is to expose the discursive, rhetorical, practical, historical, political, and so on, resources that serve in the construction of an ostensibly unproblematic (or, rather, unproblematizeable) 'nature'. In the present case, while accepting the importance of the above perspectives, I want to consider some of the ways in which 'nature' is beginning to be reintroduced into social theorizing, in particular, as an independently effectual actor. So, to rephrase the central issue outlined in the introduction: what reason could we possibly have for treating non-humans – whether 'natural' or 'technological' – as autonomous participants, whether agential or not, in the world as opposed to 'merely' the social constructions of human discursive collectivities?

Such an intellectual query is, of course, not altogether novel. Indeed, we find it appearing in several sub-disciplines such as sociological theory, feminist theory, SSK and environmental ethics. Thus, we witness attempts to problematize the division between human and social sciences. For example, Horigan (1988) has shown how the 'natural' was variously differentiated from the 'social' in an attempt by social anthropologists to separate anthropology from its parent discipline of biology and natural philosophy. The long-term result, according to Horigan, is that there has been a privileging of social factors to the extent that the influence of natural factors upon human social behaviour and structures, by and large, has been bracketed (also cf. Ingold, 1989). Horigan's work entails a critical analysis of the emergence of traditional disciplinary boundaries, and as such it is an exercise in reflecting upon their social construction. At issue is the reflexive question: if we assume that it is important to deconstruct the ostensibly obvious (whether these be 'social' or 'natural' entities), is it not also equally important to unravel the roots of the divisions between the 'social' and the 'natural' (sciences)?

If Horigan's task has been the excavation of the historical and institutional conditions that led to the differentiation of 'social' and 'natural' science discourses, Benton (1991) has concerned himself with the historicity of what he perceives as the re-emergence of 'nature' on the social science agenda. In other words, he has attempted to identify some of the pressures placed upon the social/biological divide and the dichotomies that characterize it (mind/body, culture/nature, society/biology, meaning/cause, human/animal) by contemporary social movements such as feminism and environmentalism. These political interests, fundamentally concerned as they are with the role that 'nature' has to play in constituting and delimiting present-day social dynamics, are not satisfied with purely sociological explanations and characterizations. The limits of body and environment also need to be taken into some sort of account.

Horigan and Benton have produced programmatic analyses of the (possible) return of 'nature'. Dickens (1992), on the other hand, attempts to formulate the broad outlines of a coherent (social) theory that encapsulates the roles of both the 'social' and the 'natural'. Drawing upon the young Marx, he develops a critical realist account of society that hinges on 'nature' that is at once socially constructed but also 'transcendental'. The latter refers to 'causal powers', that is, the way that 'organisms are seen as having necessary, latent or potential ways of acting . . . but [these] critically depend on contingent circumstances' (p. 178). Thus, 'nature' is constitutive of people insofar as they have 'particular kinds of latent tendencies and potentials (natural and species being) which may or may not be realized in their association (or lack of association) with the natural world' (p. 64). In relation to (social) psychology, both Parker (1992) and Greenwood (1992) have advocated this epistemological position (though they have not directed it to 'external nature' in the same way as Dickens).

By and large, the approaches mentioned above tend to treat 'nature' as a mechanistic component in the (re)production of the social. It is as an, albeit contingent, causal influence on social processes that 'nature' is to be reappropriated and theorized. In contrast, there are alternative perspectives that attempt to reintroduce 'nature' as a semiotic player. Here, 'nature' adopts the part of another interlocutor in the discursive/practical community that (re)constructs both the 'social' and the 'natural' or 'technological'. This can take various forms. For example, there are efforts to recover the agential status of 'nature' or to retrace its fall from the heights of personhood (Adorno & Horkheimer, 1979; Berman, 1981; Merchant, 1980).

Perhaps the most elaborated accounts of treating 'nature' as a subject in interaction with humans can be found in the burgeoning field of environmental ethics. Much of the intellectual effort expended in environmental ethics seeks to find a philosophical (e.g. Heideggerian, aesthetic, phenomenological) or theological (e.g. Christian, American Indian) basis for 'ecological consciousness' (cf. Rodman, 1983). In some treatments, 'nature' is elevated to a 'Thou' – a full participant, equivalent to a human interlocutor, in conversation with the human 'I' (e.g. Buber, 1970; Tallmadge, 1981; however, also see Kultgen, 1982; Michael & Grove-White, 1993; Reed, 1989). In this latter case, 'nature' is merely 'humanized': 'nature' is attributed characteristics typical of humans conceived in humanistic terms. The agential status of 'nature' is here assumed or argued for (as is that of humans). As we will see below, such 'semiotic' (broadly defined) interactions need not trade on pre-existing agents – these may emerge from the interaction. Indeed, the production of agency, as with the production of 'society' or 'nature', can be seen as an accomplishment.

These efforts of some humanistic environmental ethicists are essentially attempts to articulate what it might mean to broaden the 'linguistic' collective to include 'natural'. On this score, we might interrogate Harré's (1992) transcendental conditions for the possibility of discursive practice. If discourse must create and sustain persons, do these necessarily have to take human form? If discourse is person-produced in joint action, what happens if we impute to 'natural entities' the status of persons? If the 'real for social constructionism, properly formulated [*sic*] . . . must be whatever is intransigent to individual desires [and that is] the human conversation' (Harré, 1992, p. 157), what happens when we suggest, following Latour (1988a, pp.

158, 166), that non-human actors offer their own gradients of resistance in the process of interaction with others (whether humans or not)? The point is that such transcendental conditions do not preclude other 'reals', properly formulated.

Knorr Cetina (1988) likewise gives analytic priority to the interactional situation in the context of the macro–micro controversy in sociology. Methodological situationism is seen as the appropriate way to theorize the way in which the macro is rooted in the micro, specifically through the way negotiating, that is to say, broadly political, actors situationally accomplish representations of the macro. Obviously, the macro refers to the macro-sociological – the state, classes, epistemes, and the like. However, what happens if we broaden the interactants in the micro-situation to include non-humans who contribute not only to the generation of representations of macro-social entities, but also to the representation of macro-natural entities? Again, here, we prioritize the micro-situation but one that can be constituted with numerous, so far neglected, non-human 'characters'.

In contrast to those approaches which attempt to reinstitute 'nature' as a subject or as an object, we can draw upon actor-network theory, which, while it ascribes autonomy to 'nature' (and to technological artefacts), nevertheless conceptualizes these as historically contingent entities which can, with further analysis, be shown to be constructed out of further 'natural' and 'social' entities (or actors or actants). In other words, the object or subject status of 'natural', artefacts or humans is one topic of analysis. I will now briefly consider this perspective.

Actor-network Theory and Identity

The actor-network perspective (e.g. Callon, 1986a, 1986b, 1987; Callon & Latour, 1981; Latour, 1986, 1987, 1988a, 1988b; Law, 1987) rests on three tenets: generalized agnosticism – analytic impartiality as to whatever actors are involved in controversy; generalized symmetry – the use of an abstract and neutral vocabulary to understand the conflicting viewpoints of actors; and free association – the repudiation of a priori distinctions between the social and the natural or the technological. Within this meta-theoretical framework, scientists are treated not simply as scientists but as multifaceted entrepreneurs who, with skill and aplomb, engage in political, sociological and economic activities, as well as in those practices tradi-tionally assigned the label 'scientific'. Thus scientists harness a multiplicity of materials and techniques to extend their influence beyond the laboratory. To do this they must enrol others. Actor-network theory (ANT) has evolved a variety of terms with which to conceptualize this process.

At a general level there is *interressement* – 'actions by which an entity attempts to impose and stabilize the identity of other actors it defines through its problematization'. This broad term encompasses a variety of strategies and mechanisms by which one entity – whether that be an individual like Pasteur, a small group like the three researchers of St Brieuc Bay or an institution like the Electricité de France – attempts to 'corner' and enrol other entities such as scientists, publics, institutions, scallops, electrons. This is achieved by interposing oneself between the target entity and its pre-existing associations with other entities that contribute to its identity. Only with the successful disconnection from these other associations can enrolment be said to have, albeit temporarily, succeeded.

However, enrolment is not a unilateral process of imposition: it entails both the 'capturing' of the other and the other's 'yielding'. It is a multilateral process. For Latour (1986), power is not a possession, but an arrangement of assent:

> 'Power' is always the illusion people get when they are obeyed . . . [they] discover what their power is really made of when they start to lose it . . . it was 'made of' the wills of all the others . . . power [is] a consequence and not a cause of collective action. (p. 173)

Enrolment has been fleshed out through a consideration of a variety of other concepts, each examining how it is that some entities are in the thrall of others.

'Translation' is the means by which one entity gives a role to others, from the macro-sociological to the subatomic. In the process, the translator sets itself up as their spokesperson. If these identities are to take hold, then it is also necessary to invent a geography of 'obligatory points of passage': for those elements and entities that wish to continue to exist and develop, and which the enrolling entity wishes to enrol, such points constitute unavoidable conduits – narrative bottlenecks – through which they must pass in order to articulate both their identity and their raison d'être. Another mode of translation is 'displacement': this refers to the ways in which entities organize and structure the movement of materials, resources and information. By the organization of meetings, the making and maintaining of contacts, the carrying out of experiments, an entity can accumulate just those materials that render its actor-network more durable.

Now, the processes of enrolment are particularly problematic when they are conducted across longer distances. One of the prime modes by which the disruptive potential of distance is combated is that of the 'immutable mobile'. The immutable mobile is some form of text – writing, graphs, figures, formulae – which can be moved, remains stable, and can be combined with other such texts. It facilitates the capacity of particular entities to centralize and monopolize such meanings at centres of calculation, such as laboratories, where these materials, traces, and so on, can all be tied together.

However, the whole system is unreliable. In Callon's (1986b) terms, the actor-world can convert or revert into an actor-network. That is to say, particular traces, immutable mobiles, materials, can suddenly become problematized (un-black-boxed). The roles and identities assigned by one entity to another may suddenly be challenged, undermined or shattered.

Where once the 'enrolling' actor had organized the obligatory points of passage for others, it finds itself forced to traverse the obligatory points of passages that are 'dictated' by others. And it is not only social others who intervene: the heterogeneity of the networks means that any entity can begin to step out of semiotic character within the network – electrons, microbes, scallops, the Atlantic.

The notion of identity has arisen several times in the above accounts of ANT. Through various techniques, scientists construct identities for other actors who are then 'persuaded' to adopt them – to define themselves through these identities (at least in relation to the scientists). Thus, in Callon's (1986a) classic study of the scallops, researchers and fishing community of St Brieuc Bay in their effort to develop techniques for cultivating the scallop *Pecten maximus* in order to restock the bay, the biologists constructed an actor-network in which they narrated the roles of the component actants. Specifically, the local fishermen were represented as fundamentally interested in the restocking the scallop population and as committed to its long-term viability and sustainability. For a while, it seemed that the fishermen accepted this identity. In Callon's (1986b) study of the efforts by the Electricité de France (EDF) to institute a programme of research into an electric vehicle, he shows how they represented the public as undergoing a change of lifestyle. In the not so distant future, the public would become highly anxious about the environmental threat posed by pollution from combustion engines – their preferred alternative would be electric vehicles. The EDF also portrayed Renault not as a major French car manufacturer, but (given its lack of expertise in electric alternatives to the combustion engine) as a builder of specialized chassis for the electric vehicle. For a while, at least, it seemed that Renault, by virtue of its silence, had accepted this new identity. As things turned out, both the fishermen and Renault betrayed their enrolling actors. However, the point is that identity was something that was constructed by certain others, who, with the aid of translation techniques, immutable mobiles, *interressement*, seemed to have managed to enrol crucial others to their network, necessarily persuading them to adopt new or modified identities in the process.

Obviously, this sort of approach can be applied to actors outside of science: parents and children, state and civil society, church and worshippers, doctor and patient, and so on. In relation to most linguistics-oriented social constructionist treatments of identity, it shows how identity is 'socially distributed'. Most social constructionist approaches in social psychology have considered the discursive or narrative resources available to participants in their construction and exemplification of identity (e.g. Shotter & Gergen, 1989). What we find here is a detailing of the way that particular linguistic resources are deployed in the expression–reproduction of identities. How such resources became available, how they were set in place, is left vague or is implicitly ascribed to the general discursive contents of the linguistic community to which the speaker belongs. In contrast, ANT attempts to lay out some of the routes by which such resources came to be entrenched in a particular actor (individual or collective). It looks at those junctures at which texts of identity were made available by one actor for the use (and hence enrolment) of another actor. It is the textual, social and physical mechanisms by which such historically located 'persuasions' were accomplished that is of key interest to ANT and which distinguishes it from other (social) constructionist perspectives.

Commentaries on ANT: Perspectives, Marginality and Ambiguity

Criticisms of ANT have focused on, for example, the ambiguous role of interests or de-prioritization of the social. Thus Shapin (1988) argues that Latour's eschewing of interest explanations is by no means convincing: it is only by conflating interests and accounts of interests that Latour manages to make his case that 'interests' are the consequences of negotiation. In contrast, Callon and Law (1982) acknowledge that their use of interests falls more closely on the side of the Edinburgh school than on Woolgar's (1981) ethnomethodologizing of interests, where accounts of interests are afforded analytic priority.

Collins and Yearley's (1992) critique addresses the radical symmetrism of ANT: the 'actant' status that technological artefacts and natural entities have within ANT is seen as highly problematic. The de-prioritization of the social that gives an autonomous voice to 'things' disguises the fact that these voices in actuality depend upon the mediation of human actors: this pivotal role of second-hand reports of human actors reinstates the social as the real site of SSK investigation. Callon and Latour's (1992) response is, in part, that technological artefacts are implicated in the very fabric of the social – they are social relations viewed in their durability and cohesion: as such the techniques by which meaning is drained out of artefacts become the objects of study.

There have, however, been more sympathetic commentaries that have attempted to elaborate on ANT.

(1) *Perspectives:* In the recounting of an ANT story, where does the analyst situate him/herself? Schwartz Cowan (1987) has argued that ANT tends to take up a perspective outside of the network: it studies networks from the outside in. By studying the 'consumption junction', as Schwartz Cowan calls the temporal and spatial point at which consumers make choices between competing technologies, it is possible to ascertain how a network may have looked from the inside out.

(2) *Multiplicity:* How should we incorporate into a network entities that possess a range of attributes and identities? Within any network, constituent actants have multiple membership in many worlds at once. For Star (1991), this is used as the ground for examining the potentially critical positions of actants on the margins of a given network. Where the network is multi-dimensional and contains within it obscure associations and roles – that is, where there is a network-within-a-network – actants

have many resources to draw upon which, while problematizing certain components of the original network, can ultimately contribute to its durability (also cf. Law, 1991; Singleton & Michael, 1993).

(3) *Marginality and critique:* What voice should be attributed to those actors who are systematically excluded from a network? How is it possible to turn ANT to critical ends that 'champion' particular actors with which the analyst can be said to identify? Those who are marginalized should not, Star argues, be conceived as simply 'outside'. They occupy a position that is 'as yet unlabelled' and which can serve as a latent subverting influence upon the network.

The main interest in the present context is actor-network theorists' ambition to grant sociological, or, perhaps more accurately, narrative, rights to non-humans. Accordingly, 'natural' entities also enrol – they, too, have their resistances and goals (however mysterious or other-worldly). In relation to the construction of identity, the questions that we are faced with can be phrased in the following way: how might 'nature' intervene in the construction of identity? Here, I focus upon the way that the 'natural' serves to enrol human actors, and how its resistance – a resistance that is always already historically contingent – begins to shape the construction of a social identity. However, such resistances as they are expressed in the micro-situational interaction need not always be linguistic. Indeed, to capture the range of the media through which the interactions between humans and non-humans are conducted, one needs an expanded definition of semiotics. Fortunately, Akrich and Latour (1992) provide just such a definition. Semiotics is

> The study of how meaning is built, [where] the word 'meaning' is taken in its original nontextual and nonlinguistic interpretation: how a privileged trajectory is built, out of an indefinite number of possibilities; in that sense, semiotics is the study of order building or path building and may be applied to settings, machines, bodies and programming languages as well as texts. (p. 259)

What concerns us here is the notion of 'building a privileged trajectory out of an indefinite number of possibilities'. The point is that the 'natural' can play a part in such structuring. Through a variety of media, the natural can enrol humans by giving them (or getting them to accept) particular identities. In the process, order (behavioural as well as linguistic or narrative) comes to be generated out of an indefinite number of possibilities.

ANT, 'Nature' and Identity

This section deals with two examples of the way that ANT might be used to theorize the construction of identity in which non-humans play an independent part. Rather than press this claim to the limit and look for the most difficult cases, I have been rather cowardly and opted for easy illustrations where the conduits of communication or semiosis are relatively unmediated. Thus, I deal with those non-humans that are traditionally thought to fall within the limits of human perception: animals rather than viruses; immediate environment rather than the cosmos. In keeping with the focus upon the micro-social context of construction (see above), it is at this locus that 'conversation', however formulated, *can* take place (of course, there is no guarantee). At all other levels, some mediation must presumably take place.

Animals

In regard to the role of the 'natural' in the constitution of identity, we can draw upon Callon's (1986a) classic study of the scallops, researchers and fishing community of St Brieuc Bay mentioned above. This we can reinterpret in terms of the production of identity that was partially shaped by the intransigence of both social and natural entities. The researchers attempted to construct an actor-network in which they narrated the roles of the component actants. We have seen how the local fishermen were represented as fundamentally interested in the restocking; the scallops were represented through the various scientific techniques as potentially cultivable; and the relevant scientific community was represented as an assenting constituency. The influence of the three researchers derived from the fact that they headed these three heterogeneous populations. In effect, their constructed identity was constituted across these three domains, each of which apparently supported their self-narration as experts, representatives, scientists, advisers and so on. However, this complex of identity could only survive as long as each of the actors in the researcher's network played their allotted part. When the fishermen betrayed the scientists by, contrary to their supposed long-term aims, fishing to the point of decimating the scallop beds, then it was no longer feasible for the three scientists to claim to represent the interests of the fishermen. Likewise, when the scallop larvae 'refused' to be cultivated and levels became hopelessly low, the stories the researchers could tell about themselves as scientists and cultivators became subverted. In sum, their identity, dispersed and decentred across the network as it was, became suspect – their texts of identity were effectively exploded. In terms of the micro-social context, the biologists' interactions with the larvae produced a certain response, namely that they as cultivators had failed.

An easier example, from my perspective, comes from accounts of interactions with putatively 'more overtly responsive' (i.e. interactive) animals. Animal pets have long been said to have therapeutic effects upon their owners, though obviously this will depend on the precise nature of the relationship. In particular, owners say that 'their animals are sensitive to their [the owners'] moods and feelings' (Serpell, 1986, p. 114; also cf. Sanders, 1992). The processes of communication that are evident here are clearly not linguistic, but vocal, visual and tactile. However, animals' lack of linguistic capacity may be one of their prime assets. As Serpell (1986) puts it:

Lacking the power of speech, animals cannot participate in conversation or debate but, by the same token, they do not judge us, criticize us, lie to us or betray our trust. Because it is mute and non-judgemental, their affection is seen as sincere, innocent, and without pretence. It is essentially reliable and trustworthy. (p. 114)

Sanders (1992) echoes this point when he says that the

. . . chief pleasure they [owners] derived from the animal–human relationship was the joy of relating to another being who consistently demonstrated love – a feeling-for-the-other which was honestly felt and displayed and not contingent upon the personal attributes or even the actions of the human-other. (p. 16)

However, this intimacy does not preclude humans from 'speaking for' their pets. As Sanders notes:

Because the animal is 'mute,' caretakers often find themselves in situations in which they must 'speak for' their nonhuman companions. In so doing, they make use of a rich body of knowledge derived from an intimate understanding of the animal-other built up in the course of day-to-day interactional experience. Dog owners commonly give voice to what they perceive to be their animals' mental, emotional, and physical experiences. (pp. 6–7)

Such talk suggests a process of re-narration by humans of their own and their animals' experiences with the aid of more or less familiar stories. These stories, which suggest that companion animals communicate with humans in certain non-linguistic ways both to give comfort to their owners and to express their own inner states, tend to anthropomorphize, in the sense of attributing human qualities to animals which are essentially 'other'. To take such accounts seriously, and then to argue that companion animals enrol their owners in various ways, is to practise a double anthropomorphism. Any such account which regards the animals as autonomous co-conversationalists (albeit outside the medium of language) will neglect to give due weight to the discursive trajectories by which such animals are constructed by owners and ethnographers/sociologists for particular interactional/social functions as autonomous actors. However, in response, we might draw on Latour's (1992) counter-queries: what role does such an accusation have for the critical social constructionist? Should we not follow this communicative process seriously (not via some pure empiricism as Latour occasionally seems to suggest), but through an analytic posture that aspires to agnosticism as to the form of the interaction and attempts to remain sensitive to extra- or quasi-linguistic shaping of human identity?

However, though a convincing social constructionist account of pet owners' anthropomorphizing of animals can no doubt be provided, it is also possible to derive another story. It is possible to detect in owners' accounts a view of the animal as an 'Other World'. Noske (1989), in her critique of the social sciences' neglect of the animal (as something other than 'symbol'), suggests that the 'otherness' that the social anthropologist confronts and respects in her ethnographic endeavours should be extended to animals. If social anthropology is 'the science of the other', then social scientists need to immerse themselves in contexts that contain animal others to understand the what and how of animal–animal and animal–human conversations while retaining a sensitivity to animals' otherness. This point is underlined by Haraway (1992) in her meditation on Noske's book (amongst others). In addition to not being objectified, Haraway suggests that

> The last thing 'they' [animals] need is human subject status, in whatever cultural–historical form. . . . We need other terms of conversations with animals, a much less respectable undertaking. The point is not new representations, but new practices, other forms of life rejoining humans and not-humans. (pp. 86–7)

Out of this emerges, Haraway hopes, a new form of human being:

> Once the world of subjects and objects is put into question, that paradox concerns the congeries, or curious confederacy, that is the self, as well as selves' relations with others. A promising form of life, conversation defies the autonomization of the self, as well as the objectification of the other. (p. 90)

What Haraway is getting at here is that to engage in those non-linguistic processes of communication with animal others is to diffuse one's self – to admit of its multiplicity and dispersion. It is perhaps just this dimension of 'dissipation' that enrols the human actor to its animal companion. The identity that is thus generated is one that no longer follows the linearities of narrative, but is one mediated by and realized in the many channels of human–animal communication. Thus, over and above the identities that are reflected in owners' narration of the animal–human dyad, it is *the form of non-linguistic communication that becomes the content of human identity* in the association between human and animal companions. So, animals, in all their other-worldliness, enrol humans but the identity that they offer them is of a different order from the typical modes of the human social self. (As Noske notes, babies and disabled people can offer similar identities.) Constructed but not socially constructed, micro-situationally negotiated but not linguistically mediated, these human identities serve the animal's network which is none other than the dyad itself. In terms of ANT, the network, obligatory point of passage and the identity begin to fuse into a whole: the animal–human dyad.

Immediate Environment

In this section, I look at some of the ways that we might consider 'nature', this time in the guise of the local environment, as an independent player. In keeping with my cowardly strategy of choosing the easiest cases, I will focus on the environment in its more conducive incarnation – the sunny scenario, so to speak. The reason why will become clearer below.

Above, we saw how various accounts of 'nature' as a co-conversationalist – a Thou – explicitly tried to construct 'nature' as a subject. This was implicitly criticized for its humanist stance (of course, as Soper, 1986), has noted, there is a strategic place for humanism). Given the short but glorious history of post-structuralist critiques of the centred subject, I will not reproduce the arguments here, but turn to an account that aims to broaden community to include 'nature' but which does not, in the process, attribute subjecthood to 'nature'. Here, we turn to the work of Jim Cheney. Cheney (1989) attempts to articulate an environmental consciousness, and a relation between humans and 'nature', that draws upon the postmodern project of avoiding the essentialization of the self. His solution is to develop a notion of bioregional narratives grounded in geography:

Narrative is the key then, but it is narrative grounded in geography rather than in a linear, essentialized narrative self. . . . Totalizing masculine discourse (and essentializing feminist discourse) give way to a contextualized discourse of place. (p. 126)

Thus,

Within the geography of the human landscape the contextual voice can emerge in clarity and health only through a 'constant recontextualizing' which prevents the oppressive and distorting overlays of cultural institutions . . . from gathering false, distorting and unhealthy identities out of 'the positive desire for unity, for Oneness. (p. 128)

Clearly, Cheney is wary of essentializing discourse. His partial answer is to

. . . expand the notion of a contextualizing narrative of place so as to include 'nature' – 'nature' as one more player in the construction of community . . . [he proposes] that we extend these notions of context and narrative outwards so as to include not just the human community, but also the land, one's community in a larger sense. (p. 128)

The medium through which this could be achieved is, according to Cheney, myth. If 'bioregionalism can "ground" the construction of self and community' (p. 134), it will proceed through the narratives and metaphors of mythology which are derived from the landscapes and the localities themselves. Obviously, this begs a lot of questions as to how such a process of derivation might come about. While it expresses an albeit normative hope (this is ethics, after all) that 'nature' can be regarded as a voice in the community that constructs such sociological givens as identity, the way in which 'nature' actually intervenes in such a community remains painfully vague.

In terms of ANT, 'nature', qua bioregional locality, is an actant. Elsewhere, I have suggested that Cheney's 'nature' is an actant that is not given to the coherence of a unitary entity.

Rather, its very diversity and richness serves to disaggregate the texts of identity of its human inhabitants. Again, in terms of actor-network theory, we might say that it has enrolled human actors who begin to formulate, that is to say, narrate themselves in like fashion – they are dispersed and decentred – in short, they are 'postmodern selves'. The obligatory point of passage is one in which the core texts of identity are those of fracture, of the forgoing of 'coherence, continuity and consistency' (Cheney, 1989, p. 126). In the process, the power of 'nature' does indeed take the form of an association in which the human actants give up their stories of unitary self if they wish to 'carry on'. (Michael, 1992, pp. 83–84)

However, in retrospect, how this process of fragmentation is conveyed remains somewhat opaque. Once again, in terms of ANT, how 'nature' 'interresses' and eventually enrols the human actor – the semiosis by which this is mediated – is left uncomfortably obscure.

Drawing on Latour's (1991, 1992; Latour/Johnson, 1988) work on the social intervention of technological artefacts, we observe that door grooms and hotel key weights take on their supposed moral standing by acting against the body of the human actor. The aim, in true Foucauldian form, is to discipline the human actor by delegating certain functions to non-human actors. Door grooms – the hydraulic mechanism which both offers resistance when opening a door and then slowly closes it – discipline humans who must exert additional energy when opening the door (the point of the groom is to avoid slamming and broken noses). As Latour (1992) notes:

> . . . neither my little nephews nor my grandmother could get in unaided because our groom needed the force of an able-bodied person to accumulate enough energy to close the door later . . . these doors *discriminate* against very little and very old persons. (p. 234; emphasis in the original)

At issue here is the way in which the artefact acts upon the capacities of the body to shape and discipline the human actor – to give them a particular identity. Here, a physical constraint is imposed, which, while not overly inconveniencing some humans, forces others to enrol other humans to do their door-opening for them. If these relatively 'dis-abled' humans succeed in such enrolments, they have, in an almost literal sense, grown bigger. Nevertheless, the centrality of the *capacities of the body* to Latour's story remains. In what follows, however, I want to draw out some of the ways in which 'nice nature' interacts with the body to recover previously suppressed possibilities, where the environment – 'natural' instead of 'technological' – potentially enables, rather than constrains, the movement of the body in light of the body's capacities.

Drawing on Gibson's (1979) notion of 'affordance', Michael and Still (1992) suggest that the interface between organism and environment generates behavioural options for the individual with which to challenge power/knowledge (in the Foucauldian sense). 'Affordance' refers to the way in which the (optic) array of surfaces and structures in the environment specify a range of possible actions for the organism. A flat horizontal surface thus affords sitting on, lying across, rolling out dough, and so on. As such, there are a range of options that are *implicit* within a physical milieu and this implicitness is directly connected to the bodily capacities and limits of the organism. It is important here to stress the *optionality* of afforded actions: the environment does not determine what happens, it implicates a repertoire of possible happenings. This non-determination by the environment brings to mind Deleuze's (1988) treatment of Foucault's distinction between the discursive and the non-discursive. The former is constituted by statements and is determining, whereas the latter is visible, constituted by visibilities, and is determinable. These visibilities 'are not the forms of objects . . . but rather luminosities which are created by the light itself and allow a thing or object to exist only as a flash, sparkle or shimmer' (p. 52). Deleuze firmly historicizes these visibilities such that the 'visibilities of one epoch become hazy and blurred to the point where "self-evident" phenomena cannot be grasped by another age' (p. 57). However, while these visibilities are 'determinable' by discourse, they are not *determined*: as Deleuze argues, there is a rift between what we see and what we speak, between the visible and the articulable. As such there is a potential slippage between what we 'see' – in Gibson's terms, what is afforded – and what the discourses of power/knowledge dictate. In a sense, affordance serves to map out some of the corporeal *resources* for resistance against Foucauldian discipline.

Returning to the effort to constitute the local 'natural' environment as a semiotic player in the micro-situation, we can make the following tentative observations. First, such an environment incorporates a variety of affordances for the human individual. The discourses and narratives that the individual brings to bear within such a physical milieu are potentially subverted or challenged by the affordances and visibilities of local 'nature'. That tree in the local wood is not just an object of beauty and contemplation. (MacNaughten [personal communication] is examining the way that, in Britain, policy documents and tourist/user guides produced by such institutions as English Nature, the Tourist Board and the Countryside Commission serve as manuals imparting techniques and technologies of the self – (Martin, Gutman & Hutton, 1988.) A tree is also a thing to climb, to scratch oneself against, to sleep under, and so on. None of these options might be realized – however, in being afforded in relation to bodily capacities and limits, they serve potentially to challenge particular disciplined views of the tree and the human identities which attend these.

The point here is that local 'nature' enrols by virtue of opening up behavioural vistas – that is, by expanding the potential range of identities for an individual. In contrast to Latour's view of enrolment by non-humans/technology in which limits are placed upon the enrolled actor, here limits are potentially removed and repertoires implicitly revealed.

As noted above, this story rests on the sunny scenario of 'nature'. 'Nature' is represented as benign and its prime narrative role is as a world of surfaces. (As such it is no different from the built environment – nevertheless, the point holds: affordance still operates in 'non-natural' environments.) However, 'nature' can also be nasty: it can serve up its own resistances – rain, cold, mud, and so on – which in the context of bodily capacities serve to constrain options. Moreover, throughout this account, I have focused upon the individual human. Missing from the storyline is a vision of the expanded or collective physical individual. This expansion can involve both humans and non-humans. Thus, the affordances offered by a local 'nature' can multiply in the company of some humans (e.g. friends) or decrease in the company of others (e.g. wardens). Likewise, affordances can be expanded with the aid of some technologies (e.g. Landrovers, boots, grappling hooks), and reduced by the presence of others (e.g. electric fences, barbed wire, walls).

Nevertheless, the point remains that 'local nature' can enrol through the expansion of identity, formulated in physical/behavioural terms: this is part of its attraction for humans. For humans who wish to expand their identities, to become liminal perhaps (cf. Michael, 1992), it can be said to be a possible point of passage. Like animals, the 'local nature' of the situational interaction is an 'other world' – its motives and purposes remain obscure. However, it is still an actor or actant that, in the above story, enrols and the medium through which it does so is not just linguistic or symbolic but also corporeal/perceptual.

Concluding Remarks

This chapter has advocated, or at least told a story about, a form of construction of identity that adds to the typical conduits of communication: parallel with the linguistic are other semiotic modes. I have attempted to tell a tale about what we might call a 'corporeal semiotics'. This is a medium that, as with its linguistic counterpart, falls within the compass of individual human perception (left unproblematized). It is the human body, with its capacities and faculties, that sets out the parameters for such communications (and thereby the constitution of identity and enrolment). Such an individualistic account is, inevitably, contentious, especially in light of some of the recent writings on cyborgs (e.g. Haraway, 1991) which reformulate the individual as an entity extended across space and time by virtue of its integration with technological systems. This point has already emerged in relation to the above considerations of human–animal dyads and affordance. Both of these reflect a process by which the unity and integrity of the human individual is broken down, and out of which emerges a distributed self (physically, as well as in the post-structuralist sense). The actor becomes a collective one; the unit of analysis is broadened to encompass the human-other (animal/local environment) complex. At such a point, as with Haraway's Cyborgs – which she clearly states are historically novel entities – we might say that enrolment by the 'other' has been successful, and the actor that was the animal or local environment has grown bigger. In terms of ANT, the association is (albeit temporarily) secure, appropriate human identities are in place, the enroller has enlarged and, in relation to the human, black-boxed its network: the network so produced is the new actor.

In sum, the present chapter has been an elementary attempt to map out a different direction for constructionism to follow. The task, so woefully broached here, and so spectacularly accomplished by Latour and his co-workers in relation to technology, is to elaborate a vocabulary that begins to accommodate the 'natural' as an interlocutor in a non-linguistic conversation. But this would be too limited a programme. The simultaneous task would be to integrate this so far neglected dimension of the construction of identity with the processes and resources that have typically concerned social constructionists.

Note

1. I could have added a third category of non-humans to this chapter, namely technological artefacts. However, while he does not focus primarily upon identity, Latour (1991, 1992; Latour & Johnson, 1988) has provided a number of demoralizingly brilliant accounts of the ways in which non-humans/technological artefacts are implicated in the constitution of social order. It is hoped that the import of this category for identity will be more fully explored at a later point.

References

Adorno, T., & Horkheimer, M. (1979). *Dialectic of enlightenment*. London: Verso.

Akrich, M., & Latour, B. (1992). A summary of a convenient vocabulary for the semiotics of human and nonhuman assemblies. In W.E. Bijker & J. Law (Eds.), *Shaping technology/Building society* (pp. 259–263). Cambridge, MA: MIT Press.

Beck, U. (1992). *Risk society*. London: Sage.

Benton, T. (1991). Biology and social science: Why the return of the repressed should be given a (cautious) welcome. *Sociology*, *25*, 1–29.

Berman, M. (1981). *The reenchantment of the world*. Ithaca, NY: Cornell University Press.

Buber, M. (1970). *I and Thou*. New York: Scribner's.

Callon, M. (1986a). Some elements of a sociology of translation: Domestication of the scallops and fishermen of St Brieuc Bay. In J. Law (Ed.), *Power, action and belief: A new sociology of knowledge?* (pp. 196–233). London: Routledge & Kegan Paul.

Callon, M. (1986b). The sociology of an actor-network: The case of the electric vehicle. In M. Callon, J. Law & A. Rip (Eds.), *Mapping the dynamics of science and technology* (pp. 19–34). London: Macmillan.

Callon, M. (1987). Society in the making: The study of technology as a tool for sociological analysis. In W.E. Bijker, T.P. Hughes & T. Pinch (Eds.), *Social construction of technological systems* (pp. 83–103). Cambridge, MA: MIT Press.

Callon, M., & Latour, B. (1981). Unscrewing the big Leviathan. In K.D. Knorr Cetina and M. Mulkay (Eds.), *Advances in social theory and methodology* (pp. 275–303). London: Routledge & Kegan Paul.

Callon, M., & Latour, B. (1992). Don't throw the baby out with the Bath School: A reply to Collins and Yearley. In A. Pickering (Ed.), *Science as practice and culture* (pp. 301–326). Chicago: University of Chicago Press.

Callon, M., & Law, J. (1982). On interests and their transformation: Enrolment and counter-enrolment. *Social Studies of Science*, *12*, 615–625.

Cheney, J. (1989). Postmodern environmental ethics: Ethics as bioregional narrative. *Environmental Ethics*, *11*, 117–134.

Collingwood, R.G. (1960). *The idea of nature*, New York: Galaxy.

Collins, H.M., & Yearley, S. (1992). Epistemological chicken. In A. Pickering (Ed.), *Science as practice and culture* (pp. 301–326). Chicago: University of Chicago Press.

Deleuze, G. (1988). *Foucault*. London: Athlone Press.

Dickens, P. (1992). *Nature and society*. Hemel Hempstead: Harvester Wheatsheaf.

Edwards, D., Ashmore, M., & Potter, J. (1992). Death and furniture: The rhetoric, politics and theology of the bottom line arguments against relativism. *History of the Human Sciences*, *8*, 25–49.

Gibson, E.E. (1979). *The ecological approach to visual perception*. Boston: Houghton Mifflin.

Greenwood, J.D. (1992). Realism, empiricism and social constructionism: Psychological theory and the social dimensions of mind and action. *Theory & Psychology*, *2*, 131–151.

Haraway, D. (1991). *Simians, cyborgs and women: The reinvention of nature*. London: Free Association Books.

Haraway, D. (1992). Other worldly conversations; terran topics; local terms. *Science as culture*, *3*, 64–99.

Harré, R. (1992). What is real in psychology? A plea for persons. *Theory & Psychology*, *2*, 153–158.

Horigan, S. (1988). *Nature and culture in Western discourses*. London: Routledge & Kegan Paul.

Ingold, T. (Ed.). (1989). *What is an animal?* London: Unwin Hyman.

Israel, J., & Tajfel, H. (1972). *The context of social psychology: A critical assessment*. London: Academic Press.

Knorr Cetina, K. (1988). The micro-social order. In N.G. Fielding (Ed.), *Action and structure* (pp. 1–47). London: Sage.

Kultgen, J. (1982). Saving you for real people. *Environmental Ethics*, *4*, 59–67.

Latour, B. (1986). The powers of association. In J. Law (Ed.), *Power, action and belief: A new sociology of knowledge?* (pp. 264–280). London: Routledge & Kegan Paul.

Latour, B. (1987). *Science in action: How to follow engineers in society*. Milton Keynes: Open University Press.

Latour, B. (1988a). *The Pasteurization of France*. Cambridge, MA: Harvard University Press.

Latour, B. (1988b). The politics of explanation – an alternative. In S. Woolgar (Ed.), *Knowledge and reflexivity: New frontiers in the sociology of knowledge* (pp. 155–176). London: Sage.

Latour, B. (1991). Technology is society made durable. In J. Law (Ed.), *A sociology of monsters: Essays on power, technology and domination* (pp. 103–131). London: Routledge.

Latour, B. (1992). Where are the missing masses? A sociology of a few mundane artifacts. In W.E. Bijker & J. Law (Eds.), *Shaping technology/Building society* (pp. 225–258). Cambridge, MA: MIT Press.

Latour, B./Johnson, J. (1988). Mixing humans with non-humans? Sociology of a few mundane artefacts. *Social Problems*, *35*, 298–310.

Law, J. (1987). Technology and heterogeneous engineering: The case of Portuguese expansion. In W.E. Bijker, T.P. Hughes & T. Pinch (Eds.), *Social construction of technological systems* (pp. 111–134). Cambridge, MA: MIT Press.

Law, J. (1991). Introduction: Monsters, machines and sociotechnical relations. In J. Law (Ed.), *A sociology of monsters: Essays on power, technology and domination* (pp. 1–23). London: Routledge.

Martin, L.H., Gutman, H. & Hutton, P.H. (Eds.). (1988). *Technologies of the self: A seminar with Michel Foucault*. London: Tavistock.

Merchant, C. (1980). *Death of nature: Women, ecology and the scientific revolution*. London: Harper & Row.

Michael, M. (1991). Discourses of danger and dangerous discourses: Patrolling the borders of 'nature', society and science. *Discourse & Society*, *2*(1), 5–28.

Michael, M. (1992). Postmodern subjects: Towards a transgressive social psychology. In S. Kvale (Ed.), *Psychology and postmodernism* (pp. 74–87). London: Sage.

Michael, M., & Grove-White, R. (1993). Talking about talking about 'nature': Nurturing 'ecological consciousness'. *Environmental Ethics*, *15*, 33–47.

Michael, M., & Still, A. (1992). A resource for resistance: Affordance and power–knowledge. *Theory and Society*, *21*, 869–888.

Moscovici, S. (1981). On social representations. In J.P. Forgas (Ed.), *Social cognition* (pp. 181–209). London: Academic Press.

Moscovici, S. (1984). The phenomenon of social representations. In R.M. Farr & S. Moscovici (Eds.), *Social representations* (pp. 3–70). Cambridge: Cambridge University Press.

Noske, B. (1989). *Humans and other animals*. London: Pluto Press.

Parker, I. (1992). *Discourse dynamics*. London: Routledge.

Reed, P. (1989). Man apart: An alternative to the self-realization approach. *Environmental Ethics, 11*, 53–69.

Rodman, J. (1983). Four forms of ecological consciousness reconsidered. In D. Scherer & T. Attig (Eds.), *Ethics and the environment* (pp. 82–92). Englewood Cliffs: Prentice Hall.

Sanders, C.R. (1992, 5–6 March). *Perceptions of intersubjectivity and the process of 'speaking-for' in canine–human relationships.* Paper presented at the International Conference on 'Science and the Human–Animal Relationship', Amsterdam.

Schwartz Cowan, R. (1987). The consumption junction: A proposal for research strategies in the sociology of technology. In W.E. Bijker, T.P. Hughes & T. Pinch (Eds.), *Social construction of technological systems* (pp. 261–280). Cambridge, MA: MIT Press.

Serpell, J. (1986). *In the company of animals.* Oxford: Blackwell.

Shapin, S. (1988). Following scientists around. *Social Studies of Science, 18*, 533–550.

Shotter, J., & Gergen, K.J. (Eds.). (1989). *Texts of identity.* London: Sage.

Singleton, V., & Michael, M. (1993). Actor-networks and ambivalence: General practitioners in the cervical screening programme. *Social Studies of Science, 23*(2), 227–264.

Soper, K. (1986). *Humanism and anti-humanism.* London: Hutchinson.

Star, S.L. (1991). Power, technologies and the phenomenology of conventions: On being allergic to onions. In J. Law (Ed.), *A sociology of monsters: Essays on power, technology and domination* (pp. 26–56). London: Routledge.

Tallmadge, J. (1981). Saying you to the land. *Environmental Ethics, 3*, 351–363.

Tester, K. (1991). *Animals and society.* London: Routledge.

Thomas, K. (1984). *Man and the natural world.* Harmondsworth: Penguin.

Turner, J.C. (1987). *Rediscovering the social group: A self-categorization theory.* Oxford: Blackwell.

Williams, R. (1980). *Problems of materialism and culture.* London: Verso.

Woolgar, S. (1981). Interests and explanation in the social studies of science. *Social Studies of Science, 11*, 365–394.

16

What Scientists Do

Karin Knorr Cetina

The Need to Explore What Scientists Do

As Bryant (1992) pointed out, the mechanical materialists of the eighteenth-century enlightenment were among the first to recommend, with great anticipation and confidence, the application of the methods of mathematics and the physical sciences to human affairs. From that time onward, there has been no shortage of calls for the human sciences to model their procedures after the natural sciences. One of the last incidences of this is a resurgence of a positivist disposition on the micro-level, for example in social psychological approaches or in action theory of the rational choice brand, and, on the other end of the scale, in recent macro-theoretical discourse (e.g. Lenski, 1991).

The foundation of this call to refashion ourselves after the methods of the natural sciences is a set of beliefs which can be stated as follows: they assume the methodological unity of the sciences, they deny the existence or relevance of distinctive ontologies of different phenomenal worlds, and they assume that the social relationships implicated in how a science conducts its business are of no concern to scientific outcomes. These beliefs, I maintain, are without empirical merit. They do not represent natural scientific practice, but at best its philosophical reconstruction detached from any empirical investigation of these sciences. It can be shown that the methodological unity of the sciences, which we must assume if we are to recommend the application of natural scientific methods to the social world, does not exist – except perhaps on a level of abstraction devoid of information. Detailed investigations of different natural sciences reveal different *epistemic cultures* – different strategies of creating and warranting knowledge. For example, the sciences exhibit radically different understandings of the meaning of experiment and measurement, and they may base their approach to the world on a variety of epistemic procedures, including on 'negative' ('liminal') strategies that probe the limits of knowledge.

The preference of the recommendation given to us to emulate the natural sciences for ignoring the distinctive ontology of the social world – for example the ontology of human agency – cannot be warranted by reference to the natural sciences either. Different natural scientific fields work with different reconfigurations of their object domains. Moreover, these reconfigurations stand in relation to the conception of the human agents, scientists, that we find implemented in a scientific field. Epistemic strategies such as the 'negative' and 'liminal' approach mentioned earlier are embedded in social strategies, and relations with objects are embedded in social relations. How a science configures its social relations also has implications for its ethnomethods of consensus-formation.

I cannot, within the space of this chapter, give detailed examples of the disunity of the natural sciences. Works on this subject exist (see Galison & Stump, 1996; Knorr Cetina, 1995, 1996, in press). Instead, I shall give a brief account of the recent history of science studies, followed by a description of relevant areas of the empirical investigation of natural scientific practice – the ones which dominate today. In the third part of the chapter, I shall provide two illustrations of the kinds of results of this line of research – one referring to what the sciences can teach us about interesting social forms, the other referring to what we might have to teach some sciences about themselves.

Recent studies of scientific practice suggest that the natural sciences harbour extraordinarily complex cultural traditions of epistemic procedure that are not obvious from natural scientific writings. These traditions are specific, and provide no ground for wholesale recommendations to the human sciences to perform empirical research in particular ways or to script theories according to positivist ideals. The positivist model of what the natural sciences are about fails on account of its own lack of positivism – its own failure to ground its recommendations in empirical investigation.

The Development of Science Studies

Natural science, we all know, is the epitome of the will to knowledge with respect to the natural order. It has had its fall-out with earlier authorities like religion from which it wrought the right to say something about nature religion did not like. Perhaps because natural science always was so much on the doing side of this development – because it is the most important agent of the will to knowledge – it has not focused much upon itself, upon how it does what it does, empirically speaking. Science embodies the will to knowledge, but it has not been penetrated by it. Empirical penetration is the project of *science and technology studies*, which arose since the late 1930s stimulated in the US by the social theorist Robert K. Merton at Columbia. It is a project which came late compared with, today, two hundred years of studies of social problems; and when it came, it remained, for a while, curiously timid toward the internal side of science. While values and norms which sustain science from the outside and the organizational settings within which it takes place were brought into the picture early, the live animal which lived in these frameworks was not. Science became encircled, but its real being, science in action, stayed closed off.

In fact, it stayed not exactly closed off so much as concealed – that is, 'well covered' by hypotheses which, in a nutshell, said that what scientists do was spelled out by *the scientific method*, explicated as science's progress through the verification of theories by observational testing (through its reliance upon theory-neutral sense data about which agreement could be reached),[1] and, later, as its progress through a non-inductive logic of refutation (theories could not be verified through sense data but they could be falsified). These were pleasing hypotheses put forward by thrifty rational philosophers; they were highly selective and parsimonious and thrust into focus notions of rational scientific progress which sustained and reinforced our tendency to see Western modernity as a process of institutional and economic rationalization. But they also shrank a historically grown massive social institution which is arguably at the centre of modern culture and consumes and produces substantial percentages of gross national products to one spot, the spot of the logical and rational reconstruction of scientific growth. It is something that could not work in the long run; compressed states of this sort are inherently unstable, the stable state being the rather more luxuriant chaos of everyday life. The rational state could only be purchased at the price of a very restrictive hold on the field, a hold that involved refraining from looking at what scientists do empirically and of working with highly reconstructed historical materials. Once this hold was loosened, real life was upon us, much as it is upon a molecular biologist who tries to tackle the intricacies of the genetic code with actual viral DNA, or the experimental physicist who confronts his or her simulations with the real events in a detector: none of the prior neatness of the problem obtains, much of what we thought was the case is unrecognizable or wrong, and the spot explodes into a plethora of dimensions, activities and levels which one cannot hope to come to grips with through one approach, let alone a few principles.

This is what happened in science studies in the late 1970s, when the exclusionary approach of earlier thoughts on what scientists do was replaced by an inclusionary view. Instrumental in this happening was, among others, the late Tom Kuhn with his book called *The Structure of Scientific Revolutions* (1970; 1st ed. 1962). What Kuhn's theory did was change the terms of the discussion by switching the approach to science – by making it plausible that besides a logic of discovery and the rational reconstruction of scientific progress we should have historical (empirical) theories of scientific change, and more generally empirical examinations of the internal workings of scientific practice – of real-life scientists with interests and affiliations, or of networks of laboratories running huge experiments and disciplines, or of threads of communications stitching together the discourse of a field. To be sure, awareness of these empirical states of science sank in slowly, and often took even the social analyst by surprise. I remember well, when I made my first steps into the scientific laboratory as a social scientist in Berkeley in 1976, I was quite convinced that this was a silly thing to try, because, I imagined, what scientists did primarily was thinking, which would not offer much to see. Social analysts had to *retrain* themselves and their own conception of science, and they did it, felicitously, not by arguing things out, but by letting the experimental sciences they studied train them (they did it through detailed empirical investigation). As a consequence, the field of science and technology studies rearranged itself.

How Science Studies Picked Up What Scientists Do

In the following, I shall briefly comment on four distinct waves of studies corresponding to different layers of what scientists do which have marked the exploration of this social institution since the 1970s. The first wave of studies took on the scientist and his or her making of knowledge; the second the laboratory; the third scientific discourse; and the fourth socio-technical networks.

I begin with the first. There had been in the 1930s a movement called the sociology of knowledge associated with two sociologists, Mannheim (1954) and Scheler (1926), who devoted themselves to exploring the social and existential conditioning of thought. The hypothesis was plausible – who would deny today that all human thought, scientific or other, must some-how be influenced by the social and historical context in which it is rooted? Yet like many good hypotheses it proved difficult to measure, and Mannheim and Scheler, who had a case to build, rested it on the more easily accessible social thought. What the first wave of studies in the new sociology of science did was remember the plausibility of the idea and pursue it in the 'hard' sciences. In essence the argument went that a scientist's preferences for, say, a particular model, theory or thought style could be linked to their cognitive investments and interests and to the thought styles of the groups they associated with. For example, the prefer-ence for a particular statistical coefficient like the one Pearson proposed for continuous variables as opposed to the one Yule proposed for discontinuous ones was sustained, in the case of Yule, by his involvement with groups that believed and had a stake in discontinuous evolution, and in the case of Pearson, by his roots in, and involvement with, groups which harboured correctionist notions of continuous incremental social improvement (MacKenzie, 1981). The argument suffered from having to rely on similari-ties in forms of reasoning rather than on firm causal connections; but this is no news in social and historical fields where the causal road is often the most bumpy and obstructed, and the least clear to lead to success. Its true limitations are that the approach seems most applicable to a time, and to fields, in which the relation between scientists and social and political groups is close and on the record. It seems ill suited for disciplines which have differentiated from the rest of society much further and in which the epistemic subjects – the procurers of knowledge – are no longer individuals, for whose deeds their biography can causally matter, but groups.

This is where the second wave of studies comes into the picture, which no longer took its starting point from individual scientists but from the laboratory, the demarcated spaces in which much of modern experimental science is worked out.[2] The first four laboratory studies were started roughly at the same time in California between 1975 and 1977, a mere historical coincidence which is interesting mainly for the detail that the Europeans involved had to displace themselves to California to muster the courage to conduct this kind of research. If explorations of scientists' cognitive thought styles and preferences had brought into focus the horizontal extension of science by showing how the social context could matter to scientists' beliefs, laboratory studies showed its vertical extension – they showed that the *conduct of research* was itself a thickly layered enterprise of some depth. There had been in the past investigations of scientific experiments, but experiments had been mainly methodologically defined and inspected with a view to their role in theory testing. Hence not much was known about the actual conduct of research, notably in contemporary science. Moreover, it became quickly clear that many more things happened in a laboratory than could be subsumed under the methodology of experimentation. Scientific objects are not only cognitively thought out in the laboratory; nor are they construed merely through the interaction with natural objects. Successful empirical natural science seemed to rest on the mobilization of many skills and resources, some symbolic, involving, for example, techniques of persuasion and conversational routines, some strategic–tactical (what social scientists tend to call political), involving, for example, the outmanoeuvring of natural tendencies and events as much as the outmanoeuvring of scientific competition, some social, involving, among other things, the mobilization and maintenance of networks of exchange of specimen and communication between scientists, some perhaps even ontological, involving, for example, the redefinition of subjects and objects in the laboratory with a view to changing their relations to the advantage of scientists. In other words, the whole spectrum of human (and non-human) repertoires seemed to be present and needed in the lab. Needed to extract information from recalcitrant natural objects, needed to interact with them, needed to entice them into some form of co-operation. But also needed to create favourable or manageable conditions for this interaction with natural objects and for their acceptance by others, through the simultaneous deployment of such skills and resources to fellow scientists, and to society at large.

One of the activities laboratory studies found that scientists do was producing scientific discourse (e.g. through writing scientific papers), and this discourse proved so interesting and complex that a whole field of discourse analysis is now devoted to its study in science. Science, of course, has long been considered as an affair that has much to do with written products, but these were at the same time perceived a bit like a vast sea of noise from which one had to extract the real objects of interest like scientific theories or arguments. Discourse, of course, is noisy, even when it is approached not from a logic-of-argument viewpoint but from a linguistic one. But the noise is vastly reduced when you find that scientific writing itself is thoroughly patterned, skilfully employs techniques of representation, and transforms embodied laboratory experience in systematic ways. A comprehensive definition of discourse includes *oral communication*, whose importance in science tends to be obscured by the conspicuous presence and permanence of written texts. With respect to the production of knowledge, however, it is often forms of speech and oral communication which appear to bring forth the concepts and shifts in interpretation which move a field, and it is texts which appear like no more than the shadow of speech. Texts need to be interpreted (they are read, decoded, criticized), which re-enters them into oral communication, and, besides, they are usually too late to matter for the much faster world of science in action.

If you take scientific statements out of the laboratory and pursue their career in society, and, particularly, if you study technology *made to have* a career in society, you are confronted with science in yet a different state, a state some analysts have described in terms of socio-technical networks of translation (see, e.g., Callon, 1986; Latour, 1991). Translation networks refer to a compound reality in which statements, technical devices and human actors (researchers, technicians, industrialists, corporations, politicians, etc.) are brought together and interact with each other. Translation leads to an alliance of interests – it tells users, for example, 'you will get what you want if you support my research'. It means establishing an equivalence between, say, the biochemical study of a polymer and its absorption by certain body organs, and many other agents in society, for example the groups and institutions which support the struggle against cancer, the field of biochemistry interested in such polymers, or the pharmaceutical industry and the medical profession. When a network is established, scientists speak not only on behalf of the DNA whose properties they 'translate' in their laboratory, but also for the external actors they have interested and which have become the context of their action: biochemists, for example, 'translate' (re-represent) in their own way chemotherapy and the fight against cancer.

What translation networks bring into focus once more is what the inclusionary view has emphasized in different ways – that scientists' multiple vocabularies and involvements do not flaw the production of knowledge, nor do they just form a ring around it (as notions of embeddedness or context suggest), but they are part and parcel of the creation of epistemic effects (e.g. truth effects). These involvements and vocabularies *are* 'the scientific method' before it is codified in textbooks, when it is practised, underneath its own reductionist representations. Science and technology would not be possible today, let alone be successful, if they were *prudish* and *demure* vis-à-vis the resources and mechanisms in evidence in our societies, and exploitable for epistemic causes. It is a bad artist, they say, who does not experience all strata of personal life, including those on the dark side. It might be a bad scientist who does not exploit all strata of modern societies' institutional possibilities, including those not codified in the textbook image of science.

What Scientists Do is of Interest to Society

In the following I would like you to look with me through two windows that recent studies of science have opened up: one on how science can teach us interesting social forms, the other on what we might have to teach science about itself. I begin with the first. Science, we always thought, thrusts modernity forward through its redescription of the world and through technology, which Marcuse (1973) described as 'the racing heart of capitalism'. What I want to show you is that it also thrusts modernity forward through inventing social forms which are rare, if they exist at all, in the rest of society, and which are tempting the moral architecture of modern life. We witness at present a renewed debate in political philosophy between communitarians and liberals in which one side emphasizes that social actors are 'members' and 'participants' in a community in which they have their roots and with which they should have common identifications and bonds, whereas the other side emphasizes individual rights and choices, impersonal government and the impartial rule of law. It is the debate between atomism and holism mixed with the issue of whether civil rights and choice should be the principal virtues of social life, or whether solidarity through a strong sense of community should play a strong part in what we think is good. Now the debate resonates with the real issues of sharing that have come upon us in Europe with the recent wave of migrations from the poor East and South to the West. But it also resonates with the breakdown of communism, and the question of what sort of communitarian life forms are still imaginable and liveable under capitalism.

Experimental high energy physics, I think, provides one answer to this question. It lives a communal life form and has done so for some time, though the scale on which it manages to do so is growing more massive by the day. What I have in mind are the huge collaborations recent experiments in high energy physics string together, collaborations of a thousand physicists which can last up to twenty years, the better part of the working life-time of a member. What is impressive about these collaborations for a sociologist is that they work apparently without the huge organizational apparatus one assumes would be needed to stabilize such arrangements, without much in terms of hierarchy, formal structure or line of command, without much conflict, constant breakdowns and endless delays in goal achievement, and without even so much as legally binding contracts or a strong informal organization. In large corporations and industries which possess a huge organizational apparatus and also conflicts and inefficiencies, a whole industry of professionals from several fields (management consultants, organizational sociologists, social psychologists, human resource people and recently even anthropologists) is busily at work advising them how to engineer a unity of purpose, and integral, working human populations. There is of course the long-held notion that scientists are self-motivated, hence some of the problems rampant in industrial organizations should not occur. But self-motivation is common to most sciences, where it does not bring about communal life forms. Communitarians tend to frame these issues in terms of a moral sense which *should* make individuals think in terms of a whole (but normally doesn't, as you can see in West Germany today), or they invoke notions of rootedness and belonging which, if they were ever real, appear to have been real for life forms which are now extinct. What makes the communal life form of physics tick is neither *morals* nor *human resource styling* but a variety of mechanisms which counteract and channel forces of individuation present elsewhere in society and which unleash forces of co-operation.

How? In other fields, for example in molecular biology, a strong coupling exists between the scientist as an author, a scientific project, a career, a biography and the person – the four components sustain each other and enforce (or reinforce) individuation. One is an individual (or individually ranked) author for individually assigned and attributed projects, one's career and biography is connected to authorship and work accomplishment, and the scientist as a person blends into this. In high energy physics, however, the string is broken up: career-biography-and-person are dissociated from authorship and work, such that the latter no longer sustains and puts into focus the former. The physicist's career needs, for example, his or her institutional biography, still exists individually, and the experiment takes 'care' of it (e.g. it helps young physicists get positions). But the physicist completely *loses individualized authorship rights*, a simple but very effective mechanism that *unleashes co-operation*. Authorship in high energy physics is rigorously and indignantly collective and alphabetical; that is, it lists all members of a collaboration, with the consequence that the scientist can no longer be identified and described from authorship, or associate his/her personality, his/her 'ego', with it.

The flipside of this coin (but not quite the same, for work circulates in a collaboration whereas authorship does not) is that individual *work* is disowned and decoupled from the author, as when the outcome of several years of dissertation labour of a doctoral student is published under the names of several hundred collaboration members(!). A third mechanism institutes the individual as a competent but neutral person who *re-presents* the whole. There is the usage of the person as a 'convener' of group activities, or as a 'spokesperson' for what the group thinks, roles in which the person *sums up* the contribution of others *not* through reinterpreting them (as a social scientist might) in his or her own terms but by *presenting together* the contributions (e.g. transparencies) of others. This function is extended through the role of physicists as rapporteurs at conferences, a format of *presenting others* which requires summarization of other experiments, technological developments, or of the status of fields. But even the 'experimental' talks at high energy physicists' conferences are talks in which presenters report *not their own work* but work coming out of the whole collaboration, work in which they need *not* have participated personally at all. High energy physics completely reshuffles individuals and works through treating them as if they were infinitely combinable separate packages. In doing so it creates a second level of order which exists in parallel to the one mapped out by individuals and their biographies and career needs, a level of order in which work (and the physicists who perform it) circulates independently, and in which persons act as *intermediaries* for the whole, which they constantly incite and create.

There are other features. Most importantly, perhaps, the phenomenon that what strings an experiment together seems to be the discourse and communication which runs through it, and not, as in other areas, structural devices (e.g. stratified positions to which decision rights are attached) or political negotiation, or values and norms. Scientists constantly tell each other with different degrees of formality what happens where with what results and conclusions, such that the experiment *continually integrates itself along threads of talk, e-mails and transparency-exchanges.* Another device is the heavy use made of temporality as an integrating force on many levels, for example through schedules. There are numerous schedules continually forcing participants to perform by certain deadlines, and forcing the whole to march together on certain tasks. I shall not bore you with any further details, and just mention that these devices are interesting also in that they naturalize integration and co-operation: by subjecting everything to time and by refusing the traditional sequence of, first, individuation, and, then, social and political integration, things are made to happen '*neutrally*' and '*naturally*', *not* governed, so to speak, by human law.[3]

The Limits of Opticism

In the last example, I looked at what scientists do, not with a view to their production of knowledge but with a view to their construction of interesting social forms – their contribution to the social order. Now I want to talk about the scientist as an 'intervener' in the natural order, and about what follows from this for our current notion of objectivity and the public distrust in science. While natural science was busy studying the natural world in the last fifty years, social science was busy studying the social world, *the smallest problem of which seemed to be for a long time science itself.* But *it is no longer the smallest problem.* The attention devoted to science and technology in the last two decades also reflects a rising interest, on the part of those financing research, in understanding better this massive enterprise on which our economy and society depends, and which produces, as we have come to see it, results of not only benevolent but also malevolent and mixed consequences. There are today conversations about 'ending science' which would have been unthinkable some time ago, conversations which have started to captivate even conservative historians like Gerry Holton of Harvard. Now neither you nor I may think that such talk is serious, but the reasons we have for thinking so are discomforting, and reveal more about our problems with than our love for science. In Gerry's words:

. . . our planet is not in equilibrium; we have destabilized it with our ignorant meddling, and current knowledge is insufficient to assure a sustainable future. Life in the 21st century will not be enviable and may not be bearable without a great deal more scientific knowledge than we now have. (Holton, 1991, p. 545)

Even while physicists achieve an unsurpassed unity of purpose within a communitarian social form that one is pleased to see enacted just once, the delegitimization of science continues. On the part of the public, we are being offered a choice of worries, which range from fears about the destructive force of our nuclear, chemical and biological weapons to fraud in science. The most persistent worries surely have to do with concerns for the environment and health, and we see them enacted every day in new laws and regulations. Yet there is also the betrayal the public seems to feel from an institution whose moral and epistemological warrants for the objectivity it preaches seem no longer clear. If Kuhn in his Rothschild lecture of 1991 confessed himself and his profession to have been con-siderably disconcerted by the pliability of observation and the near circularity of scientific method that the study of actual scientific practice revealed, he is no longer taking an esoteric stance. If the Princeton historian Gerald Geison's work on Pasteur (1995) reveals 'shocking discrepancies' between Pasteur's public claims and what he knew, his 'failure to tell the truth in published papers' (in the words of the press, Pasteur, too, was a fraud and a cheat), this is one more incidence which contributes to the feeling, which is slowly sinking in, that we may have deeply misunderstood something about science. Philosophers, disciplinary scholars who reflexively study their own field, and the press, they all articulate this bewilderment differently. But it is there, and, I believe, it ought to be met not by defending science's integrity along the old lines, but by *refocusing our commitment to science* through a *changed understanding of what scientists do*.

How? Perhaps the notion of objectivity to which we hold science accountable is itself at odds with what scientists do, and has been so for some time. We tend to use this notion as a 'panhistorical honorific', but, as historians have shown (Daston, 1989; Kutschmann, 1986), it is itself a notion that developed and changed over time. What has been entangled in its history at various points were attempted 'de-anthropomorphizations' of science, the elimination of the scientist's senses, body and *subjectivity* from the conduct of research. For Galileo, Bacon and the seventeenth-century experimentalists it was wrong to believe that our senses were the measure of all things (Kutschmann, 1986, pp. 156, 168ff). Galileo, for example, 'never tired' of denouncing the senses for their deceptibility and errors, of displaying their need for assistance, and of recommending the 'sublime sense above the ordinary and the natural', his telescope. Galileo's argu-ments, of course, were self-serving, but the thought is recurring, as other incidences show. In a recently documented case the setting is medical science, the time the late nineteenth and early twentieth century, the issue anatomical atlas making or the question of how human bodies and their pathologies should be rendered. Whereas earlier atlas makers conceived of the exercise of judgement and of their interpretative skills in the selection of typical, characteristic (and so on) anatomical and pathological images not only as inevitable but as laudable and perfectly within the spirit of 'Truth to Nature', the later ones argued for a different notion of objectivity – one which meant that they had to forswear judgement and interpretation, and even the testimony of their senses (Daston & Galison, 1993).

What interests me about the history of objectivity is that its recurrent debates seem to be tied to '*opticism*', a term originally proposed by Lynch which I want to use to subsume various observational approaches, approaches for which vision (through an optical or optically derived instrument) provides the paradigm of data collection.[4] Opticist doctrines have defined objectivity as non-interventionist; they are concerned with the vulnerability of observations and scientific representations to subjective intrusions by a meddling observer of reality. This concern, however, may be inadequate to experimental laboratory sciences, whose ways with natural objects are by necessity interventionist: they *manipulate* substances and materials and subject them *to any imaginable intrusion or usurpation*. Objects are smashed into fragments, evaporated into gases, dissolved in acids, reduced to extractions, purified, washed, inhibited and precipitated, exposed to high voltage, heated or frozen, grown on a lawn of bacteria and incubated and inoculated, transfected, pipetted, killed, cut into sections and slices, and so on. Social scientists, almost as soon as they put their foot into scientific laboratories, labelled this approach *constructivist*. A philosopher, Ian Hacking (1983), called it *intervening*, which he contrasted with the procedure of representing. Paradoxically, non-interventionist experiments are today more often performed in the social and psychological sciences, which, for example, try to re-create social processes (like the deliberations of a jury) in the laboratory in order to observe their features, while taking great care that they do not interfere with the 'natural' course of events.

Opticism, then, in many natural sciences, has long been replaced by interventionism, from which the meddling, interfering, interpreting and negotiating analyst cannot very well be removed. Perhaps we should consider developing concepts of science which capture its contemporary interventionist character, which recaptures that of the technological sciences (except for the goals, experimental high energy physics and molecular biology, two most complex and advanced basic science fields, seem nearly indistinguishable from a technological science). For an interventionist science, subjectivity is no longer the most dreaded enemy – it has larger and more truculent foes to master. Perhaps such a foe is the *bias* which is possible when science becomes positioned in a field that includes, on a large scale, players such as government, industry, the military, environmentalists, 'the economy' and so on, and so forth – all those that become interested when science produces, as it now does, not only technology by design but nature by design. In this scenario, therefore, what scientists do is shot through with the interests of many players, and perspective is no longer something that has to do with an individual's viewpoint and visual location but becomes the outcome of a collective bargaining process in which many players have stakes.[5] If this is the case, the public could learn to resent not the subjectivity of expert opinion and the mixed uncertainty of scientific findings, but the consequences of this collective process of positioning science. Perhaps, also, the foe is internal, and resides in a certain disregard for natural objects which easily goes together with interventionism. As we have learned in the past, natural objects have a tendency to strike back, and they may even do this through (as a consequence of) their extinction. Perhaps we must extend our notion of the object by conceiving of it, as suggested by the philosopher Rom Harré many years ago, as agents that have powers and dispositions to react – and, one might add, that have contexts they can mobilize by affecting them, and plasticity (the power to change and adapt), and special uses of collectivity (the power to lose some members, or the power not to be tracked down individually), and so on. Perhaps such a notion could also make plausible why it is so difficult to come up with clear-cut scientific results – when the tampering scientific intervener in nature is confronted with natural objects that are his or her equal, at least over time or collectively, in their capacity to react, bounce back, change their strategy and form, interfere with and shape an environment. In this case, again, the public might learn to accept a notion of the scientist as the meddling constructor of the world, but join forces with him or her in the pursuit of the goal of a certain respect for the object and of a more interactive conception of our traffick and commerce with nature.

Whatever a new notion of objectivity (of interobjectivity?) that empowers the object while acknowledging the collective investments that run through the (scientist as a) subject may turn out to be, it seems clear is that it will not do, in the future, to go on just comforting our self-esteem with regard to science, as some parts of science studies have done in the past. We will need an entry point into the matters I have raised, if for no other reason than because public disillusionment with and distrust of science will demand it. It is because I firmly believe that science exists not by fraud *or* by mystery that I think that the visibility the study of science has achieved through its working contact with science needs to be extended, deepened and channelled into a publicly accessible reconception of science. If we want to have this reconception we cannot proceed to merely selectively, thriftily see what scientists could or should have done over the long haul of history through rationally reconstructing the growth of knowledge, but we need to copiously see what scientists do contemporaneously, in their fantastically interesting deep processing of nature, and their production of culture.

Notes

1. These were the formulations of logical positivists in the 1930s, which culminated in the contention that the language of science needed to be 'rationally reconstructed', i.e. reduced to idiom of sense data.

2. For a comprehensive review of the literature to date see Knorr Cetina (1995).

3. For a detailed description of how different sciences involve different *epistemic cultures*, see Knorr Cetina (1996, in press).

4. My usage of the term here differs somewhat from Lynch's original use in his work on digital imagery (1991, p. 86).

5. I do not think that we have even started to grasp the collective investment in a science that produces, in a wide range of fields which are not technological fields in the old sense (which range from chemical synthesis to genetic engineering, and biotechnology, but also include artificial intelligence and economics), nature and society by design.

References

Bryant, J. (1992). Positivism redivivus? A critique of recent uncritical proposals for reforming sociological theory (and related foibles). *Canadian Journal of Sociology*, *17*(1), 29–53.

Callon, M. (1986). Some elements of a sociology of translation: Domestication of the scallops and the fishermen of St. Brieuc Bay, in J. Law (Ed.), *Power, action and belief: A new sociology of knowledge?* (pp. 196–233). London: Routledge & Kegan Paul.

Daston, L. (1989, November). *Die Vorgeschichte der Objektivität*. Paper presented at the University of Bielefeld.

Daston, L., & Galison, P. (1993). The image of objectivity. *Representations*, *40*, 81–128.

Galison, P., & Stump, D. (Eds.). (1996). *The disunity of science: Boundaries, contexts, and power*. Stanford, CA: Stanford University Press.

Geison, G.L. (1995). *The private science of Louis Pasteur*. Princeton: Princeton University Press.

Hacking, I. (1983). *Representing and intervening*. Cambridge: Cambridge University Press.

Holton, G. (1991). Spengler, Einstein and the controversy over the end of science. *Physics*, *XXVIII*, 543–556.

Knorr Cetina, K. (1995). Laboratory studies: The cultural approach to the study of science. In J.C. Petersen, G.E. Markle, S. Jasanoff & T.J. Pinch (Eds.), *Science, technology and society handbook* (pp. 140–166). Los Angeles: Sage.

Knorr Cetina, K. (1996). The care of the self and blind variation: The disunity of two leading sciences. In P. Galison & D. Stump (Eds.), *The disunity of science: Boundaries, contexts, and power* (pp. 287–310). Stanford, CA: Stanford University Press.

Knorr Cetina, K. (in press). *Epistemic cultures: How science makes sense*. Boston: Harvard University Press.

Kuhn, T.S. (1970). *The structure of scientific revolutions* (2nd ed.). Chicago: University of Chicago Press.

Kutschmann, W. (1986). *Der Wissenschaftler und sein Körper*. Frankfurt: Suhrkamp.

Latour, B. (1991). Technology is society made durable. In J. Law (Ed.), *A sociology of monsters: Essays on power, technology and domination* (pp. 103–131). London: Routledge & Kegan Paul.

Lenski, G. (1991). Positivism's future – and sociology's. *Canadian Journal of Sociology*, *16*(2), 187–195.

Lynch, M. (1991). Laboratory space and the technological complex: An investigation of topical contextures. *Science in Context*, *4*, 81–109.

MacKenzie, D. (1981). *Statistics in Britain, 1865–1930*. Edinburgh: Edinburgh University Press.

Mannheim, K. (1954). *Ideology and utopia: An introduction to the sociology of knowledge*. New York: Harcourt Brace & World.

Marcuse, H. (1973). On the philosophical foundation of the concept of labor in economics. *Telos*, *16*, 9–37.

Scheler, M. (1926). *Die Wissenschaftsformen und die Gesellschaft*. Berne: Francke.

17

Participant Status in Social Psychological Research

Ivan Leudar and Charles Antaki

Introduction

Many, probably most, 'critical' social psychologists who do empirical research would be doing something involving talking and listening to people. What linguistic relation do they have with these speakers at the time, and how do they use the speakers' words later? We use an insight from Goffman (sharpened by Levinson) to help diagnose some worries about the footing on which people talk and hear. A lot of research proceeds on the basis that the researcher and respondent (and, later, researcher and academic audience) are 'ordinary speaker' and 'hearer' respectively, but there are about forty other possible combinations of *participant status* possible, some of them often much more plausible.

The argument in this chapter is going to be that we psychologists are rather bad at acknowledging different participant statuses. So, in consequence, we're sometimes bad at understanding what people are saying, and prone to misrepresent them when we write up reports for our peers. Things are not always what they seem – even among critical social psychologists, who are much more sophisticated about language than are traditionalists.

Participant Status

The 'natural' roles in a linguistic exchange seem to be signalled by the Western grammatical distinction between *I* and *you*, with perhaps the third person s/he being available to represent an 'audience' role. But Goffman's inspection of linguistic practice quickly revealed more to the story.

Goffman (1981) distinguished between the speaker as the *principal* (someone in whose interest the talk is done), the *author* (someone who has selected the sentiments and words in which they are encoded) and the *animator* (the person who does the speaking). What we traditionally think of as 'speaker' is just the occasional case when all of these come together – when I ask the operator to put me through to extension 3812 I am principal, author and animator. But the three can be separated. A spokesperson (such as the White House spokesman) will have written the script of what he's saying, but he is not saying it on his own behalf. So it doesn't mean quite the same thing as if President Clinton says it. The important thing to hold on to is that part of what an utterance 'means' depends on whether the speaker is the author, spokesperson or principal, or all combined. We'll see examples of this in a minute.

We could stick with Goffman's list, but Levinson (1988) has nicely shown that there is a bit more to it. The English language, as with other languages, has a large number of names for various kinds of speakers, and each one is subtly different. For example, consider the goings-on in a committee meeting.

Chair:	I think the Fund-Raising Sub-Committee is ready to give its report	[addressing meeting, intended for Treasurer]
Treasurer:	Oh sorry, is it me . . . now then . . . where are my things . . . oh yes.	[ordinary speaker]
	Report of income for the year ending March 31st . . .	[relayer]
Heckler:	. . . 1892	[as relayer]
Treasurer:	yes very amusing	[ordinary speaker]
	Chair, can I ask that I not be interrupted	[addressed to Chair, but directed at members]
Chair:	[*winking*] As Chair, I have to bring members' attention to rules of good conduct	[double role]

Obviously that's all made up, but we'll use proper examples later.

Levinson asked himself whether there might be an underlying conceptual structure on top of which these various statuses could lie in a more principled way. He came up with the following. We don't need to follow it in detail here, but we offer it just to show that there is a principled way of generating the variety of statuses we shall be considering later.

Producers can:

- be present or absent;
- be transmitting or not transmitting;
- have or not have the motive for the message; and
- be responsible for the form of the message/not responsible.

For example, take a barrister in a courtroom. She is present, and speaking for her client. She is responsible for the form of what she is saying, but not for the content. That is the responsibility of the 'principal' in the case – the defendant, who may be present in the courtroom, but isn't speaking, and who, although the ultimate benefactor of what is being said, is not responsible for its form.

Or consider someone like the hapless Treasurer above – her alternate turns can only be understood as shuttling between someone who is merely relaying an agreed message and someone who is speaking, as it were, for herself.

Looking now to *recipients* of messages, they can be:

- present or absent;
- the intended recipient or not;
- actively addressed or not;
- physically able to hear the message or not.

For example, take the 'judge' – this is somebody who is present, but, although directly addressed, is not really meant to be the ultimate recipient of the message (as in 'Your Honour that last point was irrelevant to the issue at hand' – addressed to 'targeted overhearer', i.e. the person who actually made the last point, or her/his spokesperson; or perhaps the jury).[1]

Never mind about the details of these dimensions, and all the possible participant statuses they can lead to. We're only really going to be concerned with two observations:

(a) that when considering speakers, the traditional psychological approach has been to assume that subjects are either 'ordinary speakers' or, in (at least some) discourse analysis circles, 'representatives';
(b) that when picturing themselves as hearers, psychologists usually completely ignore any variations in their own participant status either within the interaction, or, later, when they use their respondents' words in a new interaction (e.g. in a conference paper or a written article).

Why Is This Important?

Simply, because *we won't understand a given utterance until we know the status of who is sending it, and to whom.* Let's turn to real examples to show what we mean:

(from Schegloff, in Levinson, 1988, p. 166)

Sharon:	You didn't come tuh talk to Karen?
Mark:	No, Karen – Karen' I're having a fight (.4) after she went out with Keith and not with (me)
Ruthie:	Hah hah hah hah
Karen: →	Well, Mark, you never asked me out

How do we understand Karen's utterance? It is set out as a response, yet no-one had addressed her – on the contrary, Mark's answer to Sharon seems to be explicitly designed not to address Karen. But look how the participant statuses are being used. By naming Karen, Mark makes her the indirect target of the utterance and thereby picks her out as an appropriate next speaker. The accusation has the conversational effect of allowing her to reply with a defence.

That was an example of a subtlety about the recipient. Consider a different example, this time to do with the producer. As you read this, ask yourself: '"who" is talking?' at the arrowed utterance – in what voice, if you like, is the utterance being expressed?

S&Q S 2.1. 880

A:	get erm a bookseller such as Blackwell
B: →	Blackwells to handle it
A:	er or IUB
B:	yeah
A:	and em er it shouldn't be too bad an investment (.) I don't think

We think you'll agree that it only really makes sense as if it were a continuation of A's utterance, *in A's voice*,[2] and promoting the emergent account as a joint production.

One can draw two morals from these examples:

1   The semantics of the utterance isn't enough
2   The voice, or participant status, of the utterance is essential.

More generally, moving away from conversational talk data: sometimes we will need to understand that an author of a text need not be a single individual, but can be a structured group, in which different aspects of message production (e.g. motivating a message, formulating its content and style, and speaking it) are *distributed across the members*. The participant may be in a different relation to the text in the same way that members of a production team (managers, shareholders, supervisors, workers) are in different relationship to industrial products. It is important to be clear that the contributions of some members of a collective to the production are less visible and less valued than those of others – but the hidden should be made visible. The audience is rarely an individual, or an unstructured set of individuals. Ethnomethodological studies (e.g. Goodwin, 1981) show that recipients of messages can be on a different footing to them and that messages may actually structure an audience into more or less complex collectives (cf. Leudar, 1991; Levinson, 1988). The force of some acts of speech in fact depends on this – public reprimands, commendation, work insofar as they succeed in structuring an audience. Finally, meanings are not simply encoded, sent and decoded, implying a sharp distinction between the production and the recipient statuses.

This decomposition of the message production into a set of co-ordinated functions has an interesting consequence. Note that, apart from the 'ordinary speaker', the producer of a message is *necessarily a collective agent*. This is to say, once you get away from the case where all the statuses are embodied in one person (the 'ordinary speaker', who is present, transmitting, the agent responsible for the form of the message and its motive), there must be at least two people acting in some kind of concert to produce the message – president and spokesperson; client and barrister; and so on.

What Has All This To Do With Social Psychology?

Just this: that *it should make us suspicious about any research enterprise – be it traditional or critical – which claims to represent what 'the speaker' said.*

Social psychological investigations are communicative transactions between two people: investigator and subject. But sometimes the researcher treats the subject as speaking as the single 'ordinary speaker', and themselves as listening as the single 'interlocutor'. This is often the assumption in 'traditional' experiments, questionnaire studies and even in research interviews, even though there's no guarantee that the interaction proceeded that way. And sometimes the subject is treated as a representative of some group or other (even if that is just 'society'). That is normal in discourse analytic studies. But, again, there is no guarantee that the subject is actually speaking like that throughout the interaction.

At the time of the exchange itself, there are very many other possible combinations of participant status. It is an open question how that exchange is represented in the psychologist's subsequent report of what happened and 'who' was talking. It is an equally open question whether the 'meaning' of what the respondent said is unaffected by any transformation in participant status s/he may have undergone as a product of the report-writing.

Let us give another crude, made-up example of the sort of worry we're expressing, or at least the first stage of it. Suppose we were interested in (say) national identity and interviewed two people about being British. Somewhere in the transcript we see this extract:

A: But Brits are awful, Brits are intolerant

What shall we make of this? At first sight it looks like A is ('authentically') expressing the point of view that 'Brits are awful'. But you could alter the intonation and make it sound different. What that would do might signal that A is 'putting those words in someone else's mouth' – in turning her from authentic 'ordinary speaker' to (ironic) 'statement maker' or 'relayer'. But supposing that it was delivered 'flat', without that ironizing inflexion. Wouldn't *that* guarantee that meant that A is speaking for herself? Not necessarily. When we pull out a little bit to see more of the interactional context, we see:

Interviewer: In Spain it's like 'we're tolerant'
A: But Brits are awful, Brits are intolerant

Even 'flat', we would still want to read it as 'not-just-A speaking' because of the strong sense that it completes the Interviewer's story about what the Spanish would say. That is, A is colluding with the Interviewer to put words (still) into someone else's mouth.

Exactly whose mouth? Well, it looks like 'Spaniards', but suppose I now reveal that the third person in the room, B, is in fact a Spaniard, and the next line is:

Interviewer: In Spain it's like 'we're tolerant'
A: But Brits are awful, Brits are intolerant
B: You're awful! That's enough! [etc]

B's line might cast the Interviewer and A together as 'teasing', that is, as having B in mind when they apparently address each other. So what looked like an authentic statement about British people turns out to be a teasing joke at B's expense.

We just raise this example not to argue about how to resolve it (which probably needs a whole-hearted conversation analytic account) but to show how the 'meaning' of what is said, even in a typical discursive psychology data set, depends on participant status. We'll give real examples later.

But Surely All That is True Only About Brief Turns, Not About Larger Scale Monologues?

One objection is that discourse analysts and others are typically interested not in brief turns, but rather in larger swathes of talk which reveal serious meaning units of discourse – interpretative repertoires, themes, and the like. Presumably discourse analysts and others believe that it is in these larger chunks (nowhere defined that we know of) that 'authentic' expressions emerge. But are these larger chunks really secure?

Here's another invented example, just to make the point. Same trio as before.

A: [long story apparently complaining, in her own voice, that the French are badly dressed] so like when they say the french are chic, well it's not true
B: that's why we pay a million pounds for their clothes
A+B: [laughter]

You'll see that we mentioned 'authenticity' here and there in that example. We don't mean that psychologists have to be committed to their respondents' being 'authentic' at every turn. But they do have to know when their respondents are speaking in their own voices and when they're not.

A Little More Background

It turns out to be true that communicative games and turn-taking rituals are very often constructed to maximize the apparent distinction between the authors and the consumers. From a transactionalist viewpoint the division is, however, not necessary but a fiction which in practice is maintained with effort and self-contradictions. Why is it a fiction? One can show that the meaning of a message depends on recipients' reaction or uptake (cf. Austin, 1962; Habermas, 1984). So if meanings are co-authored, then the individual determination of meaning is an illusion. But why is this not obvious and what gives rise to the illusion and maintains it? Metonymy, where a part stands for a whole, is a common semiotic process. In representation of transactions metonymy results in recipients' contribution being minimized and (made) invisible. The problem is also that we usually say that authors produce messages for recipients. We could, however, say that authors produce meanings for collectives in which they themselves participate. This is a transactionalist (or some say mutualist) conception of meaning (cf. Leudar, 1991).

The problems are: how is co-authoring controlled and how are contributions of recipients made visible, invisible or appropriated? This framework is clearly relevant to interpretation in social psychological and micro-sociological research which uses talk. This framework makes it much harder to assume that the subjects in social psychological investigations simply express information which the investigator observes and reports. In this chapter we aim to analyse and make visible the participation of subjects in such research.

We want to apply the observations about participant status to various investigations, starting with the well-flogged horse of the traditional laboratory experiment, but going on to the uncomfortably closer territory of discourse analysis – including the 'discourse analysis', if such it is, of psychoanalytic interpretation.

Participant Status and the Traditional Experiment

Let us start the ball rolling at perhaps the easiest point on the slope: the psychological laboratory. Psychologists – or experimental psychologists at least – traditionally do not engage with subjects any more than biologists talk to plants. The psychologist effectively denies that s/he has any 'footing' (as Goffman referred to participant status) in the interaction. But it is easy to see that psychologists do indeed have speaking positions, and that those positions are crucial in understanding just what is going on in their experiments.

A Case Study of Slippery Participant Status

Let us illustrate what we mean by using the example of a lovely paper by A.J. Crowle (1978). Crowle was a jobbing experimental social scientist (actually an ethnographer by training) who was recruited to help run a cognitive social psychology experiment. The set-up was this: all subjects were put in a position, before the experiment proper, of overhearing some of its details from a supposed subject who'd just come out of the experimental room. The real subjects then went and did the experiment (it doesn't matter what it was). Half of them were asked by the experimenter if they would volunteer to come back for another session in a few days (they all agreed). This request was supposed to increase the subjects' self-perceived commitment to the experiment.

Finally they were asked whether they had overheard anything about the experiment before they went into the experimental room. This was the dependent measure of interest, about which cognitive dissonance theory had a strong prediction to make. Those who had been asked to return turned out to give less honest answers about their prior knowledge than those who had not been asked. The results nicely fit the cognitive dissonance story: the greater the commitment to the experiment (operationalized by volunteering to take part again), the less consonant it is to admit something that ruins it, so the greater the drive to disguise the fact that you've overheard its details.

But Crowle was unwilling to let it go at that. Trained to worry about such things, he asked himself what sense the respondents made of the question put to them. For our purposes, there are three 'experimental moments' in which the footing of the participants is crucial to an understanding of what the words they uttered meant.

The first moment was the 'manipulation'. The subject was asked: '*We may ask you to come back again in a few days. You will come back won't you?*' The official story was that this had one single meaning: please commit yourself to the experiment. Now you can see that this meaning only works if the Experimenter has the participant status of an 'ordinary speaker' with all the personal commitment that invokes. But the very use of 'we' might suggest to the subject that the Experimenter is actually speaking as a spokesperson, and so not particularly committed to the invitation, and certainly not personally engaged with it; if so, then the invitation might seem rather cynical, and the flavour changes.

The second moment was the respondent's reply: saying 'yes' or 'no' was taken to mean 'I hereby commit myself to this experiment' or its opposite. Again, this presupposes the natural sincerity of the 'ordinary speaker' (i.e. the linguistic role of 'ordinary speaker' – present, transmitting, responsible for the form of the message and, crucially here, with the personal motive for it) and her or his commitment to what s/he is saying; but, in the context of a peculiar laboratory set-up, the Subject may well have been speaking what s/he thought of as being the appropriate 'lines'. Perhaps s/he was speaking as a 'ghostee' – someone whose apparently authentic lines were written by someone else.

The third moment was the point at which the respondent was asked whether s/he had overheard details of the experiment in the waiting room. A denial was taken to be 'a lie to reduce dissonance'. Once again, the 'ordinary speaker' is assumed.

All that is a linguistic gloss on Crowle's attack on the validity of the experimental operationalizations, whose meanings are, as he says, so plastic that they (and therefore the experiment) will admit of a very large number of interpretations. Now, you could say that this is just a question of internal validity and it could be solved by some tighter control over the wording. But it couldn't dissolve away the Experimenter's footing, and the Subject's bewildered thrashing about for some sensible participant status. All that gets papered over in the report, where all speakers are assumed to live in the standard world of just two roles – speaker and hearer.

Participant Status in Other Kinds of Social Psychological Method

Let us now move on to three other kinds of research methodologies in the social sciences – questionnaires, interviews and 'discourse analysis'. We shall argue that the kind of transaction that we described above gets obscured by waves of presentation. Each displaces the original transaction with another, until, finally, we end up with a transaction in which the author claims no intervention in the original talk, which is held up as being the subject's own, as the morally accountable 'ordinary speaker'.

'Context'

To start us off, let us consider some very thought-provoking points made by Condor (1989) about *context*. She has in her sights what happens when researchers extract responses out of the context of a free-response questionnaire, but her message extends to other methods which use people's 'own words'.

The background is the standard discourse analytic (among other) objection to traditional questionnaires. Potter and Wetherell (1987), for example, complain (crudely speaking) that single items may mean different things to different people, that the very choice of how the phenomenon is described is itself prejudicial to the kind of answer one gets, and so on. The answer is, discourse analysts say, to look at text and conversational transcripts, in which people respond freely to the interviewer's questions.

Condor diagnoses the same problem with questionnaires, but goes a step further in seeing the dangers not only in the prejudicial setting-up of the questions, but also in what happens to the answers when they are in the hands of the researcher. She observes that it is often forgotten that the answers are situated in a question/answer sequence and dialogically understandable in that way. It will be the norm that respondents' answers are cooperative (well considered, sincere) and hence they can be reported as assertions expressing individuals' beliefs. Normally, researchers assume that the dialogical context is really transparent and irrelevant; if it isn't, that only happens in 'badly constructed' questionnaires. She points out, however, that even in 'well-constructed' questionnaires answers, and in fact the question/answer sequences, are positioned in social controversies. As Gergen (1973) remarks, the huge majority of social psychological investigations are about things in which ordinary people have an interest, and about which it would be impossible to ask wholly value-free questions. The same point extends to the questions on a questionnaire; by setting them in front of a respondent, one is challenging the respondent to guess what 'side' the questioner is on. So rather than simply expressing a belief, a questionnaire question solicits a position in a controversy and the way the respondent meets the challenge reflects the respondent's perceived side and their view of the investigator's side.

In other words, Condor's diagnosis of what can go wrong goes further than the traditional discourse analytic complaint of leading questions. She points the finger at the researchers, who all too often occlude their own part in the production of the discourse.

A Participant-status Account of 'Context'

Now we want to give a pragmatic spin to Condor's objections, by restating them as complaints about the participant status of the speakers.

As an example, consider the following response given by a student who was asked (in writing): 'If you had to explain what "democracy" meant to someone who didn't know, what would you say?' We use this example because we know a lot about how it came about, since one of us (CA) was involved in setting up the research and in analysing the data.

> Political organization of popular government. A vote on every issue for every person. Decision making not passed over to a representative who makes decisions for you, but make decisions for yourself. 'Grass Roots' politics – more chance of making change, effecting immediate initiation from bottom up. Self-government. In its best form democracy should be a situation where communities are aware of issues, are able to reach out to more people, who therefore involve themselves in all decision making and can therefore feel they have more control over their lives. Are aware of how their decisions will affect others; take more care over how they vote.

There are two things to say about this extract. The first is to admire its articulacy, and the second is to ponder what it means. If we admire its articulacy, we are in danger of forgetting the context in which it was produced. As Condor says,

> The question itself (hypothetical in tone) is reminiscent of a 'tricky' examination question and the relevance of their identity as students was indicated by the request for information concerning their major course and year of study. The social context in which the questions were asked may also have contributed to this interpretation of the situation. The questionnaires were distributed by a university lecturer in lecture theatres or through the Psychology department's 'subject pool'. If it is the case that the students 'read' the request for information as a test of knowledge, this would or might go some way towards accounting for their use of an impersonal ('essay'?) style, their tendency to stick to 'the facts of the case' and attempts to provide a formal definition (often backed up, one would imagine, by a reference to a dictionary).

Now we agree entirely, but would just add a bit more pragmatic flavour. Note the actual wording of the question: 'If you had to explain what "democracy" meant to someone who didn't know, what would you say?' That sets up whatever is said to be:

(a) addressed to someone *other* than the experimenter/interviewer; and
(b) (possibly) in the voice of the spokesperson or relayer – there is no commitment to the subject speaking for him- or herself.

And yet when we come to 'analyse' it, we consciously or unconsciously treat it as addressed to us as ordinary interlocutors, and as coming from an equally ordinary speaker. But supposing the wording of the question had been different?

In sum: Condor's argument is that decontextualization (from co-text, and from the researcher's contribution) is a temptation into which even so-called discourse analysts slip all too readily. We shall follow that reading in looking at what happens to the 'subject' in three papers which represent various degrees of adherence to (a certain form of) discourse analysis. We shall try to show how the researcher is gradually effaced from the trans-action by successive waves of presentation. Each wave lays a certain transaction over the last one, each obscuring the initial collaboration until, by the end, the transaction seems to be between the 'subject' and the reader, with the researcher – who had originally half the responsibility for the transaction – present only as an authoritative participant, disinterestedly mediating between reader and 'ordinary speaker' now constituted as absent source.

Some Discourse Analytic Examples

So far we've complained about laboratory experiments and about question-naires of one sort or another, so now let us complain about (some kinds of) discourse analysis, just to show that we are even-handed. In outline, the argument is something like this. The subject's contribution to an exchange with a researcher may, or may not, be as the traditional 'ordinary speaker'. And whatever status it had originally, that is likely to change under the literary effort of the report writer or talk-giver. One may interview a subject, subtract a question/answer sequence, discuss it with a colleague, and report its interpretation at a meeting (perhaps to block a counter-argument by one's opponent sitting in the audience; but, in any case, for some rhetorical purpose unrelated to its format of original production). The subject's reply, originally situated in an interview, changes first into reported speech and the material of a co-operative interpretative argument, and then later into a backing of one's argument against the opposition.

Now if the researcher presents him- or herself as a recipient of a message (rather than its co-author), we can still ask what kind of recipient s/he was. His or her position is relevant and will vary, depending on whether an incidentally overheard conversation, or a recording of a radio programme, or an interview is the material being reported, discussed or analysed. The dialogical positioning of the researcher with respect to the subject is not usually reported, as if it were not only transparent but irrelevant. We want to claim that it is not the case.

The investigator does not simply receive a message from the subject. S/he also reports, discusses or argues about it with his/her colleagues. So s/he participates in two transactions, one with the subject of investigation, the other with his/her colleagues. S/he is an intermediary between them, brings them together and re-contextualizes the message between the transactions. The question is what happens to a message on its journey.

In the exercise that follows, we shall take a look at three papers. One is by Wetherell and Potter (1988), which we have access to only as a published text. Because we want to say something about how things change over the development of the research from interview to written version, we will also take a look at two other papers, each of which we have some extra access to: Bowers and Iwi (1993) and Antaki, Íñiguez and Díaz (1989). These, too, are examples of the kind of 'discourse analysis' which uses interviews to collect 'data' and in which the investigators participated in the data collection; indeed, they make explicit reference to the tentative 'ten steps' of Potter and Wetherell. We don't want to give the impression that these three pieces of work are especially wicked; we've chosen them because they seem to represent a reasonably typical range of what goes on in this corner of the discourse analysis field.

Wave 1: Introducing the Subjects and What Happens to Their Talk

In Wetherell and Potter's interviews, talk with the respondents was recorded, transcribed and then, following the heuristic 'ten steps' of Potter and Wetherell (1987), dossiers of 'interpretative repertoires' of racism were extracted from the transcripts by theme or function. In Bowers and Iwi (1993) the authors interviewed subjects to explore how 'in everyday talk people make reference to society, its constituents, and its "influence" over their affairs'. They then compile a list of alternative constructions of society (e.g. society as *uniform-and-total, multiform, agent, entity*) together with some functions and effects of these conceptualizations. The constructions are *really* the subjects' constructions, the functions are really the uses *they* put them to. In Antaki et al. (1989) one of the authors (Díaz) interviewed the respondents about 'democracy' and then the researchers combed through their responses to extract 'themes' (like 'balance' and 'mentality') to support a certain political analysis of their talk. In all cases much is made of the importance of getting at the respondents' natural and spontaneous talk, and, although it is clear that each respondent was actually interviewed, nothing is made of this.

In Wetherell and Potter (1988) respondents are introduced by a paragraph and readers are referred to another source (Potter & Wetherell, 1987, p. 123) for further methodological considerations. In Antaki et al. (1989) the respondents are introduced as 'students representing each level of secondary education' (p. 232). The interviewer (perhaps) and the authors (certainly) take as unproblematic the respondents' status as 'representatives' (in participant status terms, 'spokespeople'), though whether they themselves thought so is not made clear.

Wave 2: Interview, Investigators/Investigated

In all three studies, the everyday-talk-people are 'informants', they *inform* the researchers. The transactional format of investigation is a question/answer one, with at least some questions prepared in advance and asked of most informants. The informants were interviewed by one of the investigators, either individually or in a small group (in Bowers & Iwi, 1993, the interviewer is sometimes an undergraduate student). Now if the data were gathered from interviews, and given all the authors' respect for the integrity of linguistic data, we would expect to see as much of the interviewers' talk as of the interviewees'; but in fact the interviewers' turns are not always recorded. If they appear, they precede the respondents' turn setting the agenda but hardly ever respond to it in any significant way.

For example, from Wetherell and Potter (1988, p. 135):

(1) I do this bible class at the moment, not highly religious, I just think children ought to know about religion . . . and last night we were just discussing one of the commandments, love your neighbour, and I had this child who said 'What would happen if you got a whole load of Maoris living next door to you?' and I said to him 'That's a very racist remark and I don't like it', and he shut up in about five seconds and went quite red in the face, and I realized afterwards that obviously it wasn't his fault he was, turned out to be thinking like that, it came directly from his parents.

(2) [*Racist jokes*] I don't like them I don't find them amusing.

(3) [*What can we learn from Maori culture?*] The extended family situation's brilliant, they've got this lovely idea that a child born out of wedlock would have to be the best sort of child because it was obviously born in love . . . I think their way with children is wonderful. . . . They've got a lot to show us I think.

The respondents' words are set up explicitly as 'extracts' and it is assumed that the authors' gloss is self-explanatory. In the example that follows see how the authors simply assert that the extract is an uncontentious example of their category (here 'simple explicit appearance').

From Antaki et al. (1989):

Two examples of simple explicit appearance are the following: . . .

(2) One has to have balance (*equilibrio*). Balance supported by everyone. I think balance is fundamental. Balance all the time, in everything. For me, the word balance sums it all up. One oughtn't go beyond one's reach, nor drop short of the target either (p. 234).

Wave 3: Extract and Systematize: Scientist and Assistant

The interviews are recorded and transcribed by the authors. Wetherell and Potter (1988) follow the craft procedures of Potter and Wetherell (1987), setting up dossiers of extracts and seeing how patterns emerge. In Bowers and Iwi (1993), Bowers reads the transcripts and notices the parts which contain the term 'society'. With the help of 'critical linguistics theory' he puts together a system of categories and gives these to Iwi to apply systematically to the texts. Having done this, Iwi comes back to Bowers with problems and they discuss the examples. The fragmentary records of interviews are now interpreted as instances of possible uses of 'society' but they also partly drive the construction of the system. In Antaki et al. (1989)

all three authors separately read the transcripts – even though one does not speak the language of the respondents fluently, or, in some cases, at all – then identify themes (without the aid of 'critical linguistics theory') and in a discussion extract the ones they agree on; the transcripts are then gone through again and 'nuggets' extracted.

This example, from Bowers and Iwi (1993), illustrates the use of an extract to authorize a reading of the texts:

> *I*:   if you don't have any particular prejudice against gays what do you feel is *society's general position* on the matter
> *R*:   well society it's (.) well *society always gangs up* against minorities (.) *that's the way society is* it's mob rule and if you're in the minority you expect to get jumped on but (.) well I suppose homosexuality is stamped on in the bible to start with and this country to which is basically Christian (.) you wouldn't know to look at it but most people would have their fundamental upbringing being some religious background (.) I don't know of any religion that actually accepts homosexuality um so *society is always against it* and it *has been labelled as perverse by society* (p. 368; emphases in original)

Here, the possibility that society might have a 'general position' different from the respondent is suggested by the interviewer. This is taken up by the respondent, who offers a uniform account of the nature of society in terms of society involving mob rule and being essentially Christian. The Christian nature of society is used to explain why society is always against homosexuality. This is a clear example of a uniform construction being used to depict society as having an eternal (note the two occurrences of 'always') essence ('that's the way society is'). However, in contrast to the previous examples in (4) 'minorities' and in particular 'homosexuality' are excluded from society, opposed and 'labelled as perverse' (Bowers and Iwi, 1993).

Wave 4: Transaction 4: Reports and Arguments: Allies and Opponents

In Bowers and Iwi the fragmentary records are written up in a paper and circulated to participants in a workshop. The audience are other discourse analysts. Bowers and Iwi are criticized for not including enough contextual information. In Antaki et al. the authors among themselves argue for various readings of what the 'themes' they have identified mean. This is a difficult stage to illustrate, as mention is not usually made of competing ways of organizing the data.

Wave 5: The Effacement of the Researcher/Subject Transaction Contribution in the Elicitation of the 'Data'

The papers are submitted to journals (we won't carry on the analysis into the refereeing stage). The reports are presented as free-standing data, which can be used to support arguments. The final version of the studies casts the authors into much the same model as the experimental social psychologist of old.

Every wave that washes over the respondents' talk, we argue, wears it down in various ways, and when it finally beaches at the high tide mark of a written paper, it has undergone so many transformations that easy interpretation of its 'meaning' becomes very hard. Of course, as readers and consumers of discourse analysis, we usually manage to make something of it, but that something is highly flavoured by the writers' own interpretation of the talk; it is not any more the raw data it claims to be.

Interpretation in Melanie Klein

Let us push away from these fairly familiar research genres to one outside (at least some kinds of) critical social psychology: psychoanalysis. Klein's *Narrative of Child Analysis* (1961/1975) was published in part 'to illustrate her technique in greater detail'. In this it is successful and it should be compulsory reading for anyone interested in therapeutic discourse and especially in discourse characterized by the asymmetry of power/knowledge of participants. The book reports on ninety-three analytic sessions Klein held with an eight-year-old boy, Richard. The sessions took place daily, except on Sundays, for about four months. Of relevance here are Klein's reports of her interactions with Richard and her interpretations of his activities. Some of these interpretations are accessible and seem common sense, others are striking, as the following excerpts show.

> *12th session.* Mrs K. had brought pencils, crayons and a pad of writing-paper, and put them on the table. Richard asked eagerly what they were for, whether he could use them for writing or drawing. Mrs K. said he could do what he liked with them. Richard had hardly begun the first drawing when he repeatedly asked whether Mrs K. minded that he was drawing. Mrs K. interpreted that he seemed to be afraid that by drawing he was doing something harmful to her. . . . (p. 56)
>
> *14th session.* Mrs K. had brought the toys and put them on the table. Richard was interested and at once began to play. He first picked up the two little swings, put them side by side, made them swing, and then laid them beside each other, saying: 'They are having fun.' He filled one track of the train which he called 'goods train' with small figures, and said the 'children' were off on a pleasure trip to Dover. He added a slightly larger toy woman in a pink dress, whom he at once called Mummy. . . . Mrs K. interpreted that the swings represented his parents; laying them down side by side and saying they were having fun meant their being in bed together, and the movement of swings together indicated their sexual relations. When the pink woman (whom he called Mummy) was to go away with the children on a pleasure trip, this meant that the parents should not be together. . . . He made the train run round and into the houses. As he had left too little space, the train knocked over the houses, and he put them up again. He pushed the other train . . . and a collision ensued. He became very upset and made the 'electric' train run over everything. Mrs K. interpreted that the children's pleasure trip to Dover meant that they, too, wanted to do something sexual as the parents did. . . . Richard was extremely impressed by Mrs K.'s interpretation. He expressed his surprise that his thoughts and feelings could be shown in his play. Mrs K. interpreted that his recognizing that his play expressed his feelings also meant that Mrs K. made what went on in him clear to him. (Klein, 1961/1975, pp. 64–65)

We doubt that there is a code for us to discover which allowed Klein to make such inferences, a code which would be self-evident once revealed, and which would warrant the validity of the interpretations. What is relevant for this chapter is how Klein's interpretations are situated in her dialogues with Richard, how Richard's contributions to these interpretations are managed, and how all is presented to readers. We can say that Klein, Richard, the readers of her book and ourselves and possibly yourselves are involved in a complex dialogue. Klein reports on discourse in which she positions herself and Richard. He is her patient, she is the therapist and she avoids any ordinary conversation about ordinary events outside the analytic situation. She and Richard are in complementary positions: he is the source of the material to be interpreted and the subject to be changed by her interpretations. With respect to Richard she is the personal warrant that her interpretations are true and well meant. Klein also positions herself with respect to her readers. As she says, the book aims to record her technique. The technique is dialogue and the targets are either her peers in psychoanalysis or trainee psychoanalysts. The book is, however, also on sale to the public, and, judging by the number of reprints, it does well, so one can expect a large lay audience, like ourselves.

The reports of sessions follow a relatively fixed format. Each starts typically by a report of Richard's behaviour – of what he says and does in his play – followed by an interpretation, sometimes presented as a suggestion to Richard about a meaning of what he says or does. Finally, reactions to such interpretations are also reported. In the above example, the reported conversation structure is a series of question/answer pairs. Richard's reluctance to answer is reported. The subsequent move reported is Klein's 'suggestion', which is really an interpretation, in which she ascribes Richard's fears (parents would go to bed and Mummy would be hurt when they did things with their genitals); she points out analogies in Richard's thinking (tramp who would hurt Mummy is like Hitler who frightened the cook). Klein then reports Richard's reaction to the interpretation, for example that he looked surprised and worried. So the therapeutic discourse sequence that Klein reports is question–answer, question–answer, question–answer, interpretative suggestion, reaction. These are narrated to the outside of the therapeutic situation, to laypersons, other therapists, Anna Freud, and so on. Klein interprets answers to her questions, not question/answer sequences and thus she removes herself from the interpretation. Klein reports repair. She used the word 'genital'. She writes that Richard does not seem to understand it and she initiates repair. She asks him if he knows what genital means. She writes that Richard at first says 'no', then admits he thought he knew. Klein writes that Richard went on to say that Daddy is nice and would not hurt Mummy. Richard is reported to reject the interpretation, but she does not report it as a dialogical rejection.

What can a measure of the correctness of Klein's interpretations be? In *Love, Guilt and Reparation* (1929/1988), she writes that even in analysis of young children the final result to be obtained is adaptation to reality. She continues: 'one way in which this shows itself in children is the modification which is encountered in their education' (p. 137). So you could judge the effectiveness or accuracy of interpretations according to whether the child gets better later, outside of the therapeutic situation. (And if they do not, the interpretations could still have been correct – the therapy hasn't been long enough etc.). In other words interpretation is successful or analysis is successful to the extent that the interpretations are correct and succeed in getting rid of symptoms such as anxiety attacks, *pavor noctornus*, the inability to communicate, inhibition in play, and so on. The child is not in a subject position to dialogically affect the significance of the interpretation. The child is not a psychoanalyst – the child's reactions are a source of information, not intentional counter-arguments. Just as the minds of little children differ from those of older children, so their reactions to psycho-analysis are different in early childhood from what they are later. We are often surprised when on some occasions our interpretations are accepted. Sometimes children even express considerable pleasure in the interpreta-tions. According to Klein, the reason for this is not dialogical but that in a child the communication between consciousness and unconsciousness is easier, and for the therapist it is much simpler to retrace the steps from one to the other.

Now this is a very clear example of how a dialogical process, in other words, children accepting interpretations more easily than, say, adults, is taken out of the dialogue in which it occurs and recontextualized in the discourse of psychoanalysis and presented to us as readers. It is of course the case that the interpretation is also presented dialogically to Richard, and as we have seen its effects are reported. Klein presents her interpreta-tions to Richard dialogically as suggestions, and as interpretations to readers. This means that there are two discourses running in parallel, with Richard having access to only one – that of everyday discourse with Klein – but not the theoretical psychoanalytic discourse, which will remain for ever out of his grasp.

Concluding Comments

The aim of this chapter was to think aloud about what relation we have with our respondents – what participant statuses we enjoy when we talk to them, and what participant statuses we make use of when we turn their words into the building blocks of our academic analyses. The argument has been as much about our practice as psychologists – critical or otherwise – as it has been about what our informants actually say in this or that situation, or to this or that discursive end, and in that sense, it is a piece of methodological wrangling. But, as ever, method and theory are indistin-guishable; if we want to say something about what people do, a bit of theory about what that saying involves will not go amiss.

Notes

A version of the material in this chapter appears in I. Leudar & C. Antaki, 'Discourse practices, participant status and social psychology', *Theory & Psychology*, 6, 1996, 5–29.

1. We won't go into the various kinds of evidence – from English-language role names and conversational practice, and from non-Western grammar – that Levinson adduces for all the observations so far.

2. The grounds for believing so are in the participants' own reactions to what is said. We realize that we should make the conversation analytic case more fully, but can we leave it sketchily as follows: for the analyst, everything hinges on speaker A's second utterance. In loose terms, it is A who disposes of the meanings made available in what B says. It is A's reaction to B's arrowed utterance in the example above which convinces us (the analysts) that A is construing B's contribution as consonant with A's original utterance. Imagine what we would have made of rival third parts, e.g. 'What? How dare you!' or silence, or . . . . We have a fuller and more tedious account of this elsewhere if anyone wants it.

References

Antaki, C., Íñiguez, L., & Díaz, F. (1989). Balance and mentality: An analysis of a Spanish discourse of democracy. *Revue Internationale de Psychologie Sociale*, 2, 227–244.

Austin, J.L. (1962). *How to do things with words*. Oxford: Clarendon Press.

Bowers, J., & Iwi, K. (1993). The discursive construction of society. *Discourse & Society*, 4, 357–393.

Condor, S. (1989). Constructing the construction of facts. Paper presented at the E.A.E.S.P. Meeting on Rhetoric and Social Construction, Lancaster.

Crowle, A.J. (1978). The deceptive language of the laboratory. In R. Harré (Ed.), *Life sentences* (pp. 160–174). Chichester: Wiley.

Gergen, K. (1973). Social psychology as history. *Journal of Personality and Social Psychology*, 26, 309–320.

Goffman, E. (1981). *Forms of talk*. Oxford: Blackwell.

Goodwin, C. (1981). *Conversational organization: Interaction between speakers and hearers*. New York: Academic Press.

Habermas, J. (1984). *The theory of communicative action. Vol. 1: Reason and rationalization of society*. Boston: Beacon Press.

Klein, M. (1975). *Narrative of a child analysis*. London: Virago. (Original work published 1961)

Klein, M. (1988). *Love, guilt and reparation*. London: Virago. (Original work published 1929)

Levinson, S. (1988). Putting linguistics on a proper footing. In P. Drew & A. Wootton (Eds.), *Erving Goffman: Exploring the interaction order* (pp. 161–227). Oxford: Polity.

Leudar, I. (1991). Sociogenesis, coordination and mutualism. *Journal for the Theory of Social Behaviour*, 21, 197–220.

Potter, J., & Wetherell, M. (1987). *Discourse and social psychology: Beyond attitudes and behaviour*. London: Sage.

Wetherell, M., & Potter, J. (1988). Discourse analysis and the identification of interpretative repertoires. In C. Antaki (Ed.), *Analysing everyday explanation* (pp. 168–183). London: Sage.

Index